CHRISTIANITY CONFRONTS CULTURE

A Strategy For Crosscultural Evangelism

MARVIN K. MAYERS

ZondervanPublishingHouse
Grand Rapids, Michigan

A Division of HarperCollinsPublishers

to Marilyn

CHRISTIANITY CONFRONTS CULTURE
Copyright © 1974 by The Zondervan Corporation
Copyright © 1987 by Marvin K. Mayers

ACADEMIE BOOKS is an imprint of Zondervan Publishing House
1415 Lake Drive S.E., Grand Rapids, Michigan 49506

Requests for information should be addressed to:
Zondervan Publishing House
Academic and Professional Books
Grand Rapids, Michigan 49530

Library of Congress Cataloging in Publication Data

Mayers, Marvin Keene, 1927–
    Christianity confronts culture.

    Bibliography: p.
    Includes index.
    1. Missions—Theory.   2. Intercultural communication.
3. Christianity and culture.   4. Evangelistic work.
I. Title.

BV2063.M38   1987   266   87–1839
ISBN 0–310–28901–7

All Scripture quotations, unless otherwise noted, are taken from the *Holy Bible: New International Version* (North American Edition), copyright © 1973, 1978, 1984 by the International Bible Society, used by permission of Zondervan Bible Publishers.

Appreciation is expressed to the following for the use of copyrighted material:

Evangelical Missions Quarterly for excerpts from the article "Why Pentecostal Churches Are Growing Faster in Italy."
International Review of Missions for a case study from "The Educational Value of Initiatory Rites."
Moody Monthly for "My Hippie Brother." Reprinted by permission from the October 1969 issue of *Moody Monthly*. © 1969 by the Moody Bible Institute of Chicago.
Practical Anthropology for a conflict situation from the article "The Social Context of Guilt and Forgiveness."
The Chicago Tribune for quotations from the article "The Decision-Making Process in Japan."
Word Books, Waco, Texas, for the story "If I Forbid Ken to Drink," from *Are You Fun to Live With?* by Lionel Whiston, Copyright © 1969.

Grateful acknowledgment is also made for the use of occasional Scripture verses from the following versions of the Bible:

The Living Bible. Copyright © 1971 by Tyndale House Publishers, Wheaton, Illinois.
The New Testament in Modern English. Copyright © 1958, 1959, 1960 by J. B. Phillips, published by The Macmillan Company.
The Revised Standard Version of the Bible. Copyright © 1952 by The Division of Christian Education, National Council of the Churches of Christ in the United States of America.

Printed in the United States of America

97 98 99 00 01 02 /DH/ 15 14 13 12 11 10 9 8 7

CONTENTS

PART TWO: CASE STUDIES IN CROSSCULTURAL COMMUNICATION

Model Three: The Validity of Distinct Societies

Model Four: Effective Ministry

PREFACE

Christianity Confronts Culture was first published in 1974 and has had wide usage in mission programs around the world, in formal academic programs in colleges and universities, and in nonformal educational programs designed to train and retrain recruits for mission.

In the ensuing years, a number of other books have emerged. These have found a place in laying a broader foundation for preparation in mission and crosscultural communication, but none has done just what this book has done. This book is a practical guide to effective communication in the crosscultural setting— which exists in fact when any one person meets another. It draws together insights from the various fields of the behavioral sciences, academic disciplines that are the very life and breath of effective ministry. Finally, it is in itself an academic course that provides a professor a text, viable case studies for discussion, guidelines to carry out an adequate training program, questions for discussions and examinations, and activities that increase the vitality of the educational program.

The course this book serves best in is an entry-level course in which the goal is to effect a crosscultural conversion—i.e., a paradigm shift—and to help the student begin to see just how this change of perspective influences one's personal life, social interaction, and relationship with God and his Word. Activity-oriented learning is used to teach content/principle and to have the learning applied immediately. A "conversion" is effected by placing one in an experience that demands a change of perspective. Just telling a person what salvation is all about does not change a life. Missions today demands a change of life that allows one to see the other person as valid and to relate to that one in the same way that God does—directly through his own culture. The exercises at the end of each chapter suggest activities that can be carried on in a class to simulate the real experience.

Other courses that use other kinds of books now on the market can be taught after this course. Such courses and authors may be anthropological—Grunlan and Mayers, Hiebert, and others; missiological—Reed, Luzbetak, and others; and communicational—C. Kraft, Hesselgrave, and others. One book or one course alone does not meet the needs of today's world, in which an

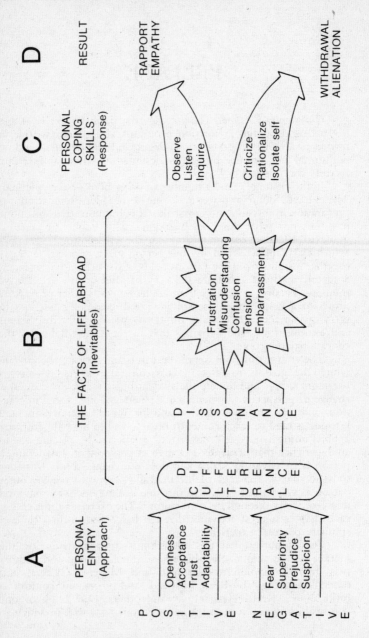

increasing number of national leaders are Ph.D.s, and in which there is a highly sophisticated exchange of knowledge, "primitive" being almost nonexistent. Learning must be at increasingly advanced levels such as in courses taught by Kraft or Lingenfelter and Mayers. In recent years two of my own books that apply crosscultural principles to Latin American lifestyles (1982) and Filipino lifestyles (1980) have been completed.

This new edition is just that—a new edition. I have rewritten obscure parts, added new cases and discussion, introduced questions for those in church work and students of the Bible, as well as for missionaries and people serving in crosscultural ministry, included more insights from Scripture, and added some specific case studies from the Bible, such as "Jesus the Educator" (chapter 17). One major change I have made from the first edition was the elimination of chapter 1, which was a theoretical introduction to the volume but had little to do with the rest of the book. (Relevant material from this chapter has been incorporated into model 2.) In its place I have provided an overview of the trust bond, the primary concept dealt with in chapters 2 through 5. Previously, I told my students to start reading at chapter 2; with this new edition, that is no longer necessary. The reader can now begin where all books begin—at the beginning.

The material of this volume is presented in four models: the contributions of social psychology (model 1), sociology (model 2), anthropology (model 3), and crosscultural education (model 4). The order of presentation is not significant, and one should consider the four models to be parts of a whole in order to grasp the total concept and apply the principles of crosscultural communication. These principles apply equally to an individual encounter as well as to a group or distinctive cultural encounter.

I have found that case-study debriefing is an effective tool for group learning. A case study is an experience from life to which all members of the learning group can relate. Most chapters in the book begin with a mini-case to which the principles of the chapter apply, and chapter 18 presents major cases to which each of the concepts of the book applies. At the end of the book I also present a selection of mini-cases that are useful in extending the teaching of the book. The intent is not to solve a case with finality, rather, to have the experience of applying the models so that through this practice an actual experience can be approached with confidence.

This is a practical book. It can serve you well if you will read portions and then go out and practice what you have learned. When you are "in the field," have the book available to you, and as you read and muse on the content, you will find solutions to the various social and ministry problems that plague you. Therefore I urge you to use it carefully and diligently in the study of interpersonal and intergroup relationships.

ACKNOWLEDGMENTS

The principles of crosscultural communication included in this volume grew out of my professional studies in social anthropology. They were first tested on the mission field while I was serving with Wycliffe Bible Translators. Late in my teaching at Wheaton College, a course began to develop around these principles. It became a very popular course both there and at other schools where I have had opportunity to teach it. As the course developed, this volume grew, and so did other supplementary materials, such as a Filipino case study, a Latin American case study, and a book of shorter cases, and out of it all a total life-way emerged. I have sought to apply principles of the course in my home, with my friends, in my teaching experience, with my colleagues—in fact, in every aspect of my life. Although the results have not always been as I might have wanted them to be, it has been exciting to see the development of sound interpersonal relationships in the cross-cultural challenges of my life. It is for this reason that I must acknowledge the contribution made to this volume by my family, my friends, my students, and my professional colleagues. Without their help and inspiration I would have given up the task long ago. Further, my appreciation extends to my beloved friends among the Pocomchi (Guatemala) and those in the Philippines who have given me the opportunity of knowing them and working with them in sharpening these tools.

Special recognition must go to my wife, Marilyn, who has suffered through my field blunders, the agonies of graduate work, and the hammering out of this material. She has been my adviser and typist in many aspects of the program. Special contributions have been made by Craig Cook, John Snarey, Carol Gene Olsen, Sam Scheibler, Ron Wiebe, and Cornelia Vergara. Also, I acknowledge the assistance of David App, Rich Butman, Carol Evans, Marjorie Garrison, Marti Hausch, Douglas Kell, Philip Yancey, Mary Arnell, Judy Fulops, and Pauline Roelofs. Dr. William Kornfield, having used the book extensively in numerous courses and workshops, has made valuable contributions to this revision.

As this approach to crosscultural communications has become a life-way, an unexpected bonus has been mine. I have found that the principles applied in the human arena of life have opened up new experiences and insights in my spiritual life, thus aiding me in developing a new relationship with my God.

INTRODUCTION

Change in Our Lives

Each change in our lives and in the world about us forces us into a change of perspective and a change of background—in effect, a change of culture. In fact, every encounter becomes a crosscultural encounter. Whenever we encounter someone, we face difference—difference of dialect, subculture, background, or perspective. We have the same reactions to difference whether we are dealing with an individual, a group, or an entire people. For each of these encounters we need the same tools to cope with the challenge of change, and we need the same attitudes. We need principles and tools that help us to communicate effectively in whatever setting we find ourselves. This book is designed to provide such tools— tools that help us to be more effective in communicating when differences of culture or subculture are involved.

This book is designed to make it easier to face the change process, to handle difference of culture and subculture more gracefully, and to communicate within diverse cultural contexts more effectively. Such effectiveness cannot be guaranteed. It will take a great deal of work to master principles and practices of crosscultural communication and to apply them in increasingly complex crosscultural settings. The differences range from changes of dress and technology to differing concepts of morality and ethics. It is not an easy thing to accept people who are different. It is even more difficult to work with people who do not think and believe as we do.

Culture is everything that is a part of one's everyday life experience. It includes:

1. Tangibles such as food, shelter, clothing, literature, art, music, etc.
2. Intangibles such as hopes, dreams, values, rules, space relationships, language, body movements, etc.

These work together to give an entity distinctiveness and unity.

Whenever two entities come together, there is a crosscultural encounter because no two individuals or groups have the same list of, or integration of, cultural details. Thus individuals in ever-expanding groupings form subcultures and cultures, and every individual has his own expression of the culture. This is a process of social and language differentiation comparable to the sudden and dramatic event that took place at the time of the Tower of Babel when God "confounded their language" (Gen. 11:1–9). People agree to recognize themselves as members of the same culture and thus obviate difference. However, when shared features are minimal and a distinctive entity emerges, people from this emergent group see themselves as a different culture. Crosscultural encounters thus occur between individuals, between subcultures and, more noticeably, between two distinct cultural groups.

In most societies and communities, a person grows up in a "one-culture" world. He may not be aware of dialectal differences in his own language. He tends to learn and accept the one-culture, self-centered approach that identifies the one who speaks with an "accent" as an oddball and an outsider, and thus worthy of rejection. The average person uses a series of defense mechanisms to show this. The superior-inferior category quickly labels the other person as inferior when he differs in language and culture. Further, the right-wrong category convinces the person that his own way of life is right and that the other person's way of life is unsatisfactory or wrong. As a result, "different" becomes "odd." The person may react to another's speech and dress as strange. Divergence of thought and belief is classified as pagan or uncivilized. Ethnic and class lines dissect sharply and serve to establish one's own identity and security rather than draw together people who seem on the surface to be incompatible.

Some people, such as the Swiss, on the other hand, live in a nation made up of linguistic and ethnic diversity. They have adapted to social and cultural changes deriving from these differences. They learn at an early age to speak several languages fluently and to deal with people of diverse ethnic backgrounds. They are aware of the differences and can more readily apply principles of sound interpersonal relations within their own nation to cope with this diversity of subcultural and dialectal variations.

However much any given individual or society is able to adapt to others who are different, there is always a degree of self-orientation and ethnocentrism that closes out the other. There is a sense that "we are the real people." Such an attitude blocks effective communication with others. Fortunately it can be helped by training, by personal sensitivity, and by prayer.

Christianity and Change

Biblical Christianity is a dynamic process born in a change setting, and since it introduces change in the life of individuals and society, it resists being bound by the narrow ethnocentrism—i.e., a self-centered focus on one's own cultural ways—and restricting legalism that often characterize the established church. In light of the unchanging nature of Christ and the continual change within the sphere of the human being, these questions are forced on us: How can the Christian work with change in a change setting? How can the Christian work with cultural difference and still maintain a sound Christian faith rooted firmly in the Holy Scriptures? The average Christian, unprepared to cope with change, responds primarily in one of two ways. His response may be to cling tenaciously to every cultural form or expression to which he has become accustomed. If that is his attitude, then every rite and ritual has significance in itself and every institution must remain constant over time. Every word must have fixed meaning. He follows the path of the traditionalist who firms and finalizes every cultural and linguistic form and expression, and responds defensively to any change or innovation introduced into his sociocultural setting.

Another choice the Christian may make is to give up all form. A continual movement persists in Christian circles to do away with rite and ritual, form and expression. And with every destructuring, new forms take hold and entrap. These forms, however, are not built on a base of principle, but on a relativistic or antinomian base: "We do it this way because we like to," or in more sacred terms, "God has led us to do it this way." The firm foundation of sound principle comes only after years of rebuilding confidence in oneself, one's associates, and one's God.

The witness of the gospel of Jesus Christ has suffered from both approaches and responses too long. It is time to instruct people to follow another way: the way of the gospel of Jesus Christ, not one's own ethnocentrism. When ethnocentrism becomes wholly identified with the gospel, a pattern of enslavement ensues. This is evidenced by reactions of nationalism, low motivation in growth, and overall spiritual death.

The mission of the church of Jesus Christ is to introduce Christ into the lives of people everywhere: "Go into all the world and preach the good news to all creation" (Mark 16:15). The missionary becomes an agent of change whether he likes it or not. The gospel of Jesus Christ is tied to no one culture and allows the individual to transcend his own culture. This does not imply that we must attempt to establish a "Christian culture." Rather, it leads to the regeneration of specific cultures by the work of grace within the hearts and lives of the Christians living within those cultures. Christianity can permeate any part of the sociocultural setting or make the whole over anew. An American can become a Christian as an American without being made over into a Nigerian. A Nigerian can become a Christian as a Nigerian without becoming an American. The excitement of Christianity springs from Christ living "in me," to make me pleasing to him through the working of his Holy Spirit.

Not only will I remain an American or a Nigerian, but I will also become the very finest American or Nigerian possible. My sense of responsibility to my nation and to my way of life will be continually refined and developed. This does not mean I will agree with whatever is labeled "American" or "Nigerian," but I will responsibly share in every aspect of American or Nigerian life that is open to me. The same potential applies to everyone who comes to Christ in the conversion-regeneration process. Ideally, he will become a full and completely responsible member of his family, his interest groups, his governmental groups, etc. Gaining fulfillment in these various ways, he will become fully responsible to God. Perfection will not come in any realm, but the progress toward perfection will show in this life and be completed in the life to come.

Training and the Change Process

An exciting aspect of today's learning explosion is that any person can be trained to face the challenge of crosscultural communication quite naturally and without anxiety. This training derives from the behavioral sciences, which when teamed up with sound theology, can help the missionary introduce the gospel of Jesus Christ without its being encumbered with the cultural baggage of the sending society. The missionary is then assured of communicating the true message of salvation in Jesus Christ. The approach presented in this book presents society as a system in balance. An agent of change, seeking to change society or to introduce something new into it, must know the system currently operating. This is done by examining the social control mechanisms that maintain the system. Once he grasps these, through studying the behavior of participants in the system, he can define the system in its operation and also come to know areas of abuse. As he aids the members of the society to live more meaningfully within their society and within their subculture of that society, he will find many natural openings to share his own interests as well as many systemic reinforcements to the effective changes he is able to introduce.

There is no experience in human life more vital and exciting than encountering someone who is different and beginning a mutual trust relationship that grows and matures through time. The experience with God is the most challenging and rewarding. The marriage experience runs a close second. Beyond that, friendship that grows and endures, whether of family or friend, enriches one's life in vital, significant ways. I personally cherish every crosscultural friendship I have ever made. Each has taught me much I could not have learned in any other way.

PART ONE: PRINCIPLES OF CROSSCULTURAL COMMUNICATION

MODEL ONE
THE TRUST BOND

THE TRUST BOND

The trust bond is the foundation for effective relationships. The trust bond model includes five submodels briefly described below.

1. The *Prior Question of Trust* (PQT) is the question asked before all other questions: Is what I am doing, thinking, or saying building or undermining trust?
2. *Developing the Trust Bond* calls attention to levels and stages of trust involvement, monitoring the relationship, and the transfer of trust.
3. The *Acceptance of Self* permits the person to accept himself as he is at any given moment, to understand his own strengths and weaknesses, and to be willing to live with them. This then prepares him to accept others, including God.
4. The *Acceptance of the Other* is the application of self-acceptance to others so that one can interact and accept them as fully responsible members of their own life-way.
5. *Mutual Respect* involves balanced reciprocity in interpersonal relations, leaving both persons intact and valid.

1

Prior Question of Trust

Case Study: Study Program Aborted

Ellen Cooper's family was one of the most respected in her part of the Ozarks. She and her three brothers had attended the state university and returned to the town where their family had lived for generations. She chose teaching and was happy in her work at the county high school.

Ellen's pastor encouraged her to go to a college in the North for several summers where she could get her M.A. in Christian education. With this training she would be a great help to her church. There were few local young people who were qualified to take a leading role in religious instruction, and she seemed perfect for the job.

Ellen looked forward with great enthusiasm to her first trip north and her studies in a Christian college. She was warmly welcomed, and she enjoyed the classes, shrugging off the teasing her classmates and teachers alike gave her about her mountain accent. She kept reminding herself that people tease only those they like.

One evening Ellen entered the reception room with her Bible in her hand on her way to the evening service. "Hi, Ellen," one of the young men called. "What's that you're carrying? Not a Bible! I thought y'all's Bible was the Sears-Roebuck catalog."

Ellen laughed along with the others, but there was a hurt down inside that did not go away, and it seemed to grow as the unrelenting teasing continued.

Entering the dining hall the last morning of school, she was greeted with, "Hey, Ellen, don't tell us you're wearing shoes! You can take them off now and keep them till next summer."

Next summer didn't come. Much to her pastor's disappointment, Ellen found that in succeeding summers she conveniently had to return to the university to take refresher courses for her high school teaching credentials. She could avoid returning to the other college.

The Trust Bond Defined

A simple place to begin in reversing such a picture is the trust bond. *The trust bond is a way of forming good relationships between people.* It is a way of dealing with tension in a relationship. It is a way of alerting people to the need for sensitivity to the other person—who that person is, what needs that person is facing, what opportunities there might be to encourage rather than discourage. Sensitivity is the ability to identify the needs and feelings of another person, assess how his own behavior and attitudes conflict with or reinforce those needs, then to adjust his behavior to communicate who he is.

The trust bond is a relationship between two people or two groups that begins to grow, that suffers slights yet continues to grow, and that ultimately forms a close bond of trust and mutual respect between the participants. The trust bond is not something that is guaranteed to grow. It is not something that one can readily put one's finger on. It is not something that is always visible or available for analysis. It is simply there. The participants feel better because something is drawing them closer together. When the bond is broken for some reason or other—because of a death, a geographical separation, or a lack of maintenance of the bond— there is a keen sense of loss and regret.

The trust bond is relatively easy to form when the participants' culture or subculture is similar. It is more difficult to form when such backgrounds are different. Formal training in trust-bond formation (and thus the development of a conscious awareness of the need to follow sound principles of crosscultural communication) is necessary when one is moving crossculturally. It is also tremendously useful when one remains in one's own culture and subculture. In fact, because every encounter is crosscultural in some way, the trust bond becomes a valuable asset in the communication process. The greatest challenge in relationship occurs when the two parties disagree, and differences in culture and cultural perspective almost guarantee disagreement. The trust bond is a valuable tool in negating the adverse effects of disagreement.

The Question of Trust

No trust bond had built between Ellen and her colleagues at the Christian college. She kept fumbling toward it by ignoring the teasing as long as she could and excusing it as something friendly. Her peers, however, never really reached out to her apart from their own stereotype of a "mountain girl." It is quite possible that if they had been taught a concept that could have let them count to ten—that is, think about what they were going to say—before greeting Ellen, the picture might have been totally different. Instead of alienating Ellen—something that affected not only Ellen, but her church and pastor as well—they might have encouraged her. Instead of pointing up a difference, they could have recognized and supported her uniqueness.

The question of trust expressed as the prior question of trust, is a tool that can help one pause a moment before acting or responding. One can take a fresh look at interaction and allow sensitivity to come to the fore—sensitivity to who the other is and what that one is feeling at that moment in time. The response made or action taken can be supportive and encouraging rather than degrading and destructive.

The prior question of trust (PQT) simply asks: *Is what I am doing, thinking, or saying, building trust or undermining trust?* Is what I am doing, thinking, or saying *potential* for building trust or *potential* for undermining trust?

When we ask the prior question of trust, we do not know what the outcome will be. We do know that a trust relationship will develop that will open channels of communication rather than close them. When the question is not asked, there is a greater likelihood that these channels of communication will close, as was obvious in the case of the "mountain girl."

When one approaches the task of mission, these questions naturally arise: How can I win these people to Jesus Christ? What mission board should I serve under? Where should I serve?

In the marriage relationship or the relationship between special friends, the first question that comes to mind on Valentine's Day or at Christmas time is, What should I give my true love—flowers, a card, a gift?

In the home, the husband or wife considers the question of correct division of labor: Who should do the dishes, sweep the floors, change the diapers?

When children have done something wrong, parents' first reaction is to punish immediately so that they will know for sure that they have done wrong. The question of punishment is therefore the first one that comes to mind.

When Sunday morning comes around, the Christian parent asks, "Should we go to Sunday school or just to church?"

When a question of ethnic difference arises, these questions also arise: What are my rights as an American? as a black? as an Anglo? as a Hispanic? What are my privileges in relation to these rights?

In business or pleasure, selling or buying, lecturing or examining, the first questions that are generally considered are questions of action, participation, and response; questions of who, what, when, and why; questions of correctness or appropriateness; questions of rights or privileges.

If one is seeking to build a relationship, none of the above questions is the appropriate first question to ask in an encounter between individuals or groups. The prior question of trust is the more useful question, the one that has the greatest hope for developing the relationship into something that is positive and helpful to the participants. An empathy will develop between the parties and will increase one's sensitivity to who the other is and what can best be done to see that person's life maximally fulfilled.

The point of mission is seeing a relationship established between man and God. To do this one must begin establishing relationships with other people. In the process of establishing such relationships, a trust bond should be developed. That trust can be transferred to God by the leading of his Spirit. The mission one wants to join will be that which permits a trust relationship to grow among members of the mission; between members of the host society and members of the mission team; and as a result, between members of the host society and God himself. The place of service will be wherever one can be fulfilled as a Christian in the ministry of serving others.

A lover will give his beloved a card if a gift in some way undermines trust, or a gift if flowers are too much, or something other than a card if a card undermines the trust bond. A husband will select the household chores he senses will strengthen the trust bond he has with his wife. A wife will do the same. A father will withhold punishment from a disobedient child if he feels that a direct, immediate punishment will result in a response such as, "I can never do anything right." He may later find opportunity to reveal to his child the wrong that was done, but he will do so in an atmosphere that will communicate to the child that he has done wrong and not in one that will communicate to him that he never does anything right. On the other hand, if the father perceives that by delaying punishment the child will think, "I got away with it," then immediate punishment may be called for.

A family will go to Sunday school if the trust relationship among the members of the family is developed by doing so. They may need to avoid going, if only for a period, if trust is undermined because of some specific condition within the experience. An Anglo will approach a black; and conversely, a black will approach an Anglo in ways that respect the person and reveal this respect in action. In every aspect of life, from the least complex relationship to the most complex, the prior question of trust will open the way to effective communication within a growing trust relationship. The trust bond will be strengthened.

An individual or group does not always do the nice or easy thing in response to the prior question of trust. Jesus overturned the tables of the moneychangers to communicate a positive message to his people about the use of God's house (John 2:14–17). A parent may punish a child; a teacher may fail a student. Participants in a trust bond need to be aware when a nice response is needed and when a seemingly not-so-nice response is called for. I had been named as sponsor, or godparent, to the child of some Filipino friends. My responses to their first "tests" of my interest to such a privilege had been nice, though naïve. I was not going to be within ten thousand miles of their home and yet was expected to deliver a gift to the child each Christmas up to the fifth birthday of the child. When the "tests" were being made in preparation for naming sponsors of a second child, I had to act in a manner that I considered rude, in order to communicate to them that I was in no position to be named sponsor of their newborn.[1]

PQT and Intercultural Relationships

The Philippines

Whenever I enter a society with which I am unfamiliar, I visit with the local authorities and tell them my reasons for being there. This was the practice I followed when I entered the Philippines to live with a Filipino family in a rural city.[2] Upon reaching the city hall, however, I found that the mayor was out of town and the associate mayor was sitting in his place. After visiting for a while, I left. Later I approached my hosts regarding the possibility of holding a luncheon at one of the local restaurants in honor of the associate mayor.

Up to this point, I had already learned a number of things about the Filipinos. For example, I had learned that the men liked to belong to clubs such as the Rotary or Lions or some other group that met together on a regular basis. On their regular luncheon days or on days when some of the members chose to get together for some special celebration, they enjoyed dining at the most exclusive restaurants in town. I had also learned that the mayor was likely to be of the highest social status in the community. Even though I was living with a very high-status, prestigious family, it was my impression that the mayor, as mayor, was above them.[3] Further, I had learned that it is common practice when beginning a relationship with Filipinos to give them favors or gifts.

What I had not learned was that though the mayor was likely of higher status than my host, the associate mayor was likely to be of considerably lower status. Further, the men eat together only when there is a formal occasion; having a luncheon in honor of someone I did not know was not sufficient reason for doing so. Besides, a luncheon was too great a favor or gift at this stage of the relationship. A simple gift from the States would have been just right.

My hosts responded to the possibility of a luncheon in two ways. Verbally, they said that they would think about it. Nonverbally, they communicated that I had really offended them. I had proceeded with a very fine principle—meeting the authorities and making sure that they knew me and why I was there; but I had failed to continue asking the prior question of trust. I had thus offended my hosts, not only by giving them the impression that I did not care for the food that they set before me, but also by suggesting that they were of lower status than the associate mayor. Had I continued asking the prior question of trust (see chapter 2), I would likely have responded to the first visit with the associate mayor by sending a small gift. Then as the relationship developed, I could have had more encounters and reciprocated in more ways to establish the friendship, assuming of course, that he was seeking to see the relationship develop. Had he not demonstrated that he wanted the friendship to continue developing, I would have considered various alternatives and may have finally come to realize that building the friendship was not necessary in light of the goal I was hoping to accomplish.

After sensing that I had offended my hosts, I began asking anew the question of trust. By being a little more careful to compliment my hostess on the food, without overdoing it, and by becoming more consciously aware of the status system operating in the society, I was able to make amends for my previous offense.

The Aguacatec Indians of Guatemala

Some colleagues of mine in an Aguacatec Indian community in Central America were thinking of building a new home. They began asking the typical questions leading to a project of this kind—questions of size, construction material, source of materials, purchase of land, and so on. The Indian believers came to them and forced them to ask the prior question of trust in relation to the nonbelievers. The believers were not only concerned with the trust relationship between the missionaries and the Indian believers, but also with the trust relationship building within the larger community. They wanted unbelieving Indian friends to respond automatically to them and to their message in trust and confidence. Were the missionaries to have too large a home, trust would be undermined. It would also be undermined were they to have too small and simple a home. The believers, not with the motivation of "keeping up with the Joneses," wanted their missionaries to have a home equivalent to that of the local Catholic priest. In this way, they felt they would have the automatic trust of their friends and neighbors. The missionaries eventually built a home that was a bit more elaborate than they had originally intended, but they found that they could handle that satisfactorily. The church grew until it encompassed 80 percent of the community. The Indian believers liked to enter the home and were at ease there. Once the question of trust had been resolved, the other questions found ready solution.

The Pocomchi Indians of Guatemala

After we had been living in the highlands of Guatemala for some time, an Indian man came to the door and said, "I have no money. I have no food. Will you give me some food?" As a Christian and a missionary, I immediately thought of a number of questions: What should I give him? How much does he need? What does the Bible say about giving to a beggar? Is he saved? Can I help his family? Why doesn't he get a job? Does he really need my help?

Answering these questions satisfactorily to myself led me to give the man something to eat. The next week he was back again. I gave him more. He came weekly for a period and then started coming daily. I was still asking the same questions and still coming up with the same answers, so the gifts of food continued. I had established a pattern of giving that had to continue until I began asking some other set of questions. I had not been asking the question of trust.

Had I begun by asking this question in the light of levels of trust, I would have very quickly found out that in that community, a beggar of this type is welcome for a few months. After that time, the community slowly closes him out and communicates to him that it is time that he moves on to another community. They had done their share for this time. The beggar, in this case, did not want to move on and was going now to those who would continue feeding him—namely, the outsiders, e.g., the missionaries, and in this case, the "suckers." The community had suggested that he move on. The missionaries, by continuing to feed him, were undermining the trust bond within the community, thus alienating themselves. The longer they would continue to feed the beggar, the more of a laughingstock they would become within the community and the less they would be respected and trusted. The commands and teachings of the Scriptures were never designed to undermine trust. It is our lack of insight in crosscultural communication that causes us, however well-meaning we are, to undermine the trust relationship, and in effect, achieve the opposite of that which we intend.

American-Filipino, black-Anglo, American-Pocomchi, and Latin-Pocomchi tensions arise from cultural differences. Asking the prior question of trust lets one seek out for the differences that are significant between peoples and then look for ways to resolve or cope with these differences. The PQT thus gives one clearer vision to see through the seemingly personal affront to the deeper meaning in the differences that do exist.

Jesus used the question of trust throughout his ministry. One day he noticed a tax-gatherer named Levi. He went to Levi's house for a meal, in spite of social opposition. This was a powerful act of building trust with Levi even though trust had to be broken with Jesus' critics (Luke 5:27-30). It was the means, however, of trust being built with millions of believers to follow as the church was founded and as it spread. Jesus also called Peter to follow him. Yet Peter trusted Jesus only as a teacher and not as a fisherman. In Luke 5:4-11, Jesus showed Peter that he could trust him even to catch fish.

The story of Jesus clearing the temple (Matt. 21:12-13) appears superficially to negate the use of such a principle. My own viewpoint is that Jesus used the trust question very effectively—in this case, undermining trust with those who were making God's house a "den of robbers," in order to correct the situation by making the temple truly a "house of prayer." He thus built trust with his followers.

Summary

Before trying to answer the other questions that arise within given situations, it is wise to ask the prior question of trust. All other questions will more readily fall into place as information is gathered and plans are executed that build the trust bond rather than undermine it.

Verbal and nonverbal cues (see chapter 15) of behavior alert one to the true nature of the trust relationship, whether it is building or being undermined. These cues are different for each society and need to be learned as part of the language and culture.

Much of life is neutral to trust, therefore one need not be

"turned on" to trust in every experience of life. Someone who is always "working" the trust question, to the exclusion of the other tools of effective crosscultural communication, may communicate another message—that he is in essence seeking to manipulate another to his own ends. Someone who does not use it sufficiently may communicate an insensitivity, a lack of awareness of who the other person really is. An agent of change can rest upon the natural bond of trust that is present between individuals and groups, but he should be aware of what he can do to correct a situation that proves to be one of undermining trust rather than building it.

> Love is patient, love is kind. It does not envy, it does not boast, it is not proud. It is not rude, it is not self-seeking, it is not easily angered, it keeps no record of wrongs. Love does not delight in evil but rejoices with the truth. It always protects, always trusts, always hopes, always perseveres (1 Cor. 13:4–7).

Such love builds trust relationships.

Questions for Discussion

Relating to the Sending Church

1. With whom have you formed a trust bond recently? Can you trace the steps that have helped you develop the relationship?
2. How might we offend others by our speech? our puns? our responses to people? Refer to James 3.
3. What conditions might exist in Sunday school that would cause us to keep a child out temporarily? Would this be wise? How could we work to correct the situation?
4. How might the question of trust appear to prevent us from getting the work of the church done? Explain. Would this necessarily conflict with serving Jesus Christ?
5. How might we "let another person down"? Discuss.

Relating to the Study of the Bible

1. How might we come to conclusions in one aspect of the Scriptures that undermines trust in another aspect? For example, we stress the literal interpretation of husband–wife relationships (Eph. 5:22–32; Col. 3:18–19)), yet we do not insist on the literal use of kneeling in prayer (Acts 9:40; 20:36; 21:5).
2. Study the story of Hannah in 1 Samuel 1, especially the response of Eli to Hannah. Would we have been as accepting of Hannah's plight as was Eli? Note her position as second wife and her emotional condition when making her petition. Discuss.

3. Compare the reactions of Sarai to her husband in Genesis 16 with the reactions of Hannah to her husband when both faced the condition of barrenness. Which woman do you feel handled the situation the best? Why do you react as you do?

4. Study the entrance of Abram and Sarai into Egypt. Was Abram justified in introducing Sarai as he did—that is, as his sister (Gen. 12:10–20)?

5. Do you feel that Jesus was asking the prior question of trust when he expressed physical violence in the temple (Matt. 21:12)? Whether you do feel this or not, argue the case that he was asking the PQT. What fresh insights does this point of view give you regarding the action? regarding Jesus' approach to others? regarding Jesus' relationship to God?

Relating to Mission and Crosscultural Ministry

1. Have you encountered a challenge to ask the prior question of trust such as is noted in the cases of the Filipino associate mayor, the Aguacatec missionary house, or the Pocomchi beggar? Explain.

2. What specific things have you had to do or say to communicate trust with the people with whom you have served?

3. In some cultures, the concept of God as Father is next to meaningless. How might you use other scriptural concepts of God to communicate the truth of God to people?

4. What have been the greatest challenges in forming trust bonds that you have had to face with your missionary colleagues?

5. What major decision or plan have you had to change recently in order to build trust with the people among whom you serve?

Group Activities and Exercises

1. *Activity*. Pass the Bod. A group of seven or eight people stand or sit in a tight circle. One person stands in the center of the circle, closes his eyes, and proceeds to fall toward one side of the circle without moving his feet. The people in the circle extend their hands and gently pass the person in the center from one to the other, at times passing him across the circle. Young people like this trust game so well that they have made it a party game. With an effective debriefing session (see below) afterwards, it becomes a significant foundation block of the course.

2. *Activity*. Lift the Bod. One person lies on the floor on his back with his eyes closed, his legs extended, and his arms crossed. Seven or eight other people proceed to lift him over their heads proceeding very gradually until the person is as high as the group can lift him. They then lower him gradually and gently

until he is again on the floor—but without the awareness that he has touched down.

Debriefing for Activities 1 and 2: How did you feel during the experience? Be sure to ask this of each of the participants, not just the one passed or lifted. When were your eyes "forced open"? This would be a sign of the undermining of trust. Why do you think this is called a "trust" game? In what ways are you called upon to cooperate with your group members?

3. *Individual response.* Distribute slips of paper and ask each member of the group to describe briefly a recent situation that left a "bad taste." When this is done, ask each one to focus on one participant in the situation—the one he blames for the bad experience. Then ask him to record briefly how the situation might have turned out differently had the one he blames asked the prior question of trust.

4. *Lived experience.* Suggest that each group member practice using the prior question of trust for a few days. Have the members report orally or in writing the kinds of things that happened when they asked the trust question. Did their relationships improve? What characteristic behavior attended the action built upon the prior question of trust?

5. *Interview.* Find a local pastor who has recently moved into the area. Probe with him the various things he feels he is having to do to build trust in the community.

6. Consult the activity section of chapter 13 for instructions for the "blind walk." It could be used at this time very effectively as a trust exercise. The debriefing would be specifically regarding the building and undermining of trust.

2

Developing the Trust Bond

Case Study: Two Administrators in Mission

Two mission administrators were working in distinct aspects of their mission program, but their responsibilities overlapped in the case of a local pastor. He was under the jurisdiction of both the administrator supervising the churches and the one supervising educational institutions. The two administrators were not friends because of unpleasant interactions in their earlier ministry together. Now they were responsible for seeing the pastoral and educational ministries move forward. Further, they were responsible for encouraging this national pastor-educator in a strategic church in the urban setting of their mission area. The two administrators had been trained in seminary, so they knew the Bible and had sound theology. They had not achieved fluency in the language of the people with whom they were working as they had not had linguistic and language learning training. They were unaware of the cultural system because they had not had anthropological training. Conflict had developed with the national leaders even though they had prayed and trusted the Lord for direction in the program they had dedicated to him. They had had no crosscultural training and were unaware that there were sound principles to follow that would enable them to develop good relationships with one another, with the young pastor, with the church, and especially with the church leaders. In fact, they were unaware that it was even necessary to be concerned about that, since they felt if they did their job and prayed, the Lord would bless their ministry.

The two administrators were likely to clash head-on in their interaction involving the pastor-educator. They were unaware that tensions existing between themselves would quickly be communicated to the young man. They were unaware that the pastor would not only be caught in the middle, but that he would also be negatively affected in his own work because of such tensions. He would not feel free to handle his job creatively for the good of the church and the good of the children in his school.

Unfortunately, the two administrators would not likely be sensitive to the pastor's reactions, even as they would not likely be sensitive to their own feelings and reactions in any time of conflict and disagreement.

There was no time for them to take formal training even if it were available. Prayer would likely only leave them with the feeling that they were handling things correctly and that the situation was in God's hands and would therefore work out all right. It was quite possible that it would. Perhaps the tension would pass and the conflict would be shallow and short-lived. However, the likelihood was not only that they would clash and clash again, but also that the pastor would despair and seek some other place of service, and the witness of the gospel would suffer immeasurably.

Levels of Trust

Trust develops within groups in keeping with levels of complexity existing within those groups (see figure 2). A person living within a family, a community, a nation, or a complex of nations assumes that what is done affects only those immediately involved with the action. This is not so, however. The impact of such action can be felt throughout the system and can even influence governmental policy.

During my years of service in Latin America, I was constantly confronted with the question of whether to teach Maya Indians to read only in their own dialect or also in Spanish. In considering the matter of levels of trust, it became clear to me that they must be taught to read in Spanish if they were to become vital members of the larger community. Teaching them to read in the language of their group could facilitate this but could not replace it in significance. If they were not taught to read Spanish and then later were to enter the Spanish-speaking community, they would not be well prepared for that society. They could, moreover, very quickly associate their unfulfilled need with those who had the knowledge and the tools to teach them Spanish. I might have a very effective growing trust relationship with them at one moment, but if I were not preparing them for life in the larger community, I would actually be sowing seeds of distrust that would later result in a breakdown of trust within the community. They needed to learn Spanish for their individual as well as their group identity.

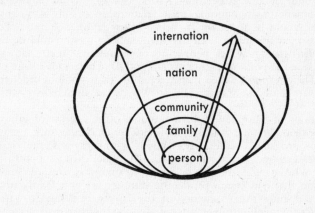

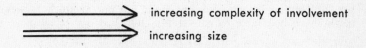

increasing complexity of involvement

increasing size

Figure 2. Levels of Trust

Reinforcing the trust bond on one level while at the same time understanding it on some other level ultimately undermines it on the starting level.

In developing the trust bond, I would not attempt to inundate the Indians with Spanish. My responsibility would be to work with them in developing a natural pride in their own language, which they had learned at their mother's knee and which was maximally meaningful to them. A good knowledge of their mother tongue would avoid unsettledness and even chaos in their everyday experience.[1] But my responsibility would not stop there. As they progressed toward involvement in the national community, it would be my opportunity to move ahead of them and prepare the way for their further development. It would be up to me to know what they needed even before they sensed their own need. I would then proceed to teach them in the light of their actual identity and with their potential in mind. A trust relationship would be building. At any point that trust was undermined, I would back off, take a new look at the larger whole, and move in again in the light of the new information I had been enabled to garner, as well as in the light of new associations I had been able to make. In the development of an ongoing trust relationship in this way, my attempt would be to *maneuver* them in their favor, not mine. To work with them solely with my own ends in view would be to *manipulate* them. When people are manipulated, their natural response at the point of awareness is "You have taken advantage of me." Their response when maneuvered for their good in order to meet their sensed or stated goals is "We're glad you are here with us."

Levels of trust development involve other aspects of group involvement. When a Sunday school teacher teaches in such a way that the program of the larger church is undermined, the class becomes a source of conflict in the church, rather than a supporting entity. When a child feels that he can go his own way irrespective of the bond that had begun to identify him as part of a family, the emotional and creative energy of the family is turned toward restoring the relationship as it formerly stood, rather than stretching and reaching out creatively for the good of the family as a whole. The family gains by this effort, but not as much as they might have been able to gain if the child had not rebelled.

Stages of Trust

Every trust relationship passes through what might be called "stages" in the development of trust. These can be any kind of milestone that indicates to the participants of the trust bond the developing nature of their trust. They could be shared experiences, new relationships developed with others, or periods of trial and testing. The relationship builds when the stages of trust are passed effectively by all participants within the trust relationship. Trust is reinforced when all move together through the relationship development. Trust is undermined when someone lags behind in the trust process. Judas, one of Jesus' disciples, lagged behind in the developing trust relationship Jesus was establishing with his disciples and became the vulnerable part of the team. He ultimately betrayed Jesus, committed suicide (Matt. 27:5), and was replaced by Matthias (Acts 1:15–26).

American young people entering on the path of courtship think in terms of dating, going steady, engagement, and finally marriage. These are milestones of a sort, but they are more static than dynamic. In order to keep up with society's expectations, the couple is likely to move from one stage to another even though trust and confidence at one stage of the relationship may not have been developed. They tend to cover up, at times, the differential development of trust. Another more dynamic set of such stages for a couple might be friendship, the building of confidence through the sharing of minor trials and challenges, the developing confidence of family, the building of confidence through more serious trials, and finally total trust and confidence. A way to chart such a developing love affair is illustrated in figure 3 below.

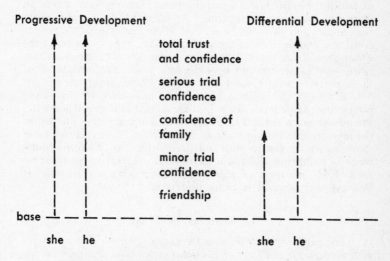

Figure 3. The Development of Trust in Courtship

When trust develops apace, with each one passing through the various stages together, the couple is ideally fully ready for engagement and marriage. Their relationship has developed personally and in keeping with their societal norms. When marriage takes place, the two are ready physically, emotionally, and spiritually for one another. Where there is a differential development of trust, one holds certain thoughts and concerns back from the other and is less than fully ready for marriage.

Recognition of a Trust Relationship

Within the crosscultural setting, verbal cues such as words, pauses, and intonations are all indicative of the nature of the trust relationship. Nonverbal cues, such as facial expressions, eye contact, positioning of hands and feet, yawns, drawl, and even vibrato connected with speech, all signal the presence or absence of trust. Even as language differs from society to society, verbal and nonverbal cues also differ and must be learned.

When the participants become aware of the nature of the trust relationship that is building, a number of developments will become evident. There will be an increase of self-confidence in each of the participants. Each one involved in the trust relationship will be self-aware and self-assured and will develop uniquely. This development will not occur apart from responsibility to the groups of which the individual is a part, however. Rather, there will be an increasing awareness of the group. A personal and a group relaxing will occur, and this can be termed "being at peace." A greater consistency in the lives of the individuals and the expression of the group should also result. It is obvious that none of these characteristics were present in our opening case study. Seldom are all of these characteristics present in a given relationship.

Although the relationship of the missionary to the target population in mission is not as intimate as that of husband and wife, the missionary must still be aware of developing stages of trust in the relationship. He must also be aware of levels of complexity as they impact the relationship and the participants. Each one must work to build trust and not undermine it, whether by word or by deed. Each one must be able to recognize when a trust bond is building and when it is being undermined.

The Transfer of Trust

The transfer of trust involves the extending of the trust one shares with one person or group to each additional person or group involved in the relationship. A trust bond can develop between two individuals or two groups, but there is no guarantee that a third party or group entering the picture will benefit from the bond already established. The transfer of trust must therefore be carried out as carefully, thoughtfully, and prayerfully as is the development of the original trust bond. In John 1:40–42, we read that Andrew first met Jesus and then went and brought Simon saying, "We have found the Messiah." Jesus looked at Simon and said, "You shall be called Peter." Jesus was constantly drawing people into his orbit. They came willingly—first the Twelve, then the Seventy, then in ever-expanding numbers. He worked with the disciples (Mark 3:13–19; 6:7–13; Luke 9:1–6) to perfect the transfer of trust.

In Christian homes, a pastor, a missionary, or even simply a long-time friend of the parents might come to visit. The children, not knowing this person, might react to the visitor as a complete stranger. Unless the parents overtly transferred the trust they had established with the visitor to the children, and again, with the children to the visitor, the children could lose a significant opportunity for establishing a new friendship, gaining some perspective regarding their future life goals, or even having an opportunity to encourage the visitor.

In education, in the church, and in business, outsiders are constantly being introduced to the group that has been established. There is a high potential for the disruption of the group unless the transfer of trust is made. The outsider is thus inserted into the group and the group process. In educational circles, a guest lecturer may be presented as a friend of the professor, as a fine person, or as a good family man. All of these factors are of interest to someone, but because such a group is gathered in an academic setting, it is vitally important to introduce the person, at least in part, through his or her academic credentials. To introduce a guest speaker to a Fundamentalist church congregation without saying anything about the guest's conversion experience is to fail the guest at the very heart of the occasion. Trust will not be fully transferred, and the audience will fail to listen to the speaker no matter how authoritative the content of the message.

Because the average person does not know how to transfer trust from one person to another in his everyday experience, he likely does not know how to transfer the trust bond from his own Savior, Jesus Christ, to another. Contemporary witness training does not take into account the need for such transfer of trust. The average Christian thinks that the key to witness is presenting the gospel message in some form—for example, through the use of "The Four Spiritual Laws" or some equivalent approach. The key to effective witness is not directing a message at someone, rather, it is the transfer of the trust bond from one's own relationship with Christ to the other person.

Monitoring the Trust Relationship

It was my privilege to go underground beneath the county building complex in a large city in the United States. Just inside the entrance was a huge console with many unlit lights on it. A man was seated before the console ready to respond if a light should light up. The lights of the console were connected to stress points in the electrical and plumbing systems that connected the giant complex. One man was able to monitor the entire system. Such a system was effective as long as the one seated behind the console was alert and knew how to make the correct response when necessary. In much the same way, *trust relationships must be monitored continually*. This does not mean that we let such observation intrude into the obvious aspects of the relationship. Rather, we need to deal with changes in the relationship that are potentially destructive to it. For example, I was late in picking up my daughter to take her to the bank where she worked, and as she got into the car she slammed the door. Then we rode to the bank in silence. Noting such signals, I quietly let her out but made it an obvious point after that time to be punctual. She let me know not long after that just how much she appreciated (1) my not jumping down her throat for her surliness and (2) my making it a point to be on time since then. Our relationship increased in strength through such difficulties as these. It could have come undone.

Jethro, Moses' father-in-law, became aware of the lack of maintenance in the relationship of Moses with God's people. He stepped in to help. He recommended to Moses: "Select capable men from all the people—men who fear God . . . and appoint them . . . [to] serve as judges for the people . . . [then] you will be able to stand the strain, and all these people will go home satisfied" (Exod. 18:21–23). Moses had been "burning the candle at both ends," and things were not much better for all his sacrifice. Jethro's recommendation took the burden off Moses to be doing everything himself.

Bonding

When an individual or a group enters another major subculture or culture, the immediate challenge is to find an entry of significance into the new setting.[2] *Role relationships that are appropriate to the overall purposes of the group will need to be sought out.* Relationships with individuals and organizations must be established. Such relationships result in bonding together participants. It is vitally important to the overall success of the effort for members of the group to know just what these social roles are and what kinds of relationships are formed. The average missionary, when entering a new mission setting, will frequently relate to known roles from his own background. It is irrelevant to him whether these are appropriate to his present purpose or not. Even more, he will relate to "his own kind of people" before he begins relating to the people to whom he has gone to serve. Such relationships may undermine trust. Bonding calls for building relationships of mutual trust.

Summary

The trust bond is developed through the use of the prior question of trust, a means of allowing us to count to ten before taking action or responding to action. The trust bond builds between two people, two groups, or a group and an individual, insuring that their relationship becomes a positive force in their respective lives. It develops through various levels of complexity, from the simplest and nearest to the most complex and farthest. Nothing can be done in a vacuum. The effects are felt throughout the system of interpersonal relationships that has been established. Trust develops by stages, and staging is important in bringing participants in a relationship to decision at the same time and in the same way so that the decision is supportive of the relationship. Trust developing may be transferred effectively to a second relationship as long as it does not undermine the first.

Acceptance of self is the beginning point of change that allows one to relate to someone who is different. Acceptance of the other communicates an equality of person and an acceptance of the validity of lifestyle that leaves the other open to influence. Mutual trust allows the relationship to grow in such a way that no one has the advantage or is taken advantage of. Such balance forms a strong foundation for trust and whatever may grow out of the trust relationship.

Questions for Discussion

Relating to the Sending Church

1. Do you believe that a trust bond has developed in the church you serve? Does it encompass the entire congregation? How does the trust relationship show? Has the bond been broken in recent days? If so, what seems to have caused this? How could it be rebuilt?
2. Likely the community has changed in recent years, and many of the members of the church have moved out of the old community yet are still attending the church. Do you know the neighbors of the church? How might you begin developing a trust bond within the immediate community? Within the larger community? Are there distinct ethnic groups now in the community? How might you develop trust bonds with the various ethnic groups?
3. List some situations in the church in which it would be necessary to have effective transfer of trust from one person to another.
4. Attempt to transfer the trust of a friend to another. Once you are aware of the steps involved, then attempt to transfer your trust

in Jesus Christ to another person. Does it work the same as in human relationships? Does it work differently? Discuss.

5. If you are attempting to reach a person or group for Jesus Christ, examine your own associations to see if you are in fact becoming bonded to the people you wish to reach or if you are becoming bonded to others with whom you feel comfortable but do not have the same compulsion to reach. In which direction do you want to go?

6. How have you felt manipulated in the church by people who want you to express your faith as they do? How have you felt maneuvered? Which type of experience did you feel best about? Which did you feel worst about?

Relating to the Study of the Bible

1. With whom did Jesus establish a trust bond? Were these always "reputable" people? Explain.

2. There were the Twelve in Jesus' experience; there were also the one hundred twenty, the five hundred, and the multitudes. Did Jesus have the same kind of trust bond with each group? Discuss.

3. How did Abraham develop trust throughout the entire area in which he lived? How did Moses?

4. Discuss the preparations in Egypt for the Exodus. What practices did the Hebrews have that built trust, and what practices failed to build trust? Answer this same question in regard to Joseph's life and Jonah's life.

5. Study the first chapters of the Book of Acts and see if you can account for the developing trust relationship exhibited there.

Relating to Missions and Crosscultural Ministry

1. With whom have you developed a trust bond in your field of ministry? How did you go about it? What were the results? Did the person(s) assume leadership in the church? Explain.

2. Did the church start in the larger community and then finally reach a smaller one, or did it begin in a smaller one and reach out into the larger community? What were the dynamics that attended this development?

3. How do you present a guest to the national church so that they gain the most from his visit? Discuss.

4. With whom did you associate upon entering your field of service—the nationals? the missionaries? others? Explain. Did this add to or detract from your ministry?

5. What actions might build trust in one culture yet undermine it in another?

Group Activities and Exercises

1. *Research.* Let each group member circulate in the larger group and write down all the cultural differences he discovers through visual or auditory stimuli—e.g., language differences, taste preferences, fashion distinctives, different expectations of goals and aspirations, etc. Share these differences in the larger group audibly through a debriefing experience or by having two members of the group collate the lists and prepare a copy for each member.

2. *Role play.* In groups of four or five, have two- to three-minute skits prepared depicting the members' perception of some aspect of mission. Suggest that the skits have two parts; e.g., how others do it and how we would do it, before and after, as outsiders and as insiders. This is for the members of the group to get acquainted with one another and also to tune into the diverse perceptions of mission.

3. *Activity.* Name Game. To get acquainted, have groups of twenty or fewer sit in a circle and let the leader give his first name. The next person will then give the leader's first name and then his own. The third person will start again with the leader's first name, the second person's first name, then his own. This will continue until everyone has had a turn. The last person will be giving everyone's first name. Repeat the process, giving full names. Let the last person start this round. Following this second round, have a specific interest added to the full name—e.g., C. S. Lewis, sports, music, or evangelism. By the end of the third round, everyone in the group should have a beginning acquaintance with everyone else.

4. An alternate experience that uses only three persons in a group is presented as Experience #1 in volume 1 of *Handbook of Structured Experiences for Human Relations Training* by J. William Pfeiffer and John E. Jones (Iowa City, Iowa: University Associates Press, 1971).

5. *Activity.* Have the students keep a list of every surprise and every irritation they face in interpersonal encounters in a forty-eight-hour period. When they report in, encourage them to indicate how the surprise or irritation is clearly linked to some cultural difference.

6. Play the game Change Agent early in your course. This game is available from Biola University (La Mirada, Calif.) and can be played in a group of fifteen to forty people. It is a good game to start training in crosscultural communication, for it shows just how difficult it is for the average person to rise above his culture and make a change of attitude or of action.

Debriefing of these various activities and others suggested in the following chapters can involve the following basic debriefing questions: How did you feel during the experience? What did you see going on? What did you learn that fits in with your other learning?

3

Acceptance of Self

Case Study: The Unwed Father

Dear Ann Landers:

Recently an irate mother wrote and asked why you never had any kind words for the unwed father. Your reply was very unsympathetic. You said you had no good-conduct medals lying around for unwed fathers and that it was always the girl who paid. You added, "The boy can go about his business. . . . Nothing changes for him." I disagree. I am not an unwed father but my best buddy is. Believe me, he has paid plenty. He got the news when he was a junior in college. He actually wanted to marry the girl but her folks were against it, and she listened to them—not to him. His life changed that very day. He began to feel depressed and couldn't study. His grades went to the dogs. He flunked out and had to take a laborer's job. He is paying child support, and he will continue to pay until the child is twenty-one. The worst of it is the guy feels so guilty and worthless now that he refuses to take out a girl. He doesn't think he's good enough for anybody. Some unwed fathers may be bums, but some are good guys who made a mistake. In this case the girl made a better adjustment than the boy. She recently married a nice fellow and seems to be very happy.—For Justice[1]

Acceptance of the Person: The Self

> Freedom to be what I am now, always . . . saying yes to
> all that has been inside of me, to all that is, to all the potential
> of the will-be. But how much easier it is to say yes to the
> possible with its hope; its, perhaps, the tomorrowness; than
> to the now that is freedom, yes, maybe yes.[2]

The subject of the above letter to Ann Landers is a young man
who could not accept himself as an unwed father, a rejected suitor,
or a child-support provider. He lived in constant conflict with all
the possibilities of today and tomorrow. He saw himself as a
failure. He had no way to turn his life around and become a fully
productive member of his society. Instead, he continued on in his
self-deprecating, self-defeating way of life, facing a most unpleasant
reality.

The poem expresses a different way, an ideal that can aid one
in restoring a more promising real experience. It suggests a plan of
self-acceptance.

The Difficulty of Accepting Oneself

Is there anything about you that you would change if you
could? One young lady responded by saying, "I hated wearing
glasses, and I resented the fact that my parents couldn't afford to
give me contact lenses." Another asked, "Why did I have to work
for money when other students had time to get to know each other
and involve themselves in organizations?" Another girl's siblings
each had a name beginning with the same letter, but hers began
with a different letter. She thought that this indicated that her
parents favored her siblings.

Displeased with his forgetfulness, one young man wrote, "I
am absent-minded when it comes to remembering errands to
accomplish, so I began writing these things down rather than
saying to myself, 'Oh, you'll remember to do that!' " Another
young man wrote, "I am a perfectionist—not that everything has
to be done exactly 100 percent perfect before I will hand it in, but I
will strive to do the best possible job I can in the amount of time
available to me. This in itself represents a change from an earlier
attitude of perfection or nothing at all. This change grew out of an
acceptance of the impossibility of gaining perfection in school
work."

There are many things in our lives that we find unacceptable.
We react to such lack of self-acceptance with rejection, a turning
aside from our good points, our strengths, and our abilities. In the
process, we find ourselves turning inward, sacrificing a creative
spirit for a self-defeating one.

It is difficult for one to accept himself as he is. The easier path is one of rejection, of dissatisfaction with what one is, with what one has.

Others reject us, why shouldn't we reject ourselves? If we are the kind of person that others cut down, turn off, reject, what is there about us that is worthy of acceptance or of self-respect? What does the young man in the case study have to live for? He faces an unwanted pregnancy, child-support payments, flunking out of college, and enduring a job that has little challenge for him. He perceives that he is rejected by everyone and everything important to him: his girl's parents, his girl, his college, and his future. He probably perceives that even his own child will reject him, even after providing for the child for twenty-one years.

Our society, represented by those influencing us, sets definitive standards for us, and we are unable to meet them all. It becomes very easy to feel that we are inadequate in some way and to succumb to an attitude of self-rejection. Many average students feel pressured to strive for grades that are in reality beyond their reach; and in striving they see the grade as an ultimate goal, obscuring for them the true goal of personal development. In the process of the grade struggle, they lose their self-respect through the rejection of their abilities.

The task of self-acceptance is further complicated by those who interpret the biblical injunction, "he must deny himself" (Matt. 16:24), as "denial" in the sense of self-rejection. Certainly this interpretation points to a truth in that we dare not be proud of what we are or have because it has been given to us from God. However, in another sense, the very moment of denial of self is the moment of acceptance of self. Whatever we reject, we are unable to turn over to someone else. When we accept ourselves at a given point—for example, we say, "I'm a worrier"—we are able to admit to God at that very moment that we worry. Then God can enter our lives and work with us as we are. That which we refuse to accept, we actually cling to, and the effect stays with us. It turns to selfishness, not selflessness.

Some segments of the Evangelical tradition suggest to us that we are not good enough as we are. We have to be what "God tells us to be." We have to follow a particular standard of Christian behavior to please him. There is a "Christian" way that must be learned. This continually leaves the Christian with a basic discontent. He is always striving to be that which he is not. Such striving ends in a life of continual struggle and dissatisfaction. One begins to cover up the truth, to whitewash it. One cannot know who he truly is, and he thus communicates to others something he is not nor ever can be. The person readily comes through as a fake to others.

Another cause for Christians rejecting themselves is that they feel they are not worthy of being Christians, of having God interested in them. A key reinforcement of this idea within the Christian community is Isaac Watts's song "At the Cross," in which the question is asked, "Would [Christ] devote that sacred head *for such a worm as I?*" One of the pitfalls of Reformed theology is that the individual is made to feel worthless before God. The Reformers, I feel, never intended this thought that has been reinforced through the centuries and now comes to us as "gospel truth." In our relationship to God, we are worth something to him. Ephesians 1:18 speaks to this with impact: "God has been made rich because we who are Christ's have been given to him!" (LB). The Reformers were trying to convey that the sinful self is unworthy. This is the tragic problem with Judaism. Its adherents do not recognize that Christ made freedom from sin and death possible for them by his death on the cross. Through Christ we no longer have to live by the law, constantly trying to make ourselves right with God. When the Jew spends all of his time and energy trying to make himself right with God, he possesses no time, no standing, no insight by which to be of any service to God. Because we are sinners, we are unworthy of meeting God *as we are,* without someone or something to make us worthy. But he has taken our sin upon himself through the blood of Christ, and this makes us significant to God, vital and enriching to him. *We are important to God, and he accepts us just as we are.*

Finally, you may be confusing self-acceptance, or being what you really are, with what you think you ought to be. Someone who lives in keeping with what he thinks he ought to be can never accept himself as he is. Any basis for change rests on a shifting base. One can easily think of new ways in which he ought to be different. Every person we meet has a different idea of what we ought to be, of what we ought to do. Until this change potential is built upon the solid foundation of what one is, it is spurious, shifting, uncertain, and inconsistent. Or, if acceptance is based on what we think we are, we may perceive what we are incorrectly.

Acceptance of Self Is the Beginning Point of Change

The person truly accepting himself as he is will not stay that way. He will change in keeping with what he is. The change process will not be erratic, not hit and miss. It will cause the person to respond, "I'm glad it worked that way." The process of self-acceptance and thus of true self-denial leads one on the path to Holy Spirit guidance of the Christian life through internal motivation. The change process starts from within the life and flows out into every contact and association beyond.

It is interesting to note that unless there is change, the person is not likely accepting himself or herself. Self-acceptance does not leave the person with a static, unchanging lifestyle. That person is constantly monitoring personal and group growth potentials and is finally free from self and self-centeredness to be able to reach out to others. This does not result in conformity, rather it leads to the enrichment of self and others.

Rejection of self, on the other hand, will continually leave a person wishing for effective change in his life, and he will be dissatisfied with the change process working in him.

James and a Formula

Acceptance of self is a process. It may not be achieved on the first try. Worked with until it becomes a way of life, it sets the scene for effective change in one's personal life, and it has beneficial results when one is dealing with others. In the New Testament, James has given us a guide to acceptance of ourselves. In 1:2, we read, ". . . is your life full of difficulties and temptations? . . ." (LB). *By accepting our difficulties which are potential for building us up, and our temptations which are potential for tearing us down, we become mature and "ready for anything"* (v. 4 LB).

James thus encourages us to accept our difficulties. They are ours and no one else's. They grow out of our uniqueness. We are to work with them and not throw up our hands and give up. All of us face many difficulties in our everyday lives. I personally do not face any difficulty in working out a problem in construction of houses, since I am not engaged in construction work. Rather, my difficulties involve working out complicated interpersonal relationships among students and between students and teachers. My difficulties lie in preparing lectures, not in preparing architectural drawings. The difficulties I face are mine. They make me what I am. Facing up to my difficulties can help me become a strong person.

Almost in the same breath, James tells us to accept our temptations as well as our difficulties. He does not say yield to them or become upset by them; he simply says accept them. The temptations we face are our own, not anyone else's. They have the potential for tearing us down if we yield to them. But they too can strengthen us toward maturity. Because I do not handle large sums of money in my work as a bank teller does, I am not concerned with being tempted by money. But I am sometimes tempted to go to class partially prepared or to recommend someone more highly than he deserves for graduate school if I particularly like him. These are my temptations, not yours. They make me uniquely me. Your temptations make you uniquely you.

Knowing yourself and understanding your own true identity

includes accepting your difficulties and temptations as you become aware of them. James is not simply telling you to accept them; he is saying that it is tremendous that they are yours. "Then be happy" (1:2 LB), he says. With each step you take in life, you will face either a difficulty or a temptation, and James simply suggests that when you take the next step, you say, "Great! That's me!"

Many people falsely think that if they want to know themselves, they have to look inward in an introvertive way. Introversion and acceptance are two completely different things. Introversion comes from looking in, from minimum action. Acceptance comes from looking out, from maximum action. Introversion will make one dwell on what one is or thinks he is. Acceptance will cause a person to move out and recognize a difficulty or temptation, and in accepting it, be on the way to resolving the difficulty or standing firm to the temptation. James is suggesting that "when the way is rough, your patience has a chance to grow" (1:3 LB). Introversion leads to impatience. Acceptance leads to patience with oneself and then with others. He goes on further, "So let it grow, and don't try to squirm out of your problems. For when your patience is finally in full bloom, then you will be ready for anything, strong in character, full and complete" (v. 4 LB).

Accepting Our Present

I was talking with a nurse recently, who said, "I just can't live with the incompetence of others. This affects what I do at the hospital and at home, and it affects my relationships with other girls. The fellows think I'm a snob." She probably is perceived as a snob by almost everyone, since she cannot accept herself as she is and, therefore, cannot accept others as they are. Her lack of patience with herself at each moment in time makes it impossible for her to accept others as they are. She is trying to be something other than what she really is, and in the process, she is trying to make others over, since she is unaccepting of them. We sat together and talked for about fifteen minutes, and with every indication from her of what she was, I said, "Great! That's you. Accept it." I suggested that over a twenty-four-hour period, every time she had some little revelation of what she was through some action or thought, she should just say, "That's me! That's great! I accept myself just as I am. That's the way God accepts me." In a very remarkable and unique way, she began to pull out of her rejection pattern and to become a person who was much more pleasant to live with.

Can I accept myself just as I am at any moment in time? Can I accept myself as a worrier? Yes! Yes, to both questions! In the acceptance of myself as a worrier, God has a solid base on which to build my life the way he wants it for me. Can I accept myself as rejected by someone? Yes, for from that moment on, I will be able to discover just why I am being rejected, and I can build toward a relationship that is meaningful with that person. Can I accept myself as having a dull spiritual life? Yes, for at that moment, I will become motivated to do something about it. Can I accept myself as being licentious? Yes, for *in the moment of acceptance, God can begin to make me a responsible person for his glory*.

Thankfulness to God for all that he does for us and "against" us is a direct route to acceptance. When rain spoils our plans for an outing and we are sitting in a worship service talking with God, it is difficult to thank him for the rain. In the moment of thankfulness, we share with him in the acceptance of his perfect will.

A summer "missionary" was working in Chicago. He was confronted by a couple of toughs who looked menacingly at him. He could have stood up to them and fought, but as he said later, he realized that he was afraid. He admitted to them that he was "chicken," and a strange thing happened. One of those toughs was also afraid but would not admit it to his buddies or himself. Not long after, the tough looked up the mission recruit and said, "I'm chicken, too. You're the first guy that ever played it straight with me. Let's talk."

A missionary went overseas to work with children. After a time she attempted to pray in the language of her host country but found it terribly difficult, since she had not mastered the language well enough. There came a point during a prayer time with the children when she just started praying in English. At that moment, the rapport between her and her friends rose sharply. They could see that she had accepted herself just as she was—an English-speaking American trying hard to learn another language.

Accepting Our Past and Our Future

Accepting ourselves as we are does not mean simply accepting ourselves as we are at this moment in time. It means *accepting our past and our future*. A young woman from a Mennonite background asked me to supervise her work in an honors project that had to do with developing an understanding of her present faith. She said, "I'm not sure of just what I do believe." I suggested to her that she study her own background. I urged her to determine what was in her own Mennonite past that she could accept, but more important, what was there that she was making significant effort to forget or to reject. I suggested to her that in knowing and understanding her background, she would have better grounds for accepting herself as she was at that time. She responded that she could never do that. I added further that in her background she would be likely to find a basis for her present faith. This is the source from which she accepted God in the first place. The more she rejected this past, the more difficult it would be for her to know where she stood with God in her present setting.

When I was a boy, I memorized many passages of Scripture, both short and long, some meaningful and others meaningless to me. When I grew older, I rejected this part of my background, feeling that I had simply memorized the passages by rote and that the memorization was useless to me. Later I began to see its value, and I accepted my Fundamentalist past, including Bible memorization. Since that time, this memory work has proven useful repeatedly as I have prepared articles for publication, lectures for classes, and discussions and special presentations. Because the Word of God is in my mind, I can scan large passages without ever having to read them, and I am able to draw out what is useful to confirm or negate the work I am doing.

When we reject our past, we often salvage the bad, i.e., that which is least useful, out of our background. We do not intend to do this, but our rejection blinds us to what is quite frequently most valuable to us. It focuses on what we do not like, rather than on what is useful to us for the present time. Acceptance allows us to consider both the useful and useless more objectively. In a rational way, we can then select out of our past that which is useful to us and what can aid us in the challenge we face at any given time. The young unwed father's rejection of his past affects his present and his future. It has delayed him in coming to terms with himself and with those about him. It has delayed his maturation as an adult.

What about the future? Some people are always looking ahead to tomorrow, and by doing this they run the risk of rejecting their past and their present. One day I saw a beautiful four-thousand-dollar organ. It was a marvelous instrument, and I was tremendously excited with the thought of owning it and being able to play it any time I chose. My first thought was that I would save and buy it "tomorrow." Then I realized just who I was—a college professor with no savings and little hope of having the amount that was called for in a reasonable period of time. I realized that even as I had begun to accept myself as I was yesterday and as I am today, that I must also accept myself with a future in which there is little place for an expensive organ. Things may change, but at the moment I accepted myself as being unable to afford such an organ, I was at peace.

Acceptance of self gives us practice accepting that which is close to us. It allows us to practice on something that is real. Then, when we move out into the world among others, we can accept them more readily. The practice of self-acceptance will become a way of life, and we will be ready to accept others as fully valid and unique. Practicing acceptance on that which we see and feel also makes it easier to accept God whom we have not seen.

Acceptance of Self in the Bible

Those persons in the Scriptures who accepted themselves as they were had a vital role to play in the development of the Christian faith. David sinned many times throughout his life, but he accepted what he was and what he did. The Psalms are full of the record of David's recognition of himself as a sinner in need of cleansing and forgiveness, and the record is a moving testimony of a man growing before God. When facing the Cross, Jesus accepted God's will for him. He prayed, "Take this cup from me. Yet not what I will, but what you will" (Mark 14:36). Paul accepted his limitations and admitted them. He wrote, "See what large letters I use as I write to you with my own hand!" (Gal. 6:11), and "I am an ambassador in chains" (Eph. 6:20). He was full of joy while in prison, and he told the Philippians, "I want you to know, brothers, that what has happened to me has really served to advance the gospel" (Phil. 1:12).

Those who failed to accept themselves had tragic lives. I think especially of Saul, the first king of Israel. Saul could never accept himself, therefore he continually drove himself and those about him mercilessly, creating all kinds of problems (1 Sam. 9ff.). Saul's lack of self-acceptance caused him to exhibit personal humility when Samuel was arranging for him to become king. It took a crisis in the land instigated by the men of Jabesh to galvanize Saul in leadership (1 Sam. 9–11). Saul was so insecure as a person that when David was anointed to replace him, Saul tried to kill him (1 Sam. 19:1).

Numerous passages of Scripture are *self-acceptance* passages. Romans 12:3 says, "Do not think of yourself more highly than you ought, but rather think of yourself with sober judgment, in accordance with the measure of faith God has given you." James 1:2 says, "Consider it pure joy, my brothers, whenever you face trials of many kinds." These verses urge believers to start from where they are—not from where they think they are, nor from where they want to be. In the process of growth and maturation, they can become what God wants them to be. The change process begins from a solid foundation. Many other passages could be mentioned (e.g., Ps. 139:13–16; Rom. 5:8; 1 Cor. 1:28; Eph. 2:10; 1 Peter 2:9).

Summary

Self-acceptance is the *beginning point of change*. At the moment of acceptance, people are not what they will eventually become, but it is acceptance that provides them with a solid foundation for change. At each step in the change process, people may achieve self-acceptance. In this way, change will be in keeping with what each individual truly is—not inconsistent with the person's life and development.

Interpersonal relations begin with the self. Some segments of Evangelical Christianity have conveyed an unfortunate message: that individuals cannot accept themselves as they are—they must always be seeing themselves as they "ought to be." This has resulted in a wholesale rejection of self and has lead to various psychological conditions. God wants us to start with our lives where he starts—in full and complete acceptance of ourselves. Then we can truly work with him in the change process, becoming what he wants us to be through the leading of the Holy Spirit. In his epistle, James says that we should accept ourselves as we are— with our difficulties, which are potential for building us up, and with our temptations, which are potential for tearing us down. We will then become mature and ready for anything.

The excitement of life lies with accepting one's past, present, and future. The degree to which individuals accept their past determines the degree to which they will be able to realize the good of this background and select from it that which is useful to them at the moment of challenge. The degree to which they are able to accept their future determines the degree of peace they have in the present.

The agent of change who, while still unable to achieve self-acceptance, approaches others will communicate this self-rejection to other people. They will always doubt to some degree the value of that change that has not provided peace in the life of the agent of change.

Questions for Discussion

Relating to the Sending Church

1. What do you find difficult to accept about yourself?
2. How do others limit or encourage your self-acceptance?
3. In what ways does self-rejection manifest itself in your life?
4. How does a partial acceptance of self become manifest in accepting yourself as you think you are or think you should be or as you would like to be; and how does this affect your relationship with others? with God?

5. Which do you think is most difficult—to accept one's past, one's present, or one's future? Discuss.

Relating to the Study of the Bible

1. Discuss the ways Saul's lack of acceptance of himself affected those about him (1 Sam. 9–15). How might his life have been different had he accepted himself?
2. Study passages on worry, such as Colossians 3:2, "Set your minds on things above, not on earthly things." How might such biblical injunctions keep us from accepting ourselves? Is this the intent of such verses? Explain.
3. Seek out verses that encourage you to grow in self-acceptance.
4. What kind of challenge did King David have in accepting his future (1 Chron. 22:8; 28:3)? How did he handle this?
5. Share some of the evidences that Paul was able to accept himself.

Relating to Missions and Crosscultural Ministry

1. Examine the relationship of nationals to the missionary who is unable to achieve self-acceptance. What might result?
2. Why will a person who has failed to achieve self-acceptance likely be a poor communicator of the gospel? Discuss. How might such lack of self-acceptance be reflected in letters sent home or in reports made on furlough?
3. Why might an international person with no previous problems with self-acceptance find self-acceptance difficult after moving into another nation?
4. How might missionaries have difficulty in accepting their future? What problems might result from this?
5. How does the sending church limit or encourage the missionary in self-acceptance?

Group Activities and Exercises

1. *Lived experience.* Have the group members seek out from among their associations someone who does not have self-acceptance and someone who does. Have them compare orally or in writing the two kinds of experiences.
2. *Conceptualization.* Plan in writing a program of change to reverse a pattern of self-rejection. Urge that the program be put into effect. Have those who put it into effect report on their progress.
3. *Creative writing.* Have the members of the group attempt to write poetry expressing their lack of self-acceptance.
4. *Competition.* Have the group divide into two and assign the first group the task of searching out Bible verses that deal with self-acceptance. Have the second group seek out Bible verses that deal with self-rejection. Discuss the results in terms of the overall intent of Scripture to build up the Christian.

The Trust Bond

4

Acceptance of the Other

Case Study: The Insensitive Roommate

I have a roommate who is very insensitive to my thoughts
and feelings, to my likes and dislikes. Just last night he came
"bombing" into the room, dropped his books on my desk,
threw his clothes on my bed; and then, to top it all off, he left
a trail of cake crumbs all over the floor. The guy knows that I
clean the room every night around six. I think I have a right
to keep this place looking neat for my friends who drop in for
the evening.

Another thing that bothers me is the way he dumps his
dirty clothes in the corner of the room. I have nothing against
the guy being an athlete, but I do have something against
peculiar odors. I wonder what he thinks the dirty clothes bag
is for. I asked him that question once, and he just walked
away as if he felt like saying, "Go hang it on your nose!" And
another thing—why can't the guy put his things on his own
desk and bed?

He knows that all of these things bother me. I have tried to
be patient with him, and I have tried to understand his
background. I have talked to him about the situation, and at
one time, I even hung up his stuff for him. But now I am fed
up with his deliberate insensitivity. I just shove his books
under his bed and throw his clothes in the closet. This makes
him mad, but that's tough! I have even come to the point of

telling him to grow up. But he'll never change. I just avoid looking at him when he is in the room or elsewhere on campus. I think this guy is in for. . . .

How difficult it is for us to accept a person just as he is and then work from that point. How frequently we hear the complaints of this young man from roommates and from mates as well. A person will put up with such practices for just so long, and then he will rebel. One reaches a point when enough is enough. Physical or social separation seems to be the only alternative.

A number of years ago I walked out onto my porch in a small mountain village in Central America. I observed my neighbor, a Pocomchi, starting down the trail. It was early in the morning for me, but he had probably been up for an hour or two. I called to him and asked where he was going. He indicated that he was going up the mountain to procure a cow for butchering for market the next day. When I asked if I could accompany him, he readily complied.

We started up the narrow, steep, and winding trail. After a while he turned to me and said, "I'm tired. Let's rest." I had become quite weary by that time, no doubt breathing heavily and thus precipitating his suggestion. I responded happily, "I'm tired, too. Let's rest."

We sat on the mountainside looking eastward down the mountain valley. While we were sitting there chatting, my friend noticed that the sun had begun to rise. He commented, "Here comes our father."

Since I was a missionary and was primed by my one-culture training, this was the "ideal" opportunity for me to give a "gospel witness." I turned to my friend and said, "Fabian, that's not our father." He surveyed me with a strange look on his face. I then proceeded to give him an hour-long eighth-grade science lecture on the topic of the sun and its relation to the earth. He did not say much after that. In fact, during the following years of our friendship, very little was said about our conversation there on the mountainside or about the gospel I had begun, so eagerly, to communicate to him.

Looking back, I realize that *in rejecting his point of view, I had failed to communicate that I was accepting him as a person,* even while disagreeing with him. When I cut down his belief and thought pattern, however wrong or right it might have been, however superstitious I might have thought it was, he also read an accompanying message that I was cutting him down and rejecting him personally.

In my estimation, Fabian was a tremendous person. I had no intention of rejecting him personally when I rejected his point of view. I did not know that we were perceiving two distinct messages. I did not even know that the possibility of two different messages existed. I assumed that whatever I said to someone would be understood by that person as I had intended it to be understood. Further, I would not have known what to do had I realized that two different messages or two parts to the same message existed. I had not been trained in effective crosscultural communication. I had not been warned that some people in the world see their entire experience as a "whole piece of cloth." Little did I realize that an attack on one aspect of life is seen as an attack on the whole; a criticism of a thought pattern is a criticism of the entire person (see chapter 11). *In rejecting Fabian's point of view, I had unwittingly rejected him as a person.* How many times in our interpersonal relations do we reject the other person's point of view, reject his action or statement, and wind up rejecting him as a person as well? We fail to recognize that there are two parts to any communication. We may want the other to know we accept him. However, he may see us as rejecting both his behavior *and* his person.

It is our opportunity and responsibility to get through to the other the message of our acceptance of him as a person, even though we might disapprove of what he does. As a person, he is loved and accepted by God, though his works may be disapproved by God when they do not meet up to his standards. Jesus was brought face to face with a woman who had been taken in the act of adultery and who, according to Old Testament law, was to be slain. Jesus did not condone the sin, but he did save her from an unjust punishment decreed from a different culture (see chapter 16). He fully accepted her as a person, though he did not approve of her behavior, and their relationship grew strong (John 8:1–11). Should we do less than accept the other person on this same basis?[1]

Instant Rejection—A Simulation Game

The game Instant Rejection allows each of us to see to what degree we are natural acceptors or rejecters of others. The rules are quite simple. One selects another person as an object of rejection. Using all the tools of rejection at one's disposal, the other is rejected, put down, alienated; and the message of such rejection is communicated clearly to him. The following methods, among many, may be used:

- Cut him off when he is talking to you.
- Laugh when he addresses you.
- Question his facts.
- Show him lack of trust and confidence.
- Attempt to overprotect him.
- Talk down to him.

- Overreact to something he says or does.
- Avoid eye contact with him.
- Forget his name.

I have guided many young people in playing Instant Rejection. The amazing discovery they make is that this is the way they actually live. They are rejecting others continually. They have been *trained* to reject others rather than to accept them. In the opening case study, the one roommate had many things to reject about his roommate: his bombing into the room, his leaving a trail of litter, his failing to regard personal property, and his dropping smelly clothing. It was quite easy to reject him without conscious thought. Unfortunately, the first roommate was totally unaware that by his rejection of his roommate, the other was being encouraged to reject him in return.

Rejection, carried out by most of us, usually produces alienation. This alienation affects all kinds of people—those within our own society and those without. The way to avoid rejecting another person is to accept him completely and fully, *just as he is*. In interpersonal relations, start from a base of acceptance rather than of rejection. Once you have an acceptance attitude in your mind, making it impossible for you to reject that other person, you will seek some way to communicate this acceptance. This again becomes an exciting game or exercise—namely, how to communicate your acceptance to the other person. As was indicated in the previous chapter, acceptance is simply the beginning point of change. We cannot predict the change, nor can we guarantee that a specific change will follow; but effective change will more likely come about through acceptance rather than rejection.

Alienation

Rejection produces alienation. Alienation, as defined by Webster, is to cause to be estranged, to make inimical or indifferent where devotion or attachment formerly subsisted. Alienation happens between two people, between a person and a group, or between two groups of any size or complexity (see chapter 12). Alienation is a cutting off, a separating from. This may occur in actual alienation where someone is cutting off another person or group, or in perceived alienation where it *appears* to the other person that he is being cut off. Either of these are equally harmful in interpersonal and intergroup relationships, for alienation gives the feeling of being unwanted, of not having a place, of not being part of a group, whether this condition actually exists or not.

Today's world has produced many experiences of alienation. Youth in American society during the late sixties felt alienated.

They responded to this feeling of alienation by withdrawing from society or by forming new groups, resulting in the resurgence of the commune. Alienation is being felt in Northern Ireland, in South Africa, and anywhere the dominant group proceeds to give minority groups—whether minor in number or power—short shrift. Alienation finds expression in war. Such alienation has caused underdeveloped nations to refuse to advance or to attempt to advance too rapidly for their own good. Some have sought to advance on their own or to seek out questionable support from nations supplying aid for ulterior reasons. Alienation has undermined aid programs, mission programs, and educational efforts.

Participants in an aid program operating in South America planned to dig a new well for a community. The ones directing the program selected a site for the well without consultation within the larger community. The well was dug on a piece of property owned by someone who was not considered an integral part of the community. Many of the villagers refused to drink the water supplied by the well either because of their own sense of alienation from the property owner or because they were convinced, however rightly or wrongly, that the well water had been poisoned.[2]

Rejection that results in alienation is likely to be reciprocated, producing further alienation. The rejected one, in fact, will do something to the other in such a way as to "get even" or to "get back."

The Snob Effect

Rejection underlies the sense of alienation. There are many situations in life in which one can either sense rejection or can reject someone. I will call the rejecter the snob. *Rejection within a society has a "snob effect" on the one rejecting. He sees himself as a member of an elite group of some type and attempts both to remain within this group and to keep others out.* His victim, in turn, rejects this group and finds some satisfaction as a member of another group, where he begins to react in the same way toward others. He closes off the boundaries of that group to the outside and thus reinforces the identity of the group. The natural formation of groups within society is not a problem except when exclusiveness is maintained by the group for selfish reasons. It is at this point that rejection of others becomes disastrous within the larger society.

Ethnocentrism is a concept denoting that a person is centered in his own culture. This is no problem as long as the person's attitude is good and others are not forced either into or out of the culture of focus. The socially healthy form of ethnocentrism causes the person to have a solid identity and to be at peace within that identity. The unhealthy form results in the snob effect.

The expression of nationalism in underdeveloped countries of the world is in part a response to rejection by outsiders. This expression may come as a formal rejection between governments or as an informal expression by outsiders criticizing the patterns of life they find in that country.

A non-American, responding to his experience of living in the United States, sensed the loss of self-respect involved in being forced to abandon what he was. "Neither can I be an American nor can I imitate them and pretend to be like them," he protested. Worst of all, he felt that he could not even be true to his own upbringing. He felt that to live among Americans he had to become something other than what he was. He just wanted to be himself— a person from a distinct source society, adapting to American society—and he wanted to be accepted as he was at that moment of the process. Becoming something other than what he was did not mean simply living a different way. To him it meant being made over into another person—that is, abandoning what he was, his principles, and his responsibilities to the whole of his former culture and way of life. How clearly this man felt the snob effect.

A young lady living in the dormitory of a Christian college left after one year, explaining, "I couldn't be myself—I couldn't dress right, I couldn't act right, I couldn't think right. I thought that I had some musical ability, but it was constantly being cut down. Nothing that I did was right, proper, or effective. I received no encouragement. I felt totally rejected." She, too, had felt the snob effect.

Conditional Acceptance

If a person accepts another on the basis of some condition, a message of rejection comes through more strongly than the message of acceptance. In fact, such an acceptance of another is no acceptance at all. When I accept my child on the basis of good grades, the grades become the strongest part of our relationship. When the grades are there, there is the uneasy feeling that acceptance is of the grades rather than of the person. The nagging effect of this results in a sense of perceived rejection. The perception of rejection is as strong as the actual rejection itself. When the grades are not there, rejection is seen as the only option.

In the opening case study of this chapter, the roommate's original attitude was, "So what, I'll clean his room myself." Then it became, "I'll accept him if he cleans his room." Finally, it was an outright rejection. My own relationship with my Pocomchi neighbor, Fabian, communicated itself as conditional acceptance based on his changing his belief system. He read the entire scene as rejection. Conditional acceptance is simply a form of rejection, and a very powerful form it is, since the one establishing the conditions believes that he is communicating a message of acceptance.

Rejection and the Christian

Rejection infiltrates our lives in very subtle ways and even reaches into all expressions of Christian ministry.

One evening I was speaking at a church that was concerned about the so-called generation gap. They had planned a three-hour session to deal with this concern. This was to include a period for spelling out the problem of mutual concern, a time of small-group discussion, a sandwich supper, a period of summing up and conclusions, and a challenge at the close.

I noted that the church members prided themselves on having effective communication with their teens, admitting only to a small gap between the two subcultures. I was interested in seeing just how correct this perception actually was. I noticed, first of all, that even though this was a rather large church, only a small number of young people attended this session designed especially to get teens together with their parents and other adults of the church. I was told later by some of the youth that their peers figured there was very little in the session for them.

An initial statement was made, and then the larger group divided into smaller groups. I had very little to do during the group discussion period, so I decided I would go from room to room and observe. I made it a point to intrude or interrupt as little as possible. After sitting in on a few of the sessions, a pattern of response to the comments of young people began to form. The pattern followed this line: Whenever an adult spoke, he was supported or his thoughts were amplified by the next adult speaker. Whenever a young person spoke, I heard a chuckle from the adult audience that sounded like a self-conscious giggle. The next statement would then come from an adult, questioning the validity of the statement the young person had made. This pattern did not occur every time a young person spoke, but it did occur enough times to make me seek to further pursue some of the implications of such a pattern of response.

In the session following the group reports, I decided to introduce this observation. I then suggested that the church had a greater youth problem than they had thought. I explained that this was evidenced not only by the small youth turnout but also by the adult behavior toward the youth.

Following the service, an attractive teenager approached me and said, "You're right! We have to live with that little laugh that degrades us so." A patterned response to youth and to their ideas thus communicated rejection to them.

I was in another church on the West Coast. After I had spoken, the young people gathered around me and questioned me further concerning my comments regarding contemporary music. Adult members also approached, some of them leaders of the church. Youth, adults, and I were all in conversation together. It seemed to me that a healthy discussion was going on. The adults appeared willing to let the young people play their kind of music in their youth groups as well as in the larger congregation. They were also to be allowed to develop this style into a gospel witness. Since the discussion was going so well, I felt free to move to another group. However, as I looked around later, I noticed that the first group had dispersed. I learned afterward, much to my disappointment, that no further discussion was held and nothing further was done by the leaders on behalf of the youth. The subtle rejection of the youth, evident in the behavior of the adults, was effectively communicated to them. As long as an authority figure was present, there could be open discussion. As soon as the authority figure left, the adults felt no further obligation to pursue the subject or to do anything about it.

The subtlety of such rejection is clearly evident when members of other ethnic groups join a conversation. They are ignored, their comments are called into question, or the conversation may even be drawn to a premature close. This type of rejection is termed "racism."

A young black spent a number of years in a white community that had a reputation of being thoroughly Christian. He reported on the comments made to him and the questions asked him during his stay there. "I bet your social life is real tough. I bet you have a really frustrating time. What sports do you play? Do Negroes sunburn?" Such statements and questions very effectively alienate through the sense of rejection. The person feels invalid, unwanted.

Too frequently the Christian feels that he will be less than discerning or that he will compromise his stand if he accepts the other just as he is. This has produced divisions within the body, which is the church of Jesus Christ, as well as alienation within the local fellowship of believers. *If our discernment or lack of compromise results in the rejection of persons, we need to reexamine the basis of our fellowship.* The love spoken of in the Scriptures does not result in alienation or rejection, rather, it results in the full-orbed experience of fellowship and belonging.

Accept-Respect Versus Accept-Believe

Acceptance of a person does not imply acceptance into one's life of all that the other person does, says, or believes. One does not have to believe the way another person does to accept him as a person. One does not even have to approve of what the other person believes to accept him as he is. In fact, it is vitally important to be wise in distinguishing between what a person is and what he does, or between accepting a person and accepting what he does. Even though we do not need to accept-*believe* what a person believes, we can still accept-*respect* what a person is and does and believes. Accept-respect means that we can accept a person no matter what he believes or does and that we can show him this acceptance or potential acceptance in the form of respect. We communicate to him in this way that he is a real and valid person in our eyes. Accept-respect allows us to know the person as he is and to begin working with him in the interaction and change process.

Acceptance of the person does not call for accept-believe, though it may develop into this. Rather, it calls for accept-respect. Accept-believe may cause us to abandon moral and ethical principles on which our lives are based. The other person does not expect us to do everything he does, to believe as he believes, or to think as he thinks. Rather, he assumes that we will be what we are. Only then will he accept us as we are and respect both our person and what we do and say. When we abandon what we are, he will lose respect for us.

Young people in American society tend to lose respect for the adult who tries to be too much like youth—wearing the same clothes, talking the same dialect, participating in the same activities. Youth do not want their elders to adopt all of their practices or all of the details of their lives. The same applies to people of other societies. They simply want the respect of others, not conformity to their lifestyle. They know that respect will lead the other to an effective adaptation to the culture and life-way. In time, conformity will undermine the trust relationship and disrupt interpersonal relationships.

People of other societies do not expect the missionary to dress just as they do, live in the same kind of houses as they do, or follow the same practices. They do not expect them to abandon principles in adapting to their way of life. They do not want the missionary to become an ethical relativist—abandoning principles to be like them (see chapter 16). They want the missionary to be a person of principle so that they can trust him. At the same time, they do expect that the outsider will use his head and adapt to the lifestyle in a dynamic and thoughtful way while being a person of principle. Then the missionary can let them be persons of principle as well, persons deserving of respect and trust.

Discernment

Acceptance of the person implies discernment; it does not negate it. In other words, *we do not accept a person irrespective of his quality of life*. Rather, our acceptance grows and develops in keeping with that person as he grows in maturity. He accepts us in return as we grow in maturity. As we mature and as we grow together, the intensity of our acceptance increases. If we grow apart, our acceptance is still there, but the intensity of our feelings lessens.

The same principle holds true insofar as the other's actions are concerned. We always accept him as a person. As his actions show increasing maturity, our acceptance increases in intensity of feeling. Thus acceptance is primary to all feelings and emotions extended toward others and is rooted in trust.

Frequently, the realization of one's worthiness for acceptance comes a long time after any initial attempt at acceptance. It takes time to gain full knowledge of another's personal and social being. This is the underlying principle involved in Christ's urging one to forgive the other "seventy times seven" (Matt. 18:22 KJV). A period of time is thus made available for each to know the other and to sense the full realization of the worth of the other within the context of individual and social differences. Christ also illustrated the principle by continually trusting and accepting when we would have given up and failed to trust and accept.

Carl Rogers spells out a number of ways that can enable us to create a helping relationship, or, in the terminology of this chapter, to become an acceptor of persons rather than a rejecter. He sums up his thoughts in this manner: "The degree to which I can create relationships which facilitate the growth of the other as a separate person, is the measure of the growth I have achieved in myself."[3]

We should ask ourselves the following questions:

1. Can I, in some way which will be perceived by the other person as trustworthy, be as dependable or consistent in some deep sense? Do I realize that being trustworthy does not demand that I be rigidly consistent but that I be dependably real?
2. Can I be expressive enough that what I am will be communicated unambiguously?
3. Can I let myself experience positive attitudes toward this other person—attitudes of warmth, caring, liking, interest, respect?
4. Can I be strong enough to be separate from the other? Can I be a sturdy respecter of my own feelings and needs, as well as his? Can I acknowledge my own feelings and, if need be, express them as something belonging to me and separate from his feelings?

5. Am I secure enough within myself to permit him his separateness? Can I permit him to be what he is—honest or deceitful, infantile or adult, despairing or over-confident?

6. Can I let myself enter fully into the world of his feelings and personal meanings and see these as he does? Can I step into his private world so completely that I lose all desire to evaluate or judge it? Can I enter his private world so sensitively that I can move about in it freely, without trampling on values that are precious to him?

7. Can I receive him as he is and communicate that attitude? Or can I only receive him conditionally, acceptant of some aspects of his feelings and silently or openly disapproving of other aspects?

8. Can I act with sufficient sensitivity in the relationship so that my behavior will not be perceived as a threat?

9. Can I free him from the threat of external evaluation?

10. Can I meet him as a person who is in the process of becoming, or will I be bound by his past and by my past?

Acceptance and Mission

There is much in missions that calls for acceptance of the other. The hosts are different from the missionary, and their behavior expresses this difference very clearly. Unless we enter into our relationship with another with an accepting attitude, we will not be able to discover all that can be known about that person and minister to his total life. As we understand his lifestyle and belief system, we can utilize what we learn to communicate the gospel message. As the individual comes to know the Lord, such knowledge can aid the one participating with him in spiritual growth. Seasoned missionaries frequently act the way they do because of their experience within a particular setting. The new missionary needs to take the time to learn what is going on before seeking to initiate change. Acceptance of the one with the experience frequently results in greater knowledge of what is actually the situation to be faced. Governments differ from the sending nation, and great understanding needs to be gained before criticism is made. Rejection in such cases tends to bring the focus on the self-centered new person. Self-centeredness and outreach are incompatible, and clash is inevitable.

Mission board personnel need an attitude of acceptance toward new recruits. Young people appear distinct from adults in numerous ways: dress, hair style, vocabulary, training, and the jargon that goes with such training. The adult often has difficulty working his way through the differences of language and fashion to find the true nature of responsibility as expressed by youth.[4] The adult needs an attitude of acceptance so that petty concerns and misunderstandings do not mar the progress of the young person through the process of recruitment. It is not only important that missionaries learn to accept others within another country or culture, it is equally significant for them to exercise this same acceptance within their own culture and subculture.

New recruits to missionary work are drawn from two different kinds of Christian educational institutions—the Bible college and the Christian liberal arts college. The former has stricter controls over the expressions of language and dress than does the latter. The latter tends to follow the lead in language and fashion of the secular college or university. Mission executives become wary of the graduates of the Christian liberal arts college, as they do not appear to be as dedicated to Christ as do their Bible college counterparts. Such a student has had more contact with what mission executives might consider humanistic studies. Such executives tend to gravitate to the graduates of Bible colleges because they feel more comfortable with them, their language, and their dress. Mission executives need crosscultural tools, for they may find, all too late, that the Bible college youth, though they dress and speak "correctly," are as radical and rebellious as those encountered in the secular university. A more worldly looking and sounding youth on a Christian liberal arts campus may be just as sincere in his dedication to Christ as his counterpart on a Bible college campus. In many ways, he may even be more capable of doing the job the mission wishes to have accomplished.

When the new recruit enters the missionary subculture overseas, he also must have an attitude of acceptance. The other missionaries probably come from his own society, but they still have sociocultural distinctions derived both from their background and from their experiences in the host country. These distinctions can produce irritations in the life of the new worker and may even be intensified because of this international setting. Every encounter within the missionary subculture must be considered as a multicultural challenge, just as any other encounter. Members within one's own mission express distinct subcultures. Members of other missions do as well. Each can be accepted for what he is, and each in turn can accept the other as valid.

In every dealing with the citizens of the host country, the missionary needs an attitude of acceptance. The national can and must be taken just as he is. This is not the way he will continue to be, nor is the missionary what he will eventually be, but it is absolutely vital that each be accepted just as he is and not be viewed in terms of the standards and practices of the other. Rogers talks about this right and privilege as being free from the threat of external evaluation. The member of the host nation can become a fine Christian in keeping with what he is. He does not need to be made over into an American, a Canadian, or a Britisher in order to know and serve God. Belief in Jesus Christ can regenerate his own life and, through this change, his society. This change will still follow the cultural ways of his people and be in keeping with it. If a man belongs to a society where men and women eat separately, becoming a Christian will not cause them to eat together. Eating together will, further, not guarantee either a closer family or a greater spirituality. The people can become fine Christians and grow in Christ yet continue to have division of the sexes in the experience of eating. It is possible that a family of that culture, by following the Western practice of eating together, might express a number of tragic non-Christian attitudes that could destroy their family and limit their testimony within the community. Though Christianity may not cause them to change their culture, it will cause their hearts to change. Whether their practice of eating together or separately changes, there will be a growing bond of Christian love and fellowship, which over a period of time will unite the family in a true unity, reinforcing the vitality of the family within that society.

Thus acceptance must become the foundation for all interpersonal relations so that the missionary can come to a sure and complete understanding of who each person is and how he can best reach him for Christ and encourage his true growth in Christ. An attitude of rejection causes the national to respond with further rejection, and the whole purpose of ministry is lost.

The missionary needs the attitude of acceptance within his own family. The missionary family is made up of a multicultural group. The parents belong to the adult subculture of their home society. They have children born either within that originating society or within the host society. Each child develops differently in keeping with the multiplicity of experiences both in his parents' home society and in the host society. The critical challenge to this attitude of acceptance is when the child returns home to enter the youth subculture of his parents' society. His preparation for this entry was made primarily in contact with the adult subculture of this society and the youth subculture of the host society. If the parents withdraw their acceptance support at this critical time, the missionary child will seek out replacement support and may find himself in the company of cop-outs and drug users.

Acceptance of the Other in the Bible

The Bible offers several clear illustrations of acceptance of the person. Only a few will be presented here.

God accepted the Israelites as they were. They were chosen by him not because they were especially holy or because they were a large nation (Deut. 7:6–8), but because he loved them. Love necessarily means acceptance. The Israelites sinned against God many times, but he did not reject them. We know that God did hate their sins, for he severely chastised the Israelites for them. But God could put up with the Israelites because he had a plan for their salvation.

God accepted David even though he sinned terribly by coveting Bathsheba and sending her husband to the front lines to be slain (2 Sam. 11:2–17). David then took Bathsheba to be his wife the very moment her mourning was past (2 Sam. 11:27). Notice, however, that it was Solomon, the son of Bathsheba, who was to be named king in David's place, for we are told that "the LORD loved him" (2 Sam. 12:24). It was through this line that Jesus was to be born (Matt. 1:6–7).

One of the most dramatic of the biblical stories of acceptance occurred between Eli and Hannah in the Old Testament (1 Sam. 1:9–18.). Eli communicated to Hannah, "You are a beautiful person, a wonderful woman; God will give you what you ask." We would, no doubt, have questioned her lifestyle, since she was a man's second wife and thus was living in a polygamous household. We would have viewed her with suspicion long after Eli did. At first, he had thought she was drunk, because she moved her lips strangely, but then he recognized his mistake and acted in accordance with his new perception without further question. Eli accepted Hannah just as she was, and he encouraged her in her request to God.

The New Testament tells us that a woman taken in adultery was brought before Jesus. In talking with her after her accusers were gone, Jesus communicated two messages to her. One was a nonverbal message that she was important enough for him to be concerned about. The second message, a verbal one, indicated his disapproval of the practice of adultery: "Go now and leave your life of sin" (John 8:11). The evidence for the two messages is quite clear. She (or another whom Jesus had helped and forgiven in much the same way) responded to the first message by returning at a later date and anointing the Savior with precious ointment—a deed she would likely not have done had she thought that Jesus was rejecting her person. She apparently responded to the second by a change in behavior (John 8:1–11).

Jesus also took the initiative to talk to a woman of Samaria. He pointed out her sins without communicating personal rejection. She then understood who Jesus was and went and called her friends (John 4:5–29).

Jesus accepted Peter, an impulsive fisherman who was ignorant in spiritual things. Knowing that Peter was to deny him three times (Luke 22:34; cf. vv. 54–62), Jesus prayed for Peter (vv. 31–32). After the Resurrection, Jesus asked Peter to tend his sheep (John 21:15–17).

When Jesus reappeared to his disciples after his resurrection, he saw that Thomas was doubting, yet he did not reject Thomas because of his unbelief. Instead, he simply asked Thomas to examine his hands and side. Rather than feeling rejected, Thomas believed (John 20:26–29).

The love chapter of the Bible, 1 Corinthians 13, also deals with the issue of acceptance. One of the most telling statements in that chapter is: "[Love] keeps no record of wrongs" (v. 5).

Summary

The acceptance of another person deals with the acceptance-rejection patterns underlying interpersonal relationships. Rejection produces alienation; acceptance reverses alienation and is t ie sound foundation for true Christian love. The average person is trained through the socialization process to reject someone different than himself. The expression of this rejection leads from self to one's neighbor, to the stranger, and ultimately to God himself. Here centers the importance of the Christian message of love, for the gospel would reverse the process of rejection and insure acceptance of the person.

The acceptance of a person as he is at any moment in time is only the starting point in change. What that person is, is not what he will become; nor will the person dealing with him remain unchanged. Both will change for the better, and a healthier relationship will emerge. The acceptance of a person precedes any involvement with that person within a change relationship. The agent of change will get nowhere if he evokes a rejection response. Complete openness in acceptance will encourage the other also to be completely open, and thus the openness will provide fertile soil for change.

Questions for Discussion

Relating to the Sending Church

1. What kinds of things do you find difficult to accept in another person? in a group or organization?
2. Describe the ways that one manifests rejection: physiologically, psychologically, sociologically; body movement, spatial arrangement, etc.

3. How can one reject a person's point of view without rejecting the person? Explain.
4. Would you say that in your church there is more acceptance or more rejection expressed? Explain.
5. How can someone claim to love someone and still express rejection through his verbal and nonverbal behavior?
6. How do church members express the snob effect within the church?

Relating to the Study of the Bible

1. How did Jesus show his acceptance of the other person? Give examples. How did he show rejection? Give examples.
2. Study the Book of Hosea and discuss the case of Hosea and Gomer. Did Hosea express acceptance of the other person? Did he go too far? What lessons does one learn about alienation and its effects in one's life?
3. Study the Book of Jonah and describe Jonah's pattern of acceptance and rejection of others. Can you explain his inconsistencies in this regard? Discuss.
4. Discuss David's struggle for acceptance by his people (2 Samuel and 1 Chronicles). Could this have been associated with his not being a firstborn son and thus not a legitimate heir to the throne as was the expectation during the period of the patriarchy? Discuss the rebellions led by David's oldest sons to usurp his role as king. Especially note his struggle not to reject Absalom. What do we learn from this about sin and forgiveness (2 Sam. 13–18)?
5. Discuss God's efforts at accepting the Israelites in spite of their constant sinning. What treatment did he give them? How did they respond? What special arrangements did he make for them to find acceptance with him in spite of their sin? What does this teach us about our own personal relationship with God?

Relating to Missions and Crosscultural Ministry

1. How might the Christian mission be carried out were one to accept others just as they are at every moment in time? What problems might one face?
2. In your experience with your colleagues, did you find it easier or harder to accept them as they were than you did the nationals with whom you worked? Discuss.
3. Provide a case study from your field work that illustrates alienation. How was this resolved?
4. Examine your marriage relationship to find what changed when you went from your own culture to another. Did any of these changes affect your acceptance of each other? Describe.

5. What have you learned about discernment from your association with members of another culture? Discuss both positive and negative factors.

Group Activities and Exercises

1. *Conceptualization.* Consider a class, church, or family situation in which group members approach the situation with a rejection attitude. Then project that same situation if acceptance were to be practiced. Discuss.
2. *Group study.* Study the Book of James to discover what James is saying about acceptance of others. Generate responses regarding what would happen if such acceptance was incorporated into the contemporary church.
3. *Observation.* Send the group members out into their everyday experiences to observe the behavior of others. Have them report back any observed behavior that has surprised them. Debrief this exercise with the following questions: What surprised you? Would this same thing surprise anyone else? Explain. How did you react? Were any of the surprises due to fresh insights into the challenge of acceptance/rejection? Discuss.
4. *Role play, corporate.* Have the group members divide into groups of four to six people and prepare a two-minute acceptance/rejection skit. For example, take a situation out of the Bible and act it out as it is presented there. Then reverse the acceptance factor. For example, if it were an acceptance scene, present it as a rejection scene. When the skits are finished, talk about the impact of rejection on the group. Then discuss the related roles and how each group member fit into his assigned role. An excellent situation to try is that of the mothers bringing their children to Jesus and having the disciples turn them away. If you do use this, be prepared to debrief the reaction to Jesus' being a "rejecter" of persons.
5. *Experiment.* Send each group member out to accept or reject someone. Let the acceptance or rejection develop for a period of time until behavior is modified. Have the person report on the behavioral response of the other person. Caution: Be careful in selecting the object of rejection since relationships can be permanently affected.
6. *Interview:* Invite someone from a different culture to discuss the acceptance and rejection practices of missionaries in this person's experience. Probe the result of such practices on the ministry.

5

Mutual Respect

Case Study: Modern Prodigal

A prominent, well-to-do family in California had a son who was expected to follow in the steps of the father and maintain the social position of the family in the community. After finishing high school, the boy joined a so-called hippie group.

Later on, he decided to go to college in England and arranged with his father to spend a year there. The father promised to pay the transportation and college costs for the first year. Without the parents being aware of it, the boy met his girlfriend in New York, and the two of them left for England where they lived together and spent the money the father had provided for college. There they did things they were interested in, but he never attended college.

When the year expired, the fellow and his girl returned to the States as husband and wife. They asked permission to live with his parents until they could get established. They also requested more money, because they needed ready cash to carry them over until they could support themselves.

Three current points of view regarding interpersonal relations leave the relationship partial and potential by loss of trust and self-respect. These points of view are that of the traditionalist, the ethical relativist or antinomian, and the situation ethicist (see figure 4). These points of view lead to partial relationships, since someone in the relationship is bound to come out on the short end. He will be the one who will abandon his principles, if only in part, and thus be less than a truly "whole person."

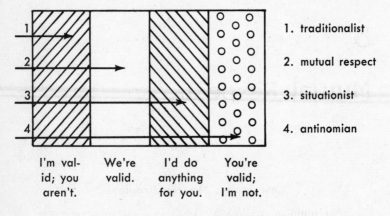

1. traditionalist

2. mutual respect

3. situationist

4. antinomian

I'm val-id; you aren't.   We're valid.   I'd do anything for you.   You're valid; I'm not.

Figure 4. Ways Interpersonal Relationships May Develop

Traditionalist

The traditionalist sees his world as one that never changes and never should change. This lays the burden of change on the other person. In order to get along with the traditionalist, one must, at least in part, abandon what he is—his principles, his beliefs, his life-way—to conform to the mind-set of the traditionalist. For the traditionalist, the focus is on form rather than meaning. The form is to remain constant whatever the cost. If the form or expression remains constant through time, it most certainly follows, as far as he is concerned, that the meaning will also remain constant through time.

While translating Luke 13 in my Bible translation program in Central America, I ran into a problem. Jesus, in verse 32, calls Herod a "fox." Since this translation effort was prior to my crosscultural conversion, I was paying more attention to form than to meaning. At first I could not understand why the nationals were having a problem with calling Herod a fox. I even used the ultimate argument with them: "The Bible says that he was a fox!" Then it began to sink in that the word implied that Herod was a homosexual. As soon as I shifted the form from "fox" to "wildcat," they understood perfectly and rejoiced that now "it made sense."

Were the father in the opening case study a traditionalist, he would insist on the couple's apology, an immediate official wedding, and a change in their appearance. He would urge the couple to return to "logical" middle-class thinking.

Being a "traditionalist" is not synonymous with being a member of a "traditional" society.[1] A traditional society is one that has changed little through time, though it may very well have effective mechanisms for change. Those coming into a traditional society may maintain their principles and operate effectively in keeping with the totality of their sociocultural background, yet they are free to adapt to the new culture as need arises. Both traditional and nontraditional societies may have traditionalists in them. Such members would focus on the form of the traditional society and seek to perpetuate it, even though the meaning of, or reason for, the form has changed or been lost.

Ethical Relativist

The ethical relativist or antinomian counts the relativity of individual behavior above all social controls over conduct. He thus abandons all that he is in order to cater or pander to the other. He forfeits principle for the sake of the other. He may become a relativist by choice or through the pressures, however subtle, of the society of which he is a part.

Were the father in the opening case a relativist, he would yield all principle and, catering to his son, welcome him back on any terms. In fact, he might even abandon his own life-way and seek acceptance by adapting the youths'. Were the young people relativists, they, too, might yield their emerging lifestyle and take on the parents' lifestyle without really wanting to. Conforming in this way, for the sake of getting along or for getting some money, could cause serious loss of self-respect.

The story of the Prodigal Son (Luke 15:11–32) may lead one to believe that the father, in welcoming back his wayward son, could have expressed ethical relativism of the type that we are referring to here. The story makes it very clear that the father never abandoned his own principles in receiving back the son. Nor did the father urge the son to become something that he was not, as a traditionalist might do. He simply welcomed the son in love. The father was effectively communicating love within a context of cultural relativism—that is, he was accepting their differences and thus allowing each to maintain personal identity and respect for one another. Cultural relativism allows for completeness; ethical relativism does not. Ethical relativism causes one to give up part of what one is (see chapter 16).

The ethical relativist is to be distinguished from the cultural relativist who holds that truth can be expressed through distinct cultural forms and that even though the form may differ across cultural boundaries, the truth can remain the same. The cultural relativist encourages full responsibility of a member within his own sociocultural setting. If for some reason change is required because of some practice or belief that is contrary to humanitarian principles or is in violation of a universal norm or moral absolute, the cultural relativist will work in cooperation with the members of the society to effect the change rather than dictating the change. The cultural relativist encourages full maintenance of principle and responsibility, whereas the ethical relativist abandons the principles in whole or in part.[2] The Christian holding to the Word of God as his authority in ethical problems is emphatically not an ethical relativist, but he equally emphatically should be a cultural relativist.

Situation Ethics

In situation ethics, espoused by Joseph Fletcher and other writers, *a person may abandon a certain amount of principle whenever necessary out of love for the other*. In the words of Fletcher,

> The situationist enters into every decision-making situation fully armed with the ethical maxims of his community and its heritage, and he treats them with respect as illuminators of his problems. Just the same, he is prepared in any situation to compromise them or set them aside in the situation if love seems better served by doing so.[3]

If the participants in our opening case study were situation ethicists, they would yield any and every principle that would be necessary out of love for the others. This sounds very beautiful and can theoretically produce a "happy" home experience for all involved. However, working from the basis of willingness to abandon principle, someone may go too far and undermine trust. This arrangement will give the recipient of the favor a good feeling at first, but it ultimately will undermine the relationship.

The primary practical problem with situation ethics is that in any decision involving another, though the other may at first like what has been done on his behalf, he may later interpret the action as an abandonment of principle in some degree and thus have his trust undermined. When the trust relationship is not affected and trust is not undermined, the result is much like the result expected of mutual respect founded on cultural relativism. However, any undermining of trust that is not adjusted for or any trust breach that is not closed can serve to disrupt and is potential for destroying the relationship.

A more basic philosophical problem with situation ethics arises in considering the decision-making process itself. Situation ethics suggests that the solution will arise out of the situation itself.

The situational factors are so primary that we may even say, "Circumstances alter rules and principles," or "Every man must decide for himself according to his own estimate of conditions and consequences; and no one can decide for him or impugn the decision to which he comes."[4] Rather, I would suggest, as an anthropologist, that everyone takes into every situation an elaborate value system with each of the values ranked in a hierarchy (see chapter 14). It is much the same with a computer program with ordered rules instructing the computer. When the computer is given a problem, the solution will reflect the input or instructional matter. So the person responding to the input of his socialization process, however unique it is for himself as an individual in society, will make a decision in keeping with that input, or rank of values. His hierarchy of values is thus tested by the situation, but the situation itself is unable to bring decision. The decision lies in the intricate programming of values, not in the situation itself.

The person responding, therefore, to his hierarchy of values may not like the choice he has made. It is at this time that he begins a careful and elaborate adjustment in his value ranking, a need that his response to a given situation has clarified for him. The adjustment in his hierarchy is thus ready to be tested by another situation. His decisions in this new situation can clarify if, in fact, his hierarchy has been changed or not and will indicate to him further direction in the change process. One's rank of values will always underlie and set up the decision within a given situation. It is thus wise to investigate the value system one has rather than simply the situation one faces. The more the decision that a person makes is in keeping with his real value system and not just his perception of his value system, the less tension he will encounter in interpersonal relations.

At times it would appear to the person that he does not respond to a situation in keeping with his value system. He falls into the trap of perceiving his values to be what they are not. As Paul commented in Romans 7:19: "When I try not to do wrong, I do it anyway" (LB). He wished that his life were pure in every way, but in reality it was not. He was responding in keeping with his true hierarchy of values whether he liked his response or not.

Mutual Respect

A fourth point of view leaves each of the participants in a relationship totally fulfilled as individuals and their lives integrated as a whole. *This approach we call mutual respect, because it involves a balanced, reciprocal relationship existing and developing between individuals, between an individual and a group, or between groups.* Effective communication unites the parties, not necessarily in agreement, but, rather, in trust development. The foundation for such a relationship is full and complete acceptance of one another as each one is at any moment. Throughout the development of such a relationship, any reflection on the relationship or on any ingredient of the relationship will always result in building trust, not undermining it. In the case of trust being undermined, both parties will extend every effort to restore the trust balance. Such a trust relationship between parties stems from and, in turn, reinforces mutual respect. Tournier speaks of a personal experience in mutual respect this way: "He felt that he was understood. More than that, he felt also that he was understanding himself better and that I was understanding him just as he understood himself."[5]

In mutual respect, each person perceives that his point of view is worthy of being heard. He is not prejudged. He has a valid point of view. His point of view can be heard and responded to by another person or by a group. His point of view can become part of the consensual process by which all societies are maintained. The consensual process may involve a formal vote or a decree by a dictator, or it may involve simply a group willingness to be part of the "scene" at the place designated by someone uninvolved in the scene itself.

The consensual process is thus based on negotiation. All the parties involved in the decision-making process, whether leader or follower, whether dominator or subject, become part of the natural, ongoing negotiation process that insures the continual development of the consensual process, and thus the process of building sound relationships within society. Each member or part of the society may enter through different roles or responsibilities to differing degrees of involvement and power. A child may enter by suggesting that the family go fishing. A subculture may enter by marching in public demonstration for or against some issue. Until consensus is reached, the negotiation process must and will continue. Any blockage of the negotiation within the consensual process limits individual and corporate development and produces disintegration to some degree. Were mutual respect operating in the relationships set up by our case, the parents and children would talk over the past, present, and future, reaching consensus at each point along the way. Such consensus would concern the amount of money involved, if there were to be interest paid, when it was due, etc. Each agreement would be upheld by each member of the group.

Reciprocity

When people are working together in a trust relationship, a reciprocity of trust must follow. *Trust is not built on a one-way basis; it must always be a reciprocating relationship.* When a given person's trust is not reciprocated, it still must be considered potential for reciprocation. So long as it is potential, the person extending trust can proceed as if the relationship were complete. Some people become weary after a few days, months, or years of trying to build a relationship with someone they feel is, or can be, meaningful to them. Parents whose child appears to ignore the trust bond may live for any number of years building toward an effective trust relationship, doing all the things necessary for laying a foundation for trust, yet not having their trust reciprocated. More and more, the child turns to his own way, and the parents tire. The reciprocating nature of trust is such that when it is reciprocated, it encourages trust; when it is not reciprocated, a rejection pattern sets in, leaving the interested party despairing over the ineffective development of trust.

Whenever a pattern of rejection has been expressed, it can be expected that final rapport will come about only after one works toward building rapport for as many days, months, or years as the rejection pattern was in effect. Any shortened period of time can be considered a bonus, something unusual. Acceptance of the person must therefore be deeply rooted within the message-sending component of one's life. Acceptance must be communicated as effectively as possible for as long as the message of rejection had been communicated, whether or not the acceptance is reciprocated and the change of attitude is recognized.

Since mutual respect is a reciprocating relationship and must be carried on between at least two persons or groups, the persons or groups must stand on equal footing in terms of validity. One cannot force the other to do that which is untrue to himself. This means that both entities involved in a given relationship will learn and change. The students learn from the teacher; the teacher learns from teaching the students. If a teacher is not continuing to learn, the course readily dries up. Parents learn from their children, even as the children learn from their parents. A reciprocating learning experience will embrace both, such as may be found in the contemporary world of music. Parents learn from their children the new forms of music, and the children learn from their parents to put their sound into perspective in relation to other sounds of music.

When reading the story in Acts 8:26–40 of Philip witnessing to the Ethiopian eunuch, we may ask, What was the Ethiopian eunuch doing out on the road? Was he on legitimate or illegitimate business? The North American would respond immediately by affirming that the eunuch was legitimately representing his government. As a bona-fide government representative, he maintained his aura of representation while he was traveling, as is illustrated in some of his conversation with Philip. On the other hand, a man from the Balue, an African society, would question the legitimacy of that trip immediately. His automatic response would be that since the eunuch was away from home, and quite a distance at that, he was up to no good. Anyone, whether on business or seeking pleasure, who is any distance from home would automatically be considered as being up to no good. The Balue has more to learn than the North American about the Ethiopian eunuch and his journey. The North American can reinforce the Bible story through his automatic response to the conditions mentioned in the story.

However, when we read some other section of the Bible, for example, the account of the wedding of Cana, we ask, Who paid for the wedding reception? The North American will automatically respond that the parents of the bride paid for the wedding reception, whereas the Balue will insist that the father of the groom did. In Bible times, it was probably the father of the groom or a third party who paid for the reception. It was definitely not the parents of the bride. Thus the North American has something more to learn from Near Eastern societies where lineage follows the male line quite rigorously and where the parents of the groom usually absorb the cost of such things as wedding receptions for their sons. The Balue thus has less to learn from us as representatives of societies where lineage follows either the male or female lines and where the parents of the bride generally pick up the tab for the reception.

Keith Miller was referring to this kind of reciprocal learning experience when he said:

> Now in the soul of our marriage it was not my vision of what a marriage, or what a husband should be, against her vision, one of us always having to be wrong; but now together we began trying to find out Christ's vision of what our marriage should be. . . . At last we can relax and be children in the soul of our marriage and find peace together.[6]

Mutual Respect in the Bible

There are numerous passages in the Scriptures that encourage such mutuality. In John 13:34, Jesus admonishes us, "As I have loved you, so you must love one another." In 1 Corinthians 12, Paul encourages us as members of one body to accept each other with our differences and weaknesses.

Possibly the most poignant story of reciprocity in the Scriptures is that of Paul and John Mark. The reciprocity of trust was missing early (Acts 15:38–39) but was somewhat restored later on, for Paul wrote to Timothy, "Get Mark and bring him with you, because he is helpful to me in my ministry" (2 Tim. 4:11; see also Col. 4:10).

On the other hand, Judas' walking out on Jesus and the other disciples, resulting in the betrayal that led to Jesus' death, was a tragic expression of a breakdown of the trust bond (John 18:2–12). The case of Ananias and Sapphira (Acts 5:1–11) was also. In both cases, there was no reciprocity, and the participants were punished for this lack.

A Check List for Mutual Respect

At times it is useful to have a check list to remind one of practices that do confirm the behavior of mutual respect. One needs to apply the check list to one's own behavior so that no aspects of mutual respect are overlooked.

1. Acceptance of the limitation of living standards of each culture. As one gains knowledge of the limits of each living standard, one increasingly accepts positive aspects of each.
2. Lack of criticism of negative aspects of each culture. Differences are not necessarily inferior. It is wise to examine the reasons why differences exist and to be sensitive to them.
3. Ability to make comparisons between the cultures without accompanying negative implications. This is expressed in positive appreciation of the other culture along with one's own.
4. Real contentment of lifestyle is experienced by each one residing there. This does not mean abandoning oneself or one's personality. One's security and satisfaction there is genuine.
5. Easy fluency with the language and idiom of each culture. Language is a living means of communication and takes time to master—especially the humor expressed in language.

6. Control of righteous indignation involving practices considered wrong, until change comes about via converted members of the culture.

7. Expression of humility within the context of either culture one is involved with, not flaunting one's own experience within the crosscultural setting.

8. Ability to distinguish between personal tastes, historic backgrounds, and moral issues (absolutes).

9. Understanding and practicing the ethical code within the other culture without strain and to the degree one's own conscience permits. When one's conscience does not permit, the ability to express this in ways that highlight the issue but do not alienate the person.

10. Understanding the basic means of communication in each culture and handling this effectively, irrespective of age, sex, status, etc.[7]

Summary

The traditionalist wants everyone to be as he is. The ethical relativist does not care what the other is, or for that matter, what he himself is. The proponent of situation ethics wants to give to the other that which he needs out of a motive of love; but there is little control to insure that the giver does not also yield principle. The one receiving may have liked the response, but upon reflection may realize the other went too far in serving him. A loss of respect may follow.

Mutual respect lets each participant in a relationship fully realize his own potential in terms of what he is. Each can be a whole, responsible person at the moment of encounter and continue throughout the relationship as a whole person. Neither need abandon his ethical and moral principles or give up what he really is. Both can learn from the other and contribute to the other for the good of each. Even upon reflection one has no reason to lose even a small degree of respect for the other nor any degree of self-respect. The relationship is always open and always potential for reciprocity. The two together are fully fulfilled because each is fully fulfilled.

Mutual respect is a reciprocating relationship. Humans so often want a one-way interaction and fail to realize that trust has not been building. Both participants must stand together on equal footing, otherwise the relationship is not balanced and one becomes enslaved to the other.

Questions for Discussion

Relating to the Sending Church

1. How do the approaches of mutual respect and situation ethics differ?
2. How do the concepts of mutual respect and Christian love compare?
3. In what ways does the average person "cop out" of the decision-making process? How does a church or religious organization do this?
4. How might a traditionalist behave in a church setting? on a church committee? in Christian education?
5. How might a situationist behave in these same three situations?
6. Can two people differ in opinion and still maintain mutual respect? How? Discuss at what point this might become impossible.

Relating to the Study of the Bible

1. In light of the model of mutual respect, discuss the relationship David had with Jonathan (1 Sam. 18–23).
2. Study the life of Ahab (1 Kings 18–22) and characterize him by one of the categories of the chapter. Why did you choose that one?
3. Study the life of Daniel and compare his behavior with that of the various kings of Babylon in keeping with the categories of the chapter. How did they differ? Why?
4. Study the life of Solomon (2 Samuel) and see if he fits in the ethical relativist or the situation ethicist category. Why did you reach that conclusion? Discuss.
5. How would you categorize Judas? Peter? Does this help you understand better their motives in doing what they did? How?
6. How might the concept of forgiveness border on situation ethics? Explain.

Relating to Missions and Crosscultural Ministry

1. How might a difficult challenge in outreach in another society cause one to become a situation ethicist? Explain.
2. How can mutual respect be maintained between a missionary and people who are obviously poorer than he? with internationals recently arrived in the United States?
3. What steps might be taken to achieve reciprocity in the community in which you are ministering?
4. How might the evangelization of a community be advanced by utilizing the principle of reciprocity? What reciprocal acts might a missionary carry out in order to internalize himself within the social context?

5. Over what kinds of things might a traditionalist missionary and a mutual respect missionary clash? Why might this be? What might result?

Group Activities and Exercises

1. *Behavioral observations*. Make it a point to discover someone practicing situation ethics, someone using a traditionalist approach, and someone using a mutual respect approach. What surprises and/or irritates you as you observe the outworking of these three approaches?
2. *Small group discussion*. Have the group members select three to five distinct situations: classroom, political campaign, church, etc., and discuss the balance of respect called for in each situation.
3. *Small group discussion*. Invite a member of a distinct culture or subculture to each small group. Have the group members discuss and compare the mutual respect demanded in this different culture in relation to their own.
4. *Self-study*. Have each group member write a statement or paper comparing the entire trust bond model (chapters 1–5) with 1 Corinthians 13.
5. *Research*. Send the group members by twos to interview overseas students to discover if the relationship maintained by the missionaries in their homeland could be characterized by mutual respect.
6. *Role play*. Use the case of the California family to experience the differences among the four categories of behavior discussed in this chapter.

California Family

PREBRIEFING:

Pass out copies of the Modern Prodigal case study found at the beginning of this chapter, and ask the class to read it.

Then ask, "What models, tools, and theories do we want to use in working with this case study?"

List all of the responses on the board or overhead transparency. Be sure the final list includes all of the acceptance-of-the-person models, including mutual respect.

Review mutual respect by having the class fill in the boxes to the following matrix:

1. Traditionalism or
   cultural absolutism

2. Ethical relativism

3. Situation ethics

4. Cultural relativity
   or mutual respect

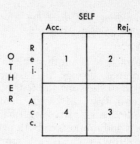

SIMULATION:

First Grouping:

Divide the class into four equal groups and place each group in a different corner of the room.

Assign one group to play the role of the father; another group, the role of the mother; another, the role of the son; and the last, the role of the daughter-in-law.

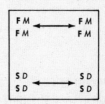

F—father

M—mother

S—son

D—daughter-in-law

Prepare questions for the various roles, and have the groups discuss them.

Second Grouping:

When there is a lull in the discussion and you sense that they are done, have half of the fathers go to the mothers' group and vice versa. Also, have half of the sons go to the daughters-in-law's group and vice versa. Each individual is to continue playing his original role in the new group.

Suggest that they again go through the discussion of the questions appropriate for their role—with two views being now represented in each group.

Third Grouping: (If there are fewer than sixteen students, skip this grouping.)

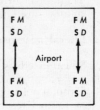

When there is another lull in the noise volume, change the grouping again. Half of the sons and half of the daughters-in-law in each couple group will change places with half of the fathers and mothers in both parent groups. Now each is a "family" group with a father, mother, son, and daughter-in-law.

Set the scene for the class role plays: The center of the room is now an airport terminal where the parents are meeting the couple as they return from England. Each group is to role play this scene of the couple meeting and "breaking the news" to the parents (see role play, below).

Give each group time to plan its role play which will be presented to the rest of the class.

Role Play:

The parents from one group will role play with the couple from another group (four plays; if there is a lack of time, do only numbers 1 and 3).

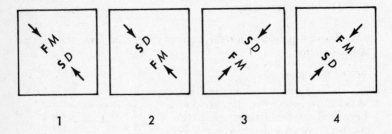

DEBRIEFING:

1. What were the different reactions taken (with reference to the mutual respect matrix discussed during the prebriefing)? Be as objective as possible. (Some students probably tried so hard to show mutual respect that they really acted like situational ethicists. And there may have been other somewhat overdrawn

efforts. Encourage the use of the prior question of trust and the self-acceptance models by those participating in the debriefing.)
2. What are some of the benefits of this type of simulation experience? (Preparation for real-life situations, seeing oneself, etc.)
3. Allow time for additional questions or comments. Give the students an opportunity to draw the conclusions on their own as much as possible. Do not allow yourself to be put in the role of judge and jury.

MODEL TWO
SOCIAL STRUCTURE

SOCIAL STRUCTURE

The model of society here termed social structure is the approach one may take to one's own sociocultural setting or to that of another in order to know who someone is within the context of society. There are seven submodels.

1. The norm of a group or of an individual within a group is the sum of all the values, norms, rules, expectations, aspirations, etc., of the group or individual. This is one's culture.
2. Social organization refers to the network of social relations structuring a social system in which a given individual operates.
3. The flow of truth directly from higher levels of the social structure to lower levels provides freedom. When "truth" is communicated via a second culture or world and life view, slavery or injustice results.
4. Identity factors of a group or individual within a group are necessary if one is seeking to know them and be sensitive to their needs.
5. The activities in which a group or an individual participates further help to define them.
6. Values underlie all that a society is and does. Cognition motivates values and establishes how they will operate within the society. The basic values model is a taxonomy of cognition that allows one to understand the underlying motivations of the members of any given society.
7. Conflict of norm is the disruptive tension that results when one seeks to change one's norm or moves into some crosscultural or cross-subcultural setting that forces a change in the norm.

6

The Norm: Culture

Case Study: Yesterday's Fool

Dear Ann:

I am 19, a sophomore in a midwestern university and considered good-looking and reasonably bright by my peers. I've been dating since I was 15 and, without boasting, I can truthfully say I've had more than my share of male attention.

During this summer, I met my ideal. We dated several times and I found myself saying "No" to others in the hope he would call. I loved being with him. On August 2 he was leaving for his vacation. We both hated to part and sat in the park two hours saying good night. For some mysterious reason all my will power and good intentions vanished and I gave in. I told myself, "This is love. Why should I deny him a true expression of my feelings?"

He sent a few postcards along the way but did not telephone me as I had hoped he would. Last night he returned—a changed man. He took me to supper and informed me that it would probably be our last date. These are his words: "You are not the girl I had hoped you were. Our last night together was a nightmare. You made me ashamed of myself. I could never marry you after that. I would always wonder if there had been others. This has been the greatest disappointment in my life."

So there's my story, Ann. I am trying to keep my chin up, but it isn't easy. I tell myself no decent man would treat a girl this way, but deep down I know it was my decision, not his, but all the rationalization in the world doesn't make it right.[1]

The Concept of Norm

The term norm has many uses in scholarly literature.[2] *Norm generally denotes what is normative, that which is the foundation for expectation within society*. In this volume, it will be used interchangeably with the term culture. If someone acts in a way expected of him, given a certain stimulus within a given situation, he is carrying out that which is normative for the society. Any deviation from this expected or normative behavior is seen as abnormal in some way. The sum of the expectations within a given society is the collection of norms of that society. Built into an individual is the sum of the norms of his society, which in reality represents a composite of the norms of all the groups and all the subcultures in which he participates. Thus we can say that an individual has a "norm" which is the sum of all the "norms" of his total experience. This total experience is in itself a composite of all the norms of all the groups of which he has been and is now a part. A social group that is a specific subculture within the society also has a composite of norms of all its component parts and a composite norm for the entire society.

Thus the norm of any social group equals the sum of its values, norms, expectations, rules, and aspirations. The norm of an individual within a society or social group equals all of the norms of the groups of which he has been, or is, a part. A convenient way for the individual to determine his own norm is to ask himself questions such as these: How am I dressed? What am I doing? What am I thinking? How am I reacting to this situation? What is expected of me in this situation? What are my hopes and aspirations at this moment? What rules of a formal or informal nature are controlling my experience? What do I believe? A convenient way to determine another person's norm is to ask these questions about him while observing his behavior (see chapter 14).

A person from a "supermarket subculture" will not automatically raise his hand to push open the door when approaching the entrance of a supermarket. He expects the door to open electronically. A member of a subculture without supermarkets will automatically raise his hand to push open the door. When he sees the door open before him, he will simply drop his hand. When the door is not automatic, the former will be forced to raise his hand or suffer the consequences—that is, bump his nose. He thus expends more energy if the door does not open than the former when the door does open.

The automatic response to a stimulus is a clear indication that a person is a member of a given culture. The automatic raising of the hand when approaching the door of a supermarket indicates that a person is a member of a nonsupermarket culture. The automatic nonraising of the hand indicates that a person is part of a supermarket culture. Such automatic responses become part of every aspect of life and literally set up a given person to live fully within the culture without undue or destructive tension. The moment one has to think of his response within a given situation, he expends energy that can no longer be made available for creative expression in his life. Society is designed to make as many experiences of life as possible completely automatic, without the need for such thinking. This leaves the person "at peace" within his culture.

In the case study for this chapter, the young woman was living within her norm until her "good intentions vanished" and she "gave in." She began to shift from automatic response to "think" response. This should have been a signal to her that she was approaching the "borders" of her norm. The thinking response was an energy consumer and occupied her thoughts then and possibly later. Her "friend" apparently considered her yielding response a great deal after the experience as well. The young man was apparently of the same subculture as the young lady insofar as this matter was concerned. By encouraging the young lady to yield to him in response to his sexual urgings, he was expressing a distinctive subculture. Once he gained what his words were communicating, he discovered he was not of that new subculture after all.

When a person is unable to respond fully and completely within the habitual patterns of a culture, he must learn what he still lacks, or he will be in conflict within the culture (see chapter 12). Conflict with the culture shows up by two significant signals: One is surprised by that which is encountered and becomes irritated when facing difference. *When entering a new culture or subculture, a person can very quickly isolate the cultural differences by being aware of surprise and irritation.* The sum of these two responses is the degree of cultural difference existing between the norm of the individual and the norm of the new culture in which he finds himself. It is therefore of value, upon entering a new culture or subculture, to maintain a list of surprises and irritations one reacts to in the everyday experience. Checking the list regularly should give a person a guide to cultural difference. For example, I was surprised every time I went on a picnic in Latin America and saw how great a number of family members attended. This was a clear indication of the extended family social structure of the Latins as contrasted to the nuclear family structure of my own North American culture. It has never been important to me to urge family members to participate in a picnic, whereas it is very important to the Latin American.

Maintaining One's Norm

By maintaining one's norm, one maintains identity and the authenticity of one's identity. For some reason, pressure is put on the person or group to remain constant in identity.

The naïve person assumes that to maintain authenticity one needs to maintain one's norm. This is the one-culture approach, and it reinforces ethnocentrism. Thus a person looking at a diagram of rain coming down straight will not interpret that as rain, since it is not blowing at an angle as one expects it to in real life. He is satisfied that his cultural perspective is sufficient to recognize rain. The people of Lystra reacted to Paul and Barnabas in this way (Acts 14:7–18), interpreting their presence in keeping with local religious beliefs. They concluded that gods had come down in human form.

Such naïve ethnocentrism is harmless in one sense, for the people simply do not know something, but as soon as the matter is clarified, they respond and take positive steps to expand their knowledge. True ethnocentrism, however, is more dangerous, for there is a studied intent to maintain the norm, resisting any experimentation in the area of excess, unless it comes naturally, and definitely steers clear of change of any kind. This is the lack of sensitivity in the change process that forces another toward an ethical relativism as discussed in chapter 16. The other must bow to the first and be made over in keeping with the norm of the first.

Resistance to the change of norm and maintaining one's norm intact are two totally different processes. True ethnocentrism is dangerous, as the first forces the second to abandon what he is and the principles on which his life is based. Naïve ethnocentrism is dangerous only if the individual or group has no way of finding out the intent of change or is unable to change because some structure of the society prevents it, thus producing the drive toward ethical relativism inherent in the true ethnocentric sense.

One can be very culturally adaptable and attempt to maintain one's norm so that there is freedom from useless error, resistance to sin, and avoidance of those things that bring no good to one's life. The virgin maintains his/her norm to remain pure for his/her mate. The youth resists drugs and alcohol to avoid what could damage and destroy his concentration or purpose in living. A person born into a class or status need not fear that he is not honoring God or is unable to fully serve God in that role. Paul tells us in 1 Corinthians 7:17, "Each one should retain the place in life that the Lord assigned to him and to which God has called him." Such maintenance of one's norm is

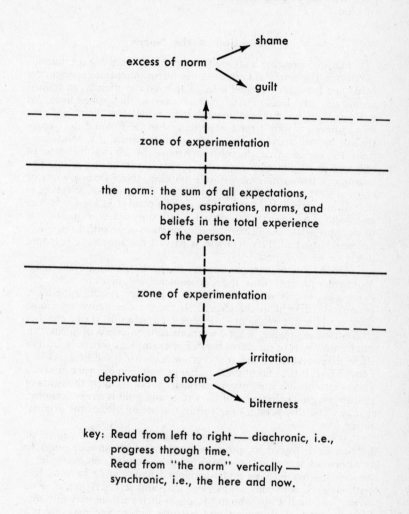

Figure 5. The Norm of the Person in Society (idealized)

done with the best wisdom possible and can be guided by the Spirit of God.

Extension of the Norm

Figure 5 presents a stylized means of representing an individual norm. The norm as known at any one moment of experience is contained between the solid lines. The lived experience can remain within the solid lines or safely extend even to the broken lines. An individual can be observed through time from left to right, and thus any moment in one's total experience can be focused on (represented by an arrow). The separation between the solid lines indicates variation of the norm. All of the allowable range of selection in response to a given stimulus is part of the norm. For example, a man who can, without thinking, select from a white or colored shirt in preparing for church has this range of selection as part of his norm. He may have received a plaid shirt for Christmas and decided to wear that to church, with only a minor question as to its appropriateness. Thus any combination of potential responses becomes a part of the norm and is part of the automatic response behavior of the norm.

Once a person extends beyond the broken lines, however, far more energy goes into the decision-making process. One can express an excess of norm, and as a positive result, experience pleasure or delight in the change. If there are negative reactions, these could result in shame or even a sense of guilt. If one chooses to continue expressing what was at one time an excess of norm, this can become part of the norm itself. For example, a formerly faithful mate may have an affair and then decide that unfaithfulness is a better lifestyle than faithfulness. That person then incorporates such excess into his life and only occasionally is bothered by thoughts of shame and guilt. However, if the shame and guilt is overwhelming, it may cause that person to return to the boundaries of the original norm.

When one is living in deprivation of norm, by choice or because he is forced to, positive reactions of pleasure or negative reactions of irritation or bitterness may result. For example, a person moving into an underdeveloped nation may have to live without such conveniences as electricity and refrigeration. A wife accompanying her husband in his job in such a nation may find this lifestyle most inconvenient and become bitter. She may force a change in her husband's job location or even precipitate a breakdown of the marriage. Frequently, one forced to live in deprivation of norm finds this very much to his taste. Some people are amazed at how easy it is for them to live in a setting where there are no conveniences. It may even change their own lifestyles upon their return to their own culture.

The practical out-working of the concept of norm for the agent of change is that he can encounter another person and, by observing behavior, begin to recognize that person's norm. Through continued experience and association with the other person, it is possible, by means of the scientific process, i.e., the hypothesizing approach, to derive a working grasp of another's norm. This can increase the potential for understanding difference and reduce the potential for adverse reaction to difference.

At this point, acceptance of the person teams up with the concept of norm to permit the agent of change to extend the foundation being built under the change program. He can then work with the person in terms of who and what he is without destroying him by making him over in keeping with the cultural demands of the agent of change.

Change of Norm

Every norm, whether individual or corporate, has a built-in mechanism for change, i.e., the zone of experimentation. One can live in excess of norm or in deprivation of norm for a period of time to test and see if this is not really part of his norm or compatible with his norm. Experimentation may be carried on in both directions, each with its own purpose: One to determine if the person is living up to the fullness of his norm or of his potential, and the other to see if he can include new things in his norm which he did not or could not do previously.

A student who has been accustomed to sleeping eight hours each night and achieving a B average in school may choose to live in excess of this norm by cutting down on sleep and studying more, thus gaining an A average. Such experimentation may leave the individual satisfied that he is living in the full potential of his norm. Or he may realize that he is living in excess of norm and revert to eight hours of sleep and be content with his B average.

People from a horse-and-buggy culture tried the automobile, and most found that they could live with it. They made it part of their norm. Individuals living in North America at the time the automobile was invented had the choice between the horse and buggy or the automobile, and they could make the automobile part of their norm. Some refused to adapt to the changing times, and the horse and buggy became one more item identifying their distinctive subculture. By rejecting the automobile, they caused any member of their subculture to feel guilt when participating in automobile riding or owning.

Generally speaking, no harm results from experimenting within the experimental zone of excess or deprivation of norm. No long-term effects will linger that will be adverse or unfortunate to the individual or group. However, in a certain percentage of cases, such experimentation can be serious and have an adverse effect. A virgin experimenting with sexual intercourse will lose virginity, which can never be regained, and she may become pregnant as well. A person experimenting with drugs may have a bad trip and die from the effects of the drug. A new driver experimenting with fast driving may blow a tire and be seriously maimed or killed in the resulting crash. A young person experimenting with various ways to enter a social group may cause offense that may never be forgiven him and may retard his social adjustment throughout the rest of his life. A mission group may experiment with a new way of raising funds and alienate some of its most faithful contributors.

Anyone experimenting must be willing to pay the price of such experimentation. A youth experimenting with drugs must be willing to run the risk of going to jail. A mission feeling the need to experiment in fund raising must be willing to adjust to a possible loss of funds.

Unfortunately, however, for those who are afraid of risking the adverse effects of the change process, progress and development will not likely come through except the route of experimentation. Without experimentation, the individual or social group will likely remain stagnant or even deteriorate. The agent of change[3] will never be an effective one unless he comes to peace with the experimental zone of the change of norm. Utilizing this zone effectively permits him to try different approaches and strategies in keeping with his sense of responsibility to meet the needs of the people he is attempting to serve.

The change of norm thus leaves one's norm "profile" through time an irregular one. The purpose of the idealized norm representation in figure 5 is simply to introduce one to the concept of norm. A more accurate profile would look similar to that in figure 6.

One's norm is constantly changing in significant ways that either encourage or discourage the growth and development of the person.

Within society, changes are programmed so that a person enculturated effectively within his own society will naturally progress without strain through the various expressions of the program. He will thus be true to himself and also not offend others. For example, the traditional American middle-class male is trained not to touch a member of the opposite sex until the dating period. Then he may hold hands or hug until a going-steady agreement is reached. From then on until the wedding, increased contact is permitted; and complete contact, of course, follows. A married man is trained not to touch a woman other than his wife in any sex-oriented way. How such culture-constrained plans are carried out depends on the participants in the drama of social interaction. Some

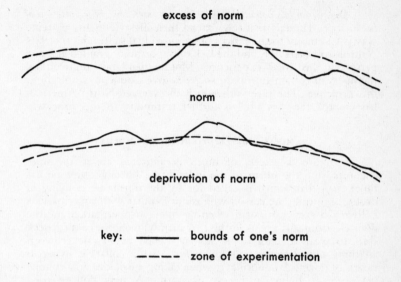

Figure 6. The Norm of the Person in Society (actual)

will follow the plan to the letter; others will modify it in some way to suit themselves.

Variation of Norm

On the synchronic plane, i.e., the person or group at a given moment in time, the norm is not fixed or set in terms of one quality. *The norm is a range of variation* in relation to every aspect of the norm. It is not one unitary expectation a person has; it is a range of expectations. In the area of education, for example, a given person may go to a college or a university. He may attend a local junior college for two years and transfer to a four-year college for his last two years, or he may attend one college for all four years without, in either instance, feeling that he has had inferior education. Another person may attend one college and, by accelerating his pace, complete his course in three years; or he may continue for four years without feeling that he is losing out either way. In each of these cases, another person may feel shortchanged or uncomfortable, a behavioral indication of a narrower variation of norm. Someone else may be free to consider and carry out some other alternatives without any adverse effect.

Any person has potential for the infinite extension of the variation of his lifestyle. The fact that few extend their lifestyle in any extreme way is testimony to the power of an individual's attitude, society's control over behavior, and the lack of opportunity granted any one person in his total experience. Multilingual and multicultural members of certain European societies give eloquent testimony to this principle. The ease with which the average North American has entered the "jet age" is further testimony to this process.

Excess and Deprivation of Norm

In figure 6, excess of norm is indicated above the lines encompassing the norm of the individual. Whenever anyone has more than that which is called for by the norm, he is living in excess of norm. The person who is not familiar with supermarkets is living in excess of norm when he enters a supermarket and the door electronically opens for him. A man who chooses a turtleneck shirt to wear to church on Sunday, when he has never worn anything other than a traditional shirt with a collar, is living in excess of norm. A nondrinker, when taking a drink of an alcoholic beverage, is living in excess of norm. A new college coed accustomed to retiring around eleven may readily begin living in excess of norm within a college community that permits her to stay out until one o'clock. A young couple, wanting to get settled before they really have the money for furnishing their home, may charge more than they can comfortably handle within their income and thus live in excess of norm. Students trained to expect examinations in a course, find their response to a nonexamination course one of excess of norm, since it appears to them that they have greater freedom in reflecting their natural ability.

Excess of norm becomes a problem to the individual and the society of which he is a part whenever the behavior of shame or guilt is expressed.[4] *Shame here means embarrassment before others, and guilt means inward embarrassment.* Embarrassment comes when a person exceeds his norm. He feels that he has no right to live as he does, but he is doing it whether he has the right or not. Shame and guilt will cause the person to behave in ways that are inconsistent within the total framework of the society and to thus sow seeds of disorganization or disruption which may have an adverse effect on the individual and ultimately on the society. The mild embarrassment derived from wearing a colored shirt when one has been accustomed to wearing a white shirt is not potentially disruptive to the society that is flexible in its expression of style in dress, but it is potentially disruptive to the society that is nonflexible in this aspect of life. It further does not affect the individual with a proclivity for trying different fashions, but it is potentially disruptive to the one whose sense of security and well-being requires him to wear white shirts. A society permitting a degree of drunkenness within socially prescribed restrictions will not be affected by a member who happens to get drunk for the first time in his life within such restrictions, for example, at a company Christmas party. However, if he gets drunk on company time, he may be fired on the spot. The person who expresses himself in excess at the Christmas party is not in any trouble so long as there is no underlying sense of having let himself, another person, or a belief system down. He could have extreme guilt and shame within this experience were the drunkenness to go counter to a deeply ingrained sense of his responsibility to shun alcohol.

In the case study at the beginning of this chapter, whatever precise degree of exceeding the norm occurred in the experience of the young woman who "gave in," the action her friend took caused him to so exceed his norm that he terminated the friendship. His guilt, or inward sense of embarrassment, was so great that he feared it would affect him the rest of his life. He directed his sense of guilt toward the girl, suggesting that she was to blame: "You made me ashamed of myself."

Forgiveness in the Scriptures, when related to the concept of norm, permits a person to snap back to his norm whenever he has sinned, by confessing his sin and being granted pardon. It is as if he had never sinned, as if he had never done that which caused him to feel guilty or ashamed, as if he had never exceeded his norm.

Deprivation of norm occurs when an individual lives in such a way that he is unable to meet the expectations of his norm. There is no serious result, either to the individual or to his society, if he makes the choice himself to live in deprivation of norm. A pastor who agrees to take a cut in pay when accepting a call to a mission church has no reason to resent living in deprivation of norm as he has made the decision himself. His wife, however, could become bitter when she is unable to live up to the level of her social and physical expectations. Deprivation of norm can be serious to the individual and society if one is coerced by forces he is unable to control to live without that which he perceives to be his right. The pastor's wife could sue for divorce. The black American who lives in deprivation of norm, or at least perceived deprivation, could do something disruptive to society, such as painting graffiti on walls or bombing a public building. A child of parents who are more than able to pay college expenses but refuse to do so may develop a deep resentment toward the parents.

The behavior of deprivation of norm is that of mild irritation, resentment, or bitterness. An employee receiving a 4 percent pay increase when he was expecting a 5 percent raise will feel mildly irritated and may work toward a more complete raise at the time of the next pay increment period. However, a person expecting a pay raise and not getting it when others given the very same conditions of employment receive it, may develop a bitterness which could seriously affect his work response within the company.

Even though the young woman of the opening case study did not sense the same degree of guilt or embarrassment due to excess of norm as did her friend, she did sense deprivation of norm. She had come to the point of anticipation in sharing her friend's life. She had no expectation of losing the friendship but of seeing it develop into a deep and lasting marriage relationship. Her irritation and disappointment, a mild reaction to deprivation, gradually developed into a more intense reaction: "I'm trying to keep my chin up, but it isn't easy," and "I tell myself . . . , but deep down. . . ."

Comparison of Norm

Since each norm is different or at least potentially different because of the unique past, present, and future experiences and associations of each one within a group, the comparison of norms becomes a challenge. Comparison of norm charts are useful in comparing those aspects of difference that are measurable or quantifiable.

When comparing a polygamous society with a monogamous society, members of a monogamous society often condemn the former without seriously considering the social structure of the other society (see figures 7 and 8). In monogamous societies, adultery is physical union with one person other than the legal mate. A more thoughtful approach would be a consideration of the norm of the monogamous or polygamous society: adultery is physical union only outside of marriage, regardless of the number of wives a man may have. In presenting the biblical ideal (norm) of monogamy, one should realize that existing multiple marriages are, in fact, legal and binding.

The Process of Enculturation

The concept of socialization in sociology or enculturation in anthropology provides insight into the transmission of the norm of the group. Through this process a person learns what is expected of him in a given situation. The process of enculturation can bring an outsider (either through birth or through migration) into a comfortable relationship to the society within a period of two to five years. This does not mean that the individual must "buy" everything that he encounters, but he must know the proper way to

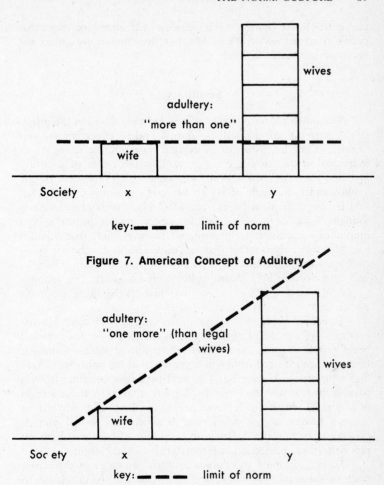

key: ▬ ▬ ▬   limit of norm

Figure 7. American Concept of Adultery

Figure 8. Polygamist Society's Concept of Adultery

do things. He must respond correctly, both consciously and unconsciously, to the various stimuli within situations, permitting others to see that he is adapting. Anything short of this dynamic, involving adaptation to the new society and its cultural ways, produces breakdown in communication.[5] The agent of change must know the system of the culture before he can effectively participate in its change. Otherwise he will introduce ways that derive from his own way of life, but these may never meet the needs of the target culture.

Summary

The norm of the group or of any individual within the group is the sum of all the values, norms, rules, expectations, and aspirations of the group or individual. Further, the norm of an individual within any group, as well as the norm of a group included in some larger grouping, equals all the norms of the groups and individuals of which he or the group is a part. That which an individual does automatically, without conscious thought, is part of his norm, and, in essence, defines the norm. If an individual must think about some action, it is likely that it is not part of his norm but, rather, part of another norm which he is being encouraged to learn and make part of his own, or from which he will turn because it is incompatible with his norm. The maintenance of one's norm is a positive process resulting in one's authenticity.

Someone living in excess of his norm will find himself experiencing a sense of embarrassment that relates to his personal belief system as guilt and to others about him as shame. Someone living or being forced to live in deprivation of his norm will likely find a bitterness developing. This will become more intense with passing time or with each reinforcing action taken by those leaders of groups of which the deprived person is a part. The only chance of such bitterness not developing is when the person himself chooses to endure the deprivation by means of personal decision, rationalization, projection, or replacement of the right.

Every individual and corporate norm is expressed through a range of variation that is developed through time and in relation to millions of interpersonal contacts and associations. This range of variation permits change of norm in that some of the range becomes established and some is rejected. Experimentation continues within the range of variation and is a healthy response to life, providing for a continual reevaluation and freshening of the norm. Resistance to the change of norm is an unnatural process and has the same effect as rejection, as the dynamics of the social process cannot work to aid the person or group in the maturation process. Whereas maintenance of norm is positive and growth producing, resistance to change is negative and destructive.

Questions for Discussion

Relating to the Sending Church

1. In what ways do churches differ? For example, in one church no music is played as background for prayer, and in another it is.
2. How does the church discourage experimentation to test for potential variation of norm? Is this helpful or harmful to growth and maturation? How?
3. Does God intend that we live only within our norm? Discuss.
4. How does our dedication to God press us to excess or deprivation of norm? How do we feel when this happens?
5. What part does the supernatural play in relation to a person's norm? a group's norm?
6. Is everything a group or society does approved by God? Explain.

Relating to the Study of the Bible

1. Study examples of the norm expressed in the Book of Ruth.
2. Can you find evidences of difference of norm between the times of Abraham early in Genesis and Joseph later in Genesis? Was there any expression of excess or deprivation of norm? Explain.
3. Discuss the apparent change of norm Daniel experienced between chapters 1 and 10 of Daniel. For example, he would not partake of the meat and drink of the king at all in chapter 1, whereas he only abstained when he was in mourning in chapter 10. How do you explain this change?
4. Discuss the difference in the norm of Jesus and that of Paul.
5. Discuss the difference in the norm of Luke (Luke and Acts) and that of John (John and Revelation).
6. How might the biblical concept of forgiveness enable one to live within his norm?

Relating to Missions and Crosscultural Ministry

1. List changes of norm you experienced moving from your own culture to the culture of your ministry.
2. When you experienced excess of norm, for example, having a live-in maid, how did this impact your life? your relationship with your mate?
3. When you experienced deprivation of norm, for example, lack of finances or change of diet, how did this impact your life? your relationship with your mate?
4. Did you carry out experimentation to see if you could extend the variation of your norm?
5. Discuss ways the two societies you know best differ. Does this knowledge provide you with fresh ideas for strategies of church planting or church growth?

6. How do internationals often live in excess of norm or deprivation of norm when living in the United States? What effect does this have on them?

Group Activities and Exercises

1. *Observation*. Observe someone close to you for a period of days to determine the patterned behavior he expresses, i.e., what he does first, what he does second, what he does next, and so on. Observe a group in the same way.
2. Observe a person you consider is living in excess or deprivation of norm. How consistent is that person's behavior? How content does that person appear to be?
3. *Experimentation*. Objectify your own norm, for example, in the area of consistent use of uniform or dress. Live for a day or two in the zone of experimentation of norm by changing your dress and observing behavioral responses to this change.
4. *Group work*. Spend a period of time individually or in a small group defining the norm of the Hebrew society, particularly the patriarchal period. Then compare this with the norm of the Jewish society of the New Testament period. How are they the same? How do they differ?
5. *Written response*. Indicate one way in which your norm has changed in the last month. Was tension associated with it? bitterness? guilt? Explain.
6. *Interview*. Invite into your group someone from another culture and have that person explain the various ways his norm has had to change since entering the United States. Seek to ascertain if he is pleased or not, if he is angered or not. Why?

7

Social Organization

Case Study: The King and Queen's Visit

In the far northwest province of Thailand, the resident missionaries, a family and two single girls, had established good rapport with the provincial governor and his wife. The governor's wife had previously taught in a Christian school in Bangkok. She even volunteered as language teacher for one of the single missionaries for a short period of time. Mutual respect had resulted in genuinely cordial relations between them.

During the furlough of the missionary family, the king and queen of Thailand planned a royal visit to this provincial town. For months in advance, preparations were being made for the royal family's visit. Houses and fences were repaired, and streets were mended and swept clean. The king had never before visited this remote province. The anticipation, the preparation, and the uncontainable joy of the people showed what a great occasion it was for them.

Shortly before the king and queen's visit, the governor's wife came to visit the missionary women. In the course of their conversation, she invited them to be present with her and the governor in order to welcome the royal couple. This was clearly a very high honor, since the king and the queen were the most important and prestigious people to the Thai.

93

At this invitation, the missionaries found themselves in a state of conflict. A believers' conference had been previously scheduled, and the first day of the conference happened to be the day of the king's visit. With other missionaries to be entertained and preparations to be made for the conference, the two women politely refused the invitation to be present with the governor and his wife in order to welcome the royal party. With little to say, the governor's wife returned home.

The royal couple arrived on schedule. The missionaries held their conference as scheduled, and during the course of the day, they caught a glimpse of the king and queen en route from the local airstrip.

A. R. Radcliffe-Brown defines social structure as a "network of social relations."[1] Social relations form through contact between two or more people or groups of people. Every addition of a person or a group increases the size and network of social relations. Every encounter with another unit of the network adds complexity to the network by establishing social relations not only with individual and individual, group and group, but also with individual and group. The sum of the network of social relations is the social structure of a given society. The sum of all of the networks of social relations of all the societies gives us the concept of world. Thus society is made up of larger groups containing smaller, less-complex groups of individuals.

The missionaries in our case study were involved in a network of social relations, including the host state in which they were serving and their field conference, a part of a larger mission organization. To the expected complexity of social relations of a person within a group within a nation, there was added the complexity of service to a second group, responsible ultimately within a second nation.

Society As System

A system is an assemblage of parts or objects united by some form of regular interaction or interdependence.[2] It forms an intricate whole. It is able to function, operate, or move in unison and in obedience to some kind of control. It is in balance when all the parts are functioning effectively together to produce the desired effect of the system. This means that all the parts or components or subsystems must also be functioning effectively for the whole system to be running smoothly. Control mechanisms keep the system operating smoothly. The system is abused when it is taken advantage of by being used for selfish ends rather than for the purposes for which the system was established, or when some control is thwarted or overlooked, or when there is some attempt to ignore or to replace some part of control unnecessarily. The system must be "serviced" or recycled periodically, otherwise it will operate less efficiently than it was designed to.

The automobile is a system with component parts that operate as wholes within the larger whole.[3] The carburetor is a part of the whole and is itself a whole assemblage, any part of which may break down, causing the whole assemblage to need replacement. Or, if a part fails (e.g., the engine), it may be economical to scrap the entire car and replace it. The automobile functions as a transportation aid. To use it as a bulldozer for moving earth or snow is to abuse it. To put regular gasoline into a high compression engine is to abuse the engine, resulting in carbon build-up that will shorten engine life. The entire system of a car needs servicing periodically, otherwise lubrication systems within the whole will dry up, producing irreparable damage. The human body is a system with component parts that function in relation to the whole. The body can be abused by lack of sleep or improper diet. It is repaired by means of rest and food. The environment in which we live is also a system with component parts that can be abused through pollution, and it needs replenishing through various means of fertilization or land rest, for example.

The Bible deals in many places with the system concept. God created three great systems and put them into operation: the universe (Gen. 1:1–2:1), the body (2:7), and society (2:18–25). He encouraged Adam and Eve to maintain the universe in effective balance (1:28), humans to care for their bodies (1 Cor. 6:19–20), and Christians to cooperate within the context of society (Rom. 13).

Society is a system and can be analyzed even as any other systems operation can be analyzed and worked with. All the parts of the system relate to the whole and give it meaning. The whole, in turn, gives meaning to the parts. Without the whole, the parts would have no reason for existing; and without any one of the parts, there would be no whole. There are many models dealing with society as a system.[4] Society can be described in terms of its social, political, economic, and religious systems and subsystems.[5] It can be described in terms of its institutions, such as the family, the church, business, and political parties. The way society as a system will be discussed in the succeeding pages, however, will be in terms of the item identification of each group; the activities carried out by the group; and the values that underlie the group, set up its activities, and give it fullness of meaning.

Systems in Equilibrium

Systems must be in balance to run most effectively. An out of tune automobile will "run rough." The subsystem termed "the engine" is running out of balance. *Equilibrium theorists* suggest that society at its heart is a system in balance, but forces within and without the system drive it out of balance. Conflict theorists, rather, suggest that society has always been in a conflict state and always will be, moving from conflict state to conflict state. Many people in evangelistic pursuits look for an individual or group in conflict to witness to, thinking that he or they might be more receptive to the gospel. Or they may even be willing to throw the one to whom they are witnessing into conflict to encourage a condition of receptivity. It is interesting that Jesus' use of "peace" is as a condition of equilibrium, not conflict.

Missionaries moving into a new society and dealing with a new culture must be careful that they do not introduce conflict unnecessarily into a setting of basic equilibrium or reinforce the conflict state that already exists within the social group. It will take many times longer to restore the society to equilibrium than it took to throw it into conflict. Not understanding the system of status within a community can cause such disruption. Often the missionary is perceived to be of high status because he owns a car and other trappings of wealth. Whomever the missionary relates to is bound to be perceived of as similar or equal in status to the missionary. If this person happens to be a low-status person within the community, achieving higher status by dealing with the outsider, others will resist such a change, for their own status position within the community could be in jeopardy. In strata-rank societies where everyone is in a status position higher or lower than others, such disruption of the social stratification system can be a powerful block to the entrance of the gospel.

On the Island of Saibai in the Torres Straits just off the northern coast of Australia, the people have developed numerous festivals involving elaborate ritual patterns and feasts. It is rare for three weeks to pass without a major feast. Such festivities celebrate events in the Anglican church calendar. Each major feast costs a great deal of money, and people save for years to participate in the various festivals of the community.

The tombstone opening is one such feast occurring when the family has been able to purchase a tombstone for a departed loved one. It does not occur on a regular basis, as it has to do with burial of some significant adult in the community. It does demand a great deal of money, however, and has become highly disruptive within the community because the public expectations for festival display have enlarged this festival out of all proportion to the community value. When a significant person in the community dies, the family begins saving for the tombstone opening. In any given home, this may take all the accumulated resources for years. If a young lady in the family is planning a wedding, she must wait until after the opening. Young people in Saibai are increasingly hesitant to wait, and this is causing an exodus of young people from the community to the mainland and causing some to live together out of wedlock, something resisted by the church leaders. The tombstone opening festivities have thrown the system of Saibai society out of balance, and it will take a great deal of patient effort to restore the balance and make the community one in which the young people wish to remain or return to.

The Mayan people of Central America engage in a two-man feud. This is a phenomenon of continuing social conflict, ending only when one of the two antagonists dies or leaves the geographic area. Family members or friends may support one or the other of the participants but are not obligated to keep the feud alive as in the case of the Hatfields and McCoys of North American history. Any kind of real or perceived injustice may keep the feud alive for years if not decades. Outsiders try to get the participants together to resolve their differences as is the approach in Western society. This only intensifies the feud and causes embarrassment to the one so persuaded.

Mayan societies achieve a state of equilibrium around such a feud. Outsiders come into the community, tune in to the feud, and try to aid in resolution only to find that they have thrown the community into conflict and forced one or the other of the participants to take action. In a church setting where the local church officials had successively negated the adverse effects of a serious feud, some missionaries began to meddle, and within a few months, one of the two participants, a very fine church leader, had left the area. His family literally disintegrated in the process, as the children lost their sense of belonging in having to choose between their old home and their parents' new home. In a traditional society such as a Mayan community, this was intense disruption. One son wound up as a vagabond, and a daughter became a maid on a ranch, eventually becoming the ranch owner's mistress. Once the conflict was resolved by the departure of one participant, the community returned to a new equilibrium, and interestingly enough, the church grew.

Culture As Expression of System

Culture is everything with which an individual is concerned and involved in a society. This sounds like a very nonacademic definition of a very important concept. Culture can be defined in hundreds of ways,[6] but the point is that every thought a person thinks, every hope he has, every step he takes, every belief he holds, and every interaction he undertakes, is controlled by his culture. Every move he makes is programmed into him by his culture.

The arena of culture is the society—American society, Nigerian society, German society, and so on. These societies are not static but are themselves divided into many subdivisions, each of which has its own subculture, i.e., a unique blending of the various cultures making up the larger society. In turn, each of these societies is changing through time, and thus each culture and subculture is itself a dynamic process.

It is therefore appropriate to talk not just of culture nor just of society, but, rather, of the *sociocultural setting* which combines these two concepts in one.

Further, it is not appropriate to talk of culture and society as unified, but as multiculture and multisociety. Each sociocultural setting is made up of many parts, each with its unique identity.

The sociocultural setting is further to be distinguished from the ecological setting, i.e., society's interaction with the environment; as well as from the products of the society, i.e., that which is produced as a result of sociocultural interaction and ecological involvement.

The socialization process is designed to prepare someone to live within his whole society, and it effectively maximizes the concept of society as one unified whole. Such a process is necessary, as it would be utterly impossible for someone to learn all the complexities of life in a given moment. The socialization process introduces to the learner only what he needs at the time. Thus the perception continues to build that the person is growing up, living, and learning within a single society. Differences are minimized or explained away; likenesses are maximized. As one grows and matures, he learns to recognize and accept differences for what they are; and to the degree he does this, he can become mature. He is also able to move from a monocultural to a crosscultural perspective. A monocultural point of view may serve a person within the narrow constraints of his own culture and subculture, but only a crosscultural perspective allows him to be fully effective in relating beyond the narrow confines of his own.

A certain family has a saying: "Walk around the rug." By itself, this saying could mean many things. It could mean that a certain rug is white; therefore, one should walk around it so as not to get it dirty. It could mean that the rug has just been washed. It could mean that this particular family has a game involving walking around a round rug but across a square one. There are many possibilities. The family that I am thinking of picked up this concept after a child became angry and walked around and around a rug to give vent to his feelings and frustrations. Since that time, whenever a family member has become angry or frustrated, he has been told to walk around the rug. You could gain this specific meaning by having someone within this particular subculture or social group explain it to you—in essence, teach you the rules of that subculture. This specific concept fits into the whole of the family subculture and gives uniqueness to that family. To enter fully into the whole, i.e., the family, the part must have been learned. The part is that network of interpersonal relations which is expressed in walking around the rug.

I can enter three different kinds of restaurants in the United States. In one, I am to sit and be served. In another, I am to pick up some of the items of the meal and be served the others. In the last, I am to pick up everything and am served nothing. These are three distinctive social groups. Many of their practices and many of the things they serve are the same. All serve American food, but each is set up differently to serve this food. They thus comprise distinct subcultures. Some members of the I-am-to-be-served-everything subculture are reluctant to enter the door of a smorgasbord or a cafeteria.

Within one ethnic-linguistic group in Central America, there are cultural and linguistic differences existing between villages just a few miles apart. In one village, the men cut firewood and carry it home across their backs in a horizontal position. In another village, the men carry firewood vertically along the length of their backs. In one village, the word *peren* is used for "rooster." In the neighboring town, it is used as a vulgar term describing a dirty-minded old man. Even though these are parts of a larger ethnic-linguistic whole, they are distinct and unique within themselves. The outsider crossing the village "boundary" must learn the system, otherwise he will be seen only as an outsider and thus a nonentity.

The four missionaries in the case study of this chapter had entered an operating system. They were individuals on a team assigned to a given station within a network of stations within a larger mission emanating from the United States. This network was plugged into a community within a state within a nation. Each missionary thus had divided loyalties. It was expected, however, that ultimate loyalty was toward the sending mission with a home board in the United States. This placed a strain on the people participating in the network operating in Thailand. That network called for response to leadership at a time when this leadership and the attendant authority of leadership was being reinforced. It was being made visible by means of a reception for the royal couple. By undermining the authority—that is, ignoring the function of the reception that was designed to bring to focus this authority for the people in the community—the missionaries abused the system that was operating and introduced a dysfunction within the system. One part of the whole (i.e., the Christian community) was not operating in harmony with the larger whole. At this point the socialization process was breaking down, since the newcomers to the society were not learning the things they needed to know for the effective perpetuation of the society.

It is easy to say at this time that the missionaries were yielding to the higher ethical law of being responsible to God. However nice this may sound, it is not likely to be the case in a large percentage of such encounters. The "object as goal" world and life view of the missionaries from the States insisted that a program previously planned had to be carried out before any other activity could be pursued. God could have been honored just as effectively had the missionaries delayed their own program, encouraged the believers to honor their king and queen, and then utilized such an experience to reinforce the meaning of God as King over all. In short, the missionaries lost the opportunity to teach their people the tremendous truths of Romans 13.

System As Control

One way of defining the social system is to describe every social control mechanism involved within the whole.[7] For an automobile, every physical property becomes a means of control. The motor block can withstand only so much heat, and this limitation in turn limits the potential top speed of the automobile. Further, there are ecological limitations as to where the automobile can go. It cannot go up the rough side of a mountain, though some kinds of automobiles can travel over rougher terrain than others. Further, there are the sociocultural controls placed on the use of automobiles. Society's rules limit their speed, their performance, their right of way, and so on. But there is another area of control by society that is informal but very real. A more economical turbine engine can be developed, but society, influenced by oil company interests and pressures, drags its feet in producing it, since this might limit gasoline sales. American Motors incorporated reclining seats in some of its automobiles, but other North American corporations did not follow the lead. This was due in part to expense and in part to possible competition with camping units, but it was also due in part to our society's reluctance to permit any pair of youths from having an instant bed, thus controlling by extension other aspects of the whole.

For a given society, *control mechanisms operate to control the immediate operation of the system, learn from its past, and perpetuate itself in the future.* Societies differ as to the amount of the past they utilize in current operations and the degree to which they prepare for the future, but each aspect of life serves as control to immediate operations. Social control mechanisms operate in the social realm to regulate marriage and mating practices, in the economic realm to regulate flow and distribution of goods vital to the society's well-being, in the political realm to control leadership and authority, and in the religious realm to control belief and practice.

Money is a social control mechanism for the economic realm. A society not wanting to use money will use barter. Another society will utilize ritual measures to insure distribution of goods. Pews in a church regulate traffic flow in the place of worship. Hallways regulate traffic flow in the educational arena. Rituals that regulate and control behavior in worship are quite distinct from those that control behavior in a Sunday school.

Network As Hierarchy

Society is organized to permit interpersonal relationships that are meaningful to each party involved. Were each individual and each group no different from any other, and were each one to be forced to relate to the other in the very same way, the energy available to the individual or group would be dissipated in meaningless pursuits. Thus society has the job of relating each of its members in an intimate way and each of the other members of other societies in ways that are less than intimate. This task calls for hierarchy,[8] for levels within a hierarchy, and for unit distinction within given levels within the hierarchy.

Hierarchy is utilized to relate smaller, less-complex parts of units within larger, more-complex wholes. Every society can be seen to have some hierarchical structuring. The American society relates families within communities, communities within corporate communities (such as cities and states), and these corporate communities within a corporation of communities that is called the nation. Latin society is organized around extended families that constitute name clans that in turn yield authority to a more or less loosely centralized government representing the state. The Hebrew society grouped extended families together in name lineages, the lineages in clans, and the clans in tribes (see figure 9). Saul finally pulled the tribes together into a nation, which was later split into two nations.

Another way of viewing the American nation is socioeconomically. This involves the placement of individuals within departments of industries and businesses, such as corporations, labor unions, guilds, and so on. Another way is to consider the American within interests groups and such interest groups within loosely structured power-prestige groups that become nothing less than a kind of pressure group within the larger society.

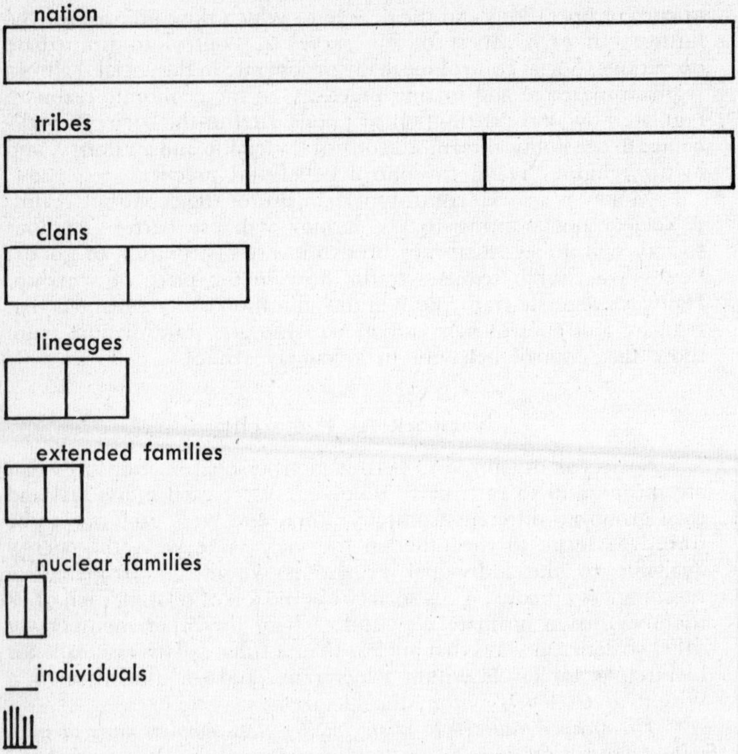

nation

tribes

clans

lineages

extended families

nuclear families

individuals

Figure 9. Hebrew Hierarchical Structuring

Some African societies have interlinked age-level groupings that bring together all the men of a given age, for example, from twenty to twenty-five or twenty-five to thirty. Alongside these age groupings there are sociopolitical groupings such as councils within the larger tribal organization. Each type of grouping has its own jurisdiction and sphere of responsibility. Each man within the society is under the jurisdiction of each group at the same time. That which a person is involved in at the moment determines which grouping has authority over him.

These various corporate "profiles" give one a quick, concise

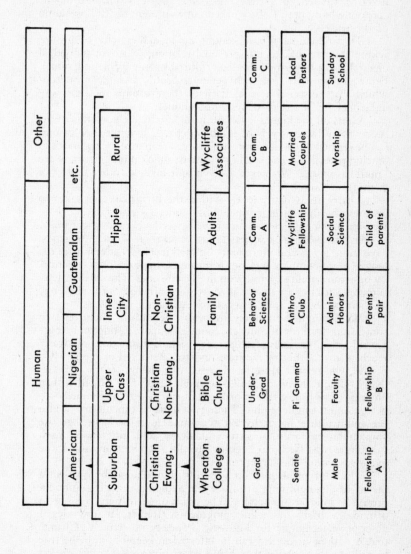

Figure 10. A Characteristic North-American Sociocultural Profile

view of the structure of the society. No one profile is sufficient to describe the entire society, however. Various profiles of the corporate body need to be worked out to present the full operation of the society.

The individual is also caught up in a hierarchy of groups within the network of interpersonal relations. Such an individual hierarchy can be termed the sociocultural profile of the individual. Figure 10 presents one such personal profile and the groups of which that person is a part. Each of these groups in some way influences his life and makes him unique.

Units on the higher levels of the hierarchy include units of the successively lower levels of the hierarchy. The latter type of unit can be termed "included unit," and these are in turn incorporated in "including units." The smallest, least-complex units of society are "minimal units." Whenever a given unit includes other units, we distinguish "levels."

There are as many levels within the hierarchy as it takes to distinguish the included/including units within the society. Smaller, less-complex societies have fewer levels and fewer units. Larger, more-complex societies, such as certain Western societies, have more levels and more units on each level. What results in the larger, more-complex societies is greater complexity, not superiority or greater ability to deal with life's challenges. The smaller, less-complex societies are totally adequate to work within the challenge of their ecological and sociocultural settings.

We distinguish units on the basis of contrast. Wherever two contrasting features of units are found, we have distinct units on a given level. Contrasting features may include distinctions of loyalty mechanisms, authority mechanisms, etc. As noted in figure 11, a person who related more to Martin Luther King, Jr., as a "hero" than to John F. Kennedy, and who spoke "hip" English rather than "nonhip" English, was part of a unit distinct from the Kennedy-as-hero, nonhip language unit. These two units or subcultures fit into the multiculture hierarchy on the same level because they are comparable in terms of shared likenesses and differences. Each subculture was likely to have comparable subdivisions and to be included within the larger society.

The concept of units on a level within a hierarchy gives us a means of distinguishing groups while avoiding branding different groups as inferior or superior. The point of such analysis is not to provide a basis for value judgments. Rather, it provides a descriptive technique for knowing a society objectively. Change that is desired or needed can be effected in keeping with the true nature of society rather than being based on some false perception of the society as compared with another in terms of superior/inferior or right/wrong evaluations. It is a means of understanding, of knowing, of recognizing difference. It provides a way for someone to determine difference, recognize it as valid, and know what to do about it in effecting sound interpersonal relations. It also provides the sound foundation for knowing what is right or wrong within the sociocultural setting.

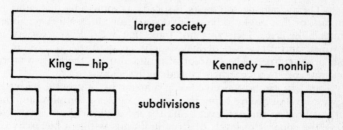

Figure 11. Comparable Subcultures Within a Society

With the concept of hierarchy, levels of hierarchy, and units on a level, we have the larger framework for understanding more completely the concept of network of social relations and the system of society built around this network. Social relations exist between individuals on an individual level within the hierarchy. Individuals group within larger more complex groupings either as individuals or as members of included groups. Finally, groups interact within groups within the hierarchy. The sum of all the social relations in the network is the social structure or system of the society. The average American, for example, is involved in one fantastic network of social relations and thus is part of a very complex social structure operating systemically. Figure 10 provides a partial glimpse of such complexity.

The individual moves within the network of social relations in two ways: as a spectator and as a participant. As a spectator, he sees and observes what occurs around him within the social group. As a participant, he fills roles within the social group. *The concept of roles is a conceptual model that describes the pattern of responsibility assigned to an individual within a social group.*[9] A given individual may have many different roles within the groups of which he is a part, such as father, manager, taxpayer, deacon, etc. He brings his personality, his uniqueness, and his idiosyncrasies to the role. The society has already prescribed the extent of responsibility expected within the role.

A given individual filling an incompatible role, for whatever reason, may play the role and wear a mask to cover the basic incompatibility with the role. Such an individual lives in conflict within the society and may begin to evidence the behavior of conflict (see chapter 12).

Summary

The average person looks at society as something that either is unitary or that ought to be so. Everyone must look alike, act alike, think alike, etc. Society is not built that way. Every society is distinct, and every part of that society has its own expressions of the larger culture. The concept of multiculture is therefore a more accurate perspective when considering society.

Society can be conceived of as a hierarchy of groups, with the lowest level of groups being the simplest and least complex, and the largest level or highest level being the most all-inclusive. Thus we have the concept of levels of structural units within a hierarchy of groups. The network of interpersonal relations that results is the web of society, with the entire structure tied together through millions of strands of interpersonal associations.

The concept of system is readily applied to the group. Each group is a system with operating parts and calls for continual systems analysis and maintenance. The system is best discovered through the study of the behavior of the people operating within that system. Once a person learns the social control mechanisms through the behavior of the participants, it is comparatively easy for him to define the system accurately. Once he grasps the system and its operations become obvious, he can clearly see which actions reinforce the system, which actions abuse the system, and which actions force the society into a disruptive instability.

Questions for Discussion

Relating to the Sending Church

1. What types of behavior could clue one in to status relationships within a given hierarchy, for example, in the military? ir the church? in your business?
2. In what ways does a local church exemplify a systems operation? Discuss. How does such insight aid in ministry?
3. In what ways might an evangelistic campaign benefit by its leaders tuning in to the sociocultural setting of the people they are seeking to reach? Describe.
4. How might God work through the system of a society to reach people and accomplish his purpose?
5. How might our social system limit the effect of God on our lives?

6. How does the system of the church control our behavior? Is this what God has for us? How is it the same? How is it different?

Relating to the Study of the Bible

1. Scan the Scriptures quickly and try to ascertain the number of different major cultures represented. Clue: For a starter, there will be at least as many cultures represented as languages: Hebrew of the Old Testament, Greek of the New. But some of the Bible was written in Aramaic, and the Jews of the New Testament spoke a dialect of Hebrew quite different from the Old Testament dialect. From this point, look for behaviors that evidence distinctives of culture, as in the Book of Ruth compared with the Book of Daniel. Discuss what makes these cultures different.
2. Study the Pentateuch (Genesis through Deuteronomy) and describe the cultural distinctives of the Hebrew people, for example, having a distinctive category of "stranger," not planting two kinds of grape vines in the same vineyard, observing certain holy days, etc.
3. Study the political hierarchy and the religious hierarchy of the New Testament period. How do they compare and contrast?
4. Study the "messiah group" concept in Acts and seek to ascertain just how this differed from the social structure of the Jewish people at the time of Christ and the early church.
5. Do you feel that the people of Jesus' day were just as controlled by their culture as we are today? Discuss.
6. Study the life of Paul to see how much under the control of his society Paul was and how this advanced as well as hindered his ministry.

Relating to Missions and Crosscultural Ministry

1. Why is it important to know our own culture when relating to internationals?
2. Describe the network of social relations that characterize the social group in which you minister. For example, how do the people communicate? How do the people influence one another? How are decisions made?
3. What social control mechanisms seem to constrain or advance your ministry? Explain. Which seem to disrupt it?
4. What has been the major structural challenge that you feel you have had to overcome in your ministry? For example, in a matrilineal society where the wife's mother can decide when a group moves, a trained male teacher may have to leave his school to follow his wife or stay and live apart from her. How could you work with this?

5. Who maintains the basic social relations of the group with whom you work? For example, in Latin America the woman maintains relationships with the extended family members. This is her responsibility. How might you work through such a significant person to further the ends of the gospel?
6. How have you seen outsiders abuse the society of your ministry? throw it into instability?

Group Activities and Exercises

1. *Conceptual*. Have each member of the group prepare his own sociocultural profile indicating all the groups of which he is a part. Then, in twos, have the team organize their groups into included/including hierarchy structures. Compare the various results and then ask, "How might your social structure hinder you from adapting to another society?"
2. *Conceptual*. Work in teams or small groups to determine the most effective aspects of North American social structure in reaching out to the unsaved. For example, how can the sports world be used to impact American society for Christ?
3. *Activity*. Have each member of a group enter a sociocultural setting new to him, for example, a new office, a different store, a different church, etc. Seek to determine the network of social relations existing in this new context. Work with space relationships, verbal and nonverbal indicators of hierarchy, etc.
4. *Experiment*. Work through the system of which you are a part to accomplish some goal. Select any systems operation you wish to work with and establish some goal that you could accomplish without rippling the waters. For example, apply for a job.
5. *Experiment*. Have each person test the existing social control mechanisms operating in his subculture by breaking one purposely. For example, stand very close to someone while talking; sit on the table to eat rather than on a chair; maintain more intensive eye contact than is normally called for; in pairs, each eat off the other person's plate. What can you learn from such an exercise? How might this help you as you enter another culture or subculture?

8

Flow of Truth

Case Study: The Decision-Making Process in Japan.[1]

In Japan, decision making in organizations of any size is an extremely complex, diffuse process in which everyone from top to bottom has a part. The views of all parties with an interest in the outcome are canvassed, and an attempt is made to accommodate each view. A consensus must be reached before a decision may be made or put into effect.

Herman Kahn, in predicting that by the year 2000 Japan may well be the world's leading industrial state, describes the uniquely effective Japanese decision-making process.[2]

There are, says Kahn, two methods of reaching a consensus: *ringi* and *matomari*. *Ringi* is a process in which junior employees initiate and reach an agreement on an idea or problem within the company. They draft a paper on the subject for the department head's approval. Then the paper is circulated among other departments. There is much discussion and change in the paper as it passes back and forth.

After a broad consensus is reached within these lower and middle levels, the paper is presented to higher corporate authorities, who are then under serious pressure to approve the plan and forward it to the highest office for final decision.

In *ringi,* it is difficult to isolate the source of initiative behind an idea, as it may come from anyone, even someone quite low in the organization. It is also difficult to determine the actual decision-maker, as the decision has been made by all the interested parties.

Matomari is a meeting attended by representatives of all departments or levels within an organization. A problem is outlined by a senior officer, and each member offers his initial thoughts on the issue. No one discloses all his thinking for fear of offending his colleagues or putting himself in a minority or, worse yet, isolated, position.

Each person slowly presents his views, listens to the others, explores their feelings, backs off, and adjusts his own views. If there appears to be agreement, the leader sums up the group view and asks if everyone agrees. If consensus has not been reached, the leader does not press for one or even ask for a vote. He suggests that more time is needed to consider the matter.

A dissident party may, however, be placated by a concession on some totally unrelated issue or by acknowledging an obligation to make up any losses he may suffer by offering a generous concession on the matter at hand. Anyone who has been generous in conceding or who has gone out of his way to facilitate consensus is remembered, whether it be an individual or a corporation.

Such decision-making processes differ profoundly from those of American business, in which decisions are either promulgated from the top, or a small group is selected to study the problem and report to higher authorities, who then make the decision. There then may be some attempt to explain the decision to employees, or there may even be an internal debate on details. But rarely is there a chance to alter the decision.

Thus there is often a tendency for junior employees who have not been consulted and who do not understand the reasons for the decision to oppose it. And the more junior the employee, the greater the likelihood of misunderstanding and opposition.

In Japan, it is unthinkable for a decision to come simply from the top down. The great virtue of the Japanese system is that the effort to keep all parties informed and satisfied prevents any demoralizing effect on junior employees.

While reading Herman Kahn on Japanese decision making and on Japanese labor unions, I could not help thinking about the trouble General Motors had with its highly sophisticated Vega plant in Lordstown, Ohio. Production lines were often shut down, and there were bitter accusations of speed-up and counter-accusations of shabby workmanship and sabotage. What a mess! Perhaps General Motors could use a management consultant team from Japan. Japan has learned much in the past one hundred years from America. Perhaps she can begin to repay the debt.

One of the implications of hierarchy and the concept of social structure being a network of social relations is the challenge of effective communication within this hierarchical network. Dominance in hierarchy is a key concept in dealing with this challenge. If within hierarchy a higher-level including group or a lower-level included group dominates another, slavery or injustice can result. The dominating group having more power or influence over the other, in effect, forces that other group through the zone of mutual respect, hence the demoralization of employees at the Vega plant. *If, however, communication is effected through the levels of the hierarchy in such a way that every lower-level unit effectively communicates throughout the hierarchy, the result is freedom or justice.* The dominance has now become part of a balanced consensus, as in the case of the Japanese industry.

The Slavery Model

The illustration in figure 12 utilizes a higher-level unit and two lower-level units.

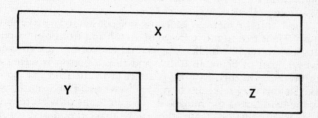

Figure 12. A Hierarchical Social Structure

When the flow of truth, or that which concerns both the included groups within the including group, is from X to Z by way of Y, then Z must wait for Y to know what to think, believe, or do in keeping with the expectations and requirements of X. This puts Z into a position of slavery or injustice (see figure 13).

For example, when the slaves were brought from Africa to the southern United States, they had to depend on the whites of the

South for a large percentage of their lived experience. Both whites and blacks were part of American society and of that society specifically involving them in the southern state of which they were a part. Yet before the black could move from place to place, select a job, form a belief, establish a standard, he had to consult with the white and follow to the slightest detail the results of that consultation. He was a slave.

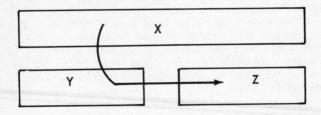

Figure 13. A Situation of Slavery

The political scientist also would call this slavery, thus reinforcing the idea of sociological slavery in this particular case. There are numerous other experiences of slavery that are not recognized in the political sense as slavery but nonetheless constitute sociological slavery.

The Central American Indian is not considered a slave of the Spanish. He is free to move from job to job and from plantation to plantation, to request higher wages, and to work or not to work. However, part of being an Indian and thus a person is seeing the earth produce. In this way, he is attached to the land that he has worked and is very reluctant to move elsewhere. The Spanish, who view the land not as the Indians do, but in terms of what they can realize as production from the land, make good use of the orientation of the Indian to the land and reinforce his obligation to the land. The result is that the Indian perceives that he is not free—both because of his orientation to the land and because of the subtle influence of the Spanish to keep him there. It does not need to be so, but the Spanish have continually interpreted the demands and obligations of the larger society to the Indian in this manner. It has not been difficult for them to do this, as they help maintain the illiteracy of the Indian by their educational processes. Injustice frequently results within this setting of virtual or perceived slavery.

A slavery experience of this kind also occurs when parents meticulously force their children to abide by the standards and requirements of the adult generation. The natural process of socialization is designed to prepare a child for living within the total society. This process is totally adequate for communicating the moral and ethical principles of the adult generation to the younger generation. However, many adults, reacting to the process as not specific enough, add restrictions and rules that they feel will aid their children as they grow up. Many of these rules and restrictions and the punishments that accompany them fail to bring children to maturity, and, in fact, often accomplish the opposite of that intended by the well-meaning parents, i.e., enslave the child.

Consider, for example, parents concerned with the strong influence of television beer commercials on their children. They may arbitrarily require that whenever a beer commercial comes on, the volume be turned down so no one can hear the words. The children have already heard the words, if not on their own sets, then on the sets of their friends. The turning down of the volume encourages the young person to commit the words to memory: the fewer times he can hear the words, the more confirmed the commercial becomes in his memory. When the volume is down, he is still letting the words go through his mind. The enslavement comes by way of restriction from the adult generation. The child, in seeking to be free from the restriction, takes steps that ultimately reinforce the advertisement and make him more aware of beer than he would normally have been. The sum of such arbitrary restrictions causes the youth to perceive himself like Z in figure 13, as living in a slavery setting, obligating him to enter the larger world of X via the requirements and restrictions of Y.

Missionaries may enter a target nation and quickly reduce converts to Christianity to virtual slavery. They establish doctrines argued out within their own cultural context, insist on their own behavioral standards, introduce a theology that has been thoroughly contextualized within their own economically oriented society, etc. Subsequent demands for national involvement, cries of nationalism, demands for national evaluation of pastors and missionaries, all indicate that the missionaries have enslaved the people to the North American culture rather than freeing them to be true Christians in the bonds of Christ.

On a visit to Papua New Guinea, I sat in on a series of chapel services in a Bible institute established by Western missionaries. Apparently, certain items from the common bathroom facilities had been taken and used privately. The chapel messages were on the subject of theft as sin. The Westerners had a concept that the one purchasing an item could establish the limits of its use. The students at the school, many of them married, had the concept that whatever was provided was for the common use of all. Who was right? Both were! Both were fully moral and ethical within the context of their own social system (see chapters 12 and 16). This was a conflict of norm that needed to be worked through together so that one Christian would not become a slave of another Christian with a distinct cultural system. If the student, on the other hand, was permitted to preach a sermon in chapel on sin, he might very well choose to speak on the sin of selfishness. The missionaries, because of their practice of purchasing items that only they could control, appeared to be extremely selfish in the eyes of the people of Papua New Guinea.

The Freedom Model

When the flow of truth is directly from the including group into the included group, i.e., from X directly into Y and directly into Z, then both Y and Z are living in a condition of freedom and justice. There is a voice for both Y and Z in the larger chambers of X (see figure 14).

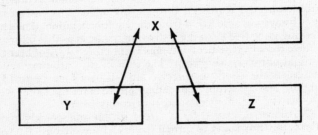

Figure 14. A Situation of Freedom

This, of course, was the cry of the American Revolution: "No taxation without representation." And this is the hue and cry of the contemporary age: "I don't want to be prevoted." And "Let me have a voice in legislature, in administration! Let me control my own destiny. Place me in the councils of government, of education, of the church." Members of the adult generation who already have their authority established vigorously resist such change. They did not have such a place when they were younger, so why should their children? They do not realize that their children, who perceive they are living in a slavery setting and are being prevoted, need such a place. The young people believe they are being taken advantage of by well-meaning adults who have effectively protected them from the full experience of life—the right to make mistakes and to do things inefficiently because of lack of experience. Youth perceive themselves as living in slavery.

A refreshing freedom experience was related to me from the work of the Wycliffe Bible Translators in southern Mexico (see chapter 18). Marianna Slocum and Florence Gerdel went to work among the Tzeltal Indians. After learning the language and culture of the people, they cooperated with the early converts to establish a program of worship and outreach that was in keeping with the Indian way of life. The worship service on Sunday was three hours long—not the traditional Western length of one hour. The missionaries at times grew tired and bored, but the people, once started in an experience, did not want it to end until it was complete. The missionaries arranged for a young man to help them in the work of translating the Bible into Tzeltal. Instead of working for pay, the young man allowed his people to take over his farming tasks so that he would not suffer from lack of food. They also assumed his other responsibilities so that he could give himself completely to the translation task. The young converts enthusiastically spread out into the entire Tzeltal region in their efforts to extend the outreach of the gospel to all their people. They organized churches, established local fellowships, carried out the discipline of the believers, and fulfilled the obligations of the ordinances of the church, except those of baptism and marriage. The church grew tremendously in such a setting of freedom.

Roy Scherer has described the growth of the church in Korea.[3] An interesting pattern emerges in his narration dealing with the development of the church. When the missionaries lived in the villages with the people for an extended period of time and knew the people and their thought patterns intimately, the church grew. When the missionaries were withdrawn from the local areas— being required to stay in the larger cities, living in Japan during the war, or remaining in their missionary compounds for an extended period—yet continued to make decisions affecting the church, the church did not grow. Whenever the missionaries had to be out of the country for an extended period, e.g., on furlough, and did not make decisions affecting the church, the church grew. Apparently, when the missionaries were on the field, in the villages and towns with the people, living with them for an extended period of time, they absorbed the thought patterns of the people and knew what the people were thinking. They saw evidences of responsibility and dedication. They made decisions in keeping with the life-way of the people. When they were in the mission compound or out of the country, however, and still making decisions for the church, they let many of their decisions be affected by their own thought patterns and their own American culture, not the Korean culture, and enslavement ensued.

The Consensual Process

The consensual process underlies the freedom model. Every member of every group must perceive that he has a voice within the larger group. The consensual process operates informally when a class is assigned to a specific classroom and every member of the class, along with the teacher, shows up in that classroom. Each member of the group arrives without ever realizing that he is making a choice, the same choice that every other member is making as well. The process also operates formally in a meeting calling for decision and operating by Robert's rules of order.

The consensual process is operating in one educational subculture when student body and faculty have separate organizations and neither feels the need for any change. It is operating in another educational subculture when both student body and faculty are representatives to a unified organization and neither group feels any need for change.

The consensual process is not operating, however, when there are two organizations and one or the other feels that it is without a voice in the operation of the larger subculture which is the immediate arena for the interaction of both groups.

The consensual process does not undermine responsibility. Rather, it reinforces and develops a sense of responsibility. It is when the consensual process breaks down that one of two groups interacting together perceives the other as irresponsible, when, in fact, the other is carrying out its obligations in the most responsible manner possible.

God and the Flow of Truth

The truth of God must come to each man completely and effectively in keeping with what he is socioculturally. Another man or group may interpret God in terms of the "good counselor" conceptual model discussed in chapter 17, but no one has the right to communicate the "God truth" in terms of the slavery model. Any attempt to do so results in the individual member of a distinct culture or subculture being reduced to slavery. The "God truth" is effectively reduced to the limit of spiritual insight of a culture.

The Reformers dealt with this concept when they spoke out for the priesthood of the believers.[4] The church had so reduced the believing body to ecclesiastical slavery that no one could read or interpret the Scriptures for himself. This limited and restricted a believer's grasp of the truth. The concept of the priesthood of believers restored each man to a freedom model of spiritual development. It thus permitted him to share equally with all other men in the consensual process that allowed him immediate access to God.

The consensual process in this discussion is not to be interpreted as man dictating to God. It simply permits each man to be a valid person, a unique entity, and a fully responsible being in the sight of God. He is no longer a slave in an injustice setting where someone else is prevoting him, making decisions for him, or interpreting God's truth to him.

Summary

Communication from group to group and from individual to individual is carried out through the social structure. Means of communication vary in keeping with the structure of the group or groups. Telephones are useful in the more impersonal American society but are of little value for a Pocomchi Indian living in Central America who uses his children to maintain effective communication with members of his extended family.

Communication that comes through an including group to an included group via another included group produces the practice of slavery or injustice. The other group defines the nature of truth as established through the larger including group. This is the point of the American revolutionary cry of "no taxation without representation." Today youth are grouped in ways distinct from the ways people were grouped when representation in the national government was established. Campus movements are one way of calling for representation and a voice in government.

Whenever the truth is communicated directly to each of the included groups from the including group, there is justice and freedom.

Questions for Discussion

Relating to the Sending Church

1. List the periods of world history most associated with slavery. Name the nations involved.
2. How could a slavery setting develop within a family? a church?
3. What kinds of things could you do were you to sense the slavery model taking hold?
4. How many "freedom" settings can you name? How can a slavery setting be changed to a freedom one?
5. How many different methods of achieving consensus within a group can you name? E.g., voting, a king's decree, etc.
6. What are the ways a teacher will use to achieve consensus? Do all help the group? Explain.

Relating to the Study of the Bible

1. Study the passages on the husband–wife relationship (e.g., Eph. 5:21–33) and discuss how applying the Scriptures literally (i.e., in keeping with the narrow parameters of one's own culture) could place the wife in slavery.
2. Discuss the consensual process that operated in Acts 1 when a replacement for Judas was to be appointed. Then go back to the Book of Ruth and see how Boaz achieved consensus in pursuing his claim to Ruth.
3. How did Jethro work with Moses to lay a more effective base under the consensual process and relieve Moses of a great deal of strain (Exod. 18:1–27)?
4. By what process did Jeroboam become king of the ten northern tribes? Was this a suitable consensual process? Did it resolve conflict? Did it leave the northern tribes free or in slavery (1 Kings 11:26–40; 12:16–19, 30; 16:16, et al.)?
5. Discuss the implications of 1 Corinthians 7:20–24 as regards enduring in an unsatisfying social role.

Relating to Missions and Crosscultural Ministry

1. At the beginning of the section on God and the Flow of Truth (p. 116), the statement is made that "the truth of God must come to each man completely and effectively in keeping with what he is socioculturally." How can we follow this advice and avoid slavery in our evangelism and discipleship of internationals?
2. How were the so-called rice Christians of the Far East enslaved by missionaries? How were the early Christians of Hawaii enslaved by missionaries? Cite other examples.
3. How could a missionary produce a slavery setting? Does he attempt to achieve this? How can he turn this around to assure freedom?
4. What are the steps you could have taken in your community of ministry to insure that the freedom model was being applied? What can you do about it today? Discuss.
5. What are the ways a missionary can use to achieve consensus? Do all help the group? Describe.

Group Activities and Exercises

1. *Research.* Have each member of the group interview an international student in order to discover to what degree the mission program in his homeland works with the slavery or the freedom model.

2. *Interview.* Invite an international student into the group to discuss consensual processes of decision making in his own culture. Then probe to see which of these could be natural forms for the church to pursue in impacting the community for Christ. Alternate choices for interviewing could be a pastor or a missionary.

3. *Simulation.* A popular exercise called "Rumor Clinic" can be adapted to illustrate the slavery model. Variations are found in Pfeiffer and Jones.[5]

4. *Observation.* Seek to observe someone using the slavery model and someone using the freedom model. Report.

5. *Research.* Send teams out into the nearest ethnic community to research the response of the people to their living in a setting of freedom or of slavery. In what specific settings do they feel they have no voice in community, business, or church affairs?

6. *Role play.* Develop two-minute small-group skits to depict a variety of slavery settings. Then in "turn about" role plays depict the same setting, but this time show how the consensual process turns the setting into one of freedom.

9

The Group: Identity

Case Study: Her Sister's Husband

I first met Tabarire when she ran away from home and came to the mission station asking us for protection. As we talked with her, we discovered that she was a Christian student at an outstation school about ten miles from us. Her parents were forcing her to marry an older heathen man who already had a wife. We gave her food and a place to stay that night.

In the morning, her parents and a brother arrived, and we all sat out under a tree and talked. This is the story we heard: Tabarire's older sister (or perhaps cousin) had been married to this man and had borne him two children. She then died while young. Since he had paid the *lobola* (bride price) for a wife and then was left without one, the family owed him a wife. Tabarire was the only girl in the family who could fill the position, so she was named as his wife. As she was just a child at the time, she had been left in her father's village. Now that she had developed breasts, her husband had come and demanded that his wife be given to him. In the intervening years, he had taken another wife.

Tabarire asserted strongly that she did not want to go to him but wanted a young Christian husband. Her parents assured us that they would not force her to marry this man, as it is against the law in Rhodesia to force someone into

121

marriage. They agreed to raise the money to refund the *lobola,* and she went home with them.

Several weeks went by, and we found Tabarire at our door again. This time she told us that she had been locked in the man's hut but had broken out. We were on our way to town for several days on a shopping trip, and so we took her with us. When the family heard this, they were frightened, thinking we were going to the European magistrate.

When we returned home, the family came again. They were having trouble raising the money, and the man was impatient and wanted his wife. We suggested that they take the case to the magistrate to be judged. The father then showed us his arms, and we saw the marks of leprosy. He feared that if he appeared before the magistrate, he would be forced to go to a leper camp. They were very afraid of the leper colonies because of stories they had heard of lepers being thrown out to be eaten by lions. It was because of his leprosy also that he had been unable to get work to repay the *lobola.* They decided to take the case to the African chief to be judged, and Tabarire went home with her parents again.

A few weeks later we got word that Tabarire had gone to be the man's wife. Surprised and disappointed, we asked what had happened at the chief's compound. We learned that the chief was the uncle of the husband; therefore, there was really no hope for an impartial judgment. Tabarire had been offered freedom on the condition that she would go and work for the chief for a couple of years. This undoubtedly meant that she would also be one of his mistresses, as the chief is allowed to take any woman he wants at any time.

Finding no way out, Tabarire went to her husband. The last time I saw her, she had a baby and was also bringing up her sister's two children. Her husband did not allow her to attend church, but she said that she loved God and prayed and read her Bible. She seemed to have accepted her role.

Society and Culture

Society is the name applied to interpersonal interaction or interrelationships. It refers to the social order, the social system within which individuals or groups interrelate. Society is distinct from environment. The environment is the physical arena in which interpersonal and intergroup relations are carried out. Whenever the interaction of environment with society is discussed, it is termed "ecology."

Society is distinct from culture. Culture results from the carrying out of interpersonal and intergroup relations. Culture thus stands as the identifying mark of the society. Every society has a culture, a total life-way that characterizes it. This involves the way people think, live, and do things within the totality of the social system.

Some people use the term society to refer to members of a specific social class, e.g., "high society." They use the term culture in reference to the arts and the patronizing of various art forms. Neither reference is particularly useful within the context of this present study. The terms society and culture are used only in relation to the interpersonal and intergroup dynamics of the social system.

Society and culture are so completely intertwined that it is impossible to determine where one begins and the other leaves off. For this reason, we frequently combine the two concepts into one and talk about the sociocultural setting. We have used other terms synonymously with sociocultural setting: the norm, the system, and culture. These are three acceptable ways of referring to the sum of the life-way within a given grouping of people.

The Bible talks about God creating the universe and the body (Gen. 1). It also implies that God created society as well, for this is what resulted when God gave Eve to Adam (Gen. 2:18–25; 3). Now there were two to interact, the basis of society and social interaction. There was no social interaction until Eve came on the scene. Once she and Adam were together, society existed. From that time on, it grew larger and more complex. The church has recognized the creation of the universe and the body. The creation of society cannot be overlooked. In some ways, it has more significance to the human than do either of the other two creations. It is through one's interaction within society that one knows his fellow human. It is in such interaction that man models and practices his relationship with God.

A Model of Society

It is impossible to sort out the various details of the life-way without some conceptual model. The model utilized for discussion of the group will distinguish the ways people group, the activities they carry out within a group, and the values that underlie all that they are and do as a group. No one conceptual model is adequate to describe all of society. Numerous models can be called into use.[1] This crosscultural model does not therefore preclude the usage of other models that work with other aspects of the reality of society. This particular model, however, is maximally useful when encountering distinct societies.[2]

A person caught up and controlled by his culture within his sociocultural setting is at home within the culture. This is his way of doing things. He is comfortable. He would not want things any other way. He responds to each challenge of life in keeping with an elaborate code of reaction that is positively directed to protect him from tension and disruption. Anyone not controlled by his culture is in effect forming some new subculture that may ultimately only represent himself or may become the subcultural manifestation of many members of the larger society.

In our case study, Tabarire was caught up in her sociocultural setting. This involved her as a marriage choice by a man who had established certain rights to her. The man was willing to work within the context of the culture as were the girl's parents. Because of her father's leprosy, Tabarire's parents stood to lose a great deal were they to seek help outside of their specific subculture. Tabarire, with the encouragement of the missionaries, was unwilling to work matters out in the context of her own subculture until she was given the choice of going with her "husband" or becoming a mistress to the chief. She discovered that she could remain within the context of her own sociocultural setting and continue as a Christian even though she was not permitted to attend church. It would have been helpful to the missionaries to have been thoroughly familiar with this sociocultural setting. They might have counseled Tabarire more effectively in her dilemma and continued to help her in her personal Christian growth and in her outreach within her community. As it was, the import of their advice was to have Tabarire step outside her own culture to maintain her Christian witness. This is advice outsiders generally give to people of other cultures though they might not consider doing so in their own experience.

Grouping

Society consists of a multiplicity of identity groups. These are termed "social groups" or "subcultures." Such groups may be informally designed with few rules and restrictions on the behavior of its members, or they may be formally designed with a multiplicity of rules and regulations. Each society has its own unique and distinctive ways of grouping its members. Every grouping within the larger society has uniquenesses that distinguish it from all other groups.

Society groups its members by age, sex, interests, status, friendship, blood and marital ties, skills and abilities, associations, and many other qualities.[3]

Sex

There is no known society that does not have some group division based on sexual criteria. Even the primitive Kaingang of Brazil, a group that assigns very few specific jobs for women within the division of labor, still permit them to select the site of evening encampment and thus establish a basic distinction of the male versus the female group within that society. Proponents of the Western sexual revolution admit that there are biological differences between the sexes. Though some try to negate these, they insist that there should be no social distinctions between them. The Western nations that succeed in this effort may become the only places in the world where there is lack of social distinction between the sexes. Missionaries need to be careful that they do not carry cultural distinctions or lack of distinctions between the sexes into the non-Western world. North Americans touring Papua New Guinea saw women carrying the family harvest of yams home from the field. They were appalled that the men followed the women, carrying only their work tools, a load that was considerably lighter than a sack of yams. The guide, well versed in the culture, commented that the women themselves would have nothing to do with the idea that the men should carry the sacks of yams. The women had planted, cultivated, and harvested them, and they were not about to let the men get their hands on them and mess them up in some way.

When a meeting is held in the highland Maya societies of Guatemala, the women sit on one side of a room and the men sit on the other. Such restrictions on the seating pattern separate and define groups. It is easy to interpret the manifestations of such groups as meaning that the men and women do not want to sit together. This is not the point at all. The society has simply established men's and women's groups. One of the manifestations of this social reality is the pattern of seating people in a meeting.

Division of labor by sex defines male and female groups in many societies. In Iran, the Iranian men urge the Americans to pull the shade when the husband does the dishes. Dish washing is one activity that defines a woman's group in Iran much more specifically than it does in many subcultures of North America. In many African societies, as well as in rural America, women cultivate the gardens where fresh produce is grown, and men take care of the fields where the money crop is raised. Division of labor also determines who leads singing, who teaches, who manages the money in a family. During the fifties, a young man would lead the singing in a youth group while a young woman would play the piano. During the sixties and seventies, it was frequently a young woman who led the singing with or without a guitar. Men usually usher during a church service in North America. The wife of the pastor takes this responsibility upon herself in the Philippines. Young women, for example, teachers and baby-sitters, are the good storytellers in North American society, whereas old men are the storytellers in Thai society.

Language often reinforces the division of labor within the sex groupings when men's and women's speech differs. Men will speak a certain dialect of the language, and though the women understand it, they will not speak it publicly. The same holds for women's speech. The Caribe of the east coast of Central America have men's and women's speech established on historical antecedents and migration patterns. A male outsider, for example, learning to speak a language from a member of the opposite sex, may learn that person's dialect perfectly but still be considered odd by the members of his own sex because he does not talk like a man. Missionaries may at times work with language helpers of the opposite sex because they are unable to find someone of the same sex or because the person appears to speak the language so clearly. As a result they fall into the trap of speaking the dialect of the other sex perfectly but inappropriately.

Age

Age distinctions serve to divide other groups within society. In North American society, the educational process with its formal and informal extensions is based on age distinctions. School classes from kindergarten to college are divided by age. The expected age in any grade level is attained by 95 percent of the members of the class prior to entrance. Such age distinctions are maintained within the church program of education known as Sunday school, as well as in the daily vacation Bible school and youth programs. Camping programs, as well as Boy Scouts and equivalent voluntary training programs, are age/grade programs. Western missionaries will frequently introduce this age-level system in the secular and religious education of the host society. They may discover, too late, that the cultural system works best with mixed ages as in the Philippines. A Bible study does well when people of all ages attend and participate. The elders bring to the group the voice of experience, and the children and young people share an enthusiasm for living.

Another type of age division is that which characterizes certain African societies (see figure 15). Everyone born during a certain period of time, either months or years, depending on the system, is placed within an age level. Even though there are other kinds of groups, such as kinship groupings and governmental councils, each member of the society relates primarily to his age level first and only then to other groups. Certain rules and restrictions apply only to the age level of the person, and correction of the member of a society in the case of such social deviance as theft must be handled first through the age level. The member of an age level remains with that level throughout his life, though the level itself moves through its levels of social existence successively as each new age level is formed beneath it.[4] In African tribes that practice cicatrization (tribal markings), the markings identify the tribe and age group to which a person belongs. The markings are different for each successive age level. Especially warm greetings are exchanged between those who have identical markings.

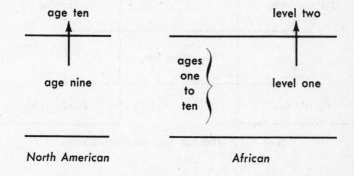

Figure 15. Age Distinctions and Groupings

Interest

Interest groups may be social, political, religious, or economic. Social groups are friendship groups that form some kind of identity through ongoing association. Economic groups draw together members of a society with the interest and ability to fulfill certain skills or obligations, such as management or sales. Political groups form the basis for governmental supervision of a society. Religious groups oversee the religious and spiritual involvement of the members of society.

Among the citizens of Gopalpur, India, two economic interest groups are linked in a total system of involvement (see figure 16).[5] Both families will remain as separate entities within separate castes. The friendship ties relate them but also prescribe behavior in the immediate relationship and in all relationships within the larger society. Efforts at ministry within such a context that fail to take such interest groups into account will be less effective than they otherwise might be. Many Westerners, when introducing an educational institution into such a society, will establish one center for the institution. This will draw only those students from the caste in which the institution is located. Further, people educated in such an institution will utilize their learning only in relation to members of their own caste. To reach all the people of a caste society, an institution must have a branch within each caste.

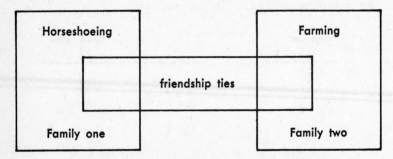

Figure 16. Friendship Ties Between Castes

Among the Pocomchi of Central America, the social and religious aspects of life are linked in a system of organization that is the primary educational group of the society. The *cofradia* is the religious brotherhood within the church context and serves as the functional equivalent to our Western university (see figure 17). A person is elected to membership in one of eight to fifteen *cofradias*, depending on the size of the community. He enters on the lowest rank of responsibility and does everything that everyone else does. After two years, he rests a year and reenters for another stint of service on a higher rank. By the time he is about forty years of age, he has served in each of the levels of the *cofradia*. By the time he completes the sequence, he knows all that the society expects him to know and all that the society has available for him to know. He has completed a very efficient educational process. He in turn is responsible for seeing that all others in the society know all that society expects them to know. Everyone within the society is related to or tied into one of these *cofradias* as an active member (men only), a resting member (men only), or a member of a "shadow" *cofradia* consisting of women only. In other words, every adult is in the Pocomchi "university."

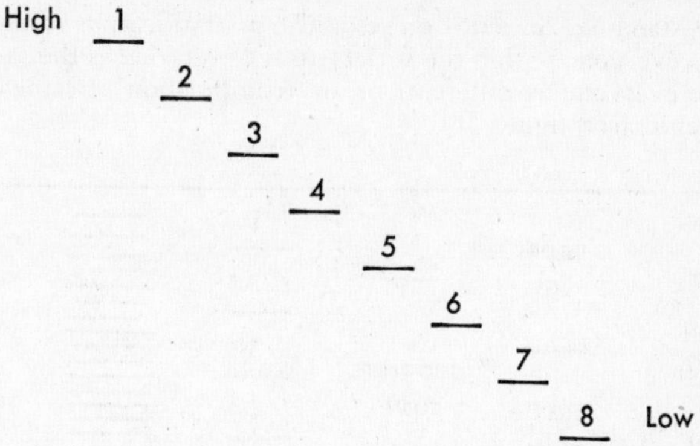

High   1
         2
           3
             4
               5
                 6
                   7
                     8   Low

Figure 17. Cofradias and Members of Cofradias

Kinship

Kinship groupings involve blood (consanguinal) or marriage (affinal) ties. A person is born into a nuclear family of father and mother, but from that point on, society establishes how he will relate to the rest of the society. American society, especially the middle class, stresses the nuclear family. A member of a nuclear family may enter interest groups but may seldom, if ever, have anything much to do with blood relatives. In Philippine society, a person who has nothing to do with relatives is an ingrate and a snob. One essential aspect of living or existence in the Philippines is to be part of an extended family, a grouping of nuclear families related by blood. Anyone not functioning within an extended family, termed an "alliance," is a nonentity in the perception of the Filipino.[6]

The Iroquois society of Indian America stressed community responsibility to the children. Each child, though he would know his biological mother, would refer to each of his mother's female peers as "mother." His responsibilities to his sociological mothers was equivalent to his responsibilities to his biological mother.[7]

Status and Stratification

Status differences produce another type of grouping. These involve prestige relationships between people—those worthy of higher prestige or standing and those worthy of lesser prestige and lower standing. Societies can establish a stratification system that causes everyone within the society to see everyone as the same, or to see everyone as different, or any combination of sameness or difference (see figure 18).

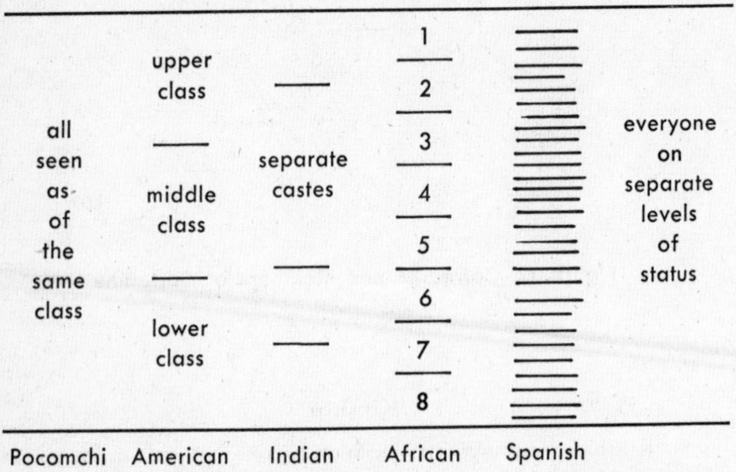

	upper class	——	1	═══	
		——	2	═══	
all	——		3	═══	everyone
seen		separate		═══	on
as	middle	castes	4	═══	separate
of	class		——	═══	levels
the			5	═══	of
same	——	——		═══	status
class			6	═══	
	lower			═══	
	class	——	7	═══	
			8	═══	

Pocomchi   American   Indian   African   Spanish

Figure 18. Class Distinctions of Various Cultures

Pocomchi society causes every member to see every other member in the same way—worthy of the same prestige. No one person is able to order any other person around. In reality, each member of Pocomchi society has more or less personal goods than any other person, but each is unable to see this distinction in viewing another member. This is a perceived egalitarian society.

American society sees some people as worthy of more prestige and others less. It is called a class system with status considerations. Upper-class people have associations and develop comparable value systems as do middle-class and lower-class members. All the members of a given class can get together in a gathering and not feel uncomfortable when members of their own class are present. They are only uncomfortable when members of a higher or lower class are present.

There are numerous societies where classes within the society are formally closed. "Caste" is the term used to describe such systems. People of higher castes do not want to associate with people of lower castes. People of lower castes are rebuffed if they attempt to go out of their caste. In India, there is a multicaste system. In Latin America, there is a two-caste system with the Latins participating in the higher caste and the Indian peoples in the lower caste.

African societies with age-level organization relate everyone by age distinctions. Older people have greater prestige and standing within the community.

Latin American or Spanish society is quite distinct from either the Pocomchi or North American. Everyone is considered to be on a rank level distinct from the next person. It is difficult, if not impossible, to get large groups of Latins together unless the concerns of status are specifically called off for that occasion or someone of higher status than all the rest calls the members together. The Catholic church operating in Spanish background communities controls this system very effectively by having mass presented numerous times during the weekend. This allows people to attend when they please. The front area of the church is reserved for those of higher status, and those of lower status are seated farther toward the back of the sanctuary. No one has to relate to any other person unless he chooses to do so. This is distinct from the Protestant service where efforts are made to have members interact with one another during the course of religious activity.

Tabarire was a member of a society with clearly defined status relationships. Her parents and her husband were on a higher level of status than she was. This meant she must accede to their wishes within the context of her own culture. Her parents and her husband were lower in status, however, than the chief. The family had to yield to his wishes if they wanted to settle their problem without becoming involved with the "colonial" government which was on a still higher status level within the larger society.

Item Identification of the Group

Every group is identified not only by sex, age, interest, status, or kinship distinctions, but also by a complex of features that give that group specific identity. Such features develop as members of the society interact. They serve as very powerful constraints on the behavior of the members of the group. They must be learned thoroughly and respected by anyone entering the group from the outside.

Each social group must have all or most of the following characteristics in order to function effectively.

Physical items:

– For example, an American family needs four walls to separate it from another family.

Social items:

- a name—either that which it calls itself or that which others call it, or both
- its own language
- greetings
- a place of meeting
- a time of meeting
- membership requirements
- means of identifying members—uniform, odor, kinesics, i.e., body movement
- leadership—the more natural the leadership is to the group, the more effective the leadership
- rules—formal or informal, written or oral
- discipline—negative or positive; by voice, force, withholding pleasures, rejection, criticism of others, evidence of pride, praise, reward, etc.
- mechanisms to induce loyalty—a mythology of sacred places and heroes, causes and issues unique to itself, memories that derive from shared experiences such as a holiday or parade
- privacy—a right to have secrets
- authority—jurisdiction over all within the group
- perpetuation—rules of inheritance, election of leaders
- means of defense—to maintain the integrity of the group

Leadership Within the Group

The key to group involvement is the nature of leadership expected within the group. *Every group has natural leaders*—those who lead it in keeping with the group expectations. Sometimes the leadership is unitary, with one person fulfilling all the obligations of leadership. At other times numerous members share the obligations, each doing that which is comfortable in terms of natural ability or training. Among the Pocomchi, all eight members of the *cofradia* lead the *cofradia* by making consensual decisions in which all share. There is no concept of "elite" within the system. Within a North American eating group, however informal, certain members take on the responsibility of either welcoming others as visitors or indicating that they are not welcome. Others take on the responsibility of making conversation. Still others shape the belief patterns of the members insofar as that group's interaction is concerned. In the more formal setting of the United States Senate, the vice-president presides over the meeting, but other members distribute the responsibility for various aspects of law making.

Tabarire's parents had a choice between two types of leadership: the colonial and the tribal. They chose the latter because they stood to lose too much if they went to the colonial power's magistrate and he discovered the father's leprosy. The tribal leadership, tied into family, in one sense did Tabarire a disservice. The chief was more closely related to the husband's family than he was to the parents' family. In another sense, however, the tribal leadership did all concerned a service, as it reinforced society's rules and let the cultural problem be resolved in keeping with what the people actually were. The missionary leadership did not enter into the decision-making process except with Tabarire. Even then it was marginal and uninformed and, therefore, ineffectual.

Leaders receive their place and attendant prestige by having it ascribed to them by birth as in the divine-right-of-kings concept, or by entering a role established within society, or by achieving prestige by dint of hard work, or by some specialized contribution. Societies distinguish the two ways quite specifically. Where leadership is ascribed, care must be taken that it be recognized and utilized. Where prestige is achieved, the tools for achieving leadership need to be made available to all members on all levels of the society.

Who leads whom is one of the most critical problems that must be worked out when one enters a new society. People are led most effectively by their natural leaders. Young women may teach Sunday school in the United States, but they are seen as inadequate to be teachers in the Philippines. Their inadequacy is not due to their inability to teach, rather to the fact that they are perceived to be of low status in relation to men and older women.

Another critical question is the way society utilizes the primary and secondary leadership roles. American society generally assigns one primary leader and makes use of secondary leaders. This is expressed in the community of the church where a pastor is the primary leader, and board members, Sunday school teachers, and ushers fill secondary leadership roles. In the Philippines, where status is so important, one of the means of achieving status is through higher education. It is assumed that part of the preparation of higher education is that of reading aloud. Every educated person is perceived to be able to read aloud fluently. If someone stumbles or stutters while reading aloud, his education is questioned, and thus his standing in the community is questioned. To avoid this undesired outcome, leaders in the religious group Iglesia Ni Cristo, a quasi-Protestant group, the primary leader never reads from the Scriptures aloud. A secondary leader reads from the Scriptures. Whenever this secondary leader stutters or stumbles, he is reduced in standing in the perception of his hearers, but the primary leader rises in comparison. Thus the primary leader never has to fear loss of status in fulfilling the obligations of his own leadership role.

Wherever there are primary and secondary leadership roles, the program or organization of a group must allow for them. In the Philippines, due to the demands of the status system, the person of highest status in the group is recognized as the leader. However, there may be another who perceives himself to be of equal or nearly equal status. He expects to have some leadership opportunity, and if it is not given to him formally, he will take it informally. For example, during a Bible study held in the home of the highest prestige person in the group, if someone else in the group makes a long statement or dissertation on the subject of the study, or if he monopolizes the floor unduly, it is evident that he perceives his personal standing in the group as equal or nearly equal to that of the primary leader. For this reason, it is good to have two leadership spots available—one for the leader who introduces the study and another for someone to sum up the study. This brings a second person into the proceedings in a nondisruptive way.

Summary

Societies group people in many ways: age groups; sex groups; interest groups—religious, social, economic, and political; status groups; and kin groups, etc.

Each of these groups has physical and social characteristics that distinguish that specific group from any other. The physical characteristics grow out of the products that the society produces, such as buildings and emblems. The social characteristics are the result of interaction of people in associational experiences. These involve name, language, rules of membership, loyalties, and many other distinctions.

Each group, no matter how subtle the distinctions, is a unique group and has certain characteristics that must be learned by anyone entering the group. Since culture is learned behavior, whenever a learning process is being undertaken, there is cultural or subcultural distinction. This is one of the behavioral approaches to people in understanding how they differ from others.

Perhaps the most significant relationship within the group process is that of the leadership of the group. Leadership can be either appointed or elected, formal or informal. It is vital to know who leads whom, how natural leaders lead, and what causes followers to follow leaders.

Questions for Discussion

Relating to the Sending Church

1. In what ways might women's liberation movements affect natural groupings in North American society?

2. Do characteristic North American groupings need to be changed? Discuss why they should or should not be changed.
3. Compare the age-grade groupings in the more typical North American church program with those in the secular educational program.
4. What problems might be encountered by grouping graduate students with undergrads in the educational setting?
5. Who are the heroes in your subculture?
6. Where are the sacred places of your subculture?
7. In what ways might prayer be used as discipline?

Relating to the Study of the Bible

1. Review the Bible quickly and indicate any evidence you find for society, social interaction, social stratification, and culture.
2. Study Genesis 3 and 4 specifically with the preceding question in mind.
3. Map the Book of Acts by marking all the social groupings you encounter there: sex, age, interest, blood lines, marriage, status, friendship.
4. Attempt to ascertain which groupings were most significant in ministry for the culture of the Book of Acts.
5. Compare various roles of leadership encountered throughout the Bible: patriarch, king, prophet, priest, disciple, apostle, etc. What was required of these primary leaders? Were there secondary roles of leadership relating to these primary roles? What significance did such roles have within the society?
6. How did Jesus fit into the leadership patterns of the New Testament?

Relating to Missions and Crosscultural Ministry

1. How can the information in this chapter help us better understand and relate to groups of internationals from the same country who tend to stick together?
2. What are the major groupings evident in the society in which you are ministering? How are these groupings manifest? What are the rules of the group? Who are the heroes? Where are the sacred places? What are the sacred times?
3. How does the culture or subculture of your group compare and contrast with that of your neighboring groups?
4. What are the areas of primary focus in the environment (streams, forests, mountains, sources of raw materials, etc.) in which you are carrying out ministry? How do these affect and influence your ministry in positive and negative ways?

5. What is the underlying stratification system operating in your group—perceived egalitarian, class, caste, age-level, strata-rank? How is this system manifest? What is the behavior of the system? How do you enter and leave the system gracefully? (See chapter 9.)

6. What leadership roles are operating within your group? Which of these leadership roles are open to you to enter? How can you be a good follower within the society? How can you become a good leader within the society? Is it wise for you to assume some leadership role? Why or why not? What might it be?

7. What is the system of influence operating in your society? How does one influence another directly? Indirectly? Is influence from outside the society perceived as negative or positive?

8. How does the language of your society tune you into the various aspects of identity of the social groupings?

Group Activities and Exercises

1. *Observation.* Observe examples of sex, age-level, and status groupings within your subculture.

2. *Observation.* Walk down a street of your business district and try to ascertain how store merchants are attempting to meet group needs.

3. *Observation.* Pick up a local newspaper and attempt to map out the social groupings evidenced in the news reporting.

4. *Ecological observation.* Walk or drive through a typical zone of your city or rural area and mark down each distinctive physical feature you encounter, e.g., streams, woods, rises, hills, buildings. Attempt to ascertain how such physical properties influence your daily life.

5. *Description.* Have each person do an item-identification description of a subculture available to him.

6. *Group discussion.* How many ways can prayer be used to reinforce the characteristics, traditions, or identity of a group? For example, how is prayer used for disciplinary purposes? How is prayer used to support someone's plans for the group?

7. *Simulation.* Play out the Broken Squares game presented in Pfeiffer and Jones.[8]

8. *Simulations as systems games.* Overpower, a game representative of the North American class system, and Strata, representative of the Latin American strata-rank system, are available from Biola University, School of Intercultural Studies, La Mirada, CA 90639. They can each be played with a group of thirty in about an hour with a brief period of debriefing.

10

The Group: Activity

Case Study: Initiation Rites in Africa[1]

Probably all the tribes of Central and South Africa have possessed from time immemorial initiatory rites which have been regarded as essential and obligatory on all young men and women of the tribe. . . . In the life of an African these rites have a paramount importance. . . . Each of these rites represents an elaborately devised portico by which one leaves all that is past to emerge a new being into a new life, with new untasted experiences and responsibilities before him.

The real meaning of the initiatory rite is that the boys are being fed from childhood and admitted to the full life of the tribe, with all the responsibilities and dangers and duties that belong to adult manhood. For example, only the initiated in the tribes with which I am familiar are allowed to take part in the burial of the dead; or to cut hair; or to take life (for instance, to kill a hen); or to attend the council of the grown men. Prior to initiation the boys are regarded as mere irresponsible children.

With the Yaos and Makuas in Tanzania, circumcision does in fact take place as part of the rite. Each boy is given a young man who will live with him, cook for him, look after him, sponsor him; in fact, behave as an ideal godparent might behave here at home. A period of seclusion in a forest camp usually lasts about three months. The teaching and training to which the boys are subjected stress manners and manliness. As an example of manners, I remember that an old chief told me that when he was a boy he was taught in the initiation to sit on the Council of the Elders; he had to be careful always to sit in the lowest place unless he was definitely invited to move up higher; and also whenever he ran along the forest paths, if he met any who were older than himself he had to slacken his pace and make a detour lest the dust raised by his feet should rest upon the clothes of his elders. The importance of not entering any room of the house without obtaining the permission of those within is stressed. The way to wear one's clothes modestly, the salutations proper to those whom he meets, the duties of a host—these and other points constitute the code of manners which is impressed on the initiates.

Their training in manliness includes endurance of heat and cold and pain, courage in meeting danger and what is fearful. Obedience is insisted upon almost unreasonably. Boys will be told that they will have no food until they have caught a particular bird visible on the bough of a tree, a task which may plainly be impossible. In the early hours of the morning before the dawn, when the air and water are as cold as they ever become, boys will be roused from their sleep and taken to stand in a pool or stream for an hour or two, and required at times to duck completely under the water. A bamboo will be split and their finger pinched in the opening and then brought close to a hot fire that they may endure heat. They will be taken out at night into a forest by their trainers or godparents, and then suddenly left alone in the pitch-black darkness, while their trainers imitate the roaring of lions and other dangerous animals and leave the boys to find their terrified way back to their camp alone. They are taught songs suitable to each occasion that may arise, and greetings to visitors, and woe betide them if they are slow in making correct response or in singing the allotted stanzas. Failure in any one of these trials is accounted as failure in all. The African proverb runs, "If one fish in the basket is bad, they all are bad," and beating and other penalties follow swiftly, and in some cases unmercifully.

The admission to this camp is preceded by careful and elaborate sacrifice, and interceding with the spirits of departed chiefs. When the three months of initiation are at length ending, the hair of their heads is shaved, new clothes are provided, finery up to the very limit of their parents' purse, and a new name is conferred, so that nothing that belonged to the past may be carried by the boy into the new life into which he is stepping.

The three months' initiation in the forest has been a time of strict training; the boy has probably grown in body; he has certainly grown in mind; and he looks upon his mother and sisters with a new awe, and they for their part recognize that he is not the child who left them, and regard him with unwonted respect. This helps to establish the desired new relationship proper to the new life.

Coupled with the teaching of much that is excellent there is an equal insistence on much that is immoral, and much that is, if not immoral, yet undesirable. Also the hardening process to which the boys are subjected becomes definitely cruel at times, at any rate from the European point of view.

When missionary work begins in an African tribe, what has happened in the past has been that at first the missionaries, knowing no details of these rites, have given them a vague benediction; then, when the passage of years has unlocked the doors of the language and the confidence of some of their converts has been won, it has become revealed to them with a horror akin to revulsion that much that they have ignorantly allowed to go on is definitely contrary to Christian morals; and so the vague benediction is exchanged for an indignant campaign of suppression, and this campaign of suppression has in many instances ended in victory. The rites have been discredited and abandoned in many mission areas, though not in all. Now the purpose of this article is to beg that we consider whether the indignant suppression has not on the whole been as unfortunate and ill-considered as the general benediction which preceded it.

Horror at the immoral element has caused us to sweep away what in itself was of a definitely striking value. Where the suppression of the rites has been complete, we have cut the African loose from the old sanctions. He is in grave danger of becoming disinherited from the tradition of beautiful manners; loyalty and reverence for his chiefs and his past have been shaken; and have we really been able to put any adequate new sanctions into the place of what we have destroyed? Man is a social animal, says the old wisdom of the Greeks, and the African tribal rites stress this point and teach each boy to regard himself not as a mere individual but as the member of a tribe, with duties to all his brethren akin to him. By the suppression of the rites he has been in danger of regarding himself merely as an individual, selfish and self-regarding.

An experiment has been made, successfully, so far as can be seen, to take the old initiatory rite, purge it of its immoral elements, enrich it from the storehouse of Christian wisdom and experience, conduct it with as elaborate a ceremonial as belonged to it of old, and then offer it as the initiatory rite for all Christian or catechumen Africans. The measure of its success may be gauged from the fact that heathen chiefs have written asking that their heathen boys might be accepted into the Christian rite. The names of the old rites have been retained.

Activities of the Social Group

Each social group has activities that it carries out by member participation. The activities of the social group cause it to have significance within the larger society. The activities of the larger society set it off from other societies and mark its significance in relation to these other societies. The specific activities each group carries out help determine how significant a given group is in relation to other groups and how important the group is to become. The societies that possess the know-how to construct giant earth-moving machines will be the ones called in for dam projects, the installation of power plants, and industrial developments. They are likely to become the richer societies of the world. Societies that introduce birth control, limiting births and thus "bodies," risk coming under the control of societies able to put millions of soldiers into a war setting. They are likely to become some of the oppressed societies of the world unless their economy makes it possible for them to maintain independence.

In this discussion, the focus will be on behavioral activity rather than the institution; on what people do and when they do it rather than with whom they do it. *The group is thus seen as a series of actions within activities. Every group develops a distinct lineup of activities.* On the Fourth of July, one town may conduct its fireworks display as just that—a display. Another town might call in the high school band and make a larger production out of the display. The North American game of football is played with an oblong ball on a rectangular field one hundred yards long. The ball is primarily thrown or carried by hand. The Latin American game of futbol is played on a larger field than a football field, and a round ball is kicked or hit with the head but never touched by the hands. North Americans call the Latin American game "soccer" and play it as a secondary sport. Latin Americans play it as their primary, or national, sport. In our case study, certain initiatory rites leading young people into adulthood are spelled out. These are not at all like North American practices or Latin practices. In fact, they are unlike practices of almost any other society in the world. They are, however, activities that make the Yaos and Makuas unique.

The Schedule Cycle—Calendar

Every social group has some means of ordering, or scheduling, its activities. It would be futile to have an activity that the members of the social group knew nothing about. Since the socialization process is designed to minimize the amount of decisions that one has to make by making many decisions automatic, society builds the activities of the group into a calendar schedule. The schedule is thus set up with all activities arranged in relation to other activities. In some societies they follow the simple rule that "after X comes Y." In other societies a specific time and place is established so that there can be no question about precisely when something is going to happen. The first society needs some type of public announcement, the second needs clocks and maps. The calendar lays out the year-by-year pattern of activity so that people will always know what to expect. New activities must be worked into the public calendar lest they be overlooked.

One of the convenient schedule arrangements is that of the cycle. It involves the day, year, and multiyear cycle. The day cycle includes the time from rising to retiring. The characteristic North American day cycle starts at about 6:00 or 7:00 A.M. and ends between 10:30 P.M. and midnight. It includes time spent in the following activities: bathing, shaving or applying cosmetics, eating breakfast, going to work or school, working or studying, enjoying breaks for coffee and the noon meal, returning home for supper, resting or relaxing in the evening (which may or may not include a variety of social activities), and preparing for bed. In some areas of Mexico, the day schedule calls for four major times for eating, not three. These are coffee and roll upon rising, a regular breakfast about 10:00 A.M., a lunch around 1:00 or 2:00 in the afternoon, and dinner sometime after 6:00 P.M.

The Pocomchi day schedule starts considerably earlier than either the North or Latin American one. The Pocom rise between 4:30 and 5:30 in the morning. A minimum of time is spent in the bath, and a maximum of time is spent preparing the food and getting ready for the chores of the day. The Pocomchi man goes to work around 7:00 and returns in the middle of the afternoon. At about 11:00 A.M., the women of the household take food to the men working in the fields. The workmen then take a break that lasts as long as they want it to. After the workmen return home, they spend three to four hours relaxing, eat the evening meal around 7:00 P.M., and then go to bed.

Conflicts in various societies ensue when subcultures have different day schedules (I observed this at two colleges and three universities). American youths tend to arise later and retire later than do the adults. American black youths tend to start later in the morning than white youths and end later in the evening. College administrators find that black students choose later-scheduled courses and tend to retire later than do white or Hispanic students.

The week cycle provides a pattern of work and rest. Every society has a period of work activity and then a period of relaxation. The North American society structures a five-day work week with a weekend of relaxation, for a total of seven days. The North American pattern formerly consisted of a six-day work week with only Sunday as the day of rest. It is moving toward a four-day work week with a longer weekend. Certain of the Mayan-derived groups of Central America have a five-day week, working four days and going to market the fifth, then starting over again on their five-day cycle.

The month cycle is one of bill paying for the average North American and of watching the changing faces of the moon for the more primitive and folk people of the world. The British capitalize on a fortnightly concept, and others emphasize the bimonthly cycle.

The physical season changes produce a scheduling of activities that generally have to do with planting and harvesting. There are also representative seasonal changes that have nothing to do with the changing phases of the moon. In North American society, the fall season is the time for starting school, for the introduction of new automobile models, for showing new television programs, etc. In some cultures, seasons also introduce fertility rites designed to cause the crops to grow better. They may or may not coincide with the actual time for planting.

The year cycle is utilized in all societies for experiences of loyalty development, bringing the annual national holidays and celebrations, town and city festivals, and religious festivals. These provide opportunity for remembering local and national heroes. The year cycle controls the celebrations for opening or closing a year, such as the Chinese New Year, the Western New Year's celebration, and so on.

Multiyear cycling of activities involves the kind of social, religious, political, and economic developments that take a great deal of time and effort to accomplish. The larger and more complex a society, the greater the demand for constancy and consistency of leadership. To change yearly would produce significant leadership gaps, and government programs would change too rapidly for significant development. Thus in North America, the higher the level of government leadership, the longer the time is between elections; for example, the election for United States president is held every four years, but city mayoral elections are generally held every two years. The Hebrew society established celebrations that incorporated the time span of seven—seven days, seven years, seven sets of seven years. This was their festival cycle, and every fiftieth year, the year after the seventh seventh (forty-ninth) year, was the Year of Jubilee. The society was supposed to start fresh after the Year of Jubilee.

Every society selects from this total range of scheduling the patterns it finds most useful. The smaller, less-complex society invokes fewer scheduling mechanisms. The larger, more-complex society will have activities throughout the year. One must be in a society over an extended period in order to sort out the various calendar-related events and their relative importance. Where two societies live in geographic proximity or are mixed, the number of activities will be greatly increased. The reason for this is that members of each society select from the activities of the other those which they wish to incorporate in their total lived experience. They may displace some of their own or simply add the new ones to their list of activities.

The Life Cycle—Rites of Passage

Societies also employ a means of advancing their members through the various stages of life. Rituals that attend the passing from one stage to another are termed "rites of passage."[2] Generally, rites of passage mark or signal four primary life crises within the life cycle: birth, the transition from childhood to adulthood, the transition from the unmarried state to the married, and the transition from life to death. The case study of this chapter concentrates on the transition from childhood to adulthood. Prior to the rites, the boys are "regarded as mere irresponsible children." Following the rites, they are admitted into the "full life of the tribe." In one sense, nothing really changes, but the perception of the tribe is that everything changes. Former boys enter the adult life of the group as new men. For North Americans, graduations are the functional equivalent of the initiatory rites described in the case study. As an educator, I am constantly amazed at the difference between the pregraduation youth and the postgraduation version of the same person. There is a qualitative distinction that is often difficult to describe, but it is certainly there.

Each society will emphasize one or more of the life crises within the life cycle. This is signaled by the extent of complexity and significance of the rites of passage. Societies, such as the Black Carib of the east coast of Central America, practice couvade. The husband, instead of the wife, goes to bed when a child is born. This practice tends to reinforce the importance of the birth-life crisis over the other life crises. For the Black Carib, marriage is not stressed nearly as much, for there is simply a taking of the bride into the household and a minimum of ritual attending this transition. When birth is not stressed, there is simply the attendance by a midwife and little more. In North American society a baby shower may be added, but little else is done at birth in the average household.

The North American tends to emphasize the transition from childhood to adulthood more than the other life crises, though a case can be made for marriage as being the most significant in the contemporary period. The rites of passage involving the transition to adulthood are so varied and complex that it is convenient to establish a fifth life crisis in the social structure. It has been termed "teen" or "youth" and separates childhood from adulthood by an entire period of development. Rites of passage involved in the transition to adulthood involve graduations, driving, voting, drinking alcoholic beverages, and numerous other practices. These so embellish the ritual of the transition that it perceptually exceeds all the other rites involved in life-crisis transitions in North American society. Very few societies stress the childhood-adulthood transition to the degree of adding a "youth period" and an entire rite of passage.

Societies stressing marriage develop an elaborate wedding ritual but also a careful set of rules regulating physical contact between the sexes prior to and following marriage. When marriage is not stressed, a man will simply take a woman to his home. There will be a minimum of ritual and a maximum of corporate support for such a practice. In North America, more ritual accompanies marriage than birth or death, and the attitudes toward marriage tend to raise it to a primary position over the others. It would appear that the rituals of marriage are lessening, especially in certain youth subcultures. The couple will live together without a formal ceremony of marriage, and if a wedding is performed, it is done at the convenience of the family and friends rather than of the bride and groom.

Societies stressing death will develop an elaborate ritual around the death-life crisis and have a detailed death belief that may even involve reincarnation. The ritual of death was so elaborate in India that some groups once called for the burning of the wife along with the corpse on the funeral pyre. Other societies called for servants to be burned with a high-status member of the society so that he would have help on the other side. Among the Pocomam of eastern Guatemala, corpses are placed on wooden platforms and allowed to lie there until decomposed. In other societies, large funerals are held with the corpse being laid to rest in elaborate structures. In North America, the ritual of death has developed to such a degree that it is vying for second place in competition with marriage. The funeral is more elaborate than ever. With the undertaker handling more and more details, the cost is also increasing. Inner spring mattresses and silk pillows are often included in the preparations for interment.

Among the Saibai of Australia, the ceremony of closing the tomb with an elaborate tombstone has produced serious disruption in the society. When a person dies, all family efforts are turned to saving for the size and style of tombstone that the family feels will most adequately honor the dead. Young people frequently are forced to put off marriage because of this expense. Some of the young people dutifully wait, hoping that no more deaths will occur before the wedding. Others simply leave and live together or elope. The island is losing many of its young people permanently, for they find that life off the island is more suitable to their own desires.

Some societies, such as the Latin American, stress a number of life crises equally, rather than highlighting just one. The transition to adulthood is attended by the ritual of godparenthood and confirmation. Marriage calls for an elaborate wedding with ceremonies at the city hall and at the church. Death calls for the all-important wake and the anniversary wake held one year after death. The postfuneral program is so elaborate that relatives may be involved with it for years following the death of a loved one, e.g., paying for his release from purgatory.

The Yaos and Makuas mentioned at the beginning of the chapter stress the transition to adulthood. The rites attending this life crisis are not only elaborate, they are made to be deeply meaningful by the isolation of the child, the assistance given him, the ritual upon his return as a young adult, and so on.

Festival Cycle—Celebration

Tied in with the calendar cycle and rites of passage is the festival cycle, which supplies every social group's need for celebration. The concept of *celebration embraces a period of mundaneness followed by a period of excitement within the group*. If every day, week, month, season, and year were the same, there would be very little interest in life. Boredom would result. If everything happened the same way year after year, the group would not build those practices that develop loyalty, as they would not be developing distinctions from others. A South American Indian group was influenced by missionaries to give up all their festivals in which their homemade beer was drunk. Within a very few years, the members of the society had little to live for and were in a state of anomie—that is, a condition of normlessness, of lack of interest in life. What the missionaries failed to realize was that these ceremonies were also the ones that stressed responsibility to the group; welcomed the stranger with the news; developed the belief system of the entire group; gave the women something worthwhile to do, i.e., make and serve the beer; and so on. Had the missionaries helped the people develop functional replacements for the ceremonies or at the very least a functional substitute to the beer, the group might have been able to maintain its sense of purpose and value. A neighboring group was provided functional equivalents and was able to make the transition to a new form, maintain its sense of worth, and become a truly Christian community.

Within the day cycle, the Latin American siesta is a festival. The North American looks at it as merely a nap or, at best, unnecessary. It is even considered a sign of laziness. To the Latin, it serves to reinforce a sense of family in a society where the family is more significant than any other unit of structure within the hierarchy. In some subcultures of North America, dinner does what the siesta does in encouraging a sense of family. Everyone is together at dinner in such American families, whereas they are not usually together at any other time. Thus for such families, the dinner time is a time for celebration within the day schedule.

Within the week schedule, religious observance brings a sense of something special to a mundane work period. Thus worship at its best is a celebration, not only of God's blessings, but also of a release from the normal everyday pressures of life. Even societies with no specific belief in God will institute in their lives some worship replacement that has a similar effect in their corporate lives.

National holidays that occur annually underscore people's sense of identity with and loyalty to the larger society. People in the United States celebrate their independence as a nation on July 4, whereas citizens of Guatemala celebrate their national independence on September 15.

Every celebration has its plan or walking pattern associated with it. This reinforces the celebration by the degree of detail and elaborateness. The Latin American procession is a vital part of celebration, and the complexity of the march indicates the degree of importance a particular festival has in the lives of the people. Perhaps the most elaborate plan of march of a festival procession is that occurring around Good Friday. There are a variety of processions during this time and each one is more elaborate than an equivalent march during any other festival. They involve more people and more of the important people within the society.

Societies focus on specific celebrations in every social group. Thus the nation, the state, the community, and the family each has its celebrations. Even an individual has his own celebration on his birthday. In small, minimally complex societies, the matter of celebration is apparent because it tends to flow quite naturally within the activity cycle and does not seem to be potential for conflict. In larger and more complex societies, celebrations may conflict with each other. A ranked code of holidays and festival periods is developed to circumvent such conflict. Such a rank establishes which are more important and which are less important. For example, in North America, family celebrations which are more potential for conflict with community and national festivals are frequently held on the same day as the larger festival, thus averting such conflict. In Latin America, however, a family festal responsibility will frequently result in a family member ignoring his social, economic, and religious obligations. One such conflict that is seldom satisfactorily resolved in American society is when a child's birthday falls on or near Christmas Day. Many families resolve the conflict by giving both a Christmas and a birthday gift, yet celebrating both occasions at the same time. To the child, however, this is less than adequate, for he sees that children having birthdays at other times have two celebrations. He considers himself cheated.

Within every social group, there will be one festival that is ranked as the major celebration of the group. It occurs at the peak of the festival cycle and is the most significant celebration within the group. It is important to note the most important celebration and be able to distinguish this from the less important ones. Primary loyalties are focused on the peak and lesser loyalties on the secondary festivals. In North America, Christmas time is the peak of the festal cycle, both in terms of national and personal concern. Even though the festival is concerned with the birth of Jesus Christ, the part that is stressed most is gift sharing, establishing a strong basis for production and distribution of toys and gift products. Thus the production cycle comes into sharper focus than does religious devotion. However, in Latin America, Christmas is one of the lesser celebrations. The most significant festival of the year is Good Friday, with festivities being completed even before Easter. Good Friday in Latin America has not been commercialized to the extent that Christmas has in North America, and the perception of religious devotion dominates the festival.

The Response Cycle

The response cycle is the expected response of an individual to a stimulus of some kind. Responses involve greetings, acceptance of gifts and the giving of gifts and favors in return, acceptance of "office" or resignation from same, religious participation, and many others. Greetings are controlled both in degree of response and timing of response. Whereas the Filipino might simply raise his eyebrows in response to a verbal greeting, the North American might totally overlook such a response, expecting a verbal one. A North American would submit his resignation to public office and expect it to be accepted, whereas in Latin America, a resignation is simply a test of strength and is seldom intended to be accepted, at least not the first time it is presented. The response in religious services is so patterned and practiced that many adherents are able to go through the motions of the religious rituals without really paying attention to what is going on.

In the Philippines, a gift extended to a person has significance only for a long-range relationship. The gift extended is to be reciprocated at an appropriate time with a gift slightly nicer than the first one extended. This pattern of reciprocity continues throughout the relationship. It comes to full fruition when a sponsor or godparent is sought for one's child. The person involved in the reciprocal gift exchange is likely to be named sponsor of the child. The relationship is sealed for all time. A person failing to return an appropriate gift at the appropriate time is not brought into a permanent relationship and is a "nobody" within the society and is thus without influence.

Walking Patterns Accruing From Activity Cycles

Every activity calls for its own unique walking pattern, and the composite walking pattern is built from the composite of activities within the society. It becomes *a map of the society as defined by the activities of the society.* The typical North American walking pattern is established through the interaction of work, school, and recreation. If work calls for a person to punch in at 8:00 A.M. and leave at 5:00 P.M., the walking pattern then involves getting to work before 8:00 and leaving work at 5:00. Such a walking pattern causes the freeways to be jammed before 8:00 and after 5:00. Another pattern, the week pattern, with its weekend of heavy traveling, is graphically indicated by the offer of reduced air or train fare for families during the off times, i.e., in the middle of the week. Resort areas feel the pressures of the yearly walking patterns during the slack times in resort activity. They have to make their money during the three months of summer or the four months of winter if they are going to survive. Motels frequently have two rates—the vacation rate and the off-season rate.

A Filipino higher-status family may own a farm, perhaps a family farm or its replacement, yet live in the city. Periodically they will go to the farm for a short visit and take friends from the city to the farm. It is there that one gains a close acquaintance with the members of the family. One missionary couple accepted the invitation of a family to visit with them. However, it was during the annual missionary conference of the mission board under which they served. Their absence at that critical time was not appreciated, and they were asked to resign from the mission. The missionaries were in tune with the walking patterns of the people they had gone to win to Christ. The mission failed them at this most critical moment.

In primitive or folk societies, the people have a market day. If that market day falls on Sunday in a given community, the walking pattern calls for the Sunday morning period to be spent selling produce and buying staples for the week—and then attending church. This is in direct conflict with the walking pattern established from the North American or Western society where the late morning is a more effective time for the rural farmers to attend the weekly celebration of religion. Farmers completed their chores by mid-morning and then needed to return home to complete others in the late afternoon. Worship of God was thus contextualized within the North American culture. A church schedule in the Indian areas of Latin America having a Sunday market should be built around the market sequence, even as the schedule in rural North America followed the chore sequence.

In contemporary North American society, people are finding that recreational activities are dominant over the religious interests, and some churches are adjusting their schedule to the pattern of a recreation weekend by having their service prior to the weekend. One church went so far as to have service on Thursday evening during the summer, another on early Sunday morning.

Summary

When studying any group, but especially one for which it is impossible to find written materials, one should focus on the behavior of the members of the society. The behavior is most clearly expressed in the activities of the group. Such activities encompass a wide variety of interests ranging across social, economic, political, and religious concerns.

One way to analyze the activities of a group is to take a look at the scheduling of these activities through the different time periods of life: the calendar, the life crises, and the celebrations. It becomes obvious which are the most important activities of the group— those around which the most ritual develops. Working from the ritual activities, it is possible to determine the peaks and troughs of festival cycles.

When the agent of change approaches the society that he seeks to influence, he needs to study the walking patterns of the people to see if that which he wishes to introduce is compatible with the activity cycling of the group. A missionary does not introduce an 11:00 A.M. worship service in the Pocomchi area during the market time if he wishes to have any Pocomchi attending the service. This is the same principle of contextualization that established the

European and the North American worship time, i.e., a time that would not interfere with milking the cows.

Questions for Discussion

Relating to the Sending Church

1. What holidays are most important to the North American? Indicate them in categories: national, religious, etc.
2. What would you say is the most important holiday in North American society? Why?
3. How has the festival cycle been adapted to meet the demands of the work/recreation cycle? Which holidays have been changed, and which have not been changed? Can you produce some generalization that is consistent with the changes as you see them?
4. What is the festival cycle of your church? How does it shape the concept of worship? of witness? of Christian growth?
5. Study the participation of the choir in worship activities and see how this confirms or negates your answer to question 4.
6. What are the stages of Christian growth that are marked within your church program?
7. How might the activity cycle, the life cycle, and walking patterns be used effectively in the witness of the gospel?

Relating to the Study of the Bible

1. Map out the activity cycles for the period of the Pentateuch.
2. Map out the activity cycles for the Gospels.
3. Study the books of Esther, Ruth, Jonah, and Acts to ascertain the walking patterns of the people living during those periods.
4. How did Jesus use the festival cycle in his approach to witness?
5. In studying the Old Testament Hebrew experience, what place did life cycle and rites of passage rituals have in the worship of God?

Relating to Missions and Crosscultural Ministry

1. Study out the festival cycle in the community in which you are serving. How are the various activities announced? Which ones do you feel free to participate in? Which ones do you not feel free to participate in? Why?
2. How might the North American activity cycle be imposed upon Christians in some other society? Give examples.
3. What are the walking patterns of the people in your community? When would you predict would be the best time, i.e., the natural time, for worship? for a church activity? for religious education?

4. How have you tended to ignore the festival cycle in carrying out ministry? the life cycle? the walking patterns?
5. How might the concept of celebration increase the vitality of your ministry?

Group Activities and Exercises

1. *Group discussion.* In small groups, probe the list of heroes, sacred places, primary and secondary holidays or celebrations, etc. of the subculture of which the members are a part, e.g., a local church, a college, etc.
2. *Film.* Show a film like "The Dead Birds," an ethnographic documentary from Papua New Guinea (83 minutes, color and sound, McGraw-Hill Contemporary Films, Inc.). This is a valuable film to use as a discussion focus on this chapter.
3. *Small group activity.* Have the members of the group generate or create all the ways a devotional program could be developed in keeping with the natural schedule of their subculture, i.e., for periods in the day, week, month, year, multiyear, etc.
4. *Large group discussion.* Introduce the four life crises that a typical society has and put them in rank order for North American society according to the amount of rite and ritual attending the rites of passage. For example, of the four life crises (birth, puberty, marriage, and death), the North American society has probably elaborated the puberty life crisis the most, as evidenced by the variety of rites attending this crisis: graduations, voting, learning to drive, drinking alcoholic beverages, etc. Once this has been completed, compare the North American practice in these life crises with that of a second society known by the group.
5. Prepare a festival or celebration that is consistent with the group of which you are a part and that adds to the sense of well-being of the members of the group. It is good to attempt this at the end of a course. The participants, in small groups, should give brief presentations (ten to fifteen minutes each) that grow out of the course and extend the learning of the course. Then take the last class period or two and allow each experience to develop. At the end of the last presentation, draw the group into a discussion of how the experience enlightened past learning and prepared the members of the class for future learning.

11

The Group: Values

Case Study: The Seven-Month Baby

Phairote, a young Thai Christian, brought his bride with him to Bible school when he returned for his second year. He had lived previously in the boys' dorm, but during vacation he had married a young nurses' aide at the Christian hospital where he was working.

They entered easily into Bible school life and continued their studies together. Before long it was announced that they were expecting their first child. Everyone looked forward happily with them to the child's arrival. They had talked of returning to Central Thailand for the birth of the child; then, as the time drew near, they decided to remain and have the baby in the government hospital nearby. The awaited day came, and they proudly announced the arrival of a son.

The missionaries who were teaching on the staff of the school began to be uneasy. One of them had attended the wedding of the young couple some months before. When they compared the wedding date with the birth of the baby, it appeared that the child was born about six weeks earlier than they felt it should have been. Since the baby was above average size and weight and normal in every way, it seemed clear that he was not premature, and so the missionaries concluded that the newlyweds had lived together prior to their wedding day.

Before long the matter took on crisis proportions in the eyes of the missionaries. As they gathered to discuss it, it was felt that since the purity of the church was at stake, the young couple must be faced with the issue. Since confrontation is the Western method of solving conflicts, they decided to visit the young couple in their quarters and talk the matter over. One evening while the other students were studying, three men and two women visited Phairote and his wife. After prayer, one of the missionaries broached the subject, informing the proud parents that their behavior had been improper by Christian standards. Silence filled the room.

One of the aspects of the Thai value system is that of saving face. They will always approach things indirectly so that no one loses face in the situation. Without an intermediary, which Thais would have used in such a case, the young couple somehow felt "naked" in the overpowering presence of the five missionaries. There was no one to remind the missionaries for them that the Thai betrothal is considered as binding as marriage and that sexual relations during the period covered by the betrothal are not considered particularly improper, since the couple is in fact married.

There was little that Phairote and his wife could say, so they listened while the missionaries proposed a solution. They suggested that the couple should stand up before the assembled Bible school students at one of their chapel meetings and confess their misdeed publicly. The young couple was not especially pleased at this suggestion, so they remained noncommittal. After considerable consultation, the missionaries departed and awaited the chapel hour when this confession would be made. It never came. The couple refused to comply; the missionaries were disappointed; and at the close of the term, the couple returned to their home.

Values in Society

Values are whatever a group or an individual within a group considers of importance. Values refer objectively to the worth of an object, thing, action, belief, etc., or subjectively to the perceived worth of the same. In each automatic or consciously made decision, some value underlies the choice of one thing over against another. Since the socialization process is designed to make as much action as possible automatic in response, it thus is responsible for developing or underscoring values. The entire life of an individual can be plotted simply by indicating the choices by which the individual lives. These choices reflect values that underlie the social groupings of which an individual is a part within society. The values cause an individual or a group to select out from the total range of activity and identity those specific aspects that the individual and group chooses to make a part of the everyday life experience.

Every social group, subculture, or community has its own pattern of values. In part, these are derived from the sum of all the values of the members of the community. In part, they are in addition to any and all individually held values. These values make a community unique. They are what causes a community to grow and maintain interest in life. Without them, life would become ordinary and humdrum, boring and dull.

The Basic Values Model and Cognitive Styles

The basic values model underlies all choices and thus all values within an individual or group. *The basic values model is a taxonomy of cognitive styles.* A taxonomy is a device utilizing categories of thought that permit the observer to objectify the behavior of the members of any given society. Utilizing such a taxonomy, one avoids value judgments based on one's own cultural experience; e.g., something I do is better than something you do. Value judgments, when applied to the known, aid discernment. Value judgments applied to the unknown distort and confuse. They often result in falsehood and injustice.

Cognitive styles are models of human thought. Behavioral scientists have been describing and classifying behavior and attitudes for years. H. A. Witkin in psychology and Parsons and Shils in sociology introduced some of the first styles models.[1] Witkin distinguished field-independent thinkers from field-dependent ones. The field-independent thinker is able instantly to draw some pattern of focus out of the background, or field, in which the pattern is imbedded. The field-dependent thinker is unable to do so even after the pattern is pointed out to him. The imbedded figures test is administered, and subjects are instructed to look at a simple geometric pattern, examine its shape, and then find that same shape within a more complex geometric design. The field-independent thinker is able to ascertain the shape immediately. The test becomes symptomatic of his ability to draw the point from a discussion, conceptualize any part within a larger whole, or focus on some aspect of the background, all of which are difficult if not impossible for the field-dependent person to do.

Whereas Witkin's study works with two categories, Parsons' study deals with a multiplicity of categories in ever-expanding matrices of thought, e.g., affectivity, orientation, universalism/particularism, ascription/achievement, specificity/diffuseness.

Among the numerous popular cognitive taxonomies of values are McLuhan's concept of "hot" and "cool" media; DeBono's vertical versus lateral thinking; Reich's "Consciousness" I, II, and III; Blake's Managerial Grid; and others. Each of these is reduced to a pair of values with extended discussions. Numerous other taxonomies are utilized by researchers in communication, education, sociology, anthropology, etc. These are variously called communication styles, learning styles, thinking styles, etc. In Christian literature, a noted styles model has been presented by LaHaye, who introduces the categories of sanguine, choleric, melancholy, and phlegmatic. One of the styles models relating back to some of Jung's writings has been developed into a professional testing program called the Myers-Briggs Type Indicator (MBTI).

The basic values model posits that there are certain values that are basic and present in all human beings. This model of human behavior bases itself on the premise that once these values and their order of importance have been established for an individual or group, one can predict behavioral response in any given situation. When applying the generative principles of the model, human behavior becomes predictable at a very high level of accuracy. This in no way implies that human behavior is determined, rather that it is effectively controlled within a social context. Knowing the model and applying it in a variety of contexts, frees one from the burden of such control and allows one to gain fresh insight into his own and another's behavior. Such insight releases a person from taking himself too seriously and assuming a personal affront due to another's actions or words.

Change and the Basic Values

Social existence is constantly subject to change. New agreements of social contracts are being made whenever two or more people come into direct or indirect contact. The sum of such agreements makes up what is termed "culture." With each change of association, a new contract emerges, based in part on the former one, yet distinct to the degree that these new associating people are distinct. Such change is difficult to observe and control because much of it is covert, lying behind existing social structures and behavioral expressions. Further, the change process is gradual, and certain aspects of change will lie covertly behind the social structures for many generations before coming to the fore. The basic values model permits the field investigator to tune into the culture at any moment of experience through the profiling technique; to grasp the dynamics of the culture by means of the generative approach; and perhaps most importantly, to project ahead of the moment of experience and predict the variety of ways the culture could change in keeping with its social dynamics.

This is not to say that the culture will predictably change in one way; rather, it means that the agent of change, by projecting possible changes, can be better prepared for the particular change expressed through the culture. The agent of change, by utilizing educational methodologies such as "game theory," i.e., inductive rather than deductive thinking approaches, can run through the possible change alternatives, design possibilities in keeping with each potential change, and thus be ahead of the actual overt expression of behavior. Such advantage comes in (1) being better prepared for the actual change, whether or not it happened to be one of those inductively predicated, and in (2) having developed an adaptive attitude which allows for and respects the change process.

The Basic Values Model

The basic values model is a multicategory taxonomy which includes the following patterns of behavior:

1. Dichotomizing
   a. A dichotomizing person will tend to polarize life in terms of black and white, here and there, me and the other, right and wrong, etc.
   b. A dichotomizing person will tend to evaluate the other (person, program, or idea) on the basis of his dichotomies.
   c. A dichotomizing person must feel that he is right, that he is doing the right thing and thinking the right thoughts, to be satisfied with himself.
   d. A dichotomizing person will tend to adapt well to computers, which are based on binary conceptualizations. However, for some, fear of computers may result from seeing them in terms of "the other."
   e. A dichotomizing person is likely to be highly systematized in classifying and organizing people, experiences, and ideas in his mind.
   f. A dichotomizing person finds that his organization of where he fits in life and where others fit provides him security.

2. Holistic
   a. For the holistic person, the parts will only have a vital function within the whole.
   b. For the holistic person, no consideration can be given any part unless it is also considered within the whole. Situations in which one must consider one part without respect to the whole produce frustration.
   c. A holistic person when faced with such frustration will utilize some defensive measure as the "mock" which strikes at the whole scene.

d. A holistic person derives his satisfaction through integration of thought and life, whether planned or unplanned.

e. The holistic person feels very insecure whenever he is placed in a category.

3. Crisis or Declarative

a. A crisis person seeks an expert or someone with extensive knowledge of a particular area to advise him in a crisis. Following such advice gives him confidence in making decisions.

b. The crisis person likes an easily accessible authority to which he can turn and to which he can direct others seeking knowledge. Consequently, he reads a great deal and uses the best written authorities as the basis for his decisions.

c. The crisis person will have a keen interest in, and a deep respect for, history. He believes that crises similar to his have been faced before and that he can find a solution through looking at past solutions.

d. For the crisis person in a learning experience, much emphasis is placed on comprehending the instructor and being able to reverbalize what one has been taught. The responsibility for the learning experience primarily belongs to the instructor. He is expected to be stimulating and motivating, thus guaranteeing learning on the part of the student.

4. Noncrisis or Interrogative

a. A noncrisis person will expect to have to select an answer to the question from various alternatives. Security and satisfaction will derive from selecting among these alternatives. Frustration will come if no alternatives are available.

b. For the noncrisis person, a new problem arises out of the alternatives selected. Personal satisfaction comes with the alternatives considered and the ones selected, as well as from the vitalness of questions or problems arising from the ones selected.

c. A noncrisis person can, through the events of life, be brought back to the same situation faced earlier and then choose a different answer, another alternative.

d. The noncrisis person will be frustrated with a lecture situation or any type of instruction in which an expert speaks, not allowing for viable alternatives.

5. Time-Oriented

a. A time-oriented person will be concerned with the time period in terms of seconds, minutes, and hours, not years and multiyears.

    b. For the time-oriented person, the time period will be a certain length depending on what is the intent or purpose of the time spent. It cannot be too long nor too short in relation to this intent. It will be carefully planned to accomplish the most possible in the time allotted.

    c. The time-oriented person will be concerned with the "range of punctuality" at the beginning and end of each timed session.

    d. The time-oriented person sets long- , middle- , and short-range goals that are related to some type of time period. He feels most comfortable when he has planned ahead in this manner.

    e. The time-oriented person will attempt to condense into a given time period as much as he can of that which he considers worthwhile.

    f. The time-oriented person will have in his mind a time/dollar equivalence, or a time-spent/production equivalence in his way of life. If he spends a certain number of hours studying for a test, he expects a certain grade.

    g. The time-oriented person will not fear the unknown too greatly. It will be quite predictable due to temporal control.

    h. The time-oriented person will recall and try to reinforce certain times and dates.

6. Event-Oriented
    a. An event-oriented person is not overly concerned with the time period.

    b. The event-oriented person will bring people together without planning a detailed schedule and see what develops.

    c. The event-oriented person will work over a problem or idea until it is resolved or exhausted, regardless of time.

    d. The event-oriented person lives in the here and now and does not plan a detailed schedule for the future. Therefore, he is not interested in, nor is he much concerned with, history.

    e. The event-oriented person trusts his own experience rather than the experience of others.

7. Goal-Conscious (Object As Goal)
    a. A goal-conscious person is concerned with a definite goal and with reaching that goal. Achieving the goal becomes a high priority. He will dedicate all that he is and has for the sake of attaining the goal.

    b. A goal-conscious person forms his deepest friendships with those who have goals similar to his. When necessary he will go it alone.

8. Interaction-Conscious (Person As Goal)
   a. An interaction-conscious person is more interested in dealing with people than achieving a goal. He will sacrifice a goal for the sake of talking with or helping a person.
   b. The interaction-conscious person will break rules or appointments if they interfere with his involvement with another person.
   c. The interaction-conscious person will find his security within the group by getting to know the people in the group and being involved with them.

9. Prestige-Ascribed
   a. A prestige-ascribed person will show respect in keeping with the ascription of prestige determined by society.
   b. The prestige-ascribed person will expect others to respect his rank and standing in the community.
   c. The prestige-ascribed person will play the role his status demands and will associate with those of his own prestige or rank.

10. Prestige-Achieved
    a. A prestige-achieved person will tend to ignore formal credentials and consider rather what the person means to him.
    b. The prestige-achieved person will struggle constantly to achieve prestige in his own eyes and will not seek to attain a particular status in society.

11. Vulnerability-As-Weakness
    a. A vulnerability-as-weakness person feels that to be vulnerable is to be weak. He takes every step possible to keep from error by double-checking everything he does and being methodical and organized.
    b. A vulnerability-as-weakness person hates admitting mistakes, so he will argue a point to the end or cover up his errors.
    c. A vulnerability-as-weakness person will not expose his weaknesses or tell stories about himself. He will speak vaguely about personal areas of his life, and he is likely to be unwilling to become involved in something new.

12. Vulnerability-As-Strength
    a. A person who feels that vulnerability is a strength is not too concerned about making errors, nor does he find it difficult to admit mistakes.
    b. A vulnerability-as-strength person will tell stories about himself exposing his own weaknesses, will talk freely about very personal areas of his life, and will likely be eager to get involved in new experiments.

The twelve categories of the basic values are not the only ones that could be considered in such a taxonomy. In studying many societies, however, these appear to be some of the most significant aspects of behavior. The analyst observing and participating within a distinct society is able to derive the primary motivational values of a society. Eighty to ninety percent of behavior within a given society opens to understanding once the relationship of these values to the society is discovered.

Application of the Basic Values Model

These individual categories of thought or conceptualizations within the basic values model can be applied to a society as individual items. In other words, a society can be described in terms of its time orientation and its response within a time setting, or in terms of the ascription of prestige. In any such description, a second culture is in the mind of the analyst. As you study the following description, keep in mind your own social setting and culture and compare the two without value judgments against either.

A Value Profile: Philippine (Tagalog) Society[2]

The insights below imply a comparison with North American culture.

1. *Time*. The following principles appear to guide the Filipino in range of punctuality: (1) The more important the individual, the narrower the time range of punctuality. (2) The business event demands a narrower range of punctuality than does the social event. (3) The more prestigious the social event, the wider the range of punctuality. Examples: An appointment with a V.I.P. starts at the set time. For mass, lasting an hour, one can arrive within the first half hour and not be late. Rotary Club induction may have an hour range of punctuality. To the North American, the time stated is the time intended in most cases.

2. *Schedule*. The Filipino appears to like a schedule, but not one that is tied to a narrow time pattern. In other words, he likes to have something to do over a particular time period, such as in the morning. He does not have to appear at 8:00 and leave at 5:00 to carry out his schedule. His schedule is important, but points of time reference within the schedule do not control his life. The North American is more tied to a time/clock schedule and hesitates to disrupt his schedule for fear that he will not get everything done.

3. *Event*. In nearly every experience of life, the Filipino is more concerned with the event itself and what is going on than he is with

the time the event begins and ends or whether it moves within a narrow time schedule. He expresses this in a variety of ways. If something does not get done today, he excuses it by talking about tomorrow. His making of a livelihood is built around an event. If he can make a living by selling one item, he does not need to be in the office from 8:00 to 5:00. The Filipino has what might be called a stoical approach to life. If something interferes with his schedule, he can patiently endure. Life is centered in the experience of the here and now, and the Filipino often is very good at starting something now but not continuing it later. Some refer to this explosion of enthusiasm as *ningas kogon*. For most North Americans, time and the timed program are more important than the event itself and tend to control the event.

4. *Vulnerability*. In some instances the Filipino appears to value vulnerability as a strength and will readily admit to things that the North American seldom would, such as an illicit sexual involvement. However, throughout most of his life, the Filipino is very sensitive to vulnerability, and he works within the society to cover all signs of weakness. When someone stumbles, falls, or in any way harms himself, Filipinos will stand around and laugh rather than aid the injured person. To the North American this appears crassly insensitive. The Filipino sees it differently. If someone has stumbled, the Filipino feels this is an evidence of that person's vulnerability, and if he took the accident seriously, the injured one would be embarrassed because the seriousness would underscore his weakness in having fallen.

The society supports the individual in any evidence for vulnerability through the practice of the intermediary. One arranges for an intermediary in every situation in which he might be proven vulnerable. If he needs money and the person who could lend it to him has no obligation to him and thus could easily refuse the request, a third party to whom the potential lender might be under obligation is sent. It is anticipated that then the request will be granted. The North American seldom works through an intermediary and feels that the best resolution of a problem is by face-to-face confrontation.

The Filipino appears to be a poor loser and will at times exert seeming superhuman physical effort in his attempt to win. For example, a basketball team winning against a Filipino team can be badly battered physically.

The Filipino does not want to put someone on the spot. The moment he does this, he makes the other person vulnerable and potentially disrupts smooth interpersonal relations, which are supremely important to him.

The North American adult also considers vulnerability as a weakness. His society, however, does not stand behind him in this value orientation, as does the Filipino's, to provide him with as many social mechanisms for covering up his vulnerability.

5. *Personalness is valued highly.* An announcer of a basketball game may fail to announce the score because he is talking about the personal qualities of the basketball player making the score.

In the Philippines, much personal support of another is expressed through tactile or touch behavior, showing a dependence one upon another, for example, men holding hands, one man laying hands on another's leg, women touching women in a crowd. Such gestures would be interpreted quite differently by the North American, more as sexual advances.

In certain respects, the Filipino is very sensitive to the other person. He will respond to a request with a euphemism to keep from saying no. For example, if a person wishes to borrow an umbrella and the other does not wish to loan it to him, the owner will say "I don't think it is going to rain." One says no only to a person with whom he does not want to be associated.

The Filipino does not want anyone within the society to be alone. He feels that it is his responsibility to be with the other person even though he may be ignoring his own responsibilities. If he has to be away, he will arrange for someone else to be there. If it is night, he will insist that the light be turned on.

The Filipino likes a "personality." To him this is one who relates warmly to him and who builds a network of interpersonal obligations through a sense of interest in him and his needs. The North American, on the other hand, is exceedingly impersonal in such interpersonal relationships with a patent insensitivity to others and a distaste for the "personality" type. He will attempt, by various means, to make the personality just one more of the crowd.

6. *Noncrisis.* The Filipino attempts to avoid crises. A crisis would disrupt smooth interpersonal relationships. Instead, he follows every avenue possible to feel someone out before taking a stand, making a request, extending a favor. The practice of using the intermediary is designed to eliminate the crisis experience. Noncrisis values may also explain the seemingly permissive childrearing practices of the Philippines. Parents do not want to make a scene, so they yield to the demands of the child. This does not necessarily mean that the child grows up to be immature in his adult behavior, for at a certain point in life, he is expected to evidence mature behavior in spite of this more permissive early training. For the youngest child, especially a boy, this point is delayed indefinitely. The North American does not hesitate to precipitate a crisis if it will further his own ends.

7. *Prestige.* When one is born into a family, he acquires prestige. An individual starts in the status system at the level of status of his family. However, he can achieve higher status through

education or marriage or "luck." Thus, frequently, the motivation
for education is not to gain knowledge but to gain a diploma,
which enables one to strive for a higher status level. A person's
family name causes those below the status of his family to expect
good of him, to assume that he will succeed in maintaining the
status of the family or improve it. The family name, however, is no
guarantee that the status level will be maintained. The Filipino
becomes a kind of copycat, one who is quick to sense the demands
of a higher status and fit in, whether he fully deserves this status or
not.

8. *Crisis: Authority.* The Filipino is very hierarchical and thus
exhibits an interesting authoritarianism. The one of higher status
has authority over the one of lower status, the leader of an alliance
over the follower. The sense of authority is intense; for example, a
youth accepting Christ may reverse this decision if the leader in his
alliance disapproves.

The Filipino will speak softly to the authoritarian. He will not
answer or respond when asked to do something by this authority
figure, deeming it neither necessary nor respectful to do so. He
simply goes ahead and does it. Both practices irritate the North
American.

The hold that the authority figure has over the follower is
extremely frustrating to the average North American who feels that
everyone must be free to make up his own mind as to the final
decision, though he himself does not realize just how much this too
is actually controlled by his own culture.

9. *Holism.* The Filipino sees life as a whole, as a unity, with all
parts being explainable within the whole. The North American
tends to be more particularistic, with greater attention to detail, to
linear sequence, to a sequential type organization. In comparison,
the Filipino appears to have an absence of logical thought and uses
euphemism extensively to talk around a subject rather than
speaking directly to the point of a subject.

Grouping the Categories of the Model

Certain categories of the model when considering natural
society, group together in an interpenetrating array that I term
"trend time" behavior: time, dichotomy, crisis, object as goal,
prestige as ascribed, and vulnerability seen as weakness. McLuhan
calls them "hot media,"[3] Van Leeuwen calls them "word type,"[4]
and Lingenfelter calls them "linear thinking."[5] They can perhaps
best be summed up with the concept "verbal."

The rest of the categories of the model group into an array that
I term "trend event" behavior. McLuhan terms it "cool media,"
Van Leeuwen calls it "spirit type," and Lingenfelter calls it "point
thinking." They can be summed up with the concept "visual."

It is quite possible that these two distinctions, verbal and visual, coincide with the two functions of the brain: analytic and appreciative,[6] referred to in "dual-brain" theory. Assuming this is so, it is valuable to study the respective functions of the two sides of the brain for additional insight as to how the basic values are expressed in human behavior.

Applications of the Basic Values Model

We can also use these individual categories of thought as contrasting items within a larger scheme that has binary considerations or bipolar relationships. In other words, we can select any two that appear to have relevance to each other; and through contrast or bipolar relationships, we can see that one society is more of one kind than it is of another. This was done in comparing the Filipino culture with the North American one above. One society may be experience oriented, whereas another society may be time oriented. A visitor in the United States notes a great deal of time orientation, i.e., careful attention is paid to the clock; there is extreme concern for meetings held during a specific time period; these meetings are to start and end on time; there are clocks everywhere—on towers, on banks, on filling station walls, in every room of the house, and on every wrist. Meetings and programs are established around a time concept: whatever is going on is set aside when the meeting is over—that is, when the time limit for the meeting approaches or when the bell rings. In fact, the people with whom one has spent this time period are no longer of primary importance. The contrast is striking when one enters the Philippines. The people are more concerned with who is there and what is going on than when something starts and ends. One may search endlessly for a timepiece.

One drawback of such a binary or bipolar method of contrasting items or approaches to life is that the analysis tends to polarize, and in the process, people are polarized, societies are polarized, and value judgments slip in to support one category over another in very subtle ways.

Therefore, a more significant means of utilizing the basic values than through either individual application of the categories or polar application of them, is by means of continua. In the polar approach, two categories are selected that appear to relate to each other, for example, time versus event; or two aspects of one category may be selected, such as crisis versus noncrisis. In a continuum approach a given society can be seen to fall somewhere along a continuum, for instance, anywhere from an extreme time consciousness to an extreme event consciousness. In this way, distinctions between societies can be noted, but there is less chance of applying value judgments that tend to be prejudicial. Different aspects of the same society can be described by the use of a series of considerations involving the same continuum; for example, American society would lean toward time orientation during the work week and toward event orientation on the weekend.

By taking two continua and placing them in a matrix with two axes in the matrix, one can compare individuals and societies by means of as many as four categories. In the "managerial grid" utilized in today's business and management world, the categories of person relatedness and production are considered, with axes representing a less person-oriented individual in comparison with a more person-oriented individual on a one-to-nine scale, and one representing a less production-oriented individual in comparison with a more production-oriented individual on a one-to-nine scale. Thus an individual who produces little and relates poorly to people is a one-one person, and an individual who is tops in production and great with people is a nine-nine.

All the other "boxes" formed by the intersection of columns and rows can also be filled with the types of individuals thus indicated or with the actual names of people representing these characteristics on the working staff. A person who is less than nine-nine in any way can theoretically be trained toward a nine-nine capability (see figure 19).

Another valuable matrix is that formed by the axes of time and event. The various time units of second, minute, hour, day, week, month, season, year, and multiyear, are placed along one axis, and the event in maximum focus scaled to minimum focus is placed along the second axis. At the intersection of columns and rows, it is possible to place the names of societies that trend toward the dominance of time structuring over the event itself or toward the dominance of the event over the time structuring (see figure 20). For example, American society is so oriented toward the smaller time units of second, minute, and hour that the event, whether it is completed or not, must yield to the timed unit. When the time is up, the event is over. Where the season dominates the timing within the society, the event has a large enough time arena to complete itself.

A final way of handling the categories of thought in the basic values model is through the use of wholes or unities. With wholes, it does not matter where someone falls in relation to another. It is simply important that a category exists and that there is a way of developing the whole by means of concentric circles, or "smear."

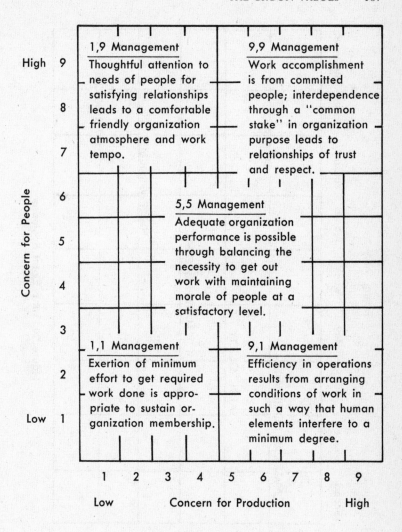

Figure 19. The Managerial Grid

Profiling

A composite of a series of evaluations derived from the basic values model will yield an individual or corporate profile. An individual may

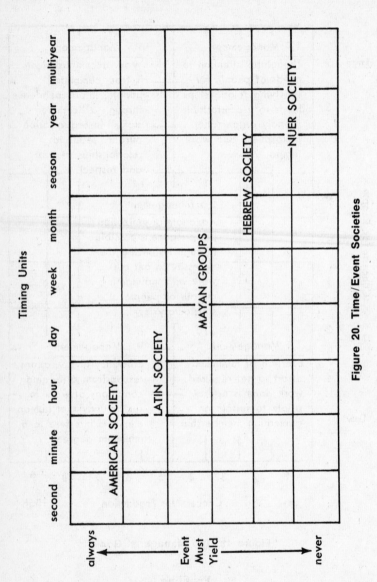

Figure 20. Time/Event Societies

trend toward time orientation in his economic experience, toward event orientation in his social experience, toward crisis when dealing with money matters and religious concerns, toward noncrisis when educating his children, toward dichotomizing in every aspect of life where he is constantly distinguishing one thing from another and where vulnerability is a weakness restraining him from ever referring personally to his personal existence and from expressing his values.

Such an individual profile is useful, first, in understanding what makes this person tick; second, in planning any program of directed activity or involvement for him; and third, in carrying out a program of change.

A corporate profile can follow from the sum of all of the individual members' profiles. This profile is generalized to a degree, but its value lies in the range of variation of the members' values within the corporate body. In a less-complex society there is greater likelihood of homogeneity; that is, more members would fall at certain points along the various continua of the profile or at some intersection of columns and rows in a matrix. In a highly complex society, such as that of the United States, there is greater likelihood that one would discover a scattering of points along the continua.

The profile approach is useful when developing educational programs for students living in the contemporary period.[7] A student who trends toward time, dichotomism, and crisis, needs one kind of approach to education—one that is fact-oriented, where these facts can be tested by objective examination, and one that focuses on the teacher as authority (see figure 21). A student who trends toward event orientation is more holistic and noncrisis, and he learns best by experiencing personally the whole of that which he is learning. This has led to the schools-without-walls concept and tour-the-world educational opportunities.

A society that is linear (dichotomistic and crisis oriented) will develop a traffic pattern that is ordered in terms of lanes and assignment of lanes to distinct kinds of traffic, e.g., "Slow vehicles keep right." Filipino society is nonlinear, and lanes are therefore somewhat meaningless, as can be seen when a street gets crowded and people move freely into lanes of the opposite direction, onto the shoulders, and even onto the walks in an effort to pass. Gigantic traffic snarls ensue that sometimes take hours to disentangle. This would be quite serious for timed, goal-oriented people, but for the Filipino who reaches goals by event scheduling rather than time scheduling, there is a certain "fatalism" that attends his attempts to get free and on his way. He tends to wait patiently for things to straighten out.

In a time-oriented, linear, and dichotomistic society, corporate prayer usually takes place at regularly scheduled prayer meetings. The members of such a society present their lists of prayer requests, and the items are prayed for, one by one, by those in attendance. In

Elements of a learning experience	Basic Values Time Dichotomy Crisis	Basic Values Event Holism Noncrisis
The classroom	Set. Four walls with blackboards, bulletin boards and windows. Plus "field trips."	Vary. In essence, one protracted field trip. World tours, city as classroom, professional quarter off-campus.
Assignments	Set units. Timed assignments, assigned in keeping with timed units of study.	Grow out of discussion, project, world concerns. Need for continual re-evaluation.
Class preparation	Units prepared beforehand and executed as planned. Lecture primary.	Total grasp needed at any moment. Material introduced where called for in class development.
Individual research	Careful detailed supervision. Little change from original plan.	General guidelines set. Plan changed as project develops.
Papers and projects	Assigned readings. Set length of paper.	General reading list; selection by cooperation of instructor and student. No set length.
Examinations	Primary basis for evaluation. Individual, objective, time limit.	One of many bases for evaluation. Individual or group, objective or essay, no time limit.
Role of professor	Carries full responsibility for learning experience. Has impersonal contact with students. Questions are of information type, not contradictory type.	Shares learning experience responsibility equally with student. Has personal contact with student. Questions are of all types and one expected answer is "I don't know; you find out."
Completion of course	At a set time, with all the material of the course completed.	Course ends only after demonstrated proficiency. The course is the beginning of learning.

Figure 21. Elements of a Learning Experience

his individual praying also, the member of such a society tends to wait for specific times of prayer. Prayer in an event-oriented, nonlinear, and holistic society tends to be something more spontaneous, happening whenever there is an impulse of a need to pray. A prayer could last a few seconds or indefinitely. "Pray without ceasing" then becomes a lifestyle where the channel of communication is never closed and prayer flows continually from the life. This attitude toward prayer expresses itself also in communal prayer. It is interesting to read the Book of Acts with the different value profiles in mind. It would appear that prayer in Acts grew from a society that was more event-oriented than timed, somewhat nonlinear, and certainly holistic. Over 90 percent of the praying in the Book of Acts followed an experience shared by the believers, after which they were literally impulsed to pray. At times the praying was brief, and at times it was quite extensive, as in the first chapter where an extensive (three-day) prayer session was held. This would create havoc in a trend time society.

A taxonomy such as that of basic values gives one perspective in dealing with a case as emotionally charged as that of Phairote in the opening case study of this chapter. Without such a tool, it is easy to be ethnocentric, thinking, "my way is right," and to have each party take the matter personally, with each intrusion in the case becoming a personal affront. There is no need for such highly charged emotional response. Further, there is no need for making judgments about behavior until one has worked through the conflict of culture and seen the specifics of motivation and intent. When this has been done, there will be ample time to work out the moral problems involved and come to a conclusion of rightness and wrongness in the matter.

Since the Thai generally consider vulnerability a weakness, any direct confrontation would be in very bad taste. The North American is defensive when his personal integrity is called into question, but he is very open and direct in seeking to determine wrongness of social and public behavior. The sexual realm is something that is liable to this openness, since fornication and adultery in the experience of a member of a group is seen as reflecting on the group. The Thai is vulnerable in both personal integrity and social behavior, since the one brings reflection on the other. The direct intrusion into the Phairote case left the participants with no other resource than to withdraw, since they had been shown publicly to be weak.

In North American society, marriage occurs at the time of the wedding, not at the time of engagement. Each step leading to marriage is part of a timed sequence that is ultimately fulfilled at the wedding. At this point in time, since the couple is married, intercourse may take place. They are committing neither fornication nor adultery if their physical contact is in keeping with the expectations of the timed sequence occasion we call marriage.

The Thai has a different timed sequence in which marriage is completed at the time of engagement rather than at the wedding. The ancient Jews had this practice, as do numerous contemporary societies. Engagement to them is as binding as the wedding is to the North American. They are committing neither fornication nor adultery when their physical relations are carried out in keeping with their timed-sequence expectations.

Finally, the North American tends to be more crisis-oriented than the Thai. He sees one solution to a problem, rather than considering natural solutions, and he sees one way to resolve an issue—namely, by confrontation—rather than considering alternate ways of reducing conflict. The North American, choosing his one way, offends, not realizing his goals could be met by alternate routes without being so highly offensive to those with whom he deals.

Generating Society

Another of the uses of the basic values is in generating society or parts of society. The process is intricate, but the results leave the analyst free to range widely through society and societies much as the linguist can range freely through language and languages.[8]

The practice of generating societies follows the following guidelines:

1. Ethnoscience—transformational grammar in linguistics and systems theory in communication provide the foundation for such an approach.

2. Process:
   a. Analyze the internal dynamics of a society.
   b. Reduce this to a core operating system.
   c. Test the operations with experiments.
   d. Examine the system for internal consistencies and inconsistencies.
   e. Evaluate the system for evidence of the various control mechanisms that keep the system operating effectively.
   f. Become aware of the malfunctions within the system or abuses of the system that reduce its effectiveness.
   g. Once the system is reduced to its minimum components, take these and generate all the rules, and only the rules, needed to operate the system.
   h. Check the rules over against the original analysis of the system.
   i. Correct the original analysis.

   j. Become aware of malfunctions and abuses. The rules appearing to be part of the systems operation may be there only to correct the system also, where part is made to be the whole or abuse is made to be the whole system.

   k. Observe these areas in comparing the logical construct with the more thorough analysis. This will show if there are ways that the control mechanism can be reinforced, corrected, or adjusted, or if the system needs modifications, or if there needs to be attention paid to the abuse—so that the system can function effectively again.

3. Dominance:

The elements of the model can be so arranged that there is a rank order of dominance to follow, much like ordered rules in linguistic science. Only when number one dominance is taken care of can number two be considered. Once two is taken care of, then three can be handled. This is the same process linguists use when they deal with ordered rules. One controls all, two controls all but one, and so on.

4. Yield of this type of approach:

It helps a society to analyze systems, evaluate existing rules, determine the extent of slavery or freedom, generate a new society, and train "doctors" of society through computer and game simulation.

Case 1

(Note that dominance is expressed in the first, then second, then third element of the model.)

In building a societal system from three basic core value-motivations—(1) time, (2) production, and (3) comfort—the following rules are derived:

1. Everyone must work.
2. Everyone must begin work on time.
3. Everyone must work a certain number of hours per week.
4. No one may undo the work another is doing or has done.
5. Everyone must achieve maximum production within a time period or schedule.
6. Everyone must have this schedule and must produce.
7. There must be a basic unit as a measure of time for all members of the society.
8. This basic unit must be stated.
9. Vocabulary must be limited to absolutes. There must be basic units of language with a one-to-one correlation of form and meaning for a minimum waste of time.

10. There will be no talking while working, except for production talk.
11. There should be centralized, dictatorial government to control the use of time.
12. Everything must be done in the shortest time possible.
13. Workers produce only what can be produced rapidly.

Now, compare this to a business or industrial system within American society. The child-labor laws were designed to guard the members of the larger society from the extremes of efficiency of such a value-based subculture, i.e., not making everyone work.

Case 2

In generating worship experience for this profile—(1) event-oriented, (2) holistic, and (3) noncrisis—we have the following:

The experience of worship could take place in an outdoor setting. The participants could be asked to arrive around dawn, to see the sun rise over a distant mountain in the background. The event could be focused on God as the Creator; and the splendor of the world awaking before these worshipers would allow them to see some of the magnitude of his power and glory. Hymns of praise could be suggested as they watch the sunrise. The participants could be asked to share God's revelation by reading from Scripture regarding the glories of God in his creation. The persons gathered could be given a choice of (1) meeting together for prayer in small groups, (2) going out in the woods alone for meditation, (3) or joining others in composing a psalm to be sung in praise of God.

Summary

Underlying all activities of the group, as well as the group structure itself, is a web of intersecting and interrelating values. Values refer to that which a society and each member of a society values or holds as important as compared to something else. Were we to define all the values in American society, large volumes would be needed to explain each value, the place that each value has in relationship to another, the individual expressions and arrangements of the value, and the corporate expressions as well.

To cut incisively into the heart of the value system, certain basic values are useful in providing clues to the larger pattern of values that motivate any member or corporate body to action. These basic values are ideal types as they stand in individual considerations, continua, matrices, and wholes or unities. Such profiles are useful when studying either a society, any group within that society, or any individual member of that society. The basic values indicate relationship of one person or group to another.

Besides profiling for understanding individual or corporate terms, the whole of a society or any part can be generated from a core of basic values. Such an exercise can aid in developing new programs and new concepts, and in applying and refining those that meet the felt need of the society and its members.

Questions for Discussion

Relating to the Sending Church

1. Distinguish values from value judgments.
2. Can value judgments ever be objective or nonbiased? When? In what ways?
3. How might church doctrine be used in a judgmental way? the basic values model? any learning?
4. How might the basic values model be utilized as a "radar"? (A radar is designed to keep two vehicles from colliding.)
5. What basic values characterize your church? How does this pattern of values advance the cause of Christ? How does it deter the cause?
6. Is there a set basic values pattern that every Christian should develop? Explain.

Relating to the Study of the Bible

1. Do a basic values analysis of great characters in the Bible, such as Jesus, Paul, Moses, Abraham, David, and others. Were they all alike? Did they need to be alike to do God's will?
2. How does the Book of Revelation exemplify a trend-event basic values orientation?
3. If you were told that Jesus was a point integrator and Paul was a linear integrator, how would you affirm this point of view?
4. Suppose Jonah had been a vulnerability-as-strength and a noncrisis person, how might his story have turned out? Rewrite the ending.
5. Contrast the openness (holistic) of Jesus to those hearing the gospel, yet the precision (dichotomistic) with which he defined the truth.
6. Review the trend-event, visual demonstrations of God's power before his people.
7. Consider the phenomenon of speaking in tongues in light of the basic values model. Would you say that the church of Corinth was more time oriented or trend oriented? verbal or visual? dichotomistic or holistic? If the verbal demands explanation but the visual does not, how did Paul stand in relation to the Corinthians?

Relating to Missions and Crosscultural Ministry

1. You, as a missionary from the West, are probably time oriented and dichotomistic in your basic values. Because you are being sent out by a conservative church, you are probably also crisis oriented. How would you assign categories to the people with whom you have worked? What impact could this insight have in your ministry? Remember that you are not to place value judgments on the categories.
2. Drama has not had a good reputation among the conservative churches in the West. Why might this be? How could drama be used in evangelizing a trend-event, visual orientation group?
3. Trend event, visual, point-integrating people will tend to use body movements, picturable presentations, tactile behavior, and even nonlanguage speech (tongues) in their worship of God. How can you work with them to assure truth content in the message they communicate to others?
4. Suppose a pocket television selling for about five dollars was available to the people of the world. How might this direct your ministry? What kinds of things might become of high value in evangelism and church planting? (Note: Television combines visual and verbal behavior.)
5. How might a missionary and a national conflict along the vulnerability continuum? How might this affect the ministry?

Group Activities and Exercises

1. *Activity.* Using the basic values model, profile a person or a group in keeping with your observation of his behavior.
2. *Activity.* Using the basic values model, profile a program such as a church service, a commencement, or a play based on your observation of the behavior of the group.
3. *Small group.* Plan for small groups to visit an art gallery, attend a concert or a play, listen to records with lyrics, or become part of some experience such as a rock concert or a church service. Discuss the experiences in light of the insights made available through application of the basic values.
4. *Generative exercise.* Prepare a set of 3-by-5-inch cards with some program named on each (worship, party, class, etc.) and another set of cards with one basic value named on each. Divide into small groups, and have each group select one card from the first set to establish its setting and two cards from the second set to establish its basic values. Let the order of selection of the last two cards become the rank order of dominance in the exercise. Present a brief version of the program developed by means of a skit, and then talk about the results after all the skits have been presented.

5. *Interview*. Invite a Filipino into the group after all the members have internalized the Filipino profile. Spend the first part of the period allowing the guest to talk about interpersonal relationships in the Philippines. Then let the group ask specific questions probing the behavior that would result from the profile. Compare what the guest says with what you discovered from the written profile and from the group's observations. Do not get to the point of who is right or wrong; rather, allow everything you see and hear to help develop a more adequate profile of the Filipino.

12

Conflict of Norm

Case Study: Dinner Decision

Helen's grandparents immigrated to America from continental Europe while their children were young. Since that time the family has lived near a large eastern city with a large group of other former Europeans who share many cultural similarities. Folk dances, food, drink, and dress are among several features of their older culture that survived, at least in part, the trans-Atlantic crossing earlier in the century.

Each person in Helen's community appreciates his heritage of distinctive traits from pre-American culture that has blended with the "American way." But Helen does not really feel any different from other American young people. During her childhood, she experienced no conflicts between the two ways. She was raised in a Christian family, and both she and her parents were eager for her to attend a Christian college. She considered many schools but finally narrowed the choice down to two. This was between a school that maintained a statement of expected standards of conduct concerning abstinence from dancing, drinking, smoking, etc., which a student was required to sign, and a school that left the student's behavior to his own discretion. She decided upon the one with the stipulated standards of conduct and signed the statement, fully intending to keep it.

One weekend in the early fall, she received an invitation to a dinner party that her aunt and uncle were giving. Several relatives and some friends from the "old country" were invited, and she excitedly accepted the invitation. She eagerly awaited the day and was glad when it arrived.

The party was entertaining, and Helen was enjoying herself. There were several relatives she had not seen recently, and it was refreshing to hear the native tongue of her parents and ancestors. Cocktails were served, but she refrained from drinking, more from a dislike for the beverages than because of the standards of conduct pledge. In the back of her mind, however, was the wine that would be served with the meal. She had always enjoyed this. Then a handsome young cousin whom she adored asked her to join him in a traditional folk dance. . . .

Conflict is the result of tension that grows within an individual, between individuals, between individuals and groups, and between groups. It stems primarily from a relationship that goes awry. Our concern here is conflict resulting from tension within the sociocultural setting—not the effect of this breakdown of relationship on the person—and the ensuing personality problems. In our case study, tension arose from the contact between a drinking subculture and a pledged-not-to-drink subculture.

Where the individual alone is concerned, conflict involves the gap between what a person really is and all the ideals that he is forced to, or seeks to, live up to. When individuals conflict because of underlying tensions, we talk about personality conflict or an inability to get along with others. When an individual conflicts with a group, we suggest that he lacks social graces; has not been effectively socialized; or, in the case of encounter with a distinct society, is in culture shock. When a group conflicts with a group, we say they are at war or in a cold war, as in the case of nations; or competing, as in the case of subcultures. Each case represents, in some way, the effect of tension within the interpersonal relationship or within the network of interpersonal relations.

Creative Tension

Tension can be constructive and useful, or it can be destructive. *Useful tension within the group can be called creative tension.* Such creative tension has a number of functions.

Creative tension aids a group or an individual in achieving authenticity. Group identity is involved. This can be developed through loyalty mechanisms, selection of heroes who are important to the group, delineation of issues significant to the group, and kinds of festival expressions that produce group solidarity. In one sense, Helen experienced creative tension that was helping her define her identity in her new context of life.

One way the group achieves its identity and authenticity is by extending its political control to the full limits of its cultural unity. Even though it was not immediately apparent to the respective thirteen colonies, there was a cultural unity that extended from north to south. Political control slowly extended throughout the cultural entity by means of numerous social and political efforts, not the least of which was the Revolutionary War. On the other hand, social and religious values differed enough from those of Europe and Great Britain so that the war also allowed the separation of the two cultural entities (The Colonies and Great Britain) and the development of separate political control over each.

In Nigeria, a cultural entity known as Biafra, with a tribal integration named Ibo, attempted to establish its own political control over the people loyal to it, as well as over some who did not wish to be a part of it. This was a very similar situation to the colonies separating from Great Britain. In the more recent case, however, Nigeria was able to maintain political control over the Ibos, and the revolution was terminated. There was no place for a George Washington among the Ibos nor for the successive heroes of a new struggling nation.

Creative tension is a constructive part of the ongoing socialization process within society. Education is effected when men of different classes and statuses train and fight side by side during a wartime setting. Further, some of the men must be sent to schools of specialization. During World War II, for example, the field of linguistics became recognized as a full-grown, legitimate discipline, due to the challenges of war with a variety of non-English-speaking nations. Also, members of one society learned about people of other societies from being stationed in those places as allies or fighting as enemies. This is not to say that all war is constructive and creative. There are, however, benefits to any nation because of the tension. Such benefits can have a creative impact within the society.

War also affects the economic base of any nation. The skill of artisans is increased significantly. New developments grow out of the extreme needs of warfare. Such developments are useful both to the participants in the struggle itself and also to the civilian populace. Scientists are still unfolding the multitudinous uses of atomic power, the development of which was accelerated greatly because the United States and Germany were at war.

New forms of social organization that prove beneficial to

society are developed in times of world and national tension. This does not imply that it is necessary to overthrow the old. However, significant changes are made that permit the group to surge ahead in progressive development. Japan is a good example of this. Prior to World War II, Japan looked back many centuries for its traditions and its place in the world. The emperor ruling Japan was the primary symbol tying all of Japan to its deeply rooted traditions. However, following the war, with the emperor removed from the seat of power, enough changes in the social organization of the society took place to allow the Japanese people to develop as one of the leading industrial nations of the world.

Along with change, however, comes no guarantee that the result will necessarily be better than before. The Philippine nation is an example of a people who may have lost a great deal because of a shift from a more Spanish type of social organization before the Second World War to a more American postwar type. The Spanish authority was rooted in the extended family. The Philippine nation, to pursue national development, was forced to pay attention to the needs of the various families of the Philippines. The postwar American system placed greater power and authority in the hands of individual leaders, to the detriment of the families and possibly of the total populace.

Tension effects a rude and imperfect selection from among leaders and organizations within society. This selection is made between those defeated and those made great by victory. The Crusades initiated a breaking up of the stagnation of the Dark Ages and an emancipation of the social forces of Europe. In American society, we may perhaps never know the full effect of the rise of John L. Lewis to prominence in the labor unions. His more militant approach to union negotiations have not only been with us as prototypes of subsequent patterns of negotiations, but they have also spelled the virtual death knell of coal mining in the United States.

Tension serves to keep groups together that need to be together and to separate those that need to be separate. Tension also determines how groups are to be kept separate and what the depth of involvement between those needing to be kept separate or together should be. Latin American nations have a long history of internal tension within the contemporary world. Because the Spanish type of government is based primarily on the extended family, the smaller the national unit, the more likelihood there is of each family having its needs met by the government in power. If a number of national units were put together, as is the case in the larger nations, many families would suffer injustice. It is this sense of injustice that lies behind much of the political unrest in Latin America.

Nevertheless, Latin American countries need to cooperate with one another for the full development of their economies. No one Latin nation, with the possible exceptions of Brazil and Argentina, can fully develop without some kind of trade relationship with its neighbors. Yet Latin nations dare not go beyond this cooperative trade arrangement to permit rule by an outside aggressor, for then the structure of the national government or alignment of national governments would be too restricting and could easily produce injustice against many family units.

Creative tension, therefore, can be said to play a vital role in society. It results in conscious effort to affirm the borders of the group, establish its unique identity, reinforce known rules, and cooperate with compatible groups in further progressive development.

Malfunction of Tension

Malfunction of tension results when an individual or a group attempts to modify or to control another. The result is slavery or injustice.

War is classically defined as an armed contest between two independent political units, by means of organized military force, in the pursuit of a tribal or national policy. Thus war is the most extreme expression of the malfunction of tension in society.

Intergroup relations on other levels of the society may result in a malfunction of tension. It is in these experiences that the members of the society train for their interaction on the national level. If interpersonal and intergroup relations on lower levels of society result in outbreaks of fighting, mob action, rebellion, confrontation, resistance, and other violent and forceful practices, there is little hope that international relations will be handled any differently.

On the local or community level within the society, any family that seeks to modify or control another family creates an undue tension between those families. A family has various means of accomplishing its wish. It can bring religious beliefs and sanctions to bear on another family. It can dominate it by sheer personality. If the attempt is simply to modify the family, resistance to the dominant family could become manifest through the one ignoring the other. If the attempt is to control the other, legal means may be brought to bear on the dominant family.

In the malfunction of tension existing between youth and adult in North American society, the youth is likely to contradict his parents when they try to modify his behavior patterns. In cases of all-out parental control, youth will be even more rebellious.

Within subcultures of the larger society, demonstrations or feuds break out if one group attempts to modify another. If an attempt is made to control the other, then riots and even blood feuds result. Such reactions have been evidenced between Indian and Latin peoples of Spanish America, black and white peoples of North America, and mountaineer clans of the eastern United States. This same type of conflict is also observed between members of the same culture or subculture.[1]

Whether a conflict between groups results in a court battle or in rebellion, rioting, feuding, or war, these expressions are behavioral indications of one group attempting to modify or control some other group. If one family ignores another, or if a child is always contradicting his parents, or if demonstrations take place against a group, or if feuding erupts between familial groups, or if there is some strong expression of nationalism within a group, there is reason to believe that one person or group is attempting to modify or control the other.

Any malfunction of tension on any level within the society calls for the use of weapons in keeping with the level and with the type of the malfunction. On the family level, the door lock becomes a very effective defense weapon if a neighbor continually enters unannounced and seeks to influence the choice of furniture, fabrics, wall decorations, or paint color within the house. Social ostracism is another weapon in a neighborhood where the people are somewhat close and do many things together.

The surliness of a youth is a weapon he uses to defend himself against an overaggressive parent who is forever trying to make him "shape up." The *mock* is also a useful weapon turned against adults. The mock can be a devastating weapon when used selfishly and a highly rewarding one when used to protect a young person from unreasonable control by an adult. In a noted Christian college, during a period of adult reaction against popular music, a reaction that caused jazz and rock music to be restricted in public performance, student organists would weave a jazz theme into the postlude following the chapel service. The *judgment* is a kind of weapon used by many adults to decide whether someone is "their kind" or not. The judgment can be used to discern between a good and a bad person, or it can be used to cut down someone who does not agree with one.

Demonstrations, petitions, breaking of laws, sit-ins, and other similar weapons have been utilized by members of different subcultures within a larger society. They are used to protect the group from injustice or perceived injustice. Guns and rocketry are used on the international level. Terrorism is becoming a forceful weapon to avenge perceived injustice and to free members of a group from being imprisoned by another.

Two questions arise out of a discussion of weaponry in a war arising from a malfunction of tension. These are: What effect do these weapons have on the "enemy"? and Is the effect of one weapon worse than the effect of another? The guns and rocketry of a nation kill the body. The other weapons tend to kill the spirit. In other words, even though the one takes life, is not the effect of a "spirit killer" more serious to the person and his society in the long run? The breaking off of fellowship and of communication between people produces alienation. This, in effect, is living death. Perhaps this is why divorce is so devastating to families. Divorce underscores alienation between parents, between parents and children, and between children; and it models most powerfully the kind of alienation that can separate God and man.

Taking the issue a step further, Jesus said: "Do not be afraid of those who kill the body but cannot kill the soul. Rather, be afraid of the One who can destroy both soul and body in hell" (Matt. 10:28); and "Things that cause people to sin are bound to come, but woe to that person through whom they come. It would be better for him to be thrown into the sea with a millstone tied around his neck than for him to cause one of these little ones to sin" (Luke 17:1–2).

Tension and the Individual

The individual's central conflict involves the gap between the real person and the ideal that is held up or that he holds up to himself. Discrepancies between the real and culturally defined ideals produce emotional unrest, a state of living in tension[2] (see figure 22).

the person

Figure 22. The Person in a Tension Situation

An attitude or approach of rejection becomes extremely dangerous when it builds into a pattern of rejection. When someone rejects someone or something, that other person or thing will in turn reject him. Thus when a person rejects what he really is—namely, the real—the real in turn rejects him. When a person strives to attain his ideal and finds it elusive, he will get rejection feedback and will likely discard the ideal. What results is a four-way flow of rejection in which each stage in the rejection process reinforces each of the other stages and a thrust of rejection that in turn produces a counterthrust (see figure 23).

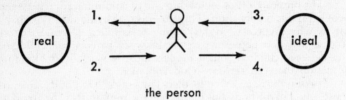

the person

1. The person rejects the real in striving for the ideal.
2. The real rejects in return.
3. The ideal is impossible of attainment.
4. The person rejects the ideal.

Figure 23. A Four-Way Flow of Rejection

Within conflict situations among individuals and groups, the first step of rejection is almost impossible to overcome, for it results in a responding reaction of rejection. Once this pattern begins to build, a variety of things begins to happen within the person. Irritation grows, ushering in further irritations. Eventually, given sufficient stimulus, there can be rebellion, reaction, or neuroses of some kind. These may even build into psychoses. Such resistance to the ideal or to the other person within the rejection pattern can result in psychological or sociological anomie. A reduction of standards and disintegration of life-way are likely to ensue. In time, a person will feel the tension building and seek to free himself from the burden of conflict (see figure 24).

People utilize a series of characteristic ways of resolving such conflict (see figure 25). Some of these ways are therapeutic. Others only increase or reinforce the tension.

Escape or *withdrawal* is one of the immediate responses to the burden of tension. Suicide is the ultimate means of escape. There are other means that one may use: entertainment, such as television or movies; fast driving; drugs; developing a sexually-oriented friendship; eating or drinking; losing oneself in a work responsibility; masturbation or other sexual deviance; and many others. In one college, the piano was played more during exam time than during other periods in the semester.

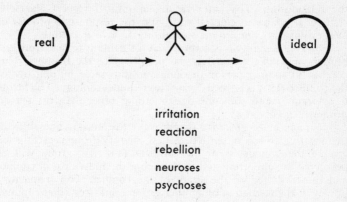

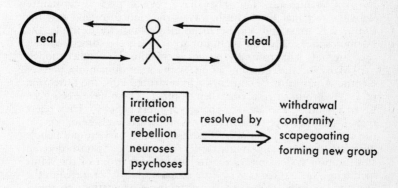

Figure 24. **Results of a Rejection Pattern**

Figure 25. **Resolution of Conflict**

Conformity is a second way of getting out from under the burden of tension. There are two kinds of conformity that are important in this regard: conformity for conformity's sake and adaptation to another's lifestyle. The former undermines self-respect and thus undermines the trust base in a relationship. It is the way a person modifies his behavior just to get along, to be seen as a good guy, to pull something off, to gain something selfishly from the relationship. The latter results in mutual respect and self-respect. It relates to cultural relativity, the responsible process of integration into one's own subculture or a new culture.

Seeking a scapegoat is a third way of gaining release from the burden of conflict. This lets the person place the blame for his conflict on another person or thing and thus sense himself free of the conflict. This is termed "projection" in psychology. The blame is associated with someone or something other than the person primarily involved.

Forming a new group is a fourth way of protecting oneself from the negative aspects of tension. A new identity group is established around the ingredients of the conflict. This new group will be perceived as supporting and encouraging the individual in conflict and thus will reduce the strain of the conflict. Too frequently, however, the formation of another group reinforces other conflicts or introduces new ones.

Case 1: Forming a New Group

The Indians of Central America, descendants of the ancient Maya civilization, have lived under the pressure of forced conformity to a Spanish life-way. They have been impressed constantly with the fact that the Spanish way is the right way and that the Indian way must and will be abandoned. Thus, for example, the Pocom cannot really be Pocom but are forced to be something that they are not. This naturally pushes them into the conflict model.

Many of the Pocom, along with other Indian peoples of Central America, have chosen, or have drifted into, the formation of a new group in resolving their conflict. These have even been given a name—*revestido,* or "change-of-dress people." They reject their Indianness and their Indianness in turn rejects them. Yet, at the same time, they can never become Spanish background people because of their appearance and because the Spanish-derived stratification system places the Indian at the bottom of the status hierarchy. Since there is very little social mobility permitted in the system, the Indian takes no less than three generations to move upward in the social hierarchy. Thus, with every step into Spanishness, the Indian is repulsed and feels the rejection and in turn rejects Spanishness. This leaves the Indian neither Spanish nor Indian. His dress so reflects his being neither the one nor the other, that the name "change-of-dress" has been that which has begun to characterize him and give him identity. The way of dressing is a cross between Spanish, or more Western dress, and Indian "costume"; for example, such a *revestido* might wear a Western-type work shirt and pants but no shoes.

The new group does much to help the person establish a new identity, but it does little to resolve the actual conflict. In fact, it introduces a new conflict involving getting established in those parts of the total life-way that can absorb such a "misfit." Many well-meaning efforts on the part of missionaries create the same tension in the areas of their ministry. People feel the need for change as influenced by the outsider and, in effect, form a new group and thus a new subculture within the larger society. It resolves some of the tensions of conflict but introduces new ones that are at times even more difficult to resolve.

Case 2: Conformity for Conformity's Sake

The missionary's child, returning from the country of his parent's ministry and entering North American society, steps into a tremendously reinforced setting of conflict (see figure 26).

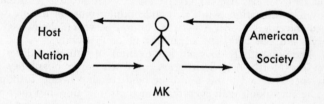

MK

1. The missionary's "kid" (MK) must leave his host nation and in essence "reject" it.
2. The host nation "rejects" the missionary's youngster, since they have nothing further to do with him.
3. The American culture which he enters is in reality youth culture rather than adult culture, and being less familiar with this, he is rejected by its members.
4. He in turn rejects members of American youth culture as "snobs."

Figure 26. An Example of the Four-Way Flow of Rejection

In the country in which he grew up, he knew adult American society, since he primarily associated with his parents and their peers. He experienced the youth subculture, not of his parents' home culture, but of the culture in which he grew up—that is, the culture of his parents' ministry. When he enters the United States, he enters the American youth subculture. It is neither like the adult North American culture that he knows, nor the country of ministry youth subculture in which he grew up. Since he is not living with his parents during this period, his contact with American adult culture is limited. Further, he has little or no contact with the youth culture of his host nation.

Young people leaving Latin society to enter North American society fail to recognize the differences between the flirtation patterns of the two cultures. In Latin America, a young man can be more aggressive in flirting with members of the opposite sex than can the North American young man. The MK learns the flirtation pattern of the Latin and, without thinking, applies it in his approach to North American young women. They react to him as being too bold and aggressive, and his approach "turns them off." The MK is looked upon as being a bit odd. He is refused dates and generally has a tough time with his social life. When the MK is a young woman returning to the States, the problem is compounded. The more aggressive flirtation she has learned through her contacts in Latin America has had no adverse effect when dealing with Latin fellows, for flirtation is just that and nothing more in most cases. When she enters North American culture, however, she is seen as "easy" and can be taken advantage of quite readily.

The typical MK does not like to think of himself as different from his North American peers, and when the possibility of difference is raised in his mind, he tends to shut it out. In doing this, he goes along with everything he finds, merging into the total picture. As he does this, however, some of the things he feels pressured to do run counter to his principles. Conforming for conformity's sake then tends to undermine his self-respect.

Unfortunately, forming a new group does not help the MK as it did the Central American Indian. Few MKs from the same host country wind up in the United States in the same place. Therefore, even though in general they have something in common with other MKs from other host countries, specific experiences differ greatly, and they find that they have little in common. Every MK is thus a separate group in himself.

Case 3: Withdrawal

North American youth are adept at using withdrawal to free themselves from conflict. They begin in the home where they have their place and their possessions. When there is something unpleasant to face, it is easier for them to go to their room, close the door, and shut out the unpleasantness. This is further trained into them in the church where they attend Sunday school and then are encouraged to go to church. They are not really mature enough to appreciate the adult type of service. They have their Sunday school papers, however, and from the first moment of unpleasantness, due to lack of understanding, they can turn to the papers. As they grow older, more means of withdrawal are made available to them. These means include the automobile, drugs (frequently used regularly by their parents under the guise of prescription drugs), eating, sleeping, and many more. Many parents are willing to make all kinds of excuses for their children to get them out of difficult spots. Even though withdrawal may be a very necessary route of escape due to the seriousness of the conflict, youth practice withdrawal as the first, and frequently only, means of dealing with the conflict, and their maturity is slowed by the process. The portable radio with headset can make the sense of isolation from the world complete.

Case 4: Scapegoat, i.e., Projection

The classic example of scapegoating is found in the early chapters of the Bible. Adam blamed Eve for tempting him with the fruit, and Eve in turn blamed the serpent: "The man said, 'The woman you put here with me—she gave me some fruit from the tree, and I ate it.' Then the LORD God said to the woman, 'What is this you have done?' The woman said, 'The serpent deceived me, and I ate'" (Gen. 3:12–13). In a society based on the value of vulnerability as a weakness, where the members seek to avoid being wrong or in error, people will readily practice scapegoating. The Latins even build this scapegoating practice into their language when they blame a thing itself for getting lost rather than explaining that they lost the thing. They say, *"se perdio,"* "it lost itself," whereas in English one would say, "I lost it."

In the opening case study, Helen is in an excellent position to work through her problem. It is in an early stage of development and not yet reinforced by other conflicts. She can accept herself as she is, i.e., a young person pledged to a school subculture where the drinking of alcoholic beverages and dancing are frowned upon, yet one who likes wine and dancing. Further, she can accept any other person in the setting as he is, i.e., enjoying alcoholic beverages and dancing, with no external restriction on either. At this point she can begin seeking out and/or making use of cultural cues that leave her a valid autonomous person in a setting of potential cultural conflict. One such cue is "No thank you," a fully acceptable cue that leaves her principles intact and leaves her in good graces with her hostess. Another is, "I've been bothered lately by alcoholic beverages." Yet another is the direct statement that she has chosen a good college in which to get the best education she can get and that while she is in the school, she has pledged that she will not partake of drinking or dancing. Whatever cue she utilizes and that is effective in leaving her as a person intact yet open to others, i.e., building trust with those about her, is a proper and a useful cue. She can build on this opportunity for further identity and further strength as a person.

However, if Helen proceeds to participate in drinking wine

and dancing, she may find a series of conflicts reinforcing her original conflict. She may question herself as a person of integrity; she may question the school that "put her in such a bind," i.e., the scapegoating route; she may form a counterculture that turns against the school and its pledge; or she may become more and more uncomfortable in the presence of her drinking and dancing friends, thus finding the association unpleasant.

A distinct route is available to her. She can experiment with the amount of participation in each cultural setting that leaves her intact as a person with no sense of guilt. Having achieved such balance, she will then need to moderate her life in such a way that one part brings no reflection on any other part. For this she must remain completely open to setting aside any aspect of any part of her total life that produces such an adverse effect. Granted, this route demands a great deal of maturity and judgment. It is a much better way, however, than the way of guilt, recriminations, and conflict.

Culture Shock

Kalervo Oberg says that *culture shock is precipitated by the anxiety that results from losing all our familiar signs and symbols of social intercourse* (see chapter 15). These signs or cues include the thousand and one ways in which we orient ourselves to the situations of daily life: when to shake hands and what to say when we meet people, when and how to give tips, how to give orders to servants, how to make purchases, when to accept and when to refuse invitations, when to take statements seriously and when not to, and on and on. These cues, which may be words, gestures, facial expressions, customs, or norms, are acquired by all of us in the course of growing up; and they are as much a part of our culture as the language we speak or the beliefs we accept.[3]

Culture shock is the emotional disturbance that results from adjustments to new cultural environment,[4] i.e., to distinctive cues.

The person in culture shock takes flight in one of two directions: either he clings blindly or immovably to his original ways, or he blindly and indiscriminately renounces his former ways and values in favor of the ways and values that are responsible for the culture shock to which he is falling prey (see figure 27). Those who cling to their original ways and values become more and more aggressively antinative, while those caught in the second current "go native." An antinativist tends more and more to pull himself back into his shell of culturally acquired beliefs, attitudes, and behavior. Thus, in his view, the local people must become like him rather than he becoming like them,[5] i.e., the traditionalist of chapter 5.

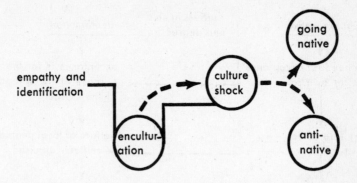

Figure 27. Development of Culture Shock and Reactions to It

Oberg presents two phases of the reactions of the antinativist: frustration and anxiety. First he rejects, and then he regresses. He rejects the environment that causes his discomfort. Regression follows, with the home environment suddenly assuming tremendous importance.

Going native differs from identification in the following ways (see figure 28).

Symptoms of Culture Shock

With the rejection of the host country (antinative), rejection is turned outward toward the host country and its people through endless complaining and faultfinding. Nothing seems to be going right, and all reactions are tinged with bitterness. Rejection of the host country leads to the development of a protective personal isolationism.

With the rejection of the home country (going native), the complaint and criticism may be directed against the home country and all the people one knows there. The rejecter lives a life of imitation of and emotional dependence on the host country and the people he has come to know there. Rejection is directed in a particular way against the mission board, the field executive committee, and the colleagues who put the newcomer in this intolerable situation in the first place. Bitter feelings about real or imagined injustice begin to arise. Field policies are bitterly attacked. Personal failures are blamed on a lack of proper orientation—on the fact that nobody had protected him from this suffering.

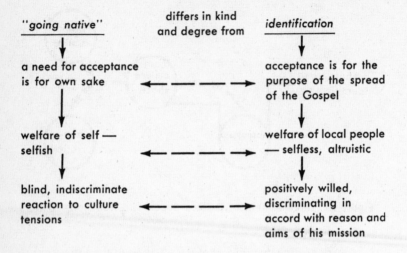

Figure 28. "Going Native" Versus Identification

Rejection may even be focused on God, for it was God who called this person into missionary work and sent him to this place. Consequently, God is to blame for making such a terrible mistake.

Obsessiveness is another symptom of culture shock. An excessive concern over germs and illness may be seen in a compulsive handwasher or a person's refusal to eat food prepared by the nationals for fear of the germs that might be ingested.

Stages of Culture Shock

Oberg discusses four stages[6] through which an individual may go. The first stage is that of *fascination,* where the newcomer has no real contact with the country into which he has moved, because friends or colleagues stand as buffers between him and the problems. He can communicate through his protective buffers.

The second stage is characterized by a *hostile and aggressive attitude toward the host country.* This hostility evidently grows out of the genuine difficulty the individual experiences in the process of adjustment. There are problems with the maid, the school, transportation, shopping, to mention only a few sources of irritation. This is the point where adjustment can go in either of two directions pointed out at the beginning of this section. If one can overcome this crisis and develop a sense of humor (see below), he is able to develop a healthy attitude and adjustment to his new environment. If not, he should leave before he reaches the stage of a nervous breakdown.

The third stage is the ability to develop a *sense of humor*. Instead of criticizing, the person begins to joke about the difficulties he faces. He is on the way to recovery. There is always someone who is worse off than he is. In wanting to help this person, he gains confidence in his ability to speak and get around.

The fourth stage is one of *adjustment*. The individual accepts the customs of the country as just another way of living. He operates within the new environment without a feeling of anxiety. There will always be moments of strain that will disappear only with a complete grasp of all the cues of social intercourse. The individual will understand what the national is saying, but he is not always sure what the national means. With a complete adjustment, he not only accepts the foods, drinks, habits, and customs, but actually begins to enjoy them. When he leaves on furlough, he takes things back with him. If he leaves for good, he generally misses the country and the people to whom he has become accustomed.[7]

Smalley adds an additional stage that is often forgotten by the secular world. This is the dimension of self-discovery, which he defines as the frank facing of utter defeat. With the facing of failure, self-discovery can assist the individual to face reality. One can come to the determination to do one's best in spite of the difficulties, to study hard, to learn well, to refuse to give in to the symptoms of culture shock. One determines to conquer them by developing a degree of bilingualism and biculturalism as fast as possible, even if the pace is slower than he would like.

The Frustration Model

When conflict is carried to an extreme of hopelessness one faces frustration. Within the conflict model, one can at least see a way out, or he can move in some way to reduce the effect of the conflict. He can withdraw either permanently or temporarily. He can form a new group that might ultimately be so therapeutic as to reduce the effect of conflict to a comfortable level. The frustration model applies when there is no conceivable hope of resolution. This appeared to be the model operating during the French Revolution, where the intensity of the conflict within the person and within the subculture built up to such an extent that the French citizen saw no hope and finally lost all sense of the rational and logical. Such a model also operates within a mission field situation or within a church conflict, for example, when a group or a board seeks change, and the field director or pastor poses as the divine representative of God who is not to be opposed.

Working With Conflict

The mistake made in working with conflict is to attempt to eliminate it altogether, or, by doing the wrong things to resolve it, to wind up reinforcing it. Neither of these alternatives is necessary. Tension can be creative within society and can help society accomplish its goals, for this accomplishment grows out of healthy interaction in working with people. When it malfunctions, however, it adds to the deterioration of the group and reinforces the conflict. Thus the task of the agent of change is to observe and correct the malfunction of tension.

The place to begin is in observing the response of irritation. Irritation is generally the first sign of crosscultural conflict, whether within an individual, between individuals and groups, or between groups. Verbal and nonverbal indicators of irritation can be read by the wise counselor (see chapter 17), who can take immediate steps to resolve the source of irritation. A missionary must constantly watch for this irritation in his contact with members of his host society. Being aware of his own irritation can help him focus on cultural difference and set up the learning process that he needs in adapting effectively to the new society. Being aware of the irritation felt by members of the host nation can guide the missionary in effectively presenting the gospel in such a way that cultural impositions are avoided. Unfortunately, so many missionaries are in culture shock during the period when they are needing to be aware of such irritation, that the irritations develop into more serious types of reactions to their ministry. Such irritations caused by crosscultural contact are frequently misinterpreted as spiritual conflict, and valuable clues to effective presentation of the gospel are lost.

Nationalism and nationalistic movements in host nations are signs of conflict. When members of the host nation feel the effect of the narrow ethnocentrism of the guests, they resist and reinforce the boundaries of their own society. The first eight chapters of the Book of Romans share with us the way Paul effectively dealt with such conflict. This can become a model for the missionary in dealing with nationalism and other conflict problems in the mission field.

Summary

Whenever there is culture contact or the contact of subcultures within the larger culture, there is potential for conflict. Such conflict is based on the flow of rejection that encompasses the association of the members of the diverse cultures.

Conflict can have numerous sources. An individual may be caught between an ideal held out to him and what he really is. Also, an individual may be caught in a conflict between himself and another individual or a group. A group may be in conflict with another group. Each of these expressions may have shared similarities, but each conflict develops in a slightly different way. The individual in conflict between the real and ideal finds irritation and reaction developing. In an effort to get out from under this burden, he may seek a means of escape, conform for conformity's sake, search out a scapegoat, or form a new group. Each of these means, when chosen carefully, may provide him with release from the conflict. The danger of such outlets from conflict is that they may reinforce the conflict or add unwanted dimensions to the conflict. The support model provides a healthy means of easing conflict (see chapter 17).

The individual in conflict with a group will find culture shock developing. A group in conflict with a group will find some expression of war developing. Frustration develops when there is conflict yet no means of resolving that conflict.

Questions for Discussion

Relating to the Sending Church

1. What has irritated you over the past twenty-four hours? List the irritations. Rank them in importance to you. Determine which could be caused by cultural differences in groupings or in activities or in values. (Note: You should maintain a list of those things that irritate you or surprise you whenever you enter a distinct culture or subculture. From time to time, seek to ascertain which of these is caused by cultural differences within the setting of contact.)

2. In what ways are you thrown into conflict by the larger society? In what ways does your church put you in conflict? In what ways do you feel tension within your work environment?

3. In what ways do you put those about you into conflict? Your parents? Your teachers or bosses? Your friends?

4. What signs of conflict do you see in the behavior of those about you in your church, home, or place of business?

5. As a pastor, try to remember when you first moved to your present church. Map out the stages of culture shock you faced as you began your ministry. Note time periods for each stage and try to recall the situations and people that aided you in moving through each stage of shock. Parishioners should do this same thing for the pastor so that he will have objective third-party reports to check his own perception.

Relating to the Study of the Bible

1. Study the Book of Daniel to ascertain the degree of culture shock he faced as he was taken captive to Babylon. Study through the first ten chapters of the book to trace the signs from his behavior that he was moving out of shock and adjusting to the life-way of the people.
2. Trace the contacts Jesus had with nonbelievers and try to gauge the degree of conflict he encountered in such relationships.
3. What did Paul have to say about his own personal tensions, i.e., with his weaknesses, etc.?
4. What kinds of things irritated Jesus?
5. Study the lives of the prophets, e.g., Elijah and Elisha, and discover how they used the practice of withdrawal to escape from unwanted conflict.
6. Discuss the case of conflict between Paul and Barnabas over John Mark's joining them for a missionary journey (Acts 15:36–41). Did they handle this well? How might they have handled the conflict in a more loving way? How did John Mark wind up?

Relating to Missions and Crosscultural Ministry

1. How might a well-meaning missionary throw a member of his host society into conflict? a member of a distinct ethnic group? a member of his own mission?
2. Discuss the possibility that Christianity must give first priority to resolving social conflict created by missionaries and church members rather than introducing Jesus Christ.
3. How might the gospel be introduced into a setting of conflict to aid in its resolution?
4. Many people have become displaced in the world and are not living in adequate surroundings. How might the gospel aid them?
5. When conflict arises in the church, are there times that it might be wise to begin a new work with some of the participants in the conflict? Discuss.
6. Observe your new workers and take note of any signs that may indicate that they are in culture shock. Are there any ways that you might help them advance toward adjustment and recovery?

Group Activities and Exercises

1. *Role play*. Select some situation involving family, class, or church, and assign roles accordingly, e.g., father, mother, child, etc., in a family setting. Assign two or three basic values, ranked in terms of dominance, to each of the roles, e.g., father: time, dichotomy; son: event, holism. Role play the family scene as the participants fulfill their assignments. Watch the conflict develop within the skit and be aware of how it accelerates or is reduced by things the participants say and do. Reverse roles.

2. Simulation: Using the exercise entitled "Hidden Agenda" in the Pfeiffer and Jones series,[8] develop a simulation that expresses conflict behavior and its resolution.

3. Panel discussion: Invite some missionaries to the group and ask that they share experiences of conflict they have had with members of their host society and with other missionaries. Especially note in the debriefing period their ways of dealing with the conflict. Also note if they appear to have been the instigators of the conflict or if they have added to the conflict in any way. How might this show in the narration of their part in the conflict?

4. Enter a distinctive subculture and try to spend time in it. Take note of your reactions in terms of Oberg's stages of culture shock (pp. 194–95). Become aware of your feelings and reactions to other people and practices within the setting.

MODEL THREE

THE VALIDITY OF
DISTINCT SOCIETIES

THE VALIDITY OF
DISTINCT SOCIETIES

The model termed "the validity of distinct societies" suggests two main thoughts. First, each society is different and worthy of respect. Second, there are certain tools necessary to make assimilation into another society natural. The model provides intercultural bridges that enable respect to be granted to the distinct society, along with tools of research that allow one to find and use these bridges. There are three submodels.

1. The form/meaning correlation permits the agent of change entering a distinct society or subculture to distinguish between the meaning and its expression, i.e., form.
2. The tools of research applied to each situation permit the agent of change to be aware of difference as well as of the effect of crosscultural contact.
3. The intercultural bridges cause one to start with the meaning and then find the proper, and likely different, form in the new society. These bridges will be called the "tools of relationship."

13

The Form/Meaning Correlation

Case Study: Praise Him With the Dance

One of the major forms of communication in Africa is the dance. Africans dance to gain power and to appease the dead, to celebrate, and to mourn. They seem to us to dance for any excuse whatsoever, and if there is no excuse they dance for the fun of it. Last April in the Camerouns I was riding . . . through a village in the evening just as the moon was coming up. We heard drumbeats—and believe me, I know of little else that has the fascination of the intricate, complicated rhythms of African drums on a moonlit night. We stopped and walked over to the open square where young men were tapping out the beat. A few others were beginning to get itchy in their feet. A couple of fellows were trying out a few steps. (Africans dance individually, of course, and not in the Western manner of ballroom dancing.) We asked what was going on. The bystanders were delighted with our interest and told us that a woman had been buried a year before, the period of mourning was over, and now the family was about to celebrate.

We did not stay to see the celebration because supper was waiting for us at home. But that evening we again heard drums, this time down over the hill from the mission station in the quarters where teachers and students lived. We rushed down, and this time the dance was a game. The fellows were in a circle, dancing and singing, while one in the center acted the fool to make the others laugh. He would then point to someone in the circle who would take his place and try to outdo the previous dancer.

Along with these and many other functions of the dance in Africa is its relation to drama and to other forms of communication. The dance is a major instrument by which Africans transmit values, ideals, emotions, and even history. It is a medium which the African understands. But more than once the African has been rebuffed by the missionary when he has attempted to worship God in dance—or, for that matter, even to tell the Good News in this most natural form of communication.

For example, a foreigner, an important church lady, was visiting the mission and church. Because the visitor was a woman, the African women of the area wanted to put on something very special for her, and so they worked out a dance-drama in which they portrayed the history of their contacts with Christianity. This was to be an expression of their appreciation for the fact that the missionaries had come to them.

They started out by portraying themselves naked—a bunch of leaves in front and another behind as their only clothing. This is the way they often dress in the fields and in out-of-the-way places where they are not likely to be seen by outsiders. Then the missionaries came to their country. There was an elaborate, intricate story unfolding and a quickening in tempo until they ended up by going to church in their brightest-colored, new cotton finery.

But the sight of these African women—nearly naked—dancing so enthusiastically, their whole bodies bouncing with every violent step, and their breasts flapping, was too much for the visitor. She berated them for this "heathen" display, unworthy of Christians. The poor Christian women were stunned, hurt, crestfallen, ashamed. This offering of thanks, this testimony of their gratitude to God and to the missionaries, this act of worship—far more real, far more deeply felt than most of our perfunctory acts of worship—had been so cruelly rejected by the distinguished visitor.

Fortunately, this sort of thing has not always been the case. There have been instances of missionaries who have been perceptive to the power and function of African dance and drama in communication, and who have encouraged them to splendid advantage.[1]

Form Distinct From Meaning

All social units consist of some basic meaning and a way of expressing that significance. *We will call this combination of meaning and expression of meaning the form/meaning correlation.* Language is a symbolic system and utilizes certain verbal and written forms to express meaning. Culture is a symbolic system that encompasses all of life, including the language one speaks. Items that identify it, activities, and values, are all expressions of some deeper meaning that lies within the culture and is expressed in social interaction.[2] As in our opening case study, the dominant symbolic system of the North American missionaries was language. For the Africans, it was drama/dance. Body movement, change of costume, and the depiction of historical progression by dramatic representation all communicated the same content of message, yet with greater impact on the lives of the African. The symbolic references of the drama/dance hit home in a way words and language were unable to. We termed the African lifestyle trend "event" or "visual" in chapter 11. The utilization of distinct symbolic systems in the African setting was no problem. The problem lay in the conflict of systems brought about by a unilateral decision on the part of a representative of one of the systems. By this means, she sought to control the behavior of the participants, manipulating such behavior for her own ends rather than for the good of the others.

People respond to what they perceive as reality. For example, they will see a large, leafy growing thing, and by agreement with others with whom they interact, will call it a tree or an *arbol,* depending on whether they speak English or Spanish. Again, depending on association patterns, a large growing thing can be called "tree" and something smaller, "bush." In Pocomchi, both large and small may be responded to with the word *che.* They are responding to the same reality that the speaker of English responds to, but they have a distinct form/meaning composite. Thus the English-speaking person uses "tree" or "bush," but the Pocomchi-speaking person uses only *"che."*

Were society not to use a symbolic system, we would be continually faced with one challenge after another to know how and what to say or do when confronted with a large growing thing or a small growing thing, or, for that matter, with any other aspect of reality. Language and the larger culture which gives it birth, as symbolic systems, thus are a convenience to us. They save us considerable time and energy in decision making so that we can expend those commodities on new and creative activities.

Language As a Symbolic System

In reality, language has two distinct symbolic systems operating: the verbal and the written. The two may or may not coincide, depending on society's response to the spoken language and the degree of training its members have had in preparing a scientific orthography for the writing of the spoken language. For example, the Spanish language is controlled by a commission that makes orthographic changes whenever there is some phonological (sound) change in the structure of the language. The symbols of Spanish thus more closely coincide with the actual phonics of the language than do, say, English symbols. An English *a* represents a number of different phonetic sounds. For example, note the different *a* sounds in "father," "rat," "share," and "amount." All the sounds of *a* are represented by the same symbol.

All of language grows out of the lived experience and represents some aspect of that lived experience. The spoken language is the basic symbolic system that is then taken and formally symbolized by the writing technique, or orthography. This symbolization passes from generation to generation, and everyone entering the society, either by birth or by migration, is expected to learn that symbolic system.

Any given symbolic system is adequate for handling all the needs of the society. In the past, some have argued that certain languages were superior to others in terms of their symbolic representation. Categories of thought, represented by members of a society, naturally divide the total spectrum of life into those divisions that can be grasped and symbolized. Such categories of thought are definitive for each society and permit that society to interact with the sum of experiences confronting it. If two systems of representation do not coincide, they appear to represent two different realities. Such is not necessarily the case; they are just different. For example, the North American distinguishes a proliferation of colors and shades, whereas the Pocomchi uses five basic colors and one "noncolor" to represent color reality. He has no lack in meeting any challenge of color put to him by either his environment or his society. The North American looks at a cornfield and talks about the experience with a more limited vocabulary than the Pocomchi, who can use a full range of vocabulary in distinguishing the various parts of the corn field, the different growth stages of the corn, and the various conditions of corn growth. The American system is not inferior because it uses fewer symbols for the same reality. The Pocom system is not superior for its greater range of symbolic reference, nor is the American system superior for its greater range of color differentiation. They are different systems but equally valid within their own culture setting.

Culture As a Symbolic System

A person's life-way is expressed through a complex symbolic system. The flag of a nation stands for its integrity and identity. Heroes are representative of the highest values of a society. A stop sign is a symbol of traffic control, as are yellow lines in the middle of the street. Uniforms are symbolic of a person's status or role within a society. Bookshelves placed horizontally are symbols of control, symbolic of a society's need for order in the arrangement of books and periodicals. The way one dresses signals modesty or vulgarity. Uncovered female breasts are part of the enduring identity of certain Africans and have no necessary vulgar or sexual connotation in such a context, however, they do for most Westerners.

The question frequently arises, Which comes first, the symbol or the lived experience? The lived experience is prior to the representation of the experience and in essence gives it birth. Something within interpersonal relations in a society calls for an expression of those interpersonal relationships. This expression can be by language, by touch, by association or relationship, or by any combination of these factors.

There is no symbolic reference, however, unless both meaning and form are present. If the form exists without the meaning, then the form is sterile and is referred to as a "survival" by anthropologists.[3] If the meaning exists without the form, the members of the society run the risk of being miscued regarding the significance of the event. In certain Mayan areas in Central America, small crosses adorn the peaks of the roofs of the houses. When asked about them, the people are at a loss to explain the meaning. One can conjecture that they have something to do with the invasion of Catholic Christianity at the time of the discovery and exploration of the New World. There is no remembrance of such among the people themselves, and they are quick to admit that they have no idea what the crosses stand for. Again, for example, as one reads the King James Version of the Scriptures, he encounters numerous survivals that need explanation. The dynamics of change have left many of the words of this version devoid of vital meaning to the average speaker of contemporary English. Thus these words have to be explained, and one of the the major roles of the minister has come to be that of explaining the words of Scripture. This does not mean that the King James Version is wrong or that it is wrong to use it. Rather, it simply means that readers must become their own translators or must leave that role to a professional, i.e., the minister.

Whenever a strictly literal translation, i.e., a word-for-word translation, of the Bible is produced, the form is wholly present, but the meaning may be deficient or garbled. Even a grammatical translation is inadequate, since it does little more than extend the literalness throughout the grammatical system of the language and not just to the words alone. A more vital translation is a conceptual one, where the concepts are translated across cultural boundaries. Such a translation is a dynamic equivalence translation. However, the translator frequently pays more attention to the culture into which the Word is being translated than to the text of Scripture itself. The most adequate translation is a life-way, or fidelity impact, translation in which both the words and the concepts are true to the Scriptures, but in which the same impact is felt on the present hearer as was felt by the original hearer when the Word of God was first presented. The translator is thus being completely true to the receiving culture, and every truth of Scripture is accurately stated and developed.

Generating Language From the Lived Experience

Most people living within society experience only the process of socialization that gives them a language to speak or a total culture to live by. The language or culture is then experienced "after the fact," and the excitement of developing new forms to coincide with dynamic meaning is lost to the average person. Occasionally, within a person's life span, new forms do develop from the lived experience itself. If a person is able to recognize what is happening, he can get a small look into the development of the symbolic system. Such occurred during the sixties with the generating of the word "happening." Life gained a new significance based on event orientation. People would be together in a social way and not be having a party (a party needs careful planning and organization), or in a political or a religious way and not be having a meeting (a meeting calls for a beginning and ending point as well as planned progression). "Party" and "meeting" are words coded to the culture of time orientation. They are linguistic symbols that have grown out of time orientation to life by which a party or a meeting is planned and scheduled, starts and stops, with its parts timed so that a certain amount of time is spent doing one thing and a certain amount is spent doing another. For people with event orientation, "party" and "meeting" would be totally inadequate as symbolic representations, so "happening" developed to represent the event nature of their experience, i.e., just being, and being together. Prior to the application of this term to the experience itself, there was meaning and significance within the interpersonal relationship, but this was not formally represented in language. For a period of time, an uneasiness ensued that came from doing or being something that did not have symbolic expression. Once being or experience produced the formal, understood expression, the unease and the ambiguity diminished.

In the early stages of the development of a social group, a club, or an informal grouping of people, there may be no name assigned to the group; and for a while, it may be referred to by a descriptive term of what the members are doing. For example, "They are the ones who stand at the corner of such and such a street." From time to time, there might be some problem that arises while they are standing there, e.g., someone is accosted. Later on they may be termed a "gang." Once they are named, the larger description is unnecessary. The formal naming has done away with the need for description.

In every language or cultural setting, the society operates to see that the expression of what is significant corresponds to the meaning. A society operating efficiently continually adapts to the dynamic change, making symbolic adjustments, and thus keeping the form/meaning composite intact. A society that is traditionalist or that has traditionalistic members will tend to thwart the change process, so forms become fixed and established. The vital flow of change is blocked or restricted, causing the society to become static or to "dry up." Such is the case in some conservative Evangelical churches where the people are resistant to the idea of change in their musical program, for example. Contemporary music can only creep into the services of the church. It is rejected out of hand until some significant leader endorses it or until the young people modify it in some way, making it more acceptable, or even until the older generation gets used to the sound. This happened with jazz, then with pop, and then with rock and roll. In some settings guitar music was played in an informal service, but the more formal music of the church was reserved for the "real" worship service. Each group needs to establish and maintain its own identity. They must also, however, be willing to live with the result of alienation of the youth generation as has happened frequently over the past decades. Youth's style of music becomes established and accepted when they are the leaders of the church, and then they resist change and tend to alienate their own youth in turn.

Summary

The form/meaning composite concept causes us to approach structural units as a combination of meaning and a dynamic way of expressing this meaning. Language is a symbolic system with two subsystems, the verbal and the written. A language maintaining the form/meaning correlation forces change of form in keeping with the dynamic process of the society. Culture is the larger framework within which language operates and which, in fact, gives birth to language. Cultural expressions in which there is form without meaning are called survivals. Cultural expressions in which there is meaning, but with no formal symbolic expression, will in time develop one. The form is generated in keeping with meaning, the normal process of change within society.

Questions for Discussion

Relating to the Sending Church

1. Which forms or rituals of your church, in your opinion, are timely and vital? Which are static and dead?
2. Are there words spoken in the church service that you have difficulty understanding and thus need explanation as to what they mean? Are there words in the Bible that you do not understand? Discuss what these are.
3. Are there words in school that you would like to ask your teacher to explain, yet you hesitate, thinking that everyone else knows and understands them? Discuss.
4. Have you ever participated in making up a code or a special language? Did this tend to bring you closer to the friend that helped you develop it? How did you feel speaking a language no one else could understand?
5. Discuss the so-called generation gap in terms of difference of language, music, values, etc.
6. Select one situation in your life when you were quite upset because of some misunderstanding. Discuss how a functioning form/meaning correlation could have averted some of your problems.

Relating to the Bible

1. Name the languages in which the parts of the Bible were written. How do you think the cultures of these languages might differ? How might the various cultures and frames of reference of the translators affect the version of the Bible that you read?
2. Did God establish a new language for the Bible, or did he utilize the languages the writers naturally spoke? How might his action affect the translation of the Bible you are using?
3. Take words like "remnant" in the Bible and discuss possible meanings, e.g., a left-over piece of cloth, whatever was left after a sale, a portion of God's people left over, and discuss how contemporary usage of words serves as a help or hindrance to an understanding of God's Word.

4. Take a portion of the Bible that is familiar to you and try to write it in the speech forms you use everyday. How does it sound to you? Does it sound irreverent? sacrilegious? trite? Realize that God spoke to the people of Bible times in the natural speech that they used in their day-to-day relationships.

5. List some of the symbols that we use to represent our belief in God and our Christian faith, e.g., fish, cross, dove. Search out the stories in the Bible that deal with these symbols. Are they used in the same way in the Bible that they are used today?

6. Does the Scripture passage "Man looks at the outward appearance, but the LORD looks at the heart" (1 Sam. 16:7) have any relevance to our discussion? Discuss.

Relating to Missions and Crosscultural Ministry

1. In your language learning, what words and concepts were especially difficult for you? Were they difficult because the form was hard or because the meaning was different from the way you were accustomed to thinking? Explain.

2. Select a half dozen words from the native language of your ministry area and try to express their meaning in English. (Note: In the translation process, this is called a "back translation.")

3. Sit down with a speaker of the language who has been a believer for a year or more. Inquire as to his or her understanding of the gospel. Try to get this person to speak without your prompting him or her. Do you feel comfortable with the things this person says to you, or are you upset by them? Do not let your attitude show, for you close off the natural flow of his thinking that you must become aware of.

4. Take the best translation of the Bible you have and sit with an unbeliever. Have that person explain to you what the Bible says, that is, what that person perceives it says. You are likely to become aware of errors in the translation, obscure usage, etc. You may even find some simple ways of explaining what is there.

5. Using the Greek, attempt to translate portions of Scripture without going through English. Does it come out the same as when you use English? Explain.

6. Have you encountered any survivals in your language or culture? Explain.

Group Activities and Exercises

1. *Role play.* Take a setting quite common to the members of the group and role play an experience using language characteristic of some other distinct setting, e.g., a church service in street-corner speech, or a weather forecast in "sacred" speech, etc.

2. *Activity*. Let the members of the group participate in a "blind walk" during which time one person serves as "eyes" for another (ten minutes is adequate time for a walk, five minutes out with one leading the other and five minutes back for the other to lead the first). Debrief the experience with such questions as: When did your eyes pop open or try to open? What did this tell you about your "eyes"? What kinds of cultural cues were needed to direct the one without the eyes? What did you do to compensate for lack of sight? The group members have moved in this experience from a sighted subculture to a sightless one. They are in need of new forms to express new meanings. Did this process work during the blind walk? (This exercise is an excellent one for illustrating the trust bond of chapters 1–5).

3. *Activity*. Let the members of the group participate in a nonverbal experience. By twos or threes, with at least one girl in each group if possible, have the group members go somewhere nearby and attempt to purchase something or gain a favor. Permit them to arrange beforehand any nonverbal cues they will need for directions and other challenges they might anticipate. Then when they begin the experience, *insist that they do not speak*. During the debriefing session, probe the kinds and usages of cues they developed as they proceeded with the experience. What kinds of reactions did they encounter? How did they feel about the experience?

4. *Skit*. First depict some aspect of Old Testament worship. Then take the same aspect of worship and show how it is done today.

14

Tools of Research

Most North Americans are acquainted with library research in which one chooses a book and takes from it information relating to his area of interest. Few Americans, however, are acquainted with the full scope of behavioral science research which involves primarily people. Most Americans do know something about scientific research and how it is carried on. *A hypothesis is made and then refined regarding some matter of concern in the field of chemistry, physics, biology, botany, or some other area, such as human behavior. When refined sufficiently, it becomes a working hypothesis which is confirmed by further experimentation.* For example, one hypothesis suggested that the earth was round. The hypothesis was tested and was proven to be accurate. The previous hypothesis that the earth was flat had to be discarded in favor of the new one.

The basis of behavioral science research is also a hypothesis.[1] Scientists observe a certain behavior and assign it a scientific explanation. This explanation or hypothesis is not a fact nor a final opinion. It merely provides reference points to open up more and more insight into the behavior observed or experienced. It develops when greater insights and more information are acquired concerning the circumstances and behavior of the event.

For example, one can observe a person walking down the street. He might then form a hypothesis that the people of that culture walk when they are on the street. However, this particular hypothesis for observing American society proves inadequate, as he may later observe a person driving down the street in an automobile. The original hypothesis is refined to include Americans walking as part of a larger complexity of walking and driving. The hypothesis would likely not include, at least at this writing, an American flying down the street. It might be expanded, however, to express some comparison of American street activity with that of Latin America, for example. The emerging hypothesis would be that the Latin American walks on the street more than does the North American.

Observing one person walking does not imply that anyone else will be seen walking. The original hypothesis involving one person walking is expanded upon seeing a second person walk, then a third, then a fourth, and so on. If one were to do a thoroughgoing statistical study based on the walking scene, he would take detailed records of all of those walking. He would then do the same for driving. Such a study, however, does not tell him why the persons were walking or driving. Some may have been walking because they chose to, others were on a health kick, others may have had no other means of transportation, still others may not have had a license to operate a motor vehicle. Participant observation has thus yielded to the interview technique to get a supportive, though different, kind of result.

The program of research would also investigate whether only lower-status people were walking while upper-status people were doing something else. Such research in North America would likely find this particular point relatively insignificant, whereas in the Philippines, it would be highly significant. In American society, anyone of any station in life can walk or ride. However, in the Philippines, the upper-status people will own their own vehicle whether they can afford it or not. They will do all in their power to avoid being seen riding a motorcycle with sidecar, a common means of transport somewhat equivalent to our taxi, and they wish never to be seen walking. A lower-status person will not be able to own his own vehicle but will ride a motorcycle with sidecar and will not hesitate to walk. The fact that a person owns his own vehicle, however battered it is, is a validating sign of his higher status. If he rides a motorcycle with sidecar, then he is admitting to being of lower status than people may have perceived him to be. Status is tied in with influence—that is, the higher one's status, the greater the influence. Therefore, where one is perceived to be on the status ladder is crucial. Outsiders, including many missionaries, have not realized the importance of status in ministry. They have walked or ridden the motorcycle with sidecar and then wondered why they had little influence with the upper-status members of Filipino society.

The researcher continues to refine his hypothesis until he has a

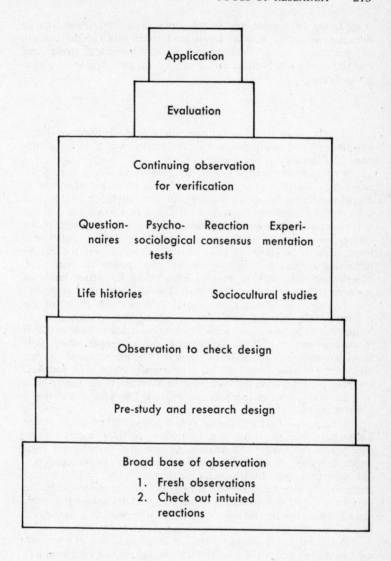

Figure 29. A Master Plan for Behavioral Science Research

(Begin at the bottom block and read upward)

complexity of hypotheses which open meaningful patterns of behavior within the society. Every person entering a second culture or subculture needs flexible and practiced research tools and methods so he can become aware of who the person is with whom he is dealing.

The Tools

The tools of research aiding in developing refined, working hypotheses are participant observation, interviewing, experimentation, and archiving (see figure 29).

Participant observation lies at the base of all sound behavioral scientific research.[2] One must observe the behavior of others in given situations in order to hypothesize anything about that behavior. Observation, in and of itself, can be carried out without participation in the society: one can look in on the members of the society. However, as we saw in the study of society as system, it is impossible to be truly objective in observation unless the person observing is also participating within the system. In this way, observation can provide a solid foundation for other kinds of research. By itself, however, it provides only beginning hypotheses. The outside observer in Central America sees many of the Indian people learning Spanish and attempting to change from Indianness to Spanishness. Such an observer is led to believe that it is only a matter of time before the Indian people make their transition fully into the Spanish life-way. The participant observer, however, entering more fully into the Indian system as it operates, and seeing all the ways the traditional culture draws the Indian back into its ways, knows the process will take decades if not many generations.

One point of critical choice comes to the Indian at about age forty. It is near this time that he makes his final decision as to whether he will enter the Spanish system and give up his own Indian life-way. In thirteen years of contact with one such group, I did not find one Indian male who made the choice to go permanently into the Spanish society. Before the age of forty, he may have toyed with the idea, changed his clothes, operated with the *revestidos,* but by the age of forty, he had become a confirmed Indian, leaving the choice now to his children.

A second, more intensive kind of research is that of *interviewing.*[3] In the interview process, the interviewer works with a subject in a way that elicits responses or answers to questions. The interviewer may choose a formal approach utilizing a questionnaire or an informal approach as in a verbal interview that is more like a conversation. The oral interview can proceed in a structured or an unstructured way. In a structured interview, the questions will be prepared in advance and posed to the respondent. In an unstructured interview, the interviewer will simply let the respondent talk as he wishes on a given subject, following his own chain of thought. Any questions posed to him arise out of the progression of the respondent's thought. Interviews can be conversational—a very natural, relaxed way of interviewing, even to the point of the respondent not knowing he is being interviewed. Or they can be direct and posed, giving the respondent a feeling of being interviewed. Interviewing builds on the base of participant observation and grows out of what was found in the preliminary research conducted accordingly.

A third kind of behavioral science research is that of *experimentation*.[4] Experimentation takes the basic information provided and tests it. Such testing may take place on animals, as in certain psychological experimentations, and on persons in carefully controlled situations. The testing is designed to see if the information on which hypotheses are based is valid, correct, effective, and useful. In experimentation, one takes the step of proving in actual life that the research findings are valid. Careless applications of experimentation infringe on the human rights of the objects of the experimentation. Sound research will always honor the rights of the persons involved and, as much as possible, reveal to the persons involved the full expression of these rights.

Archiving is a fourth kind of research available to the behavioral scientist. Archiving involves materials that are already produced, whether they are highly unstructured materials, such as bodies of records in some institution or a book that has already thoroughly processed the data. The library is the center of the archiving research, though documents useful in such research can be found anywhere: in attics, in offices, in personal letters. Archiving is to the behavioral scientist a means of reinforcing, correcting, or adding to his own research. It follows and expands field research but is not to be used as the only or final word.

Research Design

The tools of research can be especially useful and, in fact, vital to the new missionary in the field or to a veteran missionary in a new field. In such situations, they must be worked with openly and thoroughly. The veteran missionary in a continuing ministry has been doing such research throughout his ministry, often without knowing it and usually in an inconsistent and partial way. *It is wise to project a design prior to entering a new culture or subculture and then to modify it as experience grows in the field of ministry.* The design must include an a⁴equate methodology, tools worked thoroughly and consistently into the methodology, and an analytic model capable of handling sociocultural data. An example of such a design follows:

1. Build a broad base of objective observation, seeing the people as they are, not as you think they should be. Be concerned with all the little things that go to make up the everyday life of the people. It is out of these observations that the sketches of your research will gain fullness.

2. You will be engaged in a sociocultural program of research. This involves the total man in his total society. Your village or neighborhood can be considered the total society, and it is wise to concentrate, especially in the early stages, on one or two individuals in that group. The others will all be there, but it is too confusing to try to extend detailed research beyond just a few. Such extension can come later on in research. For this second stage of research, however, you will be interested in elicited material drawn from the lives of the people closest to you. Such materials can be gained by specific questioning, keeping the following possible sources in mind:

a. Make use of your own background. As long as you recognize that the society will be basically different from your own, there is no harm in assuming that some aspects of the society will be the same as, or somewhat like, yours. This is a starting point only. For example, it is safe to assume that there is some institution responsible for the education, i.e., enculturation of the children. Probe to see just what institution in the society is designed to handle this. Is it the family or an age-level system? These points of similarities in cultures are called "universals." Among the Pocomchi, the family takes responsibility for early enculturation, and the *cofradia,* or religious brotherhood, takes responsibility for later education. In the Philippines, this later education is taken on by the public and private school systems, which have both differences and similarities to our own.

b. Get the individual to respond to specific questions about pictures you show him. *Time* magazine is available to most missionaries, but its black and white pictures are poor for this type of project. *National Geographic* pictures are in color and are thus more useful. Children's picture puzzles provide simple pictures and a bonus besides, in that the people can begin to develop certain eye-to-hand coordination useful in further education. People unaccustomed to using pictures must learn to read them much as they learn to read a book.

c. Plan some simple tests to get reaction. For example, prepare one of their own food dishes and ask the people to tell you what you did right and wrong. Have them help you prepare the food dish now and you will have a chance to observe the process more objectively.

d. Ask your language helper to act out some aspect of the culture that may not take place while you are there or that you may not have the opportunity to see in its entirety.

3. As you let the above activity flow out like an ink blot, not trying to guide it in a particular direction at any one time, you will begin to get a feel for various aspects of the whole. Begin to sketch the various relationships between people and groupings of people, the activities they carry on, and any interrelationships of values discovered. Include as many of the basic values categories as possible in your preliminary sketch. This need not be complete or sophisticated; a simple sketch or outline will do. By this time you should have hit upon the aspect of the society that serves as a key to all the rest; for example, the age-level groupings are typical of an African society, and the *cofradia* is a key grouping within Pocomchi society. From this point on, the whole of a given culture will begin to make sense. A point of focus has been discovered around which other patterns will form.

4. During the next stage of research, concentrate on specialized elicited material.

a. Select words or concepts that you met in the first three stages and suggest one word or concept at a time to your language helper. Let him respond as he wishes. It is immaterial whether he talks at length or for only a brief time. As you get more and more information, you will continue selecting stimulus words and getting short texts in response to the stimuli.

b. Ask for the life history of the language helper.

c. Secure ethnographic texts as contained in text collections.[5]

d. Learn as much about the folklore as you can. This is of help more for understanding the past than the present, for it reflects the development of values within the society.

e. Have the language helper make a map of his area.

f. Have the language helper draw pictures of cultural items. He may emphasize some part of the item that will give you a clue as to the importance of that part in the larger society.

g. Have the language helper write texts or even type them when working with someone with such abilities.

5. This stage is a transition stage from participant observation practices and elicitation techniques to a structured analysis. Make a list of all the differences you have encountered between your own society and that of your language helper. Use your imagination!

Make an exhaustive list. Spare nothing. This is vitally important to carrying out the next stage.

6. Begin a structured analysis. Refer back to chapters 6 and 7 for models influenced by sociological and anthropological theorists. These provide you with underlying principles of social theory that enable you to do a thoroughgoing analysis. Also refer back to chapters 9 to 11 for aid in filling in your item identification of the culture, the activities participation, and the underlying values and motivations of the people. Include as much as you can of the ecological setting as well with details of the physical world and demography, etc. Also, be aware of the ways different products of the culture, e.g., tools, structures, and clothing, pattern into ever larger wholes and complexes within the society and the ways they interpenetrate the structural aspects of the culture.

Once you have your lists, outlines, texts, etc., as complete as possible, select a unit of focus, e.g., the family. Define it in terms of the tools used by the family, names given the family, privacy expected and carried out, interests expressed, means of perpetuation, and so on. Consider variants of the unit, the varying sizes of families, the allowable variation in the tools of the family (we have the refrigerator and stove as obligatory tools in our society, but the freezer is optional). Contrast the family with an economic team and then with a religious team of the same perceived complexity. Then attempt to arrange your institutional and structural units on levels of complexity with those less complex on lower levels and those more complex on higher levels. Continue checking the distribution and interaction of the family within the society. Seek to ascertain how the family functions to fill needs within the society, what structures develop around the filling of such needs, and how such structures define the larger whole.

Next, select a complex of activities, e.g., burial activities. Seek to determine the beginning, the parts of continuation, and the close of the complex of activities. See if you can find units of structure in the complex of activities that are the same. Identify the various units of structure of the activities in keeping with unique parts, details of participation, and expression of the experience.

Then select a pattern of values, again identifying such a pattern in terms of its unique features, the variation of expression of the value, and the extent of its acceptance in the social grouping. Follow this with a sketch of the basic values model, using the procedures of profiling, dominance, and generation to see how such motivations of behavior are able to structure and interpenetrate the activities and identities of the culture.

You will not get very far in this particular study in a few months, but you should try for at least a sampling of each and then try to develop one area of structure more thoroughly, e.g., institutions, activities, or values.

7. Do extensive reading in your selected field. Be discriminating in your reading so that others' errors will not be perpetuated in your work. The same rule holds true for reading material. The publications a researcher reads before going into the field must be taken "with a grain of salt" so that he is not unduly influenced by them. They must be respected, but there are many ways the material may be misleading. The author may have been an ineffective researcher, the group may have changed, a different line-up of language helpers may have produced quite different results, or the material may have been processed by someone who did not have the same conceptual model as the researcher.

8. At this stage of the program, you should bring to mind or search out definitive suggestions for the introduction of the gospel into your particular group (evangelism and church planting), for the organization of a church, and for the setting up of an educational program. Each of these intentions must be carried out in light of the uniqueness of the society. Just because something worked somewhere else does not mean that it will work in every setting. Respecting and utilizing differences provides stepping-stones to truth. The sociocultural setting is our friend, not our enemy. Let's make it a good friend.

9. Check all findings and conclusions with the results of linguistic analysis. Cultural and linguistic analysis are vitally interrelated, and one cannot be considered apart from the other.

Before moving on to a case study that illustrates the research approach that underlies ministry, a few practical suggestions are called for. In this day and age, it is wise to tape all material that you possibly can unless you find it is too distracting to the people with whom you are working. Video-tape is also useful in certain situations. Do not develop a formal research approach with formal vocal expression and too formalized questions or inquiries. Get close to the people, and let friendships grow. Develop a researcher's memory. It is not wise to immediately write down material you are collecting from someone unless you are in a formal interview situation. As soon as possible after the encounter, write down all the information you can remember. You should never leave an interaction unrecorded overnight. Never throw out any field notes, however preliminary they may seem to you. When you go into a new setting, of course your reactions will be unsophisticated. There are times, however, in the analytical process, that you will want to consult these notes to see if you have overlooked anything important.

Case Study in Research: Tagalog, Philippines

A researcher entered a distinct society, the Tagalog, in the Philippines. To aid him in his participant observation, he moved into a Philippine home. After a few days of meeting people, a pattern began to emerge. About 80 percent of the people he met during the first few days were members of the family, i.e., relatives of the immediate nuclear family with whom he was living. The other 20 percent seemed to have some special relationship to the immediate family, something the researcher became aware of but could not resolve at the moment. All of the people met were not only individually named, but their relationship to the family was noted, e.g., "Maria Fernandez, my mother's brother's daughter's child." The intricacies of consanguinal and affinal relationship were always spelled out. Besides, another pattern was beginning to emerge that tied into the more obvious one. Different people were encountered in different places in the home. It appeared that the servant girls, the members of the immediate family, and the parents of the husband and wife, had access to all parts of the house. The researcher, as a guest, had access to his room and the living and dining rooms. The brothers and sisters of the hosts were "at home" in the living area of the first floor, but they never went to the second floor where the bedrooms were. Those to whom the researcher responded as nonrelated but important to the family were comfortable in the living room and ventured cautiously into the dining room and office, but they did not go farther. Whenever they were in the house at all, they were polite, waiting for indication that they could go here or there, whereas the blood relatives did not have this restraint. Finally, there was a continual progression of other people, some reaching the porch, but most of them remaining at the gate.

Participant observation suggested the beginning hypothesis: Family, including both the nuclear and the extended family, is very important to the Tagalog. This was quickly expanded: The extended family is as important as, if not more important in some ways, than the nuclear family in the development of relationships. Also, in some ways there are friends who are more important than other people.

By means of the interview process, the researcher confirmed the initial observation. A series of more formal questions was prepared and administered to a number of Tagalog. This bit of questionnaire/interview research confirmed that there were three categories of people: (1) family, (2) close friends tied into family, and (3) others. The kinds of questions used during this stage of research were as follows: With whom do you associate on social occasions? How frequently do you see your relatives? Are they considered important to you? In what order would you respond in an emergency—to a blood relative, to a member of your "alliance," to a friend, or to a stranger? A second type of survey was used, with questions such as: Anyone who fails in a commitment to his relatives is a bad person (agree or disagree).

Simple, nonmanipulative experiments were conducted with these hypotheses in mind, and all of the former developments in research results were confirmed. The family appeared to be a very important part of the Tagalog life. Finally, with archiving, the full extent of the family influence began to emerge. Further research of the earlier types also confirmed or corrected the reading material. The archiving produced a name for the extended family plus close friends brought into the family through the machinery of god-parenthood, i.e., the "alliance." Continued work with the alliance showed it to be the dominant institution of Filipino society influencing all social, religious, economic, and especially political concerns.

Summary

Someone studying a society previously unknown to him (or even one in which he has participated) needs tools of research to enable him to observe objectively the experience of the members of the culture. Such tools are participant observation, interviewing, experimentation, and archiving. Participant observation is the primary tool of the social anthropologist. He enters the other society and keeps his eyes and ears open. By applying conceptual models, he sees things that others would tend to overlook. In this way, he objectively puts together material available to him from the behavior of people. Others who are involved subjectively in the experience tend to overlook significant structural keys to the society in which they minister.

Interviewing through formal and informal means is the primary tool of the sociologist. Interviews may be verbal or written (questionnaires). They may be structured in such a way that all the questions are prepared beforehand or unstructured in the sense that questions flow from the interview itself.

Experimentation is a basic tool of the psychologist. A hypothesis yields certain conclusions, and these are tested in a simulated experience. An agent of change must come to terms with the process of experimentation if he desires to impact the people. Yet, at the same time, he cannot take advantage of the people with whom he is ministering.

Archiving is the research tool with which most people are familiar. It is used in perhaps 98 percent of the American educational system as the major means of research. It involves books and other written materials. Archiving is the primary tool of the historian. Archiving confirms and expands the other research findings.

A person entering a new culture or subculture for the purpose of ministry needs research training, tools, and approaches lest he try to cast these people into his own cultural mold. In the field, research must be carried out constantly and carefully so that one can know deeply and effectively the people with whom he interacts. Without such a research mentality, he will constantly misinterpret words and actions directed to him and thus build up a resentment toward his hosts.

Questions for Discussion

Relating to the Sending Church

1. How can effective research aid in decision making? hinder decision making?
2. How might effective, ongoing research aid the pastor in his work? the youth director? the music director?
3. How might effective research have resolved more quickly the conflict between adults and youth in the 60s and 70s?
4. How might tools of participant observation aid the pastor in preparing his sermons, without revealing confidences?
5. How might the interview process aid the church staff in measuring the spiritual growth of the lay people?

Relating to the Study of the Bible

1. In what ways did Jesus carry out effective research? Paul? James?
2. How might the experience of Paul on Mar's Hill (Acts 17:16–31) have been the result or outcome of effective research?
3. How did Boaz carry out research (Ruth 2–4)? How did Nehemiah (Neh. 2)? How did Daniel (Dan. 1)?
4. Design an interview of Adam and Eve with God that might have had a more satisfying outcome (Gen. 3:9–21).
5. Name five biblical characters who impress you as being objective in their relationships with others. What do you think the reasons for this were? Consider more than the obvious reason that God was with them.

Relating to Mission and Crosscultural Ministry

1. In what ways might effective research aid in our task of mission?

2. How do missions carry out sound research in their programs? Name some that do. How has this helped them? Ask them!
3. Does research necessarily detract from the work of the Holy Spirit? Discuss.
4. Could effective research aid a missionary returning home to do deputation? Explain.
5. What seems to be the key (or keys) that unlock the culture in which you are carrying out mission?

Group Activities and Exercises

1. *Simulation.* Koko Kolo is a scientific hypothesizing game available from the Associates of Urbanus. It involves the development and continual refinement of a hypothesis during the progress of the game. Twenty to forty group members can play it during an hour period and have time for a short debriefing.
2. *Participant observation.* Have each student become part of a new sociocultural setting and see how much he can determine of the system operating in that setting. Use a setting in the urban complex, a store, a distinct school experience such as a Montessori school, etc.
3. *Interviewing.* Have each group member try two or three unstructured interviews with a member of a different culture, and from this experience have him construct from five to ten questions that he might administer to other people to check his original findings. This does not need to be complex. It will reveal something of the need for staging in research and will give the person doing the research a sense of discovery.
4. *Experimentation.* Have each group member attempt some experiment that he can follow up by observing the behavior of the people involved, e.g., maintain excessive eye contact upon greeting, eat with the British method of filling one's inverted fork by pushing it against the knife, etc.
5. *Archiving.* Consult Louis Luzbetak, *The Church and Cultures,* for some excellent ideas for library research as it relates to missions.

15

Tools of Relationship

Case Study: The Dead Dog

One day at the dormitory where we were houseparents in Congo, there was a dead dog in need of burying, as it was attracting flies and becoming a health hazard. I asked Sebuhire, one of our hired pagan Banyaruanda helpers to bury the dog and then asked if he understood. He replied that he did, and then he disappeared around the dorm, supposedly to fetch a shovel. Several hours passed, and I happened upon the dead dog once again.

"Sebuhire! That dog hasn't been buried yet, and every moment it remains unburied it represents a greater danger to the health of the children. Please bury him immediately! *Unasikia?* [You hear?]"

"Ndio, Bwana! [Yes, Sir!]," he said as he again made off around the corner of the dorm.

Later that afternoon, to my horror, the dog still lay unburied! About to find Sebuhire and read him the riot act, I was fortunately prompted to inquire first of Musakura, a Christian Munyaruanda worker, as to why Sebuhire had not buried the dog.

"Bwana, he believes that if he buries that dog, he will be burying a member of his family within twenty-four hours!"

It was true that Sebuhire hadn't said, "Yes, I'll bury the dog." He only said, "Yes, I hear." Then when he immediately withdrew, he was silently telling me, "I hear you, Bwana, but I can't do it." And I, misreading the cue, thought he was saying, "I'll do it, and I'm going immediately to get a shovel." With my newly acquired understanding of the meaning of the dead dog in the total belief system of this pagan man, I then suggested, "Musakura, will you ask Sebuhire to relieve you at your present task so you will have time to bury the dog?"

"Ndio, Bwana."

And so the dog was buried.[1]

Need for Tools of Relationship

Tools of relationship are needed when one crosses cultural or subcultural boundaries. They are the foundation for crosscultural communication. Communication very quickly breaks down, sometimes with serious results, when one has no way of determining meaning from someone's behavior. The missionary in the opening case study could have found himself in trouble by insisting that the person he considered "lazy" get at the job of burying the dog.

Tools of relationship include the cultural cue, the functional equivalent, the principle of the adverse effect, the ranking of values, the abuse of system being made the whole, the part being made the whole, and the distinction between the real and the ideal and between the real and perceived. Not until the outsider begins to work consciously with the tools of relationship will he begin to validate the other society. Not until he works with all the tools consistently will members of the host society perceive themselves as fully human and their life-way valid when in his presence.

Tools of relationship are quite different from tools of research. Both permit the full validation of each society in which associations take place, but each is designed for a distinctive purpose. Tools of research validate society by accurately and fully representing it. Sound research must be carried out lest the investigator see only what he wants to see and hear only what he is pretuned to hear. *The tools of relationship, rather, permit the actual association with people within the society and must be used in personal interaction.* They must be applied by participation, not simply by observation; by thoroughgoing participation in the whole of the society, not in only a portion. They must be applied by full and complete interaction, not just by interview. Constant experimentation is necessary to make sure that the full kit of tools is available at any time, so that the culture in its entirety is understood as it actually is. What is in the archives is valuable for the past, but the present must be lived fully, and the tools of relationship permit this.

The Cultural Cue

The concept of *cultural cue* is taken from the acting profession. The cue indicates the point at which the actor is to make his appearance. Extended into the cultural setting, *the cue lets one do precisely what he must do, at the right time, in the right way, without manipulation.* The cue may be verbal, as in "Come in!"; or it may be nonverbal, such as a wave of greeting. It may simply be the placement of furniture in a room. A verbal cue is tied into the larger linguistic pattern. The nonverbal cue is tied into the larger structural organizational pattern. Placement is tied into that aspect of culture called "space relationships."[2] Society can thus be conceptualized as one vast, intricate network of cues permitting the participant to enter the stage of life when he needs to, accomplish what he needs to, and retire from the stage gracefully.

One way of carrying out an analysis of a society is to allow the patterns of cues to form by which one responds to society's stimuli. Our response is based on millions of such cues that guide us in every social setting to do the proper or expected thing, to recover when the unexpected has been done, or to impulse some change in the way of doing things. Another way of looking at the socialization process is to see it as internalizing all the cues one needs for living within society. Culture shock resulting from the mismatching of cultural cues may be devastating to the monocultural person, because there is a lack of correspondence between the cue responses of two societies. For example, the wave of "goodbye" in English has the fingers extended downward. This gesture in Spanish means "come here." The discomfiture of monocultural North Americans in Latin America is great when they wave goodbye to someone and that person approaches rather than departs.

A knowledge of the cultural cue is needed by the agent of change so that he can adapt to the new society without losing his own identity as a person and as a member of his own society. In other words, he must know the cues that allow him to remain a person of principle and to fulfill responsibly his role in life in whatever culture. Well-meaning missionaries who are from non-drinking backgrounds may refuse alcoholic beverages with a curt refusal designed to protect them from the evils of drinking. This is readily perceived by the host as a "slap in the face." Each society has an effective way of refusing alcoholic beverages so that the host will accept the refusal gracefully. It is the responsibility of the guest to seek out such cues, recognize them when he encounters them, and act correctly in using them. To the Central American Indian, it is enough to say "It hurts my stomach." Alcoholic beverages are thus automatically recorded in the mind of the host as being in the same category as "chili pepper," the spicy addition used to make their food tasty, but which not everyone can "stomach." The host reads the refusal, therefore, as, "This person wants to remain my friend, but he just can't drink an alcoholic beverage. There are other beverages he can drink, so I will serve him one of those." The curt refusal, on the other hand, signals to the host that one does not want to remain his friend. To the Filipino, it is sufficient to request Coca Cola in place of an alcoholic beverage. Again the message communicated is that the guest is a fully responsible friend of the host.

The Functional Equivalent

Most people expect to find in another culture exactly what they have in their own. They expect it to look the same and to have the same meaning as we discussed in the chapter on form/meaning correlation. They assume that if the form is the same, the meaning must also be the same; and if the form is different, the meaning is different also. In other words, they focus on the form of the communicated message or on the form of the cultural expression, rather than on the significance of the message or on its impact. This then is the use of the direct equivalent or the nonfunctional equivalent. The form/meaning in one culture is intended as the form/meaning in the other.

The functional equivalent[3] is based on meaning out of which form grows and develops. Equivalence of meaning is therefore sought, and from meaning one seeks out the form that is the natural means of expressing it. Whenever there is agreement to and knowledge of a form/meaning correlation, the hearer automatically comprehends the full and correct impact of the communicated message or deed. Within the crosscultural setting, complete agreement and knowledge of the form/meaning must be learned. The process of adaptation to the new is the process of learning the cues of the new and the functional equivalence of the old to the new. It is to be expected in crosscultural settings that the meaning will remain intact, though the form will differ. When this is not the case, and the form is the same for two cultures, the agent of change can consider that he has received a bonus. For example, the functional equivalent of the "goodbye" in English, with the fingers extended downward, is the fingers extended upward in Spanish. The functional equivalent of "It hurts my stomach" for the Pocomchi is "I'll have a Coke, please," for the Filipino. The functional equivalent of a bell ringing to dismiss classes in our society is the clapping of hands to dismiss classes in some Asian societies. The functional equivalent for reading in the Philippines is to know the right people, for in that society it is more important to know someone influential in order to get ahead than it is to be able to read.

No functional equivalent can be expected to equate across cultural boundaries 100 percent. Thus functional equivalence may involve a range of equivalent items or terms that do in one culture what one of them alone does in another. For example, the English word "carry" is joined with other separate words called prepositions to indicate the direction of carrying. In Pocomchi, four words form the functional equivalent of the English "carry": *camlok, camje, cambeh,* and *cam.*[4] Calvin's *Institutes,* a classic work on the theology of the Christian community, is impossible to match for its completeness and breadth in the contemporary period. Therefore, the functional equivalent of the *Institutes* is a series of volumes on the Christian view of God and the Christian responsibility to humankind in community.

The concept of the functional equivalent is used widely today in translation ministry under the name "dynamic equivalent," "life-style translation," and others.[5] It has also been used by Don Richardson as the "redemptive analogy."[6] By means of an analogy to a "peace child," Richardson was able to communicate the message of Christ's gift to save them from their sins and to grant them eternal life.

Though Richardson selected a key functional equivalent to call the redemptive analogy, in effect there are millions of redemptive analogies—as many as there are cultural cues. Each provides the communicator of the gospel a dynamic means of getting the message across. For example, in Latin America, the major orientation to life is not so much economic, social, or religious; rather, it is political. This means that the idea of Jesus as a political force when introducing the gospel, is significant to reach into the lives of Latins, especially the men. Woman is another powerful metaphor in Latin America. She is the family organizer, an intermediary whenever something significant is being decided, and also the core of reputation for the family. What a powerful concept to use in reaching men and women for Christ in Latin America! Unfortunately, Mary, as woman, is associated with the veneration of Mary and idolatry, and Protestants are unable to make use of this very significant redemptive analogy. In Melanesia-Polynesia, there is an economic trading partner who becomes one's best friend. One will tell this best friend things he will not tell his own wife. Again, what a powerful analogy to use in describing the One who "sticketh closer than a brother!"

A final example is the American middle class. The average pastor usually berates the middle class for its crass materialism. He is unable to see beyond behavior to system. Lying behind the social system of the middle class in American society is the concept of looking out to others, rather than up or down the status system to see who is rising in status to challenge one's own position. This is a powerful analogy to explain God's choice of the North American and Westerner to participate in the greatest movement in missions ever seen in the world. The American lower class spends its energy trying to rise out of the lower class. The upper class spends its energy protecting its flanks to make sure that no one overtakes it in rising in status and wealth. Age-grade systems as those in Africa are locked into age progress to gain status, so they too look up through the system. The strata-rank system of Latin America is one that fights association with those below one in status and causes the member to constantly seek associations up the status ladder for status achievement (see chapter 7). Is it any wonder then that God could not make use of members of societies in stratification systems looking up or down the status ladder? In fact, the only social strata that he could use in reaching the world for Christ is one that looks out, where there is little dynamic operating in looking up the system. This is a heritage that the middle class has to cherish and to utilize in reaching out to all men and women everywhere.

The Principle of the Adverse Effect

Behavioral signs can indicate to us *whether we have achieved what we set out to do or whether we have accomplished just the opposite*. Awareness that verbal and nonverbal indicators can alert us to errors in our approach to others opens up an entire study of how these errors are communicated and what such problems in communication tell us in the way of adjusting our approach. Many parents punish their children immediately upon finding them in the wrong. With some children, this communicates the message, "You have done wrong, shape up." In contemporary American society, however, it has been discovered that this sometimes communicates, "You can never do anything right." The two messages are quite distinct, and the American parent needs to be aware of the possibility of the two messages. The first develops positive response, the second generates negative and destructive response. One must be sensitive to possible miscommunications through cultural cues and all forms of verbal and nonverbal communications. How easy it would have been for the missionary to have insisted that Sebuhire bury the dead dog and thereby to have lost for all time the opportunity of effective witness of God's grace.

Ranking of Values

One's value system is not a series of values all jumbled up together causing erratic responses to stimuli. Order and arrangement exist based on a hierarchy of value distinctions. *Such a hierarchy of priority from greater to lesser importance determines one's choice in any given situation.* A person never makes a choice or decision apart from this rank order. A given situation allows one an opportunity to reevaluate his ranking, permitting certain adjustments to be made. But such adjustments never precede the ranking itself. This is one of the major fallacies of the approach to "situation ethics."[7] Situation ethics suggests that a decision can be made in keeping with the situation. However, one's rank of values has such a powerful control on the decision-making process that one is unable to make a decision apart from this control (see chapter 16). Some people will make a decision that appears to go contrary to this rank. They have idealized what they are, or they have perceived themselves to be one thing when they are actually something else. Many American youths perceive themselves to be free from economic control and the drive to materialism. As they mature, their choices are more and more economic in nature, and the materialism they foster, though different in some ways from that of their parents, is still materialism. For example, though the clothes they wear are different from those of their parents, they still have a studied approach to clothing and what it means to them. They have a strong focus on fashion, correctness of dress, completeness of attire, etc., and are willing to pay whatever it costs to be in their "fashion."

Young American men of the forties were willing to expend themselves in the service of their nation, whereas their counterparts of the sixties were reluctant to go to war. The behavior of the former was generated from a value ranking of nation over person. The behavior of the latter was generated from a value ranking of person over nation. In other words, there has been a shift in values but not the way many people have interpreted this, i.e., from responsibility to irresponsibility, or from self-denial to selfishness. The shift has been in personal motivation rising above group interest. The men of the forties were responsible in terms of national interest first and personal interest second. The men of the sixties were responsible in terms of personal interest first and national interest second. It is easy for members of the former subculture to call members of the latter irresponsible. A difference of subculture exists, and each may be fully responsible in terms of his value ranking. If the members of the former do not like the expression or behavior of the latter, they need to effect a cultural change. If the larger society can operate in keeping with the justice model with both subcultures working together, then there is no reason for change.

When time and production units in time periods are ranked highest within society, it is impossible to generate behavior that does other than recruit the largest work force possible, unless, of course, machines can do all the work. The child-labor laws of the latter part of the nineteenth century were designed to limit the labor force to adults only. This social change was necessary because society was holding time production units to be of such high value that it was undermining the state by failing to educate its children effectively. Today the reverse is happening. There is such an emphasis on keeping children in school, whether they are learning or not and whether they like it or not, that the ones not wanting to be there are spoiling the experience for those that do want to learn.[8]

The Abuse of System

As was indicated in chapter 7, society can be seen as a systems operation and thus lends itself to systems abuse. *Any system can and will be abused.* There is no problem with abuse of the social system if the abuse can be identified and dealt with effectively. When the abuse of the system is seen to be the entire system, however, or when one perceives the abuse as the system itself, it is possible that in regulating or destroying the abuse, one regulates or destroys the entire system. Revolutionaries are often guilty of this. They strive to destroy the system and then wind up putting the same basic system back into operation, since that is the only system they know. What they have accomplished is very little, for in destroying the abuse, they destroy the system itself. The French Revolution followed this pattern, and those who advocated overthrow were themselves destroyed. Fidel Castro sought to overthrow the system in Cuba and wound up subject to the very same system he sought to destroy. He deported or killed all the higher-strata members of the society, perceiving that they were the ones blocking progress. This left a vacuum in the stratification system operating in Cuba, and lower-status people immediately moved in to fill the vacuum. At that time, however, such people were not trained to operate on those higher-status levels and were controlling those levels in erratic and unpredictable ways. What Castro did achieve was to gain the highest office in the nation for himself, and his friends filled the newly emptied ranks of high status.

The Part Seen As the Whole

Every system consists of component parts that exist only because they are parts of a larger component within a larger system.[9] Any part gains significance only by being part of the whole. Christ used the grapevine in illustrating this principle (John 15). Paul referred to this principle when he was talking about the hand in relation to the body (1 Cor. 12). Any one part of society that sees itself as the sole recipient of truth can very quickly throw the system into an imbalance and do a disservice to the other parts involved. The Fundamentalist movement in American Protestantism claimed to be the sole recipient of the truth of God and developed an approach to other Christians that was so exclusivistic that it ultimately resulted in a movement of separatistic groups, none of which would have anything to do with another.[10]

The Real As Against the Ideal or the Perceived

The real is known only through the process of abstraction from what actually is seen to exist. These abstractions are symbolized for and by society, so there is some consensus as to what constitutes the real. The process of abstraction is a healthy one that helps develop responsibility within society. Extensions of this process may develop societal health or ill health. All societies, through their ranking of values, cause certain aspects of the real to be held up as ideals to the members of the society. For example, for years the American populace was encouraged to see smoking as a rewarding experience. Many people began to smoke because of this ideal. Later it was discovered that smoking produced cancer. By this time, smoking had become so strong a habit with people and had made so much money for some, that it became a source of individual and corporate tension.

A second extension of the symbolization process is the perception of the real.[11] Individuals or the corporate body can develop perceptions of the real that are in fact nothing like the real itself. The perception of smoking as a fulfilling habit was quite distinct from the real. It is actually a self-destructing habit that causes cancer and lung disease. The perception of the missionary in the opening case study was that the worker was lazy or that he procrastinated in failing to bury the dog. In reality, the worker was fully responsible to his family, though he did need a spokesman to make clear that he was fully responsible in his job.

Summary

The tools of relationship are necessary in permitting a society to be fully valid and responsible. These include the cultural cue; the functional equivalent; the principle of the adverse effect; the abuse of system as distinct from the system itself; the part as distinct from the whole; and the difference between the real and ideal, and between the real and the perceived. Without such tools, the culture of the guest within the society is likely to be imposed upon the host's society. This produces injustice, as discussed in chapter 16.

When the tools are used effectively, the form/meaning correlation is in dynamic operation. The means of expressing the language and culture is in full correspondence with the meaning intended within the total context of the culture. Only when these tools are perceptively used is assimilation natural and smooth for both the guest and the host. This complete assimilation also expedites effective change.

Only by using the tools of relationship can one hope to be an effective crosscultural communicator and to maintain a sound theology. Otherwise, there is a high risk of the person interpreting the Scriptures out of his own sociocultural system for the other person in spite of the significant differences between the two cultural systems. Only when meaning has ascendancy over form can there be effective communication of truth.

Questions for Discussion

Relating to the Sending Church

1. How do tools of relationship differ from tools of research? How might such tools be used to free your church to grow more?
2. Can you name other tools useful in developing and maintaining effective relationships that might be added to our list?
3. How might the person who trends toward dichotomism in value formation tend to make the part of a whole as the whole itself? Can you name instances of this in your everyday lives? in your church? in your school?
4. Distinguish values and rank of values. How else do we discuss ranking of values? What is your community's rank of values regarding marriage to people of distinct ethnic background? Are you satisfied with such ranking? What does such behavior imply for your own experience? Can the ranking be changed? How can it be changed? Apply the concept of rank of values to some aspect of your church life and discuss its relevance in ministry.
5. If a person values family over nation, how is he likely to respond to a military draft? What rank of values might a person have who is willing and eager to serve in the armed forces of his nation? How can God be glorified by the expression of each person's ranking of values?

Relating to the Study of the Bible

1. Study the Book of Ruth to ascertain the patterns of cultural cues that guided each of the participants.
2. Take such sayings as, "The axe is laid unto the root of the trees" (Matt. 3:10), from the King James Version and give the meaning in contemporary speech, e.g., "Shape up or ship out." Which

expression sounds more natural to you? Could the Bible be written in such contemporary form? Would it still be God's Word? What might be the problems in translating the Bible for people with different languages? Discuss.

3. Discuss Elijah's experience in the cave (1 Kings 19:9ff.) in light of the tools of relationship. Especially note the cultural cue, the functional equivalent, and the part versus the whole.

4. Discuss David's life in light of the tools of relationship. Especially note the cultural cue, the adverse effect, the ideal versus the real, and the real versus the perceived.

5. How do contemporary Christians react to the Jewish culture of biblical times in light of the practices of the reputation of such groups as the Pharisees and the Sadducees (cf. Acts)?

6. Compare contemporary revolutionaries with Jesus Christ. In what sense was Christ the unique revolutionary?

Relating to Missions and Crosscultural Ministry

1. Have you studied the complex of cultural cues unique to the society in which you carry out mission? What are some of them? How do these impact your work?

2. Search out a dozen functional equivalents from your own cultural background to the culture of your ministry and discuss how these affect the communication of the gospel.

3. To what degree do the missionaries around you fall into the trap of considering the part to be the whole? the abuse of system to be the system itself? Share examples.

4. How does the Western rank of values regarding ethnic groups, work styles, etc., affect ministry in the field? Explain.

5. Describe examples when well-meaning missionaries and other outsiders achieved the adverse effect because they were not working with the cultural cues of their host culture nor with the principle of the functional equivalent.

Group Activities and Exercises

1. *Small group work.* Have the members of a small group work out the various functional equivalents that provide adjustment between youth and adult subcultures, e.g., hair styles, reimbursment for work done, fashions, means of transportation.

2. *Demonstration.* Find people of distinct cultures and subcultures to demonstrate greeting patterns characteristic of their culture. Then have members of the group practice the routines of greeting. While doing this, have them suggest functional equivalents between such patterns and those of their own culture. Consult Edward T. Hall's books for examples.[12]

3. *Research.* Have each member of the group spend a few days doing participant observation of the system versus its abuse, the part taken as the whole, the perceived taken as the real, and the ideal confused with the real. Ask them to report on their findings.
4. *Translation.* Have your students translate the following into "correct" English.

The Message of the
Larutlucib Tribespeople[13]

We are the Larutlucib tribespeople from the country of Sreyam; we have come to you on a flying canoe. Our insides are sweet to be here. After the flying canoe came down, our heads were in the dirt because we had never been in a canoe that was not in the water—the water was so far below us. While we were in the flying canoe, we were shivering in our livers but now that we are in your country our livers are wide open for we have something that is very important for you to know and that you must accept.

But even though our heads are in the dirt, because we are here, our minds are killing us because we have found the only trail—the only right trail, and you don't know about our trail. The jungle is so big and there are so many trails and this jungle grows so quickly and one can get lost very quickly. But we have found a trail that goes on and on. We haven't been to the end of the trail, but some day we will be at the end of the trail where there is a place that is bigger than the big river that we crossed in the flying canoe. And in this place there will not be anything there to blacken our eyes but our eyes will be whitened. There our livers will sit down. Don't you want to know where this trail is? and how you can walk on this trail?

The one who is sufficient had a pain in his liver for the people which he had carved. These people were people with bad livers. But the one who is sufficient so hurt in his liver that he sent his Trailblazer into the jungle. And his Trailblazer blazed a trail for us through the jungle. But this Trailblazer died, but he isn't dead now.

MODEL FOUR
EFFECTIVE MINISTRY

EFFECTIVE MINISTRY

The model termed "effective ministry" provides a variety of insights into interpersonal and intergroup relations, suggesting positive means of working with a person or group and effecting change in keeping with what he or it is and releasing that person or group to the maximum expression of creativity. There are three submodels.

1. Crosscultural Ethics: The discussion of absolutism and relativism opens the possibility that a Christian can be a cultural relativist and a biblical absolutist rather than absolutizing his *own* cultural ways or negating the impact of biblical truth. This material provides a means of approaching ethics and morality crossculturally.
2. The Support Model: The support model helps people in cultural conflict bridge from conflict to rapport. It involves the setting of goals and operations to meet those goals, a regular reevaluation of goals and operations, alternate sessions with debriefing sealing the learning experiences, and true creativity deriving from what a person or group actually is.

   The support person encourages the effective development and realization of each of the aspects of the support model in the lives of those contacted. The support person is in effect the educator within the challenge of crosscultural education.
3. The Models Illustrated: Two extensive case studies point up the fact that if the models of crosscultural communication are to be effective, they must be applied. A narration case comes from Chiapas, Mexico. An overview case deals with the privilege of prayer that Christians have as they seek to minister in the name of the Lord Jesus Christ. The power of prayer increases significantly as one approaches the practice of prayer crossculturally.

16

Crosscultural Ethics

Cultural Exclusivism Versus Cultural Openness

The average member of any society is likely to react to something different from his own experience in the following ways:

What does this mean to me?
How can it be said or done so that it is meaningful to me?
How can others see life as I see it?
How can I make the other person be more like me?

This approach to interpersonal relations is one of *cultural exclusivism. All other cultures and their life-ways are approached from the point of view of the person looking in.* It may also thus be termed "monocultural" or "ethnocentric." Such an approach poses no problem as long as one remains within the confines of his own culture. The process of enculturation prepares one to live within his own sociocultural setting. Any member of a society must be able to live fully and adequately within his own sociocultural setting. The society would not survive otherwise.

When one leaves his own culture, it is necessary to adapt to the new without abandoning the principles or absolutes on which his life is based. Such adaptation calls for a *crosscultural approach to the second society, one of cultural openness and sensitivity.* Such an approach is not necessarily antithetical to the enculturative process or to the

241

goals of society itself. It may, in fact, advance the purposes of the society. But it may need to be introduced as a significant factor into the enculturation process itself. Apparently, it is not something that is developed naturally.

The approach of cultural openness would involve a different set of questions when one confronts difference:

What is the person with whom I am communicating like?
What can I say or what can I do to know that there is complete understanding on the part of the other?
Can we both stand back and evaluate the communication to be sure we have fully understood each other?

The asking and answering of such questions does not in any way imply that we believe all we hear; rather, it enables us to communicate with as full an understanding as possible.[1] One simply becomes open to others within a different cultural context. He operates crossculturally, assuming that both his own and the one he is entering are valid cultures and that members of each live responsibly within the cultural context.

By being culturally exclusive, one runs the risk of putting another person into a tension of right and wrong, of sinning or not. The person feels the pressure placed on him by the other to abandon his own culture, principles, practices, and even absolutes on which his life is based. He feels he must do this in order to please the other. To conform to the other is the essence of his ethic. The "rice" Christian concept deriving from mission experience in the Far East when people supposedly converted to Christ and followed Western practices in order to get food, is an excellent example of the pressure placed on others to get them to do what one wants them to do. The Asians abandoned their Asianness in order to eat. They gained the culture of Western Christians, not necessarily Christianity, but at least they could eat.

By being culturally open, one runs the risk of abandoning his own principles for the sake of the other. This is not necessary, however, since every culture has its own means of maintaining the ethical and moral responsibility of its own members and permitting the outsider to maintain his own sense of responsibility as well. Even though one faces such a difficulty in utilizing a crosscultural approach, it is worth the risk, since only with an effective crosscultural approach can one hope to free himself to live fully in Christ Jesus in the midst of multiculture. Only with a crosscultural approach can the other be released from the onus of feeling the need for changing his culture in order to be accepted by God and man.

Case Study: When in Rome

While working in Rome this past summer, I found myself in a very interesting dilemma. In the Italian culture, one serves wine to guests as a predinner icebreaker. The Italian does not associate use or nonuse of wine with Christian behavior as does the North American Evangelical who often uses it as a criterion for measuring the spirituality of a person.

I personally have no qualms about having wine with my meal while living in another culture that accepts this social norm, especially when I am a guest in the home of an Italian. I am also willing to limit my personal freedom for the welfare of another person.

One evening I was invited to dinner at the home of a friend named Carlo. Carlo was not a Christian, and I had been introduced to him by his close friend Mario who was a Christian. Mario had been sharing his faith with Carlo for over a year.

To complicate the situation, Mr. Long, an American Evangelical missionary, had also been invited. He was trained in the same Christian college in which I was serving as a dean of students. He totally abstained from drinking wine, feeling it was unbecoming of a Christian. He had been serving in Italy for three years, and though I had met him previously, I knew very little else about him and his missionary organization.

Just about the time I was ready to ask Mr. Long some questions about his background, Carlo walked into the room with a tray of four glasses of wine. He served me first, and I accepted. Then he served Mario and proceeded to Mr. Long. Mr. Long graciously refused.

So there I stood with my glass of wine. I did not want to offend Carlo after having accepted the wine. Neither did I want to offend the missionary who totally abstained. Mr. Long, I was quite sure, knew I was dean of students at the college, further complicating the decision I had to make. This was no time for a letter to be sent to the college and the board of trustees. What should I do?[2]

The dean of students, while visiting in Rome, faced a decision. He chose to partake of the alcoholic beverage in the host culture even though he would have abstained in his own. He communicated his respect for his host by partaking. The missionary, faced with the same choice, communicated his respect by a proper and courteous refusal. His was a lifestyle of abstaining in both cultures.

He had apparently discovered the effective cultural cue and did not seem to have offended the host. A problem arose in the conflict between the two different lifestyles of the Americans rather than in the communication process with the host. The dean's principles caused him to abstain in his own culture but to partake in another. The missionary's principles caused him to abstain in both. A further complication was the dean's employment. He was serving in a college where the group lifestyle, apparently, was to abstain in both. This left him in potential conflict with the college.[3]

If the dean had had an approach of cultural exclusivism, he could have partaken in the second culture and would have been highly indignant when the other failed to do so. This would have put great pressure on the missionary to either conform or to report the behavior of the dean to his college. If the missionary had had an approach of cultural exclusivism, he could have been indignant that the dean had partaken of the alcoholic beverage, and he most certainly would have reported him to the college.

Had both been culturally open, each would have sought to determine the attitude of the other and acted accordingly. The dean needed to examine his conscience and determine two things: his participation in light of his own value system and in light of his college's value system. The missionary needed to examine his own conscience and determine two things also: whether he had in fact offended the host or not by his definitive refusal to partake; and whether, in the second culture, he should partake or not.

The Holy Spirit would need to be actively working in the conscience of each: the dean as to whether he should partake or not, and the missionary as to whether he should change his lifestyle while in Italy. What John wrote in 1 John 3:21 gives very clear guidance here: "If our hearts do not condemn us, we have confidence before God." If one does not have that confidence, a change is likely called for.

Since the dean had the most to lose in the situation, he had the responsibility for taking the next step. He would need to establish effective communication with the missionary by developing a trust bond. This might avert an adverse-effect letter to the college. He could attempt a verbal explanation or handle the drink he had accepted in such a way that he maintain the balance of trust in each relationship in which he was engaged, e.g., drink it, hold it full, or set it aside. It is not so much what one does initially that affects the relationship, as what one does next. Effective crosscultural communication must keep all parties in mind at all times. One dare not act in one way toward the host and in another way toward another guest. Sound principles of crosscultural communication allow the one acting to express a consistency of behavior within the crosscultural setting that receives the respect of each person within the setting.[4]

The person who is culturally exclusive assumes that what he does is right for everyone. The culturally open person assumes that even his own decision may have to be questioned by the Spirit of God. The approach of cultural exclusiveness moves one toward ethical relativism. The approach of cultural openness presses one toward cultural realism and the full expression of responsibility under the guidance of the Spirit of God.

Ethical Relativism Versus Cultural Realism

Ethical relativism implies an abandonment of principle and the accompanying irresponsibility within an individual's own life experience. People make choices that place their own sense of responsibility or that of others in jeopardy. One expression of ethical relativism is situation ethics, or contextual ethics, as discussed in chapter 5.

Cultural realism is the development and maintenance of principle and the expression of responsibility in one's life experience. The point is that one is ethically and morally responsible from the inside out. This does not negate the biblical truth that all men are sinners and thus have sinned (see Gen. 3 and Rom. 3); rather, it supports that truth. Jesus put it quite well in the statement recorded in Matthew 15:11, "What goes into a man's mouth does not make him 'unclean,' but what comes out of his mouth, that is what makes him 'unclean.' " The sin that comes out of a person's heart is what makes that person unclean. Culture does not make someone sin, though it may provide the setting for and reason to sin. Cultural realism is the means human beings have of living in a multicultural world without necessarily sinning, without abandoning their absolutes, without going contrary to the principles that God and culture have planted in them. It permits the member of a society to experience absolutes and to know their true significance. Herskovits has termed this "cultural relativism."[5] We might also call it "cultural integrity" or "cultural relevance."

Unfortunately, most theologians dealing with the concept of relativism associate it with both ethical and cultural relativism. There is an easy way to distinguish them, however. If someone is talking about the abandonment of principle, he is likely dealing with ethical relativism. When someone is talking about the maintenance of principle, he is likely dealing with cultural relativism, i.e., cultural realism.

Case Study: Crosscultural "Theft"

In the United States, property is divided into public and private property in the following ways:

1. What is purchased individually is individually owned and therefore private property, irrespective of where that piece of property is found.
2. What is purchased corporately, e.g., by a political entity such as a city, state, or nation, is corporately owned and therefore public property.

A responsible member of a society in Central America maintains what he wants within his own property boundaries. He is free to use or abuse his property as long as it is in his own property boundaries. He is not allowed to use or abuse that which lies within the domain of another's property without express permission. However, anything found outside the stated boundaries of a property is to be used and may even be abused by anyone. Thus anything found on trails, roads, or properties not clearly marked as "owned" is available to all. These areas are perceived as not owned by anyone.

A North American in that society had purchased a tricycle for his child. Later he found that his maid had taken it to her little girl for her to play with. On the basis of the North American division of property, he accused the maid of theft. She was scandalized and quit her job. She had acted responsibly within the laws and expectations of her own society by taking the tricycle. She had found it on a trail and so felt free to take it home to let her daughter enjoy it for a while. She had a definite sense of moral obligation not to steal and had not intended to steal. However, her action was perceived as stealing by the North American. She was judged irresponsible by him, for he viewed her actions from his own point of view.

Each person, the North American and the maid, responding in a culturally exclusive way, had forced the other into a situation of conflict of norm. The maid had taken what she perceived to be public property. The American had accused her of theft. There was no problem of ethics in this case prior to his accusation of theft. The conflict of norm threw each person into an ethical dilemma. To accept her use of the tricycle, he had to negate his own values attached to private ownership. To be accused of theft was to strike at the ethical principles of her life. For her to remain in his household, she would have had to admit to theft, which she had not intended, and thus abandon the cultural categories that gave meaning to her life. This would have produced confusion as to her ethical and moral responsibility to her child as well as to her employer. Such an admission and pursuant abandonment of principle is a step toward an ethical relativism and its accompanying irresponsibility. It is part of the process of enslavement and injustice.

There are numerous means of stealing in the Pocomchi society. One of them is penetrating the property boundary and thus taking something that belongs to someone else. Another is harvesting a crop planted by another without paying that person for the crop. These acts would be those clearly covered by the biblical injunction "You shall not steal" (Deut. 5:19). What the maid did does not fit any of the definitions of theft for the Pocomchi.[6]

An outsider seeking to be fully responsible within a society, i.e., cultural realism, as that of the Pocomchi would first of all inquire into the distinctions of property maintained there. He would attempt to grasp them in their entirety and follow them pragmatically as fully as possible without abandoning any of his own ethical and moral principles. He would further instruct his household not to leave any possessions outside their property boundaries. If something did inadvertently get outside this boundary and was taken by another, inquiry could be made and the item repossessed. If no admission was made and the item was not discovered, he would simply have to resign himself to its loss and be more careful in the next instance. Since there was no ethical problem in the first part of the case (taking the tricycle), such effective crosscultural behavior could help one avoid an ethical dilemma in the second part of the case (the accusation). The approach of cultural exclusivism causes one to make ethical and moral problems where none existed previously.

Following the approach of cultural realism, the person could have ascertained the facts of the case, apologized to the maid, restored her to her job with perhaps a small raise if appropriate, and even offered to let her child use the tricycle from time to time.

Biblical Absolutism and Cultural Relativism

Absolutism implies completeness, being free from imperfection. Relativism implies dependence, not being free from imperfection.

Biblical absolutism deals with the interpretation of the inspired Word of God, the Bible. Culture deals with one's upbringing that helps him express responsible behavior.

A matrix forms readily from these four categories of thought (see figure 30).

Approach to Culture

		absolutism	relativism
Approach to the Bible	absolutism	1	2
	relativism	3	4

Figure 30. Absolutism–Relativism Matrix

Thus, the following combinations result:
1. Biblical absolutism and cultural absolutism.
2. Biblical absolutism and cultural relativism.
3. Biblical relativism and cultural absolutism.
4. Biblical relativism and cultural relativism.

Option 1 has often been the accepted approach of the conservative arm of the Christian church. This position assumes that the Bible is the standard for all of life and behavior in one's culture. Thus the Bible and one's culture remain constant and unchanging. If one changed, then the other would have to change, and that would be contrary to God's will. What one discovered about God and his desires in one's own culture would then become standards for everyone. If someone failed to affirm biblical absolutism and cultural absolutism, it was automatically assumed that he was abandoning all absolutes and espousing biblical relativism, i.e., that the Bible had no authority in one's life. Such an approach is based upon cultural exclusivism and potentially forces the other into ethical relativism.

Option 3 has historically been of no particular concern to the church. It has been of larger concern, however, to humanitarians. Such an approach suggests that the culture is everything, and there are no standards outside of culture to guide it or correct it. The end result of such an approach is to make the culture in question a museum on one hand, or a monster on the other, such as in the case of Germany under Hitler. As a museum, the culture is unable to change either from forces within or from forces without. There is thus no dynamic within the operations of culture, and it dies. As a monster, the culture is always right, whatever the humanitarian result.

Option 4 is held by many professionals in the behavioral sciences.[7] This approach suggests that culture alone guides its members into the expression of full responsibility within the society. Culture is a dynamic process that is internally self-correcting and can be relied upon to produce decisions that aid the society as well as the individual within the society.

A serious professional need not be stuck with only option 4. Option 2 preserves the best of cultural realism. At the same time, it introduces the potentiality of God's presence, which promises to complete man's humanness.[8] A member of any given society can know God fully without changing to some other culture and, in the process, complete his own humanness, i.e., his own maturity as a human being and a member of his culture.

Option 2 is significant to the church world-wide. The approach of biblical absolutism and cultural relativism affirms that there is a supernatural intrusion. Truth is from God. Truth does not change. The way truth is communicated in a given culture and language will change. Even as Christ through the Incarnation became flesh and dwelt among us, so truth becomes expressed in culture. However, the Word made flesh lost none of his divineness, and truth is not corrupted or changed necessarily by its expression via human sociocultural forms.[9] It is always full and complete as truth. The moment truth is wed to one cultural expression, there is a high potential for falsehood.

Referring once again to the case of crosscultural theft, there is a moral absolute contained in the commandment "You shall not steal" (Exod. 20:15). According to the Bible, one is not to take that which belongs to someone else. The commandment does not give us guidelines for knowing when an action is one of stealing within a given culture or subculture. That is left to the definition of culture and the upbringing of a member of that culture to be fully responsible. For the Pocomchi, culture has given its members guidelines stating when something is public and when it is private property. One following those guidelines is not stealing when taking a tricycle or anything else when it is on a public trail. A Pocomchi is not stealing in Pocomchi culture even though a North American acting in the same way in his own culture would be stealing. This does not make God's absolutes relative, rather it defines when someone is disobeying God's absolutes and when that same person is acting in a fully responsible way toward God and man. Even as a North American can steal within the context of no division of public and private property, so a Pocomchi can steal within the division of public and private property.

The Bible provides the standard (see figure 31). The members of distinct cultures or subcultures work with the Scriptures in the language they each understand. They can thus respond to it as the very Word of God. For certain North Americans, this will only and always be the King James Version of the Bible. For others, this will only and always be some contemporary language version, depending on their particular dialect of English. For those of distinct ethnic and linguistic backgrounds, this will be the product of a translation program for that culture and language. When the language is unwritten, translation programs, such as those of the Wycliffe Bible Translators and the Lutheran Bible Translators, and the Tyndale Living Bible translation program and Bible society programs, may provide a translation that accurately represents the finest scholarship in biblical studies and in the study of the language and culture of the translation.

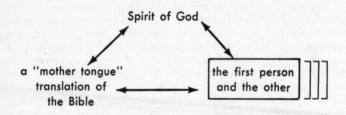

Figure 31. Resources in the Change Process

Within such a dynamic process, demands for change from crosscultural encounter, along with demands for change from within one's own society, can be worked with effectively.

A new problem may confront the agent of change once this process begins. Suppose neither norm needs changing. Or suppose a norm changes slowly over an extensive time period. Or suppose the norm of the first person changes while that of the other, seen previously as that which definitely needed changing, remains constant. This latter case is perhaps the greatest test of the missionary or agent of change. He has gone to another culture assuming that the norm will change with the entrance of the gospel. After all, aren't they heathen? There are things that will change simply because of the demand of crosscultural contact, but there may be areas of resistance that seem to the outsider to involve aspects of the culture that must change.

Many North Americans who are strongly time oriented, upon entering another culture that is definitely trend event, are determined to see the cultural norm change to time orientation. For example, one missionary spent most of his time trying to get the national pastor and the congregation to use a bulletin. Since a bulletin is designed out of a trend-time society, it does not always serve in a trend-event society. Frequently, outsiders find a culture resistant to change in this regard; and instead, the outsider himself may begin to change. Upon his return to his own society, he may find himself in conflict with the time expectations there. He has to carry out special strategies—e.g., use an appointment book—to become fully accepted by his own people once again.

When culture does not change in ways expected by the agent of change, there might be a significant reason. It is possible that the other person is not paying attention to the leading of the Spirit of God. The translation of the Bible may not be adequate. The missionary may not have interpreted the Scriptures correctly. It is entirely possible that the norm of the outsider must first change. It is also possible that change is taking place but at a pace slower than would otherwise be expected, especially in comparison with the rate of change in the guest's own culture.

Or it is entirely possible that the gospel can enter a life and a society without change being called for. This principle is probably the most difficult for a missionary to work with. He is so completely convinced that the other culture must and will change that he cannot imagine it to be otherwise. Until one is willing to accept the possibility that another culture will not change, he is unable to work effectively with the Holy Spirit, for he is decreeing what must be changed and not relying on the Holy Spirit to guide him.

Case Study: Sacrificial Adultery

As the Russian armies drove westward to meet the Americans and British at the Elbe, a Soviet patrol picked up a Mrs. Bergmeier who was foraging food for her three children. Without any clear reason for her capture, and unable even to get word to her children, she was taken off to a prison camp in the Ukraine. Her husband had been captured in the Battle of the Bulge and taken to a prisoner-of-war camp in Wales.

When he was returned to Berlin, he spent many weeks rounding up his children. Two (Ilse, twelve, and Paul, ten) were found in a detention school run by the Russians, and the oldest (Hans, fifteen) was found hiding in a cellar near the Alexander Platz. Their mother's whereabouts remained a mystery, but they never stopped searching. She, more than anything else, was needed to reknit them as a family in that dire situation of hunger, chaos, and fear.

Meanwhile, in the Ukraine, Mrs. Bergmeier learned through a sympathetic commandant that her husband and family were trying to keep together and find her. But she could be released for only one of two reasons: (1) illness needing medical facilities beyond those in the camp, in which case she would be sent to a Soviet hospital elsewhere; or (2) pregnancy, for which she would be returned to Germany as a liability.

She turned things over in her mind and finally asked a friendly Volga German camp guard to impregnate her, which he did. Her condition being medically verified, she was sent back to Berlin and to her family. They welcomed her with open arms, even when she told them how she had managed it. When the child was born, they loved him more than all the rest, since little Dietrich had done more for them than anybody else.

When it was time for him to be christened, they took him to the pastor on a Sunday afternoon. After the ceremony, they sent Dietrich home with the other children and sat down in the pastor's study to ask him whether they were right to feel as they did about Mrs. Bergmeier and Dietrich. Should they be grateful to the Volga German? Had Mrs. Bergmeier done a good and right thing?[10]

The traditionalist, i.e., the cultural exclusivist, would see her action as wrong; the ethical relativist would see it as right; and the situation ethicist would see it as right in the sense that "love" was expressed in the situation. These points of view are clarified further in chapter 5. None of these points of view, however, take into account cultural realism.

Applying the approach of cultural realism, i.e., biblical absolutism *and* cultural relativism, it is necessary to know both the biblical teaching and the sociocultural setting.

The norm model suggests that there are certain norms represented in the case: Mrs. Bergmeier, the German guard, the husband, the pastor, the person reading the case, and Joseph Fletcher, who included the case in his book *Situation Ethics*.

Fletcher's norm is expressed through the title "Sacrificial Adultery," as well as through the place given such a case in a discussion of situation ethics. He has implied that Mrs. Bergmeier committed adultery for the sake of something or someone other than herself, for she acted out of "love" for another—namely, her family. "The situationist enters into every decision-making situation fully armed with the ethical maxims of his community and its heritage, and he treats them with respect as illuminators of his problems. Just the same, he is prepared in any situation to compromise them or set them aside in the situation if love seems better served by doing so."[11]

The norm of the reader becomes expressed through agreement or disagreement with Fletcher. If there is disagreement, alternatives of norm become expressed in keeping with the way the person sees himself and thus sees Mrs. Bergmeier. It is easy at this point in the case study for the reader to respond that "biblically" Mrs. Bergmeier did the wrong thing, and then to proceed to state how she should have acted in keeping with the "objective standard" of the Bible. This is frequently expressed with the question, What is God's norm? i.e., What is normative? Were the person making such a response in contact with Mrs. Bergmeier at the time she was contemplating the solution to her problem, he would overtly or covertly begin the "self-directed" program of change of Mrs. Bergmeier. She would feel the pressure to change and either conform to get along or resist conformity. She might find reason to change in keeping with the pressure on her to "shape up." It is likely that any change thus introduced would come about through conflict, such conflict ultimately never being fully resolved.

The norm of the pastor, representing his church, was expressed in the seeming noncritical response to Mr. and Mrs. Bergmeier and the willingness to christen the child. The norm of Mr. Bergmeier evidences itself in terms of both his positive response to his wife's return and the degree of tension leading them to seek out the pastor. The norm of Mrs. Bergmeier becomes clear in view of her action in the prison camp in seeking out a German guard and requesting the impregnation.[12]

The ranking-of-values model examines the core of ranked values within the norm. In generating behavior of such an order of values, further understanding of the person's norm becomes clear. If, for example, we concentrate on the two parts of Mrs. Bergmeier's norm that could be termed "concern for family" and "personal sexual purity" and rank these in alternate ways, we can predict her behavior. If Mrs. Bergmeier's norm ranked concern for family first and concern for sexual purity second (norm A), she would have sought the impregnation as a fully responsible person within the context of her norm. Whether she actually did seek it or not would not change her norm but would only serve to give expression to the norm. She would not have chosen impregnation in light of the situation; she would have chosen it because her underlying norm or culture permitted it.

If, however, Mrs. Bergmeier's norm had the same two concerns in reverse rank—first, concern for personal sexual purity, and second, concern for family (norm B)—she would have sought out the impregnation only in direct conflict to her norm. She therefore probably would not have sought it and would have been willing to live with the consequences which would likely have caused sorrow for her.

The excess and deprivation of norm model suggests alternatives of behavior and response to behavior involving guilt or bitterness. If we assume for the moment that Mrs. Bergmeier's norm was norm A, she would be living fully and completely in her norm as a responsible person and would have no sense of guilt. If we assume, however, that her norm was norm B, she would have acted contrary to her norm, and she would probably have had a sense of guilt to the degree that she was living in excess of her norm.

If we assume that her norm was norm A, for her not to have sought the impregnation would have left her in deprivation of norm unless some other way out was provided. Such deprivation could result in a sense of bitterness intense to the degree that she was living in deprivation of her norm. Had her husband's norm also been A, he would have experienced this bitterness as well to the extent of his knowledge of the situation. If Mrs. Bergmeier's norm was norm B, she would have no sense of deprivation were she to resist the impregnation route out of prison camp. She would then have made the most of the situation.

The conflict of norm model suggests the possibility of a number of conflicts. Some were resolved, and others were impossible to resolve. Mrs. Bergmeier would have had conflict within herself had her norm been B, but no evidence of conflict would have shown had it been A. To the degree that there was ambiguity in rank, she would have had a degree of guilt or bitterness, whichever way the ambiguity revealed itself. She would have had conflict with her husband and those he represented, i.e., the children, had her norm been A and his been B, or vice versa. She would have had conflict with the church to the degree that the norm of the pastor had been different from her own. She would have had conflict with the reader had she operated on the basis of her valid norm and that of the reader was different from hers. She would have had conflict with Fletcher if she had acted on the basis of norm B and there had been no further opportunity for her to express behavior in keeping with the love ethic. Fletcher probably would not have used this case study if Mrs. Bergmeier had lived up to norm B, or he likely would have condemned her for not living up to the love ethic if he had chosen to use it.

It appears that the Bergmeiers were not without some degree of tension, for they later approached the pastor. This conflict, insofar as this case is concerned, was apparently resolved quickly, for the time being at least, with the decision of the pastor. He apparently shared norm A with Mrs. Bergmeier. Thus it would appear that there was a degree of ambiguity of rank of values, with the ambiguity suggesting a base of norm A. The ambiguity was resolved through consultation with the pastor.[13]

The effective ministry model suggests an approach to the case that would have biblical absolutism as a foundation for decision making, with Mrs. Bergmeier and her family experiencing these absolutes within a valid culture. She would be in maximum conflict with one whose norm was B if hers was A, or one whose norm was A if hers was B.

Working with her with a Bible in her own language, one would encourage her to be open to the leading of the Spirit of God. Change would thus proceed, not in keeping with what the reader thinks the biblical absolutes are, as seen through his own personal norm, but in keeping with true biblical absolutes guided into distinct sociocultural settings by the Spirit.[14]

Four Questions Insuring the Validity of Distinct Societies

The question naturally arises as to which norm or life-way is correct. The problem is resolved in the very process of asking crosscultural questions like the following:

1. What is the norm, i.e., life-way?
2. Is the person living in keeping with his norm?
3. Does the norm need changing?
4. Who is responsible for changing the norm?

The average person operating within his own norm and approaching others from the point of view of his norm, will likely begin with question 3: Does the norm need changing? Since the norm of the other person is seen from the perspective of his own, it is a foregone conclusion that the other's norm needs changing. If the norm of the other is seen to be in need of change, then the person deciding that it needs changing becomes responsible for changing it. The process of changing the norm of the other thus lies completely with the one deciding that the norm needs changing. No one else needs to be involved in the final decision. Thus the parent decides for the child, one mate for the other, the missionary council for the national, the faculty for the student body, the pastor for the layman. Within the Christian context, in case the one making the decision feels the need for support, he need only refer to a proof text of Scripture or to the "leading of the Spirit of God" with whom he has counseled in the matter. No one is able to question the final decision. The cultural exclusivism approach has struck again for ethical relativism.

The person approaching the action, thought, or belief of another from a crosscultural point of view will start with question 1: What is the norm?[15] He will thus seek to understand fully the system on which the action, belief, or thought is based and then ask if the person is acting responsibly in keeping with that system. He will have searched out the meaning by going to the basis of motivation. He will be concerned with what the person intended in the first place, whether it was responsible or irresponsible action. Then, and only then, will he proceed to question 3. When the change agent asks this question, he will be doing so, not in terms of his own norm, but in terms of the norm of the other. This will immediately involve the other in the change process. But even more significantly, it will open the norm of the change agent to the possibility of change for himself. Once the norm of each is open to change, there is a viable role for the Spirit of God to enter and guide either or both in the change process. In a dynamic way, three become responsible for the change of norm: the Spirit of God, the one whose norm supposedly needs changing, and the support person. Thus a true reciprocity of change develops, opening either or both to the effective change of norm (see figure 32).

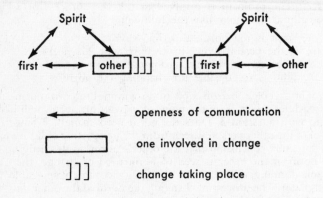

Figure 32. Reciprocity in Change

The change agent is now open to a number of possibilities: his own norm needs changing, the other's norm needs changing, both need changing, or neither needs changing. He now needs something other than the existential validation of behavioral change. He senses the need for some objective, external standard. Carnell,[16] states that "orthodoxy determines its view of the nature of man from propositional revelation." Niebuhr, on the other hand, determines his view from "the existential witness of the heart." In reality, both are involved. There must be the existential validation of the religious experience, which, when prior, gives tremendous

motivation to know God. This then drives one to seek propositional truth. When the reverse is true, one shapes experience by the
application of cultural form which readily gets bogged down in
traditionalism and cultural exclusivism and does not always reveal
truth.

Case Study: The Filipino Samaritan

In the Bible, the Good Samaritan saw a robbery victim
beside the road who had been ignored by a variety of passers-
by. He attended to the man's wounds, carried him to town,
secured a motel room, provided food, paid his bills, and
returned later to check up on him (Luke 10:25–37).

The Good Samaritan was acting honorably and unselfishly,
seeking the well-being of the wounded man and receiving in
return the latter's appreciation. Those who passed by without
becoming involved were selfish, putting their own plans and
interests over those of the wounded man, ignoring the
wounded man's pain and suffering and finally almost insuring
the man's death.

Any way we look at the action of the Good Samaritan we
see responsible action ending responsibly. The culture of his
period permitted him to assist such a man with few if any
adverse side effects. The wounded man was obligated to him
for expression of appreciation, but we see no indication that
there was anything further expected of him. The Samaritan in
no way brought dishonor or embarrassment to him, and
there was no lingering regret on the part of either party.

A Filipino Samaritan was driving along a road leading to
the capital city of his nation. He came upon the scene of an
accident in which the driver of one car was seriously injured.
A local policeman came upon the scene of the accident but
had no vehicle to transport the wounded man to the hospital.
The Filipino thus was in the first vehicle to arrive, and the
policeman requested that he transport the wounded man to
the hospital. The Filipino refused. The policeman drew his
gun and insisted, and the Filipino driver acceded and took the
man.

Had the driver initially acceded to the request, the wounded man would, had he lived, been tremendously embarrassed
that someone had found him in such a condition of weakness
(to have been in an accident in the first place) and further
would have been morally obligated to his benefactor for the
rest of his life. Such obligation would have meant giving gifts
and granting favors of any type and expense to the man

throughout the rest of his life. These are moral obligations placed on the responsible Filipino, and he would never want it any other way.

Responsible behavior would have been to ignore the wounded man until, in some way, the rules of the society would have been "called off." Then, and only then, could the wounded man be released from his moral obligation of servitude to his benefactor. The policeman, drawing his gun, effectively accomplished this and left the wounded man free of obligation. Had the benefactor sought his own selfish interests over those of the wounded man or had he been insensitive to his interests, he would have immediately accepted and taken him to the hospital. The body would have been saved, but the spirit of the man would have been enslaved. It is no small decision to aid a Filipino in evident display of weakness or personal need.

In applying the four questions, an outsider with a distinctive world view would likely have entered at question 3 and sought to be of service. Considering the norm or responsible behavior, he would have immediately responded in keeping with his own style of responsible behavior. The man's physical life would likely have been of primary importance. Only later would he have been shocked to find the man in moral obligation to him for life. The outsider would have sought to argue him out of such a "strange idea."

The effective agent of change goes in at question 1 and asks first, "What is the norm?" Responsible behavior in the Filipino culture is to aid the wounded man in such a way as to avoid embarrassing him or placing him in one's debt, even if it means the physical death of the individual. Responsible behavior in biblical culture was to aid the wounded man, irrespective of consequences.

Irresponsible behavior in Filipino culture would include either aiding the person before the rules governing this setting were called off or refusing aid after they were set aside. Irresponsible behavior in biblical culture was, among other things, to ignore the wounded man.

By initial noninvolvement and later service, the Filipino Samaritan was acting toward the accident victim as the biblical Samaritan was acting toward the robbery victim. Initial noninvolvement produced the same effect as the initial involvement of the biblical case.

Variation of Norm

Crosscultural experiences introduce an ever-widening range of variation within the lifestyle of the individual. Anyone living for a period within a distinct culture, having approached that culture with a degree of acceptance, can witness to such increase of variation. If one is seeking to influence short-haired people, he can trim his hair; if long-haired people, he can let his hair grow. If one is approaching time-oriented people, he can pay particular attention to time scheduling; if approaching event-oriented people, he can pay attention to those things that encourage the event type of behavior. If one is approaching families where the father is a strong figure, he can stress the father nature of God; if approaching families where the father is not a strong figure, then some other teaching from the Scriptures about God can be sought out and used, e.g., a friend who sticks closer than a brother (Prov. 18:24). If one is a person with norm B and is attempting to reach someone with norm A, he can put into effect change potential and learn from the insights of the other in those areas where his life is needing such insight. Paul said it this way: "I have become all things to all men so that by all possible means I might save some" (1 Cor. 9:22).

This is not an approach of compromise, but of enrichment. To compromise is to abandon principle, however much or little. *To extend one's range of variation of lifestyle is to incorporate as many lifestyles into his own as possible without producing destructive tension or causing abandonment of principle or absolute.* One can therefore be comfortable or at peace when crossing cultural boundaries. He can also become maximally available to the members of the culture or subculture with whom the gospel of Jesus Christ is shared. Christ did not condemn the woman taken in adultery; rather, he opened the way for an effective change and extension of norm that would leave her free to worship him fully and completely. In light of the above discussion, we could paraphrase his comments to her, "You are a beautiful person, now go and let your behavior be as beautiful as your person."

God has provided those who witness of his grace maximum opportunity to enter another culture or subculture without strain, to introduce the gospel message clearly and without conflict, and to permit the Holy Spirit to be effectively in control of all operations. To the degree that one is monocultural and forces his own life-way on another, the Spirit is bound, and his converts to Christ will be forced into some degree of ethical relativism. The biblical teaching will be confusing, and people will seek ways to misinterpret it to their ends. To the degree one is crosscultural, each life-way will be open to the ministration of the Spirit, and individual and group norms will change in keeping with his direction. The Scriptures will speak directly and fully to such people and become the powerful tool in their lives that God intended them to be.

Summary

The culturally exclusive approach to the behavior of others is to see in what ways that behavior is understandable to the one viewing it and how it can be changed to conform to the expectations of the one viewing it. The other is pressed into some degree of ethical relativism. The approach of cultural openness lets man be man and God be God in evaluating behavior. Thus in the approach of cultural realism, biblical absolutism is teamed with cultural relativism so that a Nigerian can be a Nigerian and be fully open to God. A North American can be a valid, responsible North American and be fully open to God. Such an approach effects maximum responsibility of the person and allows him to have those sociocultural uniquenesses that reinforce his identity and encourage mature growth in the Christian faith. Spiritual conflict is thus not intensified because of unnecessary social conflict.

The sacrificial adultery of the Fletcher case study can be seen not so much as sacrificial, but as the woman's living out her norm as a responsible individual. It can be viewed not only as adultery, but as the recognition of the precise nature of a norm that is potential for change by the Spirit of God speaking through the Scriptures to the persons involved. It further opens any norm to the influence of the Spirit of God so that any specific concern, e.g., family, will not be totally dominated by other considerations of lifestyle. A truly crosscultural individual can introduce the gospel in any culture or subculture without the accompanying "cultural baggage" that is potential for enslavement of the person and falsification of truth. His range of variation of lifestyle or norm is increased, so he is comfortable and at peace with people of diverse styles or norms. At the same time, he is protected from abandonment of his own principles. He also gains perspective that objectively enables him as a wise counselor to aid others in effective change of norm in keeping with the expressed will of God. Four questions give one tools and flexibility to maintain the validity of culture:

1. What is the norm, i.e., life-way, culture?
2. Is the person living in keeping with his norm?
3. Does the norm need changing?
4. Who is responsible for changing the norm?

Questions for Discussion

Relating to the Sending Church

1. Is there anything you do, which you notice no one else does, but which you feel is a very important part of your identity? Describe.
2. Can a person praying in an upright position be as close to God as one who is praying while kneeling? Discuss in relation to biblical teaching and practices within your church.
3. Describe two distinct patterns of "hospitality" existing side by side in North American society. Which one is correct?
4. Work with the problem of divorce in North American society in the way the author worked with "sacrificial adultery." Does the person seeking a divorce place the value of personal fulfillment over concern for the family? Is that a biblical ranking? If you feel it is, or isn't, how would you proceed to relate to this person?
5. Does your church press you toward ethical relativism? If so, describe how.
6. How can we use the model of biblical absolutism and cultural relativism to prepare Christian internationals to live biblically when they return home?

Relating to the Study of the Bible

1. Discuss Abraham's relationship with Hagar and Sarah in light of the guidelines of this chapter. Describe the conflict of norm encountered between Abraham and Sarah. How was the conflict resolved? Was the resolution effective (Gen. 16, 20)?
2. Discuss Abraham's entry into Egypt with Sarah and his explanation to Pharaoh of their relationship, in light of biblical absolutism and cultural relativism. Was Abraham wrong in introducing Sarah as his sister? Discuss (Gen. 12:10–20).
3. Discuss Daniel's stand regarding the king's meat and drink when he was a young man (Dan. 1) and his behavior while fasting and not fasting as presented in Daniel 10. Does he make apology for his change of norm (not partaking of the meat and wine when he was young, and only failing to partake while fasting when he was older)? Was he still honored by God? What are the implications for your life? Does his change condone drinking alcoholic beverages in the contemporary age?
4. Discuss the difference of response of Judas and Peter in the experience of the betrayal and subsequent denial of Christ from the point of view of biblical teaching and cultural experience. (Luke 22). Were they operating from the same cultural norm? What were the cultural features involved in their respective resolutions? The spiritual ones?

5. In the Book of Acts, how did the disciples adapt to the various demands of culture? How did such adaptations affect their ministry? How did they rise above culture? Does their experience give us insight in dealing with our own cultural demands?

Relating to Missions and Crosscultural Ministry

1. When you have sought to change something in your host culture, did you begin with question 1 or question 3? Describe. If you started with 3, how might your ministry have been aided by starting with question 1?
2. Take a significant case of discipline from your field experience and work through the various concepts presented in this chapter to see if you can gain clarification of the degree of effectiveness of the discipline.
3. Assuming you are a "teetotaler," how were you able to maintain this stance in your field without offending your hosts? Explain.
4. Select one of the continua of the basic values, e.g., time/event, and discuss the conflict of norm you encountered in the field between missionaries, between nationals, and between nationals and missionaries.
5. Did you create any ethical problems in the field? Explain.

Group Activities and Exercises

1. *Small Group*. Have the members discuss the cultural relativism evident in the progress of the Hebrews from the Old Testament period to the New Testament period. Was this bad? How did such development prepare more fully for the coming of Christ? How might Jesus have been introduced into the world had there been no culture change through the centuries of Hebrew/Jewish experience?
2. *Panel Discussion*. Have three members of the group prepare a panel on the subject of biblical absolutes versus cultural expressions as reflected in the Bible. Have each prepare a five-minute statement of a specific subject, such as "The Bible says nothing of dress styles except to indicate that one should be modest whatever his style." Then open the discussion to the larger group.
3. *Case Study*. Have the group work with the problem of divorce in North American society much as I worked with the case of sacrificial adultery in this chapter. Divide up the various models among the members of the group/class so that each of the models of crosscultural concern are covered in the discussion.
4. *Presentation*. Invite a guest from a distinct society that has a lifeway distasteful to the average American, e.g., arranged mar-

riage, to discuss his point of view within the group. Urge him to discuss just how his Christian life is enhanced by being fully responsible within the context of his own culture.

17

The Support Model

Case Study: If I Forbid Ken to Drink

When Ken Harris was a sophomore in college, he wrote home to his parents that he had begun to drink with some of the fellows. Ken's mother Ethel was frantic, and she said to her husband Sid, "Write and tell him to stop drinking at once."

After thinking about it a few moments, Sid replied, "No, I won't. If I forbid Ken to drink, he may stop, but it will be because I made the decision for him, not because he had come to a decision on his own."

Ethel found this reasoning very unsatisfactory. "Why shouldn't Ken have the benefit of our experience?" she protested. "Anyway, it's difficult enough these days to get through college sober."

After some further discussion, the parents decided to make it possible for Ken to spend several weekends at home that fall. During those days together, Sid tried subtly to get close to Ken, not pressing for an abnormal intimacy but giving his son numerous opportunities to talk about whatever was on his mind.

Several times the two of them went hiking along mountain trails. As it turned out, very little was said about college social problems in general or drinking in particular, but a new friendship developed between the father and son which eased communication.

One day Sid told Ken about a member of the family who had died of alcoholism. "I have quite an affinity for alcohol myself," he admitted, "so I've decided to leave it strictly alone. Not only for my own sake, but for your mother's and yours."

Ken didn't comment on this. They resumed their climb up the mountain, and some hours passed in the deep silence characteristic of men who enjoy being in the woods. Occasionally one of them would make a comment, but what passed between them was largely unspoken.

Three months later, Ken again raised the question of drinking in one of his letters, but this time the emphasis had wholly changed. "I've decided not to drink," he wrote. "Some of the fellows in the dorm have been going off the deep end. I've come to the conclusion that drinking is wrong for me. I hope I can get some of my friends to take a good look at themselves, too."[1]

When someone rejects another, conflict likely results. Conflict undermines interpersonal relations. The behavioral response is a kind of inconsistency and unpredictability that tends to undermine the trust bond. With the undermining of the trust bond, relationships are strained at best and may even be terminated.

Acceptance reverses the rejection process leading to broken relationships. From the moment the message of acceptance gets through to the other, conflict in relationship can be worked with effectively.

The Bridge From Conflict to Rapport

Acceptance of a person as he is causes those involved in interpersonal and intergroup relationships to seek out a bridge (see figure 33) that will lead the one(s) in conflict out of conflict into a basic reconciliation. The various means of resolving conflict utilized by the average person in conflict are one or more of the following: scapegoating or projection, withdrawal, conformity for conformity's sake, formation of a new group, etc. (chapter 12). They serve as a kind of therapy but will just as likely reinforce the conflict as resolve it, and they may even lead the person or group into new patterns of conflict. The bridge or bridges sought for, therefore, must lead the person out of the conflict setting completely and not be simply therapeutic.

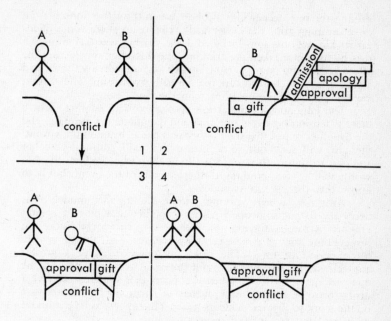

Figure 33. Bridging Conflict

Bridges may be:
information
clarification
an admission
an explanation
a gift
a favor
use of a metaphor
a show of power
correction
a counterstatement
verbal apology
action apology
approval
a compliment
flirtation
levity, such as
    punning, joking,
    teasing, heckling
a game or
    recreational activity
acquiescence

In Whiston's illustration of a college man who took up drinking much to the displeasure and disappointment of his parents, the mother kept after the father to order the boy to stop drinking. The father was aware that by ordering his son to stop drinking he would likely achieve the adverse effect, in essence, driving the boy deeper into alcohol. When the father took his son on a camping trip, the father had a chance to share some of his earlier life with his son. Included in his sharing was the admission that he had once taken up drinking but that after considering the effect of drinking on his personal health and considering that he had a wife and new child to care for, he had given it up. The sharing experience had quite an impact on the boy.

The Filipino uses the action apology to end conflict. Where there is tension between a mother and daughter, for example, and the daughter senses that the mother sees her as being in the wrong, the girl will seek out some action that will communicate her apology to the mother, e.g., washing the dishes voluntarily. No words will be said. Nothing further is made of the event, but both know that the conflict is ended.

At times, when working within the support model, it is necessary to put someone back into conflict to achieve a greater rapport. A parent, for example, who senses that a child does not respect him, may eliminate certain privileges, e.g., the allowance, for a period of time. The child may need to have a greater appreciation for that privilege and thus gain greater respect for the one making it available. When it appears that students perceive a professor to be an easy mark, it may be necessary for him to pour on the work so that the students, trained to expect a certain amount of work, will restore full respect for him.

Support

Once a bridge is built, those involved in interpersonal relations become support persons for one another (see figure 34). For the sake of this discussion, however, only two people will be referred to: the one changing and the support person. The support person is increasingly cognizant of what the other is within the context of his sociocultural setting. He begins to work with him by letting him progress in the change process. He allows him to be himself, trying not to force him to change his culture to accommodate the other.

The point of the support model within the context of effective ministry is to have the person eliminate the distinction between the real and the ideal. When they are separate, they may become polarized; and the individual may find himself in conflict between the real and the ideal. There is no problem with an individual having an ideal as long as it is a simple extension of the real and no one is forcing the ideal itself to become the real. As the real and ideal merge within the person's mentality, gradual change is permitted. The person involved with him is thus the one supporting him in this process of growth and development.

The support model involves the establishment of goals, setting operations to meet those goals, the ongoing evaluation of the goals and operations, resetting of each, the alternate session, and the encouragement toward creative expression. In other words, the support model encourages the full development and maturation of the person or the group. The support person has the delightful opportunity of seeing another develop fully in keeping with the maximum range of goals and opportunities available to him.

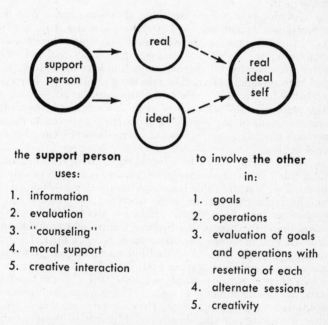

the **support person**
uses:

1. information
2. evaluation
3. "counseling"
4. moral support
5. creative interaction

to involve **the other**
in:

1. goals
2. operations
3. evaluation of goals and operations with resetting of each
4. alternate sessions
5. creativity

Figure 34. The Role of the Support Person During the Change Process

Goal Setting

Goals are anything toward which a person strives. They may be formal goals that are written down, sworn by, and carried out to the letter; or they may be hopes and aspirations that are nebulous in conception but nonetheless real. They may be short range, middle range, or long range. Time-oriented persons will establish timed goals involving timed periods of achievement. Event-oriented persons will establish goals of being with people and embellishing the event. Though the two kinds of goals may differ in form, they are the same type of goal, motivated by a distinct world and life view. Timed goals will throw an event person into conflict. Event goals will frustrate the timed person. Short-range goals will likely be specific, and long-range goals will likely be more general and nebulous. A person needs both to enable him to move maturely through life.

Anyone who values one thing above another, a trait that is characteristic of humans, will establish goals and strive for them. The support person has the opportunity to work with the other in establishing these goals and confirming their personal and ultimate value. He may suggest alternative goals in keeping with the person and his motivation. His task of providing information, however, is probably his greatest single contribution in the goal-setting area. The person himself seldom has all the information he needs to set effective goals of any type. The support person extends the other person's objectivity and scope and opens the way to more effective goal setting.

A missionary may have a long-range goal of reaching men for Christ, but in his day-to-day goals, he may not know exactly what to do. The Wycliffe Bible translator has the day-to-day goals built into his training so that he works from one aspect of the language to another until he is fluent within the whole. This then opens many doors to witness that become fruitful in accomplishing his ultimate goal of seeing men and women accept Christ. The formal training program of the Wycliffe Bible translators has gained such a good reputation for preparing a translator for the short-range goal achievement that many people not associated with the mission are attracted to the training program. The nonlinguistic missionary needs day-to-day goals as well. They can be in the area of witness, church planting, or church growth. Missions of this type should develop training institutes in such areas of specialization for attracting recruits and developing an adequate literature of such practices. This type of missionary also needs short-term goals in the areas of learning the language and culture, and the accompanying training to be able to accomplish them effectively. His strategies of evangelism, church planting, and church growth must be culture and language specific in order to be most effective.

In the Philippines, the long-range goal of winning men and women to Christ was established, and each member of the missionary team held firmly to that goal. They were unable to operationalize their day-to-day goals, however, for they freely admitted, "We really don't know just how to open Filipino society to the gospel." They were doing numerous things that had seemed to work in other areas, such as holding tent meetings and conducting door-to-door evangelism, but these did not seem to be working too well there. The Filipino was very receptive and responsive at first, but later on he turned cold to the message and ignored the missionary as well. Middle-range goals, besides, were almost nonexistent.

Working with the family and the alliance (the extended family) opened up a most critical area of the social structure and suggested some day-to-day goals that could effectively meet the long-range goals of the missionaries. It was suggested that because of the centrality of the alliance and the importance of the head of the alliance (the highest status person in the alliance), a short-range goal would be to get to know who the heads of alliances were within a given community. Middle-range goals would be to know specific heads of alliances within a two-year period and to have begun Bible studies in the homes of those who were most receptive. The long-range goal would continue as before, but a further long-range goal would be to let the Bible study in the home of the leader of an alliance develop into the local church. Along with this, the church could become related to other local churches through a loose alignment of groups under a leader who was of even higher status than any of the other alliance leaders. In one area where such a program was tried out, five Bible studies were established within the space of two years, much to the encouragement of the missionaries. They were beginning stage two of letting the groups that wanted to, relate to others in the formation of a more formal church organization.

Operations to Meet Goals

Operations help the person achieve his goals and therefore must be in keeping with both what the person is and the nature of the goal itself. The operations of a blind person must necessarily be different from the operations of a sighted person. The operations of a time-oriented person will differ from the operations of an event-oriented person. For example, in establishing a devotional program, a person who is blind and time oriented will concentrate on the use of verbal thought forms rather than visual forms. These will be scheduled, especially for the time-oriented person, according to some regular time sequence. A sighted person who is event-oriented will be able to utilize visual as well as thought forms and build these into an experience of devotions that will not be controlled by time. The two types of operations are not mutually exclusive, for both together can be formed into a total pattern for either person. However, the time person is more likely to develop timed operations even as the event person is more likely to develop operations that extend personal association or that embellish the event through visual means.

The Alternate Session

The alternate session involves taking action and then reviewing that action as a foundation for new action built on the first. There are times when a person in the change process needs to operate alone, and there are times when he needs supervision. The concept of the alternate session permits both eventualities. Jesus would at times be with his disciples (cf. Mark 5), and at times they would be off alone doing that which was suggested during their period of contact (Mark 6:12–13). The concept has come into contemporary use-fulness through the program of social work and the practice of psychological counseling. One does not, however, need to be a social worker or psychologist to use the alternate session with others.

The social worker, marriage counselor, or psychologist will meet with a person for a consultation. The client is then urged to go out and to put into practice the things he has learned during the insight session with the trained professional. In reality, church is one such alternate session, for a member is with the pastor for an hour or two and away from him until the same time the next week. Hopefully, he has been applying what he learned the prior week. School also has alternate sessions built into the educational program in that each holiday becomes a break from the learning process and the summer vacation permits a variety of experiences that could be debriefed at the beginning of the new school year. Unfortunately, the typical school program fails to gain much from such an alternate session, as the child is seldom debriefed regarding what went on during the time away and is not likely to be returned to the same classroom for the first days of the new term.

The debriefing session is what makes the alternate session of maximal worth. This involves talking through the experience with the counselor. Everyone learns covertly from experiences. At times, however, it is necessary to make that learning overt. The person involved in the experience is all too frequently caught up in it subjectively and is unable to see all the factors that are available to be learned and to be of help to him. The support person thus sets up the debriefing session either formally or informally to let the person himself see what he has learned through the experience.

Evaluation of Goals and Operations

Part of the debriefing time in the alternate session becomes a time for evaluating and reevaluating goals and operations. The time-oriented person will likely set scheduled times for the debriefing session and will have the session planned out in detail. The event-oriented person will have to "be caught" between events. Scheduling for the event-oriented person may not necessarily be time scheduled, but it can be effectively carried out nonetheless.

A teacher will encounter numerous students who trend toward the event side of the time/event continuum. It is impossible to tie them down to a specific time schedule. Any set appointment will be broken a large percentage of times. Therefore, it is necessary to look to other machinery to effect the evaluation of goals and operations. Whenever one meets them, it is wise simply to continue the earlier conversation, tuning into their progress. What results is an ongoing conversation that you simply take up where you left off. Naturally, this is not convenient for a large number of people. Where the program is small, however, such personal contact can effectively provide the alternate session for the evaluation of goals and operations. This plan also places a great load on the memory process.

If certain goals are not being met, they can be restated and reformed in keeping with the new information and insight available at the contact session. When one approaches a new program, he idealistically sets up some goals. After experience, they can be limited, restricted, and reshaped more effectively.

Feedback

Feedback is any kind of information one receives following communication of some kind that causes a change in the original message. Feedback is vital in any communication process because it provides a guide to the correction of the message so that the message is received as intended. It is of special importance to determine the speed at which change is introduced. The support person should not be limited by a time schedule. When there is feedback that shows him what change can transpire rapidly, he can move forward as rapidly as possible. When he senses verbal and nonverbal indicators of resistance, he can take a look at this resistance objectively, analyze the true message contained, and gear the program and its speed to the new situation. Overall, in the process of change, that which takes a week to develop will take a week to change or resolve; that which takes a year to develop will take a year to change. Any change effected in a shorter span of time than that which might be expected is like a bonus in the change process.

The missionary vitally needs to learn this lesson of feedback. He wants to introduce Jesus Christ, but so often he does this irrespective of the need for response of the person or group to whom he is witnessing. He does not realize that the person is frequently resisting on sociocultural grounds, not necessarily on spiritual grounds; and until these are dealt with, the person will never be able to commit himself spiritually. The missionary can read the true message of resistance, back up, and establish a new relationship with the person involved in witness. Later, when he reads the signs of response, he can move just as rapidly as that response indicates. Verbal and nonverbal cues provide red, amber, and green lights to the change process. Some people can grow rapidly in their Christian lives, and others take a very long time. We do not have to insist on an identical or constant rate of growth for everyone we encourage in the Christian walk.

The message may need to change in a given culture so that the truth does not change. In Pocomchi, the word for fox implies one who speaks with a falsetto, i.e., a homosexual, not one who is sly. In Luke 13:32, where Herod is referred to as a fox, the Pocomchi relate to him as a homosexual, and the text makes no sense at all. It was not until the word for wildcat was introduced that the passage made sense, for the wildcat, not the fox, is seen as sly by the Pocomchi. Since feedback has shown that nonsense was being communicated, the message could be changed in time to avoid falsehood. Truth could now be communicated regarding the character of Herod.

The Good Counselor

The good counselor is the support person who encourages the other to develop, change, and mature in keeping with what he is personally (see figure 35). Such a person provides information and moral support so that the other person or group can be truly creative in keeping with his own uniqueness. He never dictates to others; he simply lets each one tap into the truth of the larger group in keeping with the justice model (chapter 8). In this way, each person or group develops uniquely and learns from the other but does not become enslaved to the other.

Thus the good counselor needs objective knowledge of himself and of the other. He accepts each as worthy of respect and thus understands the distinctives in the sociocultural settings involved. He works with the various possibilities of bridges from conflict to rapport, attempting to release the other from the web of conflict. He provides information and thus is available in the formation of goals and operations. His "feel" for the other, and his true needs will involve him in the ongoing process of evaluation and reformulation of goals and operations. In being available in this way, he need never abandon his own principle and can thus encourage the other to be fully responsible individually and corporately. By becoming involved in the alternate session, he does not become a crutch; rather, he is there when he is needed to talk or work through a problem. This is most effectively set up through the debriefing process when opportunity is provided to let the covert learning of the lived experience become overt and known. Debriefing provides the opportunity for the other person or group to provide feedback information that will show the true nature of the learning experience and effect change in the communicated message so that it can get through correctly. Finally, the support person, creative himself, encourages the truly creative expression of the other.

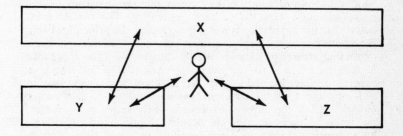

Figure 35. The True Counselor

One of the most difficult aspects of youth work is allowing the youth to develop as youth and not pressing them to be made over into adults before they can have the conversion and early growth experiences of the true Christian. The good counselor is one who lets the youth be youth and lets them grow in Christ. Likewise, he lets the adults be adults and lets them grow in Christ. He thus accepts each group as it is, letting the truth flow through the various levels of the hierarchy into each group so that each may maintain its true identity.

Master-Apprentice Role

One form of the good counselor is the facilitator of learning in the educational process. *The facilitator works with his student more as an apprentice who can ultimately become his master,* rather than viewing himself as a teacher who can never be mastered. After the learner hears the principles explained and watches the teacher put them into practice, he then can imitate the teacher by applying them in his own setting. The teacher is the model his students observe and emulate. They in turn become masters, passing on their learning to their apprentices.

The teacher-student model, practiced increasingly in the Western world, has two positions: teacher and student. The student provides response but seldom feedback to the teacher. The teacher simply needs to know that the student has learned what the teacher has taught. This is generally done in the examination process. The teacher seldom calls for feedback that is potential for changing the message of the teacher, the teaching style, or the educational philosophy.

The facilitator, or master-apprentice, model, on the other hand, calls for feedback to make the communication of the message more accurately targeted to each apprentice. The master must know that the apprentice is not only grasping the principles being dealt with but also is applying those principles effectively in ever-expanding aspects of life. The master thus involves the apprentice in various projects to test such application. The apprentice is expected to have learned so well that in certain areas of application and refinement of principle, he becomes master to the master himself. This is the ultimate expression of the learning experience.

In trend-event settings, the master can give himself totally to his apprentices. In the trend-time settings, however, time schedule and the numbers associated with viewing time as production expectation (i.e., large classes) hinder the master from entering all aspects of a person's life. Strategy is called for in order to produce an apprentice pattern in a time-structured society.

I developed a pattern of recruiting apprentices from among my students. Such recruitment was covert in that the student himself chose to become interested in something that I knew or did well. Seeking to avoid making the role too pronounced and thus forcing a change of behavior on the part of the apprentice, various subroles were built into my program. One young person wanted to become involved in writing professionally. A project I was working on was turned over to the emerging apprentice to edit. I wanted to become involved in writing in a more popular vein, a skill the apprentice had been developing prior to the association. A number of outcomes were the result: The apprentice coauthored a professional article with me and went on to become a noted author and lecturer, herself master to new apprentices. I gained greatly in the area of writing skills, never to the degree of the apprentice become master, however.

Originally, I began working with one apprentice, developing

the skills necessary to have a good experience. Later apprentices were added in various positions of teaching and research assisting and in other roles. Now, in a given educational year, I service some twenty apprentices, each involved in some area of my interest and expertise.

Consulting in Papua New Guinea with a noted mission board, I observed that the members were constantly calling for new workers. Each office needed help, each field worker needed some project accomplished that he himself could not find time to do. Near the center of operations of the mission in that country was an educational institution full of some of the brightest young people in the country. They were invited to the center from time to time to see what the missionaries were doing, but only to look, not to touch, not to participate. I recommended that each missionary, each office worker, and each administrator begin cultivating friendship with someone in the school and begin to make that person an apprentice in some area of shared interest. In time, these young people would be able to take on specialized projects in the field and even become missionaries themselves. One objection was that these young people were in the school to prepare to make money, and there was no money in mission. Such a shortsighted point of view was keeping them from one of the most significant sources for recruitment. The young people who achieved a mind challenge would think twice before they placed it as second choice to a money challenge. Even if all the young people did not choose the mind challenge, there would be enough to have made the effort quite significant in the development of the mission program.

Creativity

Creativity grows out of what a person is, and is in turn shaped by what he is. Creativity can develop when a person lets all the various aspects of his life be integrated and blended in its uniqueness. Everything that is involved in his internal, personal life experience, along with everything that is involved in the external life about him, becomes part of that uniqueness. Uniqueness does not imply irresponsibility to the group, rather, it enhances responsibility. Since a person is the sum of all the groups of which he is a part, his uniqueness will feed out of their uniqueness and in turn help form their uniqueness. Note the following characteristics of a creative person.

Profile of a Creative Person

1. *Inherited sensitivity*. The creative person has a propensity for a greater sensitivity to certain types of experience: mathematical, artistic, musical, mechanical, literary. This appears to be well established by studies of families which exhibit high creativity in certain fields over several generations. The apostle Paul put it this way: "God has given each of us the ability to do certain things well" (Rom. 12:6 LB).

2. *Early training*. The creative person, more likely than not, had his childhood in a home atmosphere that encouraged rather than discouraged, inquisitiveness. Creativity is as much a matter of attitude as anything else.

3. *Liberal arts education*. The creative person is more likely to express his creativity if he is exposed to teachers and curricula that place a premium on questions (i.e., noncrisis) rather than on answers (i.e., crisis) and who reward curiosity rather than learning by rote and conformity.

4. *Asymmetrical ways of thought*. The creative person finds an original kind of order in disorder; it is as if he sees the reflection of nature in a distorting mirror, whereas "ordinary" people are able to see the image in a plain mirror only. Most highly intelligent people (as measured by tests) have symmetrical ways of thought, and for them, everything balances out in some logical way.

5. *Personal courage*. The creative person is not afraid of failure or of being laughed at. He can afford this risk, because what is important to him is not what others think of him but what he thinks of himself.

6. *Sustained curiosity*. The creative person never stops asking questions, even about his most cherished ideas. A capacity for childlike wonder carried into adult life typifies the creative person.

7. *Not time-bound*. Morning, noon, and night are all the same to the creative person; he does not work by the clock. Problems may take years to solve, discovery may take decades. With his personal "window on infinity," time has a personal, not a social, meaning. Truly creative persons seldom respond well to "deadlines" arbitrarily set by someone else.

8. *Dedication*. The creative person has an unswerving desire to do something, whatever it may be and whatever the obstacles to doing it may be. The problem will not be left unsolved; the feeling will not remain unexpressed.

9. *Willingness to work*. It is quite possible that no one in our society works harder than the artist; the same may be said for the creative scientist, inventor, composer, or mathematician. This may not express itself in the number of hours put in on the job or in obvious physical labor, but in the fact that even in sleep or reverie the creative person is constantly working for a solution.

This definition of the creative person is different from the point of view stated in the opening paragraph of this section. His list has been included for a specific reason. Every person is creative! God made humans to be like him, and he is creative. He is even the Creator of the universe, of man, and of society. But each person would like to be more creative than his own natural gifts allow him. This list can provide the kind of insight that one can work on to enhance his own creativity.

In working with many kinds of students, whether in the school system or the church system, I have found that they tend to minimize their strengths and abilities. They feel that they cannot really effectively develop them. I encourage them to branch out, to try new things, to be creative. In essence, I free them to create, to do something that only they can do, to do something even they have never done before. This encourages them. They know they can do it. They know they can achieve. The student then takes these lessons and applies them to the rest of his life experience. He is a new person. He is uniquely free. He personally gains, and the groups of which he is a part gain also.

A Formula for Creativity

Many educators want to be creative and to encourage the people with whom they work to be creative as well. *A simple formula for developing creative expression may involve what one is learning, an interest, and an art form.*

What one is learning can be just about anything. It can be the principles of effective crosscultural communication presented in this book. An interest grows out of one's everyday life. It may relate to the urban challenge to missions experienced by someone living in the city. It may be a challenge to live with a new roommate or a new mate.

An art form may be painting, sculpture, music, creative writing, poetry, drama, etc. It may even be a lecture, though few teachers utilize the lecture as an art form. An art form is anything that enables one to communicate with another effectively. An art form replacement can be use of some electronic medium, such as radio, television, tape, or film.

In the teacher-student relationship involving two positions— teacher and student—the teacher simply does what is natural to him. The assumption is that that should be sufficient. Why develop more than one way to communicate? Usually, that one way is a lecture that is not necessarily developed as an art form. The students gain information but are seldom taught how to think.

In the master-apprentice relationship, there are three positions in focus: the master, the apprentice, and the apprentices of the apprentice. The master must prepare his apprentice for his own experience with his own apprentices. Whereas the lecture might be adequate in his own society, the apprentice may be called to minister in a visual, trend-event society where the lecture is ineffectual. The master is responsible to introduce the apprentice to other legitimate means of educating so that he is free to choose that which is most effective to his own apprentices. He, of course, has the responsibility for introducing his own apprentices to effective means of communication to their apprentices, extending the model now to the fourth position.

When the master-apprentice relationship is working effectively, with each one developing apprentices, the progression is geometric rather than arithmetic. This means that by the third position, we are close to dealing with an infinite progression. We are literally covering the world. Compare this with the two-position response of the teacher-student relationship. The progression is only arithmetic, and the results simply increase two by two. In Genesis 12:2–3, God says that through Abraham all the people of the earth will be blessed. The master-apprentice three-position model underlies this prediction: Abraham is in the first position ("I will bless you"), those to whom Abraham will be a blessing (his seed) are in the second position, and "all peoples on earth" are in the third position. In 1 Corinthians 3:6, Paul speaks of himself as having "planted" the seed (the first position), of Apollos as having "watered" it (the second position), and then of God as causing it to "grow" (the third position). Note what that growth is in verse 9. We are given an illustration from agriculture, where the product is not one stalk of grain, but an entire fieldful. We are also given the image of blocks being put together in such an orderly manner as to form a building. Jesus (the first position), selected twelve disciples (the second position), and these became the "about 120" of Acts 1 (the third position). They became the church by the fourth position and the church universal from that time on.

Jesus the Educator

Everything about the ministry of Jesus was complete at its beginning. It simply needed time to mature. It was like a living organism, complete within the seed. Jesus had been aware of those about him. He had been tuned in to the people with whom he associated. When the time came, he just "roped them in." They began doing all the things he was doing and would need to be doing after he left them. He said, "I will make you fishers of men" (Mark 1:17). He meant, "You will fish and be fishing fishers of men," since the form in the Greek is in the subjunctive. While they were doing, they were also being. While they were beginning, they were also completing. Whatever I want to complete in my course work is built into the beginning. If I want my students to know each other, I start with activities that mix and match them, even as they are learning the content of the course. Otherwise they will likely end the course as strangers.

Jesus was the master of twelve apprentices. His apprentices learned while doing. He entered their lives as a living presence, and they continued this style of ministry after he was gone. Mark 6:12–13 says, "They went out and preached that people should repent. They drove out many demons and anointed many sick people with oil and healed them." This is just exactly what Jesus did. My students use simulation activities including out-of-class assignments using the same activities we do in class. When they go into teaching, they not only have the experience of the classroom, they have their own validating experience.

Jesus made use of the case study with the attendant debriefing. Every parable Jesus taught was a case study which he afterward debriefed with his disciples. This led to additions, clarifications, and further insights not available to the others. Scripture says: "He used many such illustrations to teach the people as much as they were ready to understand. In fact, he taught only by illustrations in his public teaching, but afterwards, when he was alone with his disciples, he would explain his meaning to them" (Mark 4:33–34 LB). Jesus later told his disciples to "Teach these new disciples to obey all the commands I have given you" (Matt. 28:20 LB). Only they had them all, via debriefing. In much of my teaching, I will pause and ask a number of students to provide a fifty-word statement of what they have heard in the past period of time. Hearing it in their words, I know if I have successfully communicated my message.

Jesus made effective use of the alternate session. The key is that it looks back and stages toward the future. He sent the disciples to go and do and then return to talk about it. After the disciples had gone out to preach and heal, they "gathered around Jesus and reported to him all they had done and taught" (Mark 6:30). Each return brings greater trust and confidence. The Second Coming is the ultimate in providing hope within the alternate session concept. At the Ascension, the angel said, "This same Jesus, who has been taken from you into heaven, will come back in the same way you have seen him go into heaven" (Acts 1:11).

Jesus urged creativity. He encouraged those about him to live in keeping with their own uniqueness (see, e.g., Matt. 18). He was not bound by nonfunctional practices that had lost their meaning (Mark 7:1–16). His teachings were life expanding, like reversing a funnel and pouring in life from the small end and letting it flow out the wide end. Creativity is best expressed in celebration to reveal what is happening in the lives of the hearers, not just to know what is being said or done.

Celebration

Celebration is a time to look back and affirm social achievement. It is a time to look ahead and integrate all the experiences of learning and development and prepare for the future.

For the person in Christian ministry, celebration opens the opportunity to affirm the members of the group in loyalty and dedication to the task of spreading the gospel to the glory of God. Many servants of God grow weary in the day-by-day performance of their task in world outreach. They are in the valley of the mundane experience of life. They need time in the mountain peaks of life. Celebration affirms the need for the mountain peak.

In every class I teach, I attempt to get the work of the course completed prior to the last week of class. Then the larger group is divided into small groups, and these are given fifteen minutes during the last class periods to present some group experience in which all members of the class will share. In the process, they integrate the learning of the class far more thoroughly than they would during the final exam. They look forward to their respective ministries and bring the rest of the class into the experience of knowing and praying for their classmates.

The church today, existing in a multicultural setting, needs the concept of celebration to encourage the unity of the church. Normally, in a church setting, one ethnic group founds the church and a second emerges within that congregation or moves into it. The second must follow the plan of the first for worship, praise, prayer, and outreach. To please the mother church, they must abandon their cultural expressions as they pertain to worship and service. One way the church has resolved this conflict has been to make two completely separate entities. Each has gone its own way, whether both use the same church building or not.

The celebration church is one that maintains the identity of the various ethnic/language groups within the church yet brings them together from time to time in celebration. At such a time, each group ministers to the others in its own language, musical forms, praise forms, etc. No one group sets the standard or plans the program for the other. Each is enriched by learning the other's language, the music, and the lifestyle lying behind worship and education. Interestingly, there were no Old Testament examples of such balanced reciprocity, the Hebrews being such a dominant socioreligious group. The clearest New Testament expression was that which reduced the conflict between the Gentiles and the converted Jews. This does not mean the celebration church should not be used by the church. Few other practices have worked to achieve oneness in the body when ethnic and language differences have divided. Celebration is a way of bringing culturally different peoples into the church in social unity that has hope of founding and growing into spiritual unity.

Summary

Destructive tension or conflict is best worked with in a way that will reduce the tension effectively. A vital way is sought to bridge from conflict to rapport. Such a bridge or bridges provide a means of moving from a setting of conflict to one in which the various individuals or groups are seen as valid, are cooperating with shared "voices," and are potential for mutual respect.

Once a bridge is built, the individual or group needing the help is the center of focus and has the privilege of setting his own goals, establishing operations to meet those goals, evaluating the goals and resetting them accordingly, and developing creativity. The other person, the one helping the individual or group, then becomes the support person or good counselor. He associates freely with the individual or group needing help and offers insight into goal setting, operations development, and reevaluation of goals and operations. He encourages creativity. He is the moral support. He is the encourager, the provider of information, the interested one, the true friend. He provides the alternate session with the opportunity of debriefing the person involved so that learning can be made obvious. He encourages celebration to become free from the past and to move with confidence into the future.

The result may not be exactly that which the support person seeks, but it will be meaningful to the other person. Each will be a free person. Each will be a person growing toward maturity. When the cues indicate movement, the support person can move rapidly; when they indicate a need for slowing, the support person can slow down. Verbal and nonverbal communication will serve as guides to the support person in his ministry.

The support person becomes a facilitator of learning. This is effectively carried out through the master-apprentice relationship where the master is preparing his own apprentices for dealing with their own apprentices, and also becoming master to the master. Only then can each person be full and complete. Only then can people of every culture truly know God from the depths of their own being and grow spiritually in keeping with God's best for them. When members of various linguistic and ethnic groups come to know God and seek to praise him in worship, they can do so in a celebration church where they can maintain their own cultural and linguistic forms yet minister to the body of Christ as fully equal and valid. Such a plan enables each believer to know the other more fully and to do so by learning the other's language and cultural usage and insight.

Questions for Discussion

Relating to the Sending Church

1. How can you serve as a support person and still maintain your own principles? Illustrate your response.
2. Are there times when you might need to put a person into conflict to achieve effective rapport? Explain and illustrate from your own experience.
3. How might a typical Sunday school class operate were it to be conceived as an "alternate session"? How might a church service be designed? Would such a plan help the member? How?
4. How might the church encourage creativity in ways that would encourage its program and growth?
5. In what ways can the pastor or youth director develop as a "good counselor"? Compare such a possibility with the role each fills at the present time.
6. How might the concept of the celebration church work within the context of your ministry? Examine your ethnic/language constituency, and if there is a nucleus of members, design a fully open and equal celebration. Be educating your members so they can appreciate the language and praise forms of others.

Relating to the Study of the Bible

1. Study passages on the Holy Spirit and discuss in what ways he matches the design of the good counselor and support person, and in what ways he is more than this.
2. If someone were to suggest to you that Jesus never put anyone into conflict without also providing a "bridge" to more effective rapport, could you discover some of those bridges? Describe them. For example, study the conversation Jesus had with the woman of Samaria (John 4:1–30) or his "raid" on the temple (Matt. 21:12–16; Mark 11:15–17).
3. Compare the life of Jonah with the ideal of the support person. How does he compare? Explain.
4. Compare the lives of Nehemiah, Naomi (Book of Ruth), and Daniel with the ideal of the support person. How does each compare? Explain.
5. Compare the lives of Jesus, Paul, or Luke from the point of view of a support person, a creative person, and a good counselor; and try to derive further principles and operations to guide you in your dealings with others.

Relating to Mission and Crosscultural Ministry

1. What bridges have you consciously sought to build with your people? Explain.
2. Have you worked with a person in your ministry that exemplified the support person and good counselor models? Describe.
3. Have you had to put someone back into conflict to try to achieve greater rapport? Explain.
4. List the long-range, middle-range, and short-range goals for your participation in the program of ministry you are now carrying out. Are your activities supporting your goals? Are the people with whom you associate aiding you in attaining your goals? Is your value orientation consistent with such goals? What kinds of changes in your life might be called for in view of your goals?
5. Select two or three categories of the basic values model with which to work, and state ways that you might use to encourage greater creativity in the life of the person so designated.
6. Begin working with the master-apprentice model and let people begin to relate to you as you help them grow and develop in areas of your knowledge and expertise.

Group Activities and Exercises

1. *Simulation.* Bridges or Bombs can be played by any number within the larger group. Each person is given a 3-by-5-inch card indicating a "bridge" for developing relationship or a "bomb" for undermining relationship. (Consult the chapter listing of bridges as well as chapter 4 for bombs, i.e., rejection behaviors.) This information is confidential and is to be divulged only during the role play. With a specific setting in mind—e.g., family—the first person begins a conversation growing out of a specific situation—e.g., the son asks the father for the use of the family car. The second person—in this case, the father—responds in keeping with his bridge or bomb, and the first person responds in turn in keeping with his instruction. After a minute or two of such conversation, shift to the third person, who may take the mother's role, for example, and respond in keeping with her assignment. The exercise is helpful in permitting the group to see how a "soft answer turns away wrath."
2. *Creative project.* Let each member of the group prepare some project that grows out of his experience in the course. Let this be a full expression of the person; and involve a paper, a creative writing presentation, or something that captures the uniqueness of the person, such as a pictorial or photographic essay, a simulation game, a painting, or something else.

3. *Corporate creative project*. Have the class members in small groups of four or five prepare fifteen-minute impact presentations to share with the larger group. Use the formula: the principles of the course, some issue of concern, and these joined together by means of some art form, such as painting, music, drama, etc., or by means of some electronic media, such as tape, TV, film, etc. Let the presentations function as "celebration" at the close of the course, seminar, or program.

18

The Models Illustrated: Two Cases

Case Study No. 1: Religious Conversion and Community Development[1]

What Happened?

Mass Conversion

The group of people this article focuses on has recently experienced one of the most remarkable mass conversions of Mexican Indians on record. In the late 1940s and early 1950s, about half of the four thousand Tzeltal Indians in the municipality of Oxchuc, Chiapas, were converted from folk-Catholicism to a type of Evangelical Protestantism. Their acceptance of Protestantism can be considered a people's movement inasmuch as the role of the missionaries with the Wycliffe Bible Translators was (and remains) consistently passive and low-key. The first converts decided to follow the new religion after hearing it explained, not firsthand, but on phonograph records made by the missionaries and played by the Tzeltal who helped with the translation.

Within a year, the number of converts had grown to a hundred. They then persuaded the two missionaries living in a nearby hamlet to come and teach them more about the new religion. One of these missionaries translated the New Testament into their language and taught the doctrines of the new religion to the leaders of the converts. The leaders were then responsible for preaching these doctrines to the other believers during church services.

Community Development and Postconversion Changes

Before conversion, the Tzeltals were land-poor and liquor indebted. They were land-poor because only about one-third of their land is tillable, and Ladinos (non-Indians) had expropriated large portions of it. Very few grew enough corn to last from one harvest to the next; therefore, almost all the able-bodied men had to spend three or four months each year working on coffee plantations outside the area to earn enough money for necessities. Before conversion, Tzeltals were thus almost totally agriculturists. They occasionally made nets, rope, or carrying bags to use themselves or to sell in the local markets, but that was the extent of their nonagricultural skills.

The Tzeltals were liquor indebted because Ladinos controlled the sale of liquor needed by the Indians for their ceremonial drinking. Social and religious consumption of rum left the Tzeltals hopelessly in debt to liquor merchants.

The fear of witchcraft was also a contributing factor to poverty because it was believed that anyone who saved a little money or tried to better himself in any way would become the victim of witchcraft.

After conversion, a number of Tzeltals freed from their fear of the spirit world had the courage to move to the newly forming colonies some eighty miles away. Their leaving the area helped to ease the land-shortage problem for those remaining.

Converts were no longer liquor-indebted, for now they were abstainers. They were able to save the money that would otherwise have gone for drink to buy better clothes, livestock, and houses.

Converts were also no longer intimidated by threats of witchcraft; individual entrepreneurs could own what they like, engage in a greater variety of economic activities, and accumulate wealth without suffering anxieties about witchcraft.

Disease, the second symptom of underdeveloped communities, was widespread in the Oxchuc municipality in preconversion days. Sickness was prevalent because the Tzeltals suffered the illness-producing consequences of poverty: a lack of hygiene and an ignorance of the natural causes of disease. When they were sick, they consulted shamans whose treatments were psychological at best rather than medicinal.

After conversion, Tzeltals, with increased affluence, are substituting an adequate diet for an inadequate one. They are buying such health-promoting items as washbasins and soap, and hygienic measures are now utilized in some degree by almost everyone to control disease. Almost all the converts and many nonconverts who are sick now go to the local Western-trained medical practitioners. The combination of Western medicine, hygienic measures, and an adequate diet has resulted in better health for the Tzeltals in postconversion times.

The third symptom of underdeveloped communities is illiteracy. Before conversion, the Tzeltals were illiterate and openly opposed to having their children attend school. Even when sent to school, teaching monolingual Tzeltal children how to read and write Spanish was virtually impossible, even after seven years of schooling.

After conversion, the Tzeltals are interested in reading the bilingual materials that have been written in their language. Instead of community opposition to schools, adult literacy classes are being held.

Why Did It Happen?

Socioeconomic Factors

Social tensions over land shortages led to social unrest, group conflicts, and antagonisms expressed in excessive drinking and rampant witchcraft. The extremities of this situation may partly explain why the Tzeltals turned to the new religion. In fact, witchcraft may have become so oppressive that people sought relief from it in the new religion.

Cultural Factors

The religion of the Tzeltals in preconversion times was a mixture of Mayan and Catholic beliefs, with the latter being poorly understood. The Mayan religion, this-world oriented, emphasized following the traditions of the past to maintain personal, social, and cosmic harmony with gods and shamans. The Catholic religion, other-world oriented, emphasized life after death as being of overriding importance. This was accompanied with a passive acceptance in this life of the structured inequality of people in social, political, and religious hierarchies. The mixture of these two somewhat contradictory religions produced a single belief system that discouraged social change.

The Protestant religion as introduced, on the other hand, rejected the fixed hierarchical structuring of people in this world and encouraged social mobility. The new religion made the bold claim that individuals have direct access to God and can take positive action to bring about change in this world.

Protestantism was also appealing because of its emphasis on the forgiveness of sins. As the Tzeltals listened to the message of the Old Testament prophets, they must have been reminded of the similarity in content to their own myths. Nor was the confessing of their sins to God and one another in the new religion anything unusual to them. Such confession had always been a part of their traditional healing ritual. Catholicism, of course, could have met these same needs, but it had never been presented in their own language, thus allowing them to understand it clearly.

Missionary Factors

The missionary mainly responsible for introducing the new religion to the Tzeltals was Marianna Slocum. She worked with several female partners down through the years in a team of two, her longest-staying partner being Florence Gerdel. This latter combination was an especially efficient one, with Slocum doing the translation work and Gerdel, a nurse, handling the medical practice.

The approach used was noncoercive, patient, and entirely in the Tzeltal language. The impressive medical results helped to validate the religious message, which was presented in a culturally sensitive manner.

Part of the success in introducing Protestantism was due to Slocum's personality, which has been characterized as "charismatic." There is no doubt that Slocum has made a greater positive impact on the Oxchuc municipality than any other living person.

How Did It Happen?

Conversion Experience

The introduction of Protestantism presented the Tzeltals with a choice they had never had in the past. They were all folk-Catholics because their parents had made the decision for them. Since there was no other option, to be religious was to be Catholic. The decision had been a group decision, a decision by the family. Becoming a Protestant, by contrast, involved an individual decision. However, making an individual decision on any important matter was something that Tzeltals either never did or did only with extreme reluctance. Slocum, recognizing the difficulty of such a decision and its social implications, insisted that only individuals as members of families would be allowed to join the new church. Thus, individuals could become believers in the new religion, but church membership would be withheld from them until their families were converted as well.

Individuals and families making a decision to deviate from the traditions of the past needed to be convinced that they would not suffer personal tragedy by being the victims of witchcraft. The new religion, promising power to believers greater than that held by shamans, provided such assurance. In spite of this assurance, some would-be converts wanted to see if the initial converts would die from witchcraft before making the decision. Still other prospective converts did not make the decision until a particularly powerful shaman was converted.

The new religion allayed the fears of the converts. They were now safe from the effects of witchcraft, and for the first time, they had the freedom to innovate and accumulate wealth without anxiety.

Conversion Confirmation

Once a profession of faith was made, the convert had to live up to a standard of behavior to confirm that faith in the eyes of both believers and nonbelievers. For example, that standard of behavior did not allow a believer to drink any alcoholic beverages. Sobriety as a way of life was then extended to include hard work, punctuality, fulfillment of promises, honesty, and thrift. The exercise of these minor virtues led to the accumulation of wealth and a rising standard of living for the Tzeltals.

Accompanying this economic gospel of Protestantism was an emphasis on perfection in physical well-being. Gerdel, the nurse, started a clinic in Corralito to treat the sick. She trained young Tzeltals as nurse interns who carried on this work after she left.

Perfectionism as a way of life also had implications for the literacy of the people. Although it is possible to be a believer and remain illiterate, the ideal for a convert is to be able to read the New Testament for himself; and anyone aspiring to the more prestigious leadership positions in the new churches must be literate.

Value Orientation Changes

In the process of changing from the most backward municipality in highland Chiapas to the most progressive, one set of value orientations was replaced by another. The old value orientations, based on folk-Catholic beliefs, can be summarized as follows: (1) humanity is evil without hope for improvement, (2) people live in harmony with nature, (3) the past is the time dimension of crucial importance, (4) the personality emphasis is on being, and (5) a collateral emphasis exists in social relations.

Protestantism offered a new set of value orientations: (1) the human evil condition is subject to improvement, (2) people can exercise control over nature, (3) the present and future are the dimensions of crucial importance, (4) the personality emphasis is on becoming, and (5) persons should work for the enrichment of their own household units.

Case Study No. 2: Prayer

Prayer is, by definition, conversing with God. The primary relationship in prayer is that of an individual or a group with God. The following is written with the recognition of the cultural overtones and interpersonal relationships that are also present in group praying.

Trust

1. When do you pray? When you have a selfish desire or a personal need? In a crisis?

2. Exercising the prior question of trust in prayer to God is to ask: What now? What would you have me to do? This is the counting-to-ten prayer in which one first waits to listen. It prepares the way for clear thinking and level-headed action.

3. In stages of trust development, prayer is the adjustment factor in bringing trust in God apace. Meditation in prayer gives a clarity of vision that few other types of activities do. It allows you to get things straightened out in your mind.

4. In domains of interpersonal trust, prayer brings the principles together. An arena for openness operates. We are given an indication of how we are received beyond our immediate group.

5. Reciprocity of trust opens the way to effective dialogue. We pray with another to God and then let him speak to us. What mechanisms do you provide to let him reciprocate? We can verbalize things in prayer we never could in any other way; and such honesty causes others to be honest also, giving them courage.

Acceptance

1. The prayer of confession is the acceptance-of-self prayer.

2. The prayers of thanksgiving, of forgiveness of the other, and of intercession are. acceptance-of-the-other prayers.

3. Prayer permits an attitude of total acceptance on which a life of principle and infinite variety in lifestyle is based.

4. When rejecting others, prayer and even our ability to pray is limited.

Danger: Prayer can be used to legitimize unilateral decision making; e.g., "The Lord laid it on my heart to do A rather than B, which you felt we should do."

Mutual Respect

1. The traditionalist tends to use prayer to exert social pressure—a kind of preaching in prayer intended to legitimize his way and to make others feel that they too must follow his way. For example, "God has told me," or "I prayed about this."

2. For the traditionalist, again, prayer can be a cause for inaction. For example, "We prayed about it, but the Lord didn't lead."

3. The ethical relativist (as distinct from a cultural relativist) uses prayer as a cover, a rationalization, an excuse, or an apology for abandoning principle. He tends to legitimize self-will.

4. The situation ethicist uses prayer to legitimize his acting in love and thus abandoning that which he is—if only in part.

5. Mutual-respect prayer draws out the deep inner feelings of man in the man-to-man and man-to-God relationships. Each person is seen as valid before God and can know and be known fully.

The Norm

1. Background or sociocultural experience of the person lets prayer become (or not become) a part of the norm or sum of a person's expectations. Prayer is thus carried out in keeping with this norm in terms of the form of prayer, the position of prayer, the length of prayer, the participants in prayer, the audible/inaudible nature of prayer, the role of prayer in the total religious experience, and anything else involved in the expression of prayer.

2. A person whose norm incorporates prayer and who does not pray or who is not permitted to pray, finds himself in deprivation of norm. He can find his spiritual life becoming sour, and bitterness can turn toward those who limit the prayer experience.

3. A person who has a quiet-based prayer norm and is drawn into some overt expression of prayer, body movement in prayer, or extremes of audible prayer, may find himself living in excess of norm and will react in embarrassment, if not in guilt.

System

1. Prayer is a component of a larger system (more than even the religious component which itself is part of the larger system) and is an integral part of this larger system.

2. Prayer is also a process that operates within the system, aiding in achieving balance and in letting the various components inhere in the system. It is a check on the social controls of the system.

3. Prayer provides necessary cues for interpersonal relations within the system—guide to behavior, indication of leadership, and instructions for gaining efficiency in operation.

Hierarchy

1. The style of prayer is different for each level of the hierarchy; e.g., it is intimate and informal in the small group of the lower, included units, and it is more stylized and formal in the more formal larger group.

2. Each unit on a given level has its own particular expression of prayer. One group will have one person pray, and a second group will have audible group prayer.

3. At each level of the hierarchy, it takes distinct social mechanisms to have a prayer experience. At the lower levels, prayer can be more spontaneous. With each successive increase in size and complexity, more refined means of getting a group together and having effective control within the group experience are needed.

Multisociety

1. Prayer differs by occasion, place, group, intent, need, position, form, etc.

2. Prayer can be addressed to the person of the Trinity indicated by the specific subculture.

Flow of Truth

1. Prayer can be the means of effecting justice also by the human participants, in that things spoken audibly in prayer can be heard by them when no other form of expression of the injustice is possible.

2. Prayer can be a powerful tool of social justice, bringing to the awareness of the corporate body needs of people and groups. The Spirit of God can lead them to fill those needs.

3. Prayer can also be used to enslave, in that a strong personality can create a climate of prayer in which there can be no possibility of disagreement. Prayer can then be used to rationalize the state of slavery.

Item Identification of Group

1. Every group has clear definition of who prays and when, the degree of authority as correlated with the experience of the prayer, the issues and concerns that are to be prayed for and about.

2. Prayer is a powerful means of developing the loyalty of the group.

3. Parents and church leaders tend to use prayer as a means of disciplining the group, whether family or church members.

4. Prayer is one means of making one's Christianity visible.

Activities of the Group

1. Again, each group defines just how prayer will be used within the group process, answering such questions as these: Is it to be part of an experience or is it to be the total experience? What ingredients are to be included within the experience of prayer?

2. The degree of formality is defined in keeping with the occasion and the kinds of people present.

3. Each group also defines to what degree the event itself or the controls of the event are to dominate.

Basic Values

1. The time/event continuum will set up the beginning and the end of the prayer event and the length of time for its fulfillment. It will determine whether there will be prolegomena and closure, the length of each of these, the order or sequence of the parts of the experience, the number of times prayer is to be had within an experience or a time block, the degree of control of the event itself by the time schedule, the degree of embellishment of the event that will be permitted, etc.

2. The vulnerability continuum will set up the degree of openness in prayer, how much will be revealed in keeping with the size and complexity of the group, the nature of the confession, how a group will handle an individual's confession, who will be assigned the blame for problems and trials, etc.

3. The dichotomy/holism continuum will determine the degree of detail included in the prayer, the nature of the prayer experience as it is shared by the group as a whole or the group as individual entities, the degree to which "language smearing" phenomena will accompany prayer, the degree to which persons and issues are stressed or highlighted in the total experience, etc.

Conflict of Norm

1. Prayer can highlight conflict and bring it into focus by way of summary statement debriefing.

2. Prayer can be one of the aids to recognizing conflict in light of the way a person prays. One can note the garbled utterance of a prayer or the evidence for withdrawal either from the immediate experience or from any occasion for prayer.

3. Types of prayer can be introduced to resolve conflict; e.g., conversational prayer to resolve, for the moment, the difference between time people and event people.

4. Prayer reflects the inability of one to pray because of conflict.

5. Prayer articulates conflict in times of trouble (e.g., Hezekiah's prayer in 2 Kings 20).

6. The Holy Spirit should be looked to as one who resolves conflict.

7. New groups are formed as people try to resolve conflict; Christians are urged to conform to life-ways that are incompatible with their own and to do this as a spiritual exercise; and scapegoating turns attention to perceived cause of conflict.

Frustration

This is reflected in the "cry aloud" to God.

Tools of Research

1. The prayer experience is excellent for participant observation in getting to know people, their concerns, and their challenges.

2. In essence, each prayer is a kind of interview in which a person is expressing to God and before others not only what is in his heart, but many specifics of his lifestyle or norm as well.

3. Experimentation is often accomplished under the guise or direction of prayer. It can be legitimized by prayer.

4. The prayers of the saints are excellent material for archiving research to determine the behavior of Christians at different periods of the development of the church.

Tools of Relationship

1. A prayer is one totality of cultural cues. As each cue is properly communicated and responded to, it leaves each prayer participant with a feeling of completeness.

2. The biblical source for our approach to and manner of praying comes via the functional equivalent. The prolegomena of the time-oriented person is the functional equivalent of the brief, direct, event-type opening of Jesus' prayer.

3. Well-meaning Christians can set up ideals within the context of prayer that other Christians are expected to follow. This is fine insofar as they derive from the biblical guidelines but unfortunate if they produce a slavery setting.

4. When people pray, they can leave a perception of their spiritual condition that is far from the real.

5. Prayer is one source to check out the adverse effect. A closing prayer by someone else can tell you if you accomplished your purpose in the session.

6. Prayer is one means of abusing the system. A person may pray, and the words may be right, but his intent can be other than the content and context of prayer.

7. Prayer is frequently taken as the whole of spiritual life or assigned more value than was intended by God.

Biblical Absolutes Versus Cultural Relativism

1. The content and context of prayer is totally cultural. Prayer is formed in the language of men. The order and arrangement of the thoughts as well as the regard for issues and concerns derive from the cultural context of the participant.

2. Prayer is one source for the supernatural intrusion—the most likely route into the cultural context.

3. When prayer is consistently and wholly of the person's culture, it is the most effective means of contact by the Spirit of God. The totality of prayer then makes the supernatural intrusion meaningful.

4. Prayer extends the variation of the lifestyle, for when you pray with someone, you adapt most easily to his lifeway.

Bridge

1. Prayer is a bridge from conflict to rapport. The prayer of confession uttered audibly communicates apology to the hearer and makes rapport more effective.

2. Prayer brings the principles together so that conflict can be resolved.

Support

1. Prayer is one of the most effective means of encouraging another: through promise of prayer, through the actual praying experience, or through the postexperience indication of your prayer support.

2. The Holy Spirit is our prime "support person," and he is contacted most effectively via prayer.

3. The prayer of someone who has strayed from the path of Christian growth is effective in the restoration process.

Alternate Session

1. When someone is out doing something involved in a witness, maturation, encouragement, etc., following one session and preceding another, the sustaining nature of prayer is helpful.

2. The prayer session upon leaving and upon return is useful in orientation and in debriefing the experience.

3. The Second Coming is the prime example of the alternate session, and Jesus encouraged his own to pray until the time of his return.

4. Prayer is a source of comfort to the believer who has been "in the world" for six days and worships with other believers on the Lord's Day.

Goals and Mechanisms to Reach Goals

1. These can be defined and redefined in prayer sessions.

2. The prayer session provides the opportunity to muse over action and its results and plan anew for the future.

3. Prayer can itself be a mechanism to accomplish goals, for it provides the "counting to ten" before action or the "What's next?" in the process of goaling.

4. The response of God to man's prayers is frequently that extra factor that makes things work.

5. Answers man receives in prayer may indicate the success or failure of the project, if not of the praying process. Even negative answers indicate success in prayer (see 2 Cor. 12:8–9).

Feedback

1. Again and again in prayer a person indicates how person or program is perceived, and this is excellent feedback if used to correct communication and not used against the person praying.

2. The twenty-five-word (more or less) summary statement, a most useful tool in certain stages of the debriefing process, is one kind of prayer. Frequently, after a training or learning session, the first ones to pray sum up the session and can tell the leader a great deal about the session's effectiveness.

3. The person in tune with the Spirit of God can get feedback from that source through the prayer process.

Case Study Methodology

1. Each prayer, each prayer session, each experience of prayer provides a useful case study for consideration. The prayer will tell a great deal about a person, his attitudes, his interests, his abilities, etc.; and used wisely, it can be a great aid to a pastor or Christian worker in encouraging Christian growth and maturity.

2. Prayer is one means of considering alternatives to a case. Anything considered through the prayer process is "legitimate" to the group meeting in prayer.

Creativity

1. Since creativity is the expression of the totality of fulfillment of a person and his uniqueness, prayer lets a person be himself, accept himself, and progress in maturity; and it thus provides a solid foundation for creative experience.

2. A person is not totally human until he is in fellowship with God, and prayer lets him become a total self, totally human, totally fulfilled in the creating process.

3. Prayer is also one kind of thing to be creative about.

Good Counselor

1. The good counselor makes use of every means to effect learning and insight. Prayer provides one effective means.

2. Jesus was the good counselor model. He taught his disciples how to pray.

Questions for Discussion

1. How has your life changed during this course?
2. What effect might this program have on your effectiveness in witness?
3. Had the principles taught herein been applied a hundred years ago, what might Christian missionary work look like today?
4. What aspects of your life will hinder the consistent application of these principles and thus hinder your mission in life? What might be done to avoid such pitfalls?
5. In the story of the Tzeltals, focus on one point in the narration and indicate what might have happened had rejection been the basis for action.
6. What new insights have you received about prayer from applying the principles of the behavioral sciences to prayer? What is still missing?
7. Could God be called the "Master Behavioral Scientist"? Discuss.
8. How might that which you have learned apply to the training of others in effective crosscultural communication?

Group Activities and Exercises

New course. Draw together a small group seminar and build the course around the reading of novels, the viewing of movies or plays, or the discussion and study of contemporary issues. You may want to consider using the following books: Elisabeth Elliot, *No Graven Image* (New York: Harper and Row, 1966); Juan Isaias, *The Other Side of the Coin* (Grand Rapids: Eerdmans, 1966); and Catherine Marshall, *Christie* (Old Tappan, N.J.: Revell, 1968). Movies such as *A Man for All Seasons, Fiddler on the Roof,* and *The Gods Must Be Crazy* are full of insight for effective crosscultural communication. Contemporary issues that are productive for in-depth study are abortion, sexual morality, the church, the contemporary family, communal living, war, education in this half of the twentieth century, the computer, drug usage, etc.

PART TWO:
CASE STUDIES IN
CROSSCULTURAL
COMMUNICATION

Introduction to Case Study Methodology

Purpose of the Case Studies

The pastor, missionary, and teacher are all agents of change. Without contributing to the change process, there can be no fulfilling of the Great Commission.

There are, however, certain principles one should observe. He must first of all see the society or group he is seeking to influence as composed of persons organized into an intricate system of human relationships, interacting through that society's institutions. Each society is a valid, integrated whole, organized in a system of hierarchical levels. To change behavior on any one level of such a system will result in reverberating consequences throughout the entire society. There are likely to be related and reinforcing changes above and below the actual level of the hierarchy initially changed or impacted. This can result in a disintegration throughout the entire society.

Second, he needs to enter this highly structured group in such a way that he can develop a trust relationship with anyone at any level of the structure. This takes great skill, not only in knowing what the structure is, but also in knowing how relationships form distinctively in each unit of structure at every level of the society.

Third, he needs to work with the people themselves to initiate and carry out change. Otherwise, he runs the risk of imposing his own cultural forms and structures on the receptor people, thus confusing their own structure and their own relationships.

This section of the book is designed to give the agent of change practice in conceptualizing and responding to case studies in order to practice the three responses indicated above. Unless one is thinking about cases and case resolution, it is easy to jump at the first conclusion that comes along in a situation of challenge, only to find that this conclusion is one derived from one's own world view, not that of his host. *Our goal is simply to make people think through and live vicariously a wider range of experiences than it is possible for any one of us to live in reality.* This is particularly valuable for the one who is preparing to work with people in the pastorate, on the mission field, or in the classroom, and who, from the beginning of his work, will be expected to have the ability to think through problems which only many years of actual experience normally bring.

Case studies have been used from ancient times.

> "There were two men in a certain town, one rich and the other poor. The rich man had a very large number of sheep and cattle, but the poor man had nothing except one little ewe lamb he had bought. He raised it, and it grew up with him and his children. It shared his food, drank from his cup and even slept in his arms. It was like a daughter to him.
>
> "Now a traveler came to the rich man, but the rich man refrained from taking one of his own sheep or cattle to prepare a meal for the traveler who had come to him. Instead, he took the ewe lamb that belonged to the poor man and prepared it for the one who had come to him" (2 Sam. 12:1–4).

If one wonders whether this story was effective as a stimulus to thought and action, he has only to continue reading to discover that David, the person to whom this anecdote was addressed, became furious. "As surely as the LORD lives," he vowed, "the man who did this deserves to die!" (v. 5). The prophet Nathan, who had delivered the story, then said to David, "You are the man!" (v. 7). David was being condemned for taking the wife of another man.

More than half a century ago, the Harvard Business School began using discussion based on case studies drawn from the fields of medicine and law. Since that time, the technique has been widely included in the curricula of schools giving training in business administration, anthropology, politics, psychology, counseling, and management. It has been a useful technique for learning, for it has realism and problem solving at its core.

Pastors and missionaries need case study methodology at the foundation of their training. They must work with people and so cannot simply leave the ivory towers with conceptual and theoretical knowledge from the academic setting only—knowledge that has not been tested in interaction with real, living people. With such training, Christian leaders can save themselves years of frustration as they struggle to adapt—at times gracefully, and at times not so gracefully—to the real situations in which they find themselves.

Function of the Case Studies

These cases have been organized to present problems coordinated with the preceding models in order to extend the student's thinking and problem-solving abilities.

The cases may be used in a number of ways:

1. To extend by discussion the learning experience of a class using this book.
2. To teach a course entirely through the use of case studies and extensions of case studies in the broader field of game theory, i.e., activity-oriented learning.
3. To integrate classroom teaching with laboratory sessions, using cases for discussion.
4. To extend classroom teaching by assigning cases to be worked with and written up outside the classroom.
5. To provide material for workshops where small groups may put into practice what they have learned in seminars.

I foresee these two parts of the book as being particularly relevant to pastors, teachers, and those responsible for the training of missionaries, whether in colleges, Bible institutes, or missionary conferences.

In one sense, the cases should be divided between those of particular interest to persons planning to work within the context of the North American culture and those planning to work abroad. I have found, however, that the problems of interpersonal relationships, whether at home or abroad, are basically the same, and the same principles are applicable to both situations. Therefore, I have mixed the cases. A teacher or seminar leader may choose to work with those cases that best meet the need of his teaching at any particular time.

When a teacher uses a case study, he wants it to cause personal identification with the principles in the case and to provoke an application of the principles to be learned within it. He wants to encourage a stretching of the imagination and a sharpening of the mental abilities of those who participate in case discussion.

A good case study should bring into focus a real-life situation so that others may identify with it. "How can people show greater acceptance to members of distinct ethnic and language groups?"

becomes "How shall the Johnsons act in such a way as to build trust between them and the 'foreign' family who has moved next door to them?" It should illustrate principles that may by extension be applicable to a large number of similar circumstances; e.g., "John was delighted to learn he had been named salesman of the year until he found his prize was a weekend at the Playboy resort hotel. What should he do about it?"

A case may have as its purpose a lesson to be learned. This may involve the changing of one's behavior or thought processes; e.g., "Did the wearing of ragged jeans and T-shirt to church mean the same thing to Linda, who was a member of the local Jesus People, as it had meant to her grandmother?"

At times, the main objective of a case may be to initiate group interaction and a sharing of related experiences. This interaction may ultimately add more to the learning experience than was originally intended by the use of the case.

Use of the Case Studies

Selection of the case should be done in keeping both with the intention of the learning experience and the interest of the students. The one without the other leaves learning somewhat misguided and irrelevant or leaves the students bored and ready to move on to something more interesting and exciting.

Discussion of the case should be carried out in keeping with the following guide:

1. Elicit feelings about the case. Seek to get feelings out early; otherwise, the discussion will return again and again to some aspect of feeling reaction and disrupt the flow of learning deriving from the discussion. Feelings range from "I like it!" to "I hate it!" and from "I was really pleased with . . . ," to "I'm completely frustrated with. . . ." All feelings need to be accepted at face value; otherwise, some deep, intense feelings may be hidden and may adversely affect the discussion at some later time.

2. Probe the various aspects of what went on in the case. Try to establish the basic details of information the case presents. "Where did a given person go? What did he do? What did he think?" "What do you see happening in the interaction between. . . ?" "What were the events leading up to. . . ?" Elicit the details of the case without negating what is there or adding to the facts of the case.

3. Share insights that derive from working the case. Try to integrate what you are learning in the class with what you are learning in the case. Try to relate the case to

contemporary events in which each of the participants are caught up. "This case reminds me of something that happened yesterday. . . ." "In my Bible class I saw this in the Book of Acts, and it seems that my course is saying the same thing. This case points up the idea very well. . . ."

Case study methodology is ineffectual unless participants develop the following case study abilities:

1. Agree to the details of the case and close the case at that point. It is easy to try to keep adding details and possibilities as the discussion proceeds. This only confuses the participants and keeps them from deriving consistency of learning from the case. The discussion never goes anywhere. The best plan, if someone insists on adding new ideas to the case, is to close the present discussion, agree to the new details of the case, and proceed to discuss the new case.

2. Be careful not to assign value judgments either to the participants within the case or to the participants in the discussion. The moment someone decides a certain thing about either, the group tends to close on that idea, and new ideas that might provide a more satisfactory solution fail to form.

3. Be careful not to close the discussion. The case study is not to be "solved." Rather, it is to give one opportunity to think and discuss options. The moment someone draws the case to a close, others may fail to consider options that will be useful to them in further study or in real life.

Questions on the case can be elaborated in keeping with the case and with the group discussing the case:

1. How did you react or feel as you read the case?
2. With whom do you identify in the case? With whom do you find it hard to identify?
3. How did (or did not) various persons act responsibly in the case?
4. How might the problem have been avoided?
5. What questions would you like to ask the characters in the case?
6. What models of crosscultural communication help us in working with this case? How would you apply the trust bond? norm? hierarchy? sequence of activities? basic values? etc.
7. If you were so and so, how would you resolve the problem?
8. What kind of orientation program to missions or to pastoral work would you design to prepare a person to

encounter and help resolve problems such as this case presents?

9. Do you gain any help in resolving this case from your biblical studies? sociology? philosophy? etc.

10. Do you see in this case or in the discussion of the case insights that help you understand more clearly what the Bible is saying to you? to the church?

Extensions of the Methodology

The leader of a group discussion is not to dominate the discussion. He should try to get the participants interacting among themselves without channeling everything through him. He should try not to ask a question that has an obviously "right" answer, or a yes or no answer. To keep the participants probing and thinking, it is often good for the leader's attitude to be, "You're not wrong, but I'm not sure you are right either." It is best to leave the situation open-ended and not even make a summary. The leader wants to avoid all behavior that will tend to close the mind of the participant and keep him from continuing the debriefing after he has left the group. The Christian experience can embrace differences of opinion. Some Christians, however, may not be able to do so. All sides are aided by keeping the discussion open, even after the group debriefing is over. The group leader may want to run a variation on the theme of the case study and use the case in some way that might bring it to life.

1. Role playing is one of the most effective means of bringing a case to life. Skits with different members of the group handling the different roles of the case have significant impact on one's attitude and response. (For example, role play "The California Family" in chapter 5 and see how vital the case becomes in the lives of the participants and onlookers.)

2. Have a symposium in which a group of "experts" in a field present their analyses of the case. (For example, get a group of missionaries to discuss "Praise Him With the Dance"; see chapter 13.)

3. Have a debate in which the group is divided into two parts and each side is assigned a point to argue/debate with the other. (For example, discuss "My Hippie Brother" in Case Studies Model 1, with half of the group taking the parents' side, and the other half the brother's side.)

4. Generate small group projects in which each group is assigned a distinct aspect of the case to develop. (For example, work with "Soni" in Case Studies Model 4, especially stage 2 of the case.)

5. Plan a session of brainstorming in which group members suspend all value judgment for a time to give rapid-fire suggestions, often "piggybacking" on one another's ideas. Given the right case, this can be an exciting exercise of case study debriefing. (For example, brainstorm the case, "The Foreigner's Dilemma," in Case Studies Model 4, throwing out ideas to resolve the dilemma in which both the boy's father and the outsider found themselves.)

Christ's Use of the Case Study

Every parable Jesus taught was a case study. We are told that "with many similar parables Jesus spoke the word to [the crowds], as much as they could understand. He did not say anything to them without using a parable. But when he was alone with his own disciples, he explained everything" (Mark 4:33–34).

The debriefing process of explaining everything to his disciples led to clarifications, additional stories, and the giving of further insights that were not possible in the presence of the masses. The disciples' feedback showed Jesus when his teaching was not clear, and it drew valuable insights from him as he then expanded his teaching according to their needs.

After Jesus told an immense crowd the story of the sower, his disciples came to him when he was alone and asked, "What does your story mean?" (Mark 4:10 LB). He said, "If you can't understand this simple illustration, what will you do about all the others I am going to tell?" (v. 13 LB). But after this comment on their dullness, he proceeded to retell the entire allegory, explaining it carefully (vv. 14–20).

On another occasion, he presented the case of the compassionate Samaritan in reply to a hostile questioner. After telling this story, he began debriefing with that famous question, "Which of these three do you think was a neighbor to the man who fell into the hands of the robbers?" (Luke 10:36). When the man's answer to this question showed he had received the lesson intended, Jesus told him to go and act immediately on the insights he had gained.

By the process of debriefing the disciples' own feelings and experiences, Jesus drew from them lessons and insights that could enrich the comprehension of the group as a whole. Starting with the question, "Who do people say the Son of Man is?" (Matt. 16:13), he engaged them in a conversation which drew from Peter his magnificent confession, "You are the Christ, the Son of the living God" (v. 16).

When his seventy disciples returned from their first witnessing tour to declare jubilantly to him that even the demons obeyed them when they used his name, Jesus used the occasion to launch into deeper teaching about the surpassing wonder of having their names enrolled in heaven. He shared their joy, saying how fortunate they were to see what they were seeing (Luke 10:17–23).

Thus by debriefing the illustrations he himself had given or the experiences his disciples had lived through, Jesus prepared them in three years to carry on the teaching he had begun. He felt he could leave them now. His last words to them were to go and make disciples everywhere, teaching them to obey all the commands he had given them (Matt. 28:19–20). Only his disciples had his full teaching, which they had received in their debriefing sessions together. If they were to pass these teachings on to others as they themselves had been given them, it would seem that the use of parables—or case studies—would be a prime method to accomplish this purpose (cf. Mark 4:33–34).

The following people have contributed to the collection of case studies: Helen Dunkeld, Lisa Espineli, Harry Johnson, Douglas Kell, Dave Kornfield, Dick Muzik, Gene Olsen, Roy Prester, Roland Raucholz, L. E. Read, Cornelia Vergara, and Ron Wiebe.

Model One:

The Trust Bond

The Vasca

Senora B., a wealthy eighty-two-year-old Spanish lady, lived in front of the missionary's home. Because one hip and leg were practically paralyzed, she used a cane to walk. She owned quite a bit of property, yet she acted and lived in a simple and humble way. She was from a Basque background and was very proud and outspoken about it, considering herself to be one of the few truly honest persons around. Her children were professionals and lived with their families in the *Barrio alto*. They were embarrassed by her living in the same house for fifty years in a lower-status neighborhood where she knew all the neighbors—two to four generations—by name.

Senora B. was a staunch Catholic although she had not attended mass for sixty-five years. She told the priest that she worshiped God in her home. One of the persistent comments she made to the new missionary's wife was that "all religions lead to the same place."

After several months, she began attending the Evangelical services and staying for lunch at the missionaries' home. This was fine at first. Everyone realized that she was lonely. After four and one-half years, she got sick and was with her son for four weeks. The missionary family became used to lunching alone. Upon her return, a feeling of rejection started to leak out. It wasn't easy for one of the family members to walk her slowly back to her home

313

while all the neighbors were standing in the street talking. Although the missionary's family continued to respect her because of her age and her experiences and they realized her need for a personal relationship with Jesus Christ, little things that she did began to bother them, such as insisting that the missionary run her errands, teaching and reviewing Basque words at the Sunday table, repeating family stories, and monopolizing Sunday school class time.

Many members of the local community and church had already rejected her before the missionary family accepted her. The missionary's family began feeling that way also.

When a new missionary and his family came to take over the work, the old missionary family kindly suggested that the Sunday "fellowship" be stopped. The elderly woman could not understand why.

> *Discussion.* The prior question of trust needed to be asked much earlier than it was. Mutual respect relies on each whole person maintaining vitality and authenticity. The elderly lady was enslaving the missionary family (see chapter 17), and she needed help to see this early in the relationship. How could the missionary family have communicated this then without hurting her feelings? How can they do it now?

Wine but Not Tobacco

While visiting Geneva, Switzerland, I had the opportunity of staying with the European director of a well-known Evangelical mission. This is a personal experience that he shared with me.

While living in the European culture, he did not feel that there was anything wrong with having wine at his meals at home with his family and with other European Evangelicals. He would not have wine with his meals if this would offend another person with him who totally abstained. He was willing to limit his personal freedom out of respect for another.

The director who had preceded this man was a traditionalist. He desired to totally abstain from having wine served with his meals in Europe or in the United States. This, of course, was his personal prerogative. But now the complications begin.

Upon retiring from the position of European director, the former director returned to his home in Atlanta, but his daughter came back to Geneva to be the new director's secretary. As she began to experience cultural differences and new social norms, her rigidity toward American, Evangelical social taboos seemed to lessen. For the first time in her life, she experienced the great truth of 1 Corinthians 6:12: " 'Everything is permissible for me'—but not everything is beneficial. 'Everything is permissible for me'—but I will not be mastered by anything." Her attitudes began to change so that she was willing to restrain her personal freedom—not because she had to, but because she wanted to. Thus, when she made her own personal decision to have wine with her meals while living in the European culture, this conviction was not based on a particular subcultural pressure, but was established in a relationship with Jesus Christ.

The discovery of this new truth and the appreciation of other cultural and social norms was soon shared via letter with her parents back in Georgia. You can imagine the subcultural shock! Her father thought that the new European director was behind all of his daughter's "spiritual complacency." He called the home mission office in the States and told the general director that he would cut off financial support from his southern constituency and would also excite a few people to publicly question the biblical validity of their organization.

Incidentally, the former European director owns a huge tobacco farm and supplies the major cigarette firms in the South. . . .

> *Discussion.* This case opens a number of avenues of discussion. It would be easy to condemn the former director for his concern over drinking, since he also owned a tobacco farm. This is a distraction and should not detract from the major line of discussion—namely, that the young lady had the opportunity to work carefully with her parents, whom she knew to be opposed to the drinking of wine, and to maintain their respect. How might she go about doing this?

The Statue for the Corner Shelf

A pastor and his family were asked to help his sister and her family move to another street. Finally, after transporting several loads in the pastor's car, almost everything was moved. Suddenly the pastor's wife noticed a covered mound of something, and she offered to take it. Her sister-in-law said it wasn't necessary. But the pastor's wife mentioned it to her husband. Quietly he told her that the covered object was a little handmade statue of Mary the mother of Jesus that the brother-in-law had made. They would carry that by hand so that nothing could happen to it.

Later on when the sister's family was established in the new home and the pastor's family was invited for dinner, the pastor's wife noticed the statue installed in a special place on the patio. In front of it, there was a burning candle and a beautiful bouquet of flowers. The young missionary who accompanied the pastor on the visit also noticed it.

> *Discussion.* The pastor and his family were Evangelical Christians. The sister was not. Could the two families have good relations? How could this be effected in light of the difference of viewpoint revolving around Mary the mother of Jesus? How could the pastor's wife work to educate her sister-in-law yet maintain mutual respect? How might she witness effectively of the saving work of Jesus to her husband's family?

Speak Spanish to Missionaries?

I was in my third year of missionary service when an invitation came to speak at a youth camp directed by a sister mission. Ministering to young people was always a delight, so I readily accepted. But I wasn't quite prepared for some of the experiences that awaited me.

There were twenty Bolivian campers and ten camp leaders, all missionaries. Two missionary ladies prepared tasty American meals complete with desserts. (Bolivians eat desserts very infrequently and only for special occasions.) Five missionaries served as counselors. During the first day's activities, I noticed that Daniel, a nineteen-year-old Bolivian had good leadership potential. Addressing one of the missionaries in private conversation, I said, "Tom, why aren't you using Daniel as a counselor in this camp?"

"Oh, you don't know Daniel. He is so unstable and immature. We can't trust him to do anything."

"Not even as a 'counselor in training' under the supervision of an experienced worker?" I asked.

"No way! He doesn't have it!" Just for the record, Daniel became the director of a large theological seminary after finishing formal studies, two successful pastorates, and a term as vice-president of his large denomination.

Even though most of the missionaries present were veterans who handled Spanish acceptably well, they always spoke English to each other, even in front of the young people. I felt more than a little uneasy with their habit.

One day at the meal table, Donna, a first-termer, asked me a question in English. Embarrassed, I answered her in Spanish.

"That's the way, Ron. Keep talking to her and to all the rest of them in Spanish," seethed Jaime, anger showing in his eyes. "That's for sure," chimed in the other kids.

What do you know? I wasn't the only one who felt uneasy about English being spoken in the Bolivian context.

Discussion. How was talking in English undermining the trust bond between the campers and the missionaries? How might this have been corrected? What could each group do to facilitate the growth of mutual respect?

Pig Food and Missions

My wife and I were asked to work at a small Bible school where several ethnic groups were represented in the student body. There were Thai, Northern Thai, Leo, Meo, Yao—all manifesting distinct subcultures and valid value systems.

My wife is a nurse, and I was involved in Bible teaching and practical Christian work with the students. From the start, we made it our purpose to accept each student just as he or she was. There were six Meo families living on the Bible school premises because they had been forced out of their mountain home by Communist infiltration. One of these families consisted of Mark and his wife Cho and their two children. Mark was quiet, meek, and small of stature, but he was strong in faith and a good student. It was delightful to know him and to learn of his home in the hills, his background, his family, and his burdens and desires for the future.

All of the Meo families were raising pigs to supplement their meager resources and provide a limited means of support. The men took turns gathering a green underwater plant for pig food from a nearby lake. One morning I volunteered to go with Mark in a long dugout canoe to gather this pig food. We enjoyed good fellowship together, and as we pulled in the slimy, green pig food, we talked about Meo ways, especially about Meo courting and marriage procedures.

My wife had been helping the Meo families medically for some months, and she had grown to appreciate these industrious and resourceful mountain people. One day Mark came to visit at our house. As we sat on our front porch overlooking the lake, Mark said to my wife, "Cho will soon give birth to our child. It is our Meo custom to have the mother of the husband deliver the child. My mother is not here; she is still in the hills. Will you please take the place of my mother in the delivery of our child?"

We considered this a great honor. There was a local government hospital nearby, and my wife had encouraged the Meo women to have their babies there. This was new to them, and they did not trust the Thai anyway. They could have asked one of the Meo wives to assist, but they requested that my wife fulfill the role of mother-in-law midwife on this important occasion. Although my wife is not a trained midwife, she is a qualified registered nurse. She has assisted with deliveries in the past, but always with a doctor present. When the day arrived, she accepted her new role with a bit of trepidation and a prayer to the Lord for his help. All went well, and Cho gave birth to a lovely baby daughter. Mark, of course, was delighted, and our bond of fellowship with the family was greatly deepened. As a result, our ministry of teaching the Word of God became more meaningful to Mark and to the other Meo students.

Discussion. What helped build the trust bond?

The "Manito"

My husband's grandmother is a very venerated person in the hierarchy of the family. All cater to her wishes and desires as far as possible. No one knows her exact age, but her family recently celebrated what they called her ninety-third birthday.

One day after she had indulged in watermelon, empanadas, and tomato-onion salad, she became very sick. She had terrible stomach cramps. The doctor was called after the home remedies (herbs, etc.) failed. When he arrived and began to examine her, he found a hand that had been broken off of the statue of the favorite saint of the family resting lightly over the painful area. The grandmother, being a traditional Catholic, had faith enough to believe that the saint had such miraculous powers that even the broken hand placed in the right spot could be of help.

Discussion. Assuming the author of the case was a Christian and was thus in conflict with the belief system of her husband's grandmother, how might the prior question of trust help her in dealing with this situation? Is any explanation necessary to the doctor? Can the author achieve mutual respect with the grandmother? How might she proceed? What might she avoid?

Whose Church Is It?

While working as a missionary in Thailand, I became associated with a small Christian hospital where I acted as pastor-evangelist while my wife helped as an operating room nurse. This hospital had been established by the mission in a remote area in the midst of rice farming country about twenty miles from the railhead.

The layout of the hospital grounds had been planned by medical missionary personnel and mission leaders. The compound, circled by a barbed-wire fence, consisted of a main hospital building, a nurses' dormitory, two doctors' houses, utility buildings, and a plot of land designated for a church. On this rectangular-shaped lot, the hospital building occupied the central place toward the front, and the nurses' dorm and the doctors' houses were in the background. The plot of land designated for the church building was located on the corner of the compound farthest removed from the entrance. The nearest building to the church property, not more than twenty-five yards away, was the leprosy patients' house.

A short distance from the leprosy accommodation was the hospital morgue. When a patient died at the hospital, the corpse was stored temporarily in this small building until relatives could arrange for the funeral proceedings. Thai people are naturally very much afraid of the spirits of the deceased. In order to reach the location of the church, one had to come along the road that entered the compound near the hospital and pass directly in front of the morgue and very close to the leprosy building.

For some years, the missionaries had been concerned that a church building should be erected, but there were not sufficient funds. The small group of Thai believers—consisting mainly of the hospital staff—had been meeting together on Sunday and Wednesday evenings in a basement room in the nurses' dorm. During the week, daily prayers were conducted there, and the staff was required to attend.

Then a gift of money was received from abroad for the church building, so it was decided to erect a simple structure consisting of eight main posts and a corrugated metal roof. After this much was accomplished, the money ran out. So nothing more was done for a long time.

The missionaries complained that the Thai believers did not seem to have any interest in the development of the church. No one showed any desire to use the new building for church meetings. Later on, simple wooden benches were constructed, and with much insistence from the missionaries, services were conducted in it. Yet it seemed that the believers were ill at ease and unhappy about meeting there. Tension seemed to be building up between the Thai church leaders and the missionaries. This development was a hindrance to fellowship and a detriment to normal church growth. Something was wrong, and a remedy was needed.

Discussion. How might the prior question of trust have caused the missionaries to seek out reasons for the believers' reluctance to meet in the new church? Even after the new structure was built, was it worth it to consider moving the structure and losing the money expended in order to restore trust in the community? Might a change in location of the entrance have helped? Would changing the entrance be a way to avoid moving the church? This would be a good case to role play. Assign someone to be leader of the Thai group and someone else to be a missionary. Then encourage the group to openly discuss the problem/appropriateness of the church location.

Black and White
(Elliot Jones speaks in chapel)

Coming here to college as a freshman four years ago was a big experience for me because it was something altogether new. I did not know quite what to expect. But I did know that I should expect things to be different since I went to a high school in Chicago that was all black. And I knew that when I came here, the situation would not be the same in that here it is predominately white. When I came, my roommate was probably shocked as he didn't know what he was getting. I knew what to expect, but he didn't. I was the only black person in my room; I was the only black person in my wing in the dorm; I was the only black person in my dorm; I was the only black person in most of my classes. This was really a different situation for me.

There is one verse that I want to emphasize in the things I'll be saying: "Let love be without hypocrisy."

One of the first things I noticed when I came here to college and walked into a room was that I was obvious, and I felt obvious because I was different. It was something I had never felt before, because you don't really feel that you're different until you get into a situation where you really are different. You know that in a way, when you're different, it is because society says you are. In all my experience before I came here, I didn't feel obvious because I blended in with everybody—I was just part of the whole. But here, just walking into a room made me feel eyes everywhere. And they seemed just to look on me, making me feel obvious. The eyes seemed to say that I didn't belong, like, "Are you lost?" "Can I help you?" "Which way are you going?" or "Are you sure you're in the right place?"

This wore off pretty much after a while, thank goodness, because being obvious was a pretty rough experience. I don't think very many of you have ever experienced that, and you may never experience it unless you're in a situation where you're the only white person in an all-black group. It's really a weird experience, and I was glad that people finally got used to seeing me.

Everybody seems to think that all black people look alike. For three years I was called by another black student's name. But the thing is, we don't all look alike. We all have different personalities, and we're different in every way. We're real people; and in every way that you are different from each other, we are different also.

Another thing that I experienced was a lot of kids coming up to me and asking me what country I was from. My answer would usually be, "I'm from Chicago, Illinois. What country are you from?" Then a lot of people have seemed to be really interested in my social life. I always get questions like, "I bet your social life is really rough" and "I bet you have a real frustrating time." These things made me feel obvious or made me feel different because my blackness was always reemphasized. And it is still emphasized every day through just such comments as these.

One of the questions people always ask me after first meeting me is if I play any sports. No, I don't play any sports, because I am not any good. Not all black people are athletes, especially me.

Some people tell me, "I bet you were a good dancer once." No, I wasn't, because my feet were so big that I was kind of clumsy.

Or I'd get a question like this: "Does sunburn hurt? Oh, I forgot; I'm sorry." The next question would be, "Do Negroes sunburn?" And my answer is, "I don't know; I never had one." Or I may be walking down the street one evening from the library back to the dorm, and I see a friend, and he says, "Smile, Jonesy, so I can see you." So I smile. These are things that make me feel obvious and that make me constantly aware of my blackness.

Another "good time" for me is usually on parents' weekends. I've been through four of them now, and every time parents come, I really get a kick out of watching their reaction at seeing me. It's usually one of two reactions. Usually fear, because they might be afraid that I'm taking out their daughter or rooming with their son. Or the other reaction is one of interest. They come up, shake my hand, and say, "How are you? Pleased to meet you. Where are you from?" You know, extreme interest. And I know they don't just walk up to any kid and react to him this way. And so this too makes me constantly conscious of my blackness.

I think one of the reasons that parents react the way they do, especially parents with kids here, is because everybody comes from middle-class suburbia, which reeks! And I have come to dislike it quite a bit after having been here. I really didn't know too much about it while I was at home in Chicago where I lived. Middle-class suburbia to me is so stifling, and people don't seem to me to be free. Everyone is in a box, in a system where they follow through with certain norms and certain things which they just feel they have to do in order to survive within the system. And I reject this because the people don't seem real. They seem like mannequins.

I went to a high school a couple of weeks ago to speak to some English classes on race relations. It was very interesting to me to note how ignorant most of the students there were of what was going on in the world just because they live in suburbia. They were so sheltered from the realities of life that they had no idea, no concept of what was really going on in the world. This was really surprising to me.

Another thing I noticed was that there were two types of students there. The students classified themselves as "greasers" and "rahs." The rahs were students much like you—clean-cut, good dressers, hard workers at school. I would say they were probably conservative compared to the other kids. The greasers were the kids that were, I guess, the hoods, sort of. You know, slick heads and leather jackets—stuff like that. One class I talked to was predominantly rahs. I found that within the group of greasers there was a lot more freedom of expression, and I felt freer to express myself. They seemed to be more alive and able to react to me more quickly than the other kids did, because the other kids seemed to be out of it. I think the "system" had become so much a part of them because of their living where they lived and their wanting to follow through with it and its norms. And because I've been here at college, I've come to reject all of these.

Being here at school has helped me tremendously to know myself—I've been forced to. Being black can be an exciting and challenging thing, especially in a place like this. The situation here has helped me to assert my blackness like never before, because I was definitely different from everyone else. Being here, I became initially very conscious of my blackness. So I was forced to think more about me, about what and who I was, why I was here, and how I was to relate to everybody around me.

But that caused somewhat of a problem at first, because I'd always been taught to be proud of the fact that I was black. At the same time, I was supposed to look at myself as equal to everybody else. But at first, this was hard for me because my being black connoted that I had to be superior to be proud of it. But I learned through experience that it didn't mean that. It meant that I shouldn't be ashamed of my blackness, but that I should accept it as part of me, and hopefully that you should accept it as part of me.

There were times when I wanted to forget my blackness; I wanted to throw it away because its presence became a nuisance to me, because I was a part of the whole, but then again, I wasn't. I thought that my blackness would be a barrier at first to my acceptance in the group, especially in relationship to females. So I wanted to throw it away; I wanted to reject it. But actually what I really wanted to do was to throw off the implication that came with being black, rather than throwing off being black itself. I wanted to be accepted as a man who happens to be black, rather than as a man whose blackness means that he should be treated in a certain way.

What's important, I think, is to realize that I am black and you're white, and be realistic about it. Look at me as an individual just as Christ looks at you and me as individuals. My blackness does not cloud my relationship with Jesus Christ. He doesn't attach any special connotations or conditions because I'm black. He accepts me for what I am as a man.

I was going to speak at a youth meeting once, and a lot of problems arose because they usually had the meeting in a lady's house, but she didn't want to have it when I was coming because she was afraid of what the neighbors might say. Okay, that was fine. So then they were going to have it in a church. But she didn't want to have it in the church because she was afraid of the reaction the pastor might get from the neighborhood. So, finally, we had to have it in a high school in a different community. That was exciting to me because I'd never caused so much trouble before.

"Let love be without hypocrisy." When you say you love, do you really love? Or are you just saying it? How would you react, or how do you think Christ would react? If you were on a new job and your boss was black, how would you react? Or if you arrived at grad school to find that your roommate was black? Or if you saw an interracial couple walking down the street? Or if your brother or sister fell in love with a beautiful black person? Would your reaction be, "What will the neighbors think?" or "What about the children?" Or how would you react if a black child wanted to join your lily-white Sunday school? How would you react if social pressure said, "Stay away from him because he's black. If you don't, we will ostracize you"? Are you willing to put some teeth into your commitment to Christ? Are you willing to let Christ's love be expressed through you to others in a sincere, genuine way? He wants us to be able to love a person for who he is and not because of what he is.

Discussion. This is an excellent case to use in acceptance/rejection discussions. Discover all the ways Elliot was rejected either covertly or overtly. How might the prior question of trust have helped people approaching him? Is mutual respect possible in such a situation? How might it be effected?

Conflicting Philosophies

"Why don't we invite some of the ladies from our neighborhood in for afternoon tea and see if they would be interested in studying God's Word? If you'll do the teaching, I'll hostess it in my home," said Janet to Carol.

"That's a great idea, Jan. I've been burdened for the upper-class people in our neighborhood for a long time, although I must admit their pretty clothes, hairdos, and gorgeous homes frighten me a bit. But we have something worth more than gold to share with them."

Jan and Carol knew that if they were going to reach upper-class people, it would probably not be done by inviting them to church. The Evangelical churches were made up mostly of Indian and Mestizo people, and the educated people usually did not mix with the other classes. The indigenous peoples were the first to be reached with the gospel, and thus many felt that the Evangelical church was not for the educated. The Catholic church had also forbidden its members to attend the Protestant churches, but the pope had made a new law encouraging people to read the Bible. That ruling and several other factors were contributing to increasing upper-class interest in the Word of God. Many were traveling and coming into contact with "transformed" Evangelical Christians; and they were also seeing the effective life witness of Christian maids, repairmen, and builders. Some were responding to the prestigious ministry of evangelists like Luis Palau. And others suffering socioeconomic problems were looking for new answers.

The first afternoon, only three ladies came to the tea. Carol and Janet concentrated on getting to know them, slowly feeling their way. One lady was the wife of a commercial jet pilot and the other two were engineers' wives.

After enjoying the cheese turnovers and cream puffs, Carol gave a short and low-key lesson on the value of studying God's Word. The ladies asked for a weekly time together. The next week Carol asked, "What is God like to you?" After they shared their ideas and experiences, she suggested, "Well, let's see what God says about himself." They dug into the Scriptures, finding passages by page numbers. After this she closed in prayer, asking God's help and blessing upon each lady by name. When she finished, there was not a dry eye in the place, and out poured stories of unfaithful husbands, problems with teenagers, etc. The group began to grow from that point on as ladies invited their friends and relatives.

During the studies, the air was often blue with cigarette smoke. Janet thought the ladies should be told not to smoke during the Bible studies and was quite upset by this lack of respect and reverence for spiritual things. Carol, who had been raised in a non-Christian environment, thought that this was secondary and that forbidding the ladies to smoke would only confuse them. She felt it was not right to impose Christian "Evangelical" standards on non-Christian people. She thought that would give the impression that a real Christian was someone who didn't do certain "outward" things. Janet still showed her displeasure and made comments from time to time, but the ladies continued to light up.

Upper-class people are quite different from the lower class in that they love to talk. They are quite uninhibited, and at their teas, they talk fast and furiously. Carol's style of teaching was that of using stimulating questions, participation, and investigation of the Word so that they discovered the truth for themselves. She felt that they needed to be loved and accepted just as they were and that God could guide them concerning these secondary habits in his time. She felt the most important thing was to bring them to a personal relationship with Christ. She encouraged the ladies to share, and sometimes everyone began talking at once to the person beside her about her thoughts and views on the Scripture passage. This bothered Janet greatly. She thought they should be quiet and listen to the teaching of God's Word.

But the greatest difference between the two missionaries was their approach to these Roman Catholic ladies and their beliefs. Janet thought Carol should confront them with the errors of the Catholic faith about Mary, the saints, etc.; and if a lady accepted Christ, she thought she should immediately begin attending the Evangelical church and forget the cultural differences among the classes.

Carol felt that confrontation would only serve to turn the ladies off before they had the opportunity to know the scriptural plan of salvation through Christ and would also cause them to embrace their erroneous doctrine more strongly. She preferred to commend them for their faith in God, Jesus Christ, and the "sacred Scriptures" (a Catholic term); but at this early stage she also clarified through the Word how anyone (Catholic or Protestant) could not be a true Christian without having a personal redeeming relationship with the Lord Jesus Christ. There were many things she wanted to teach them, but she observed as Jesus said, "Ye cannot bear them now." She waited until the ladies raised questions about Mary or saints or festivals and then calmly said, "Let's see what God's Word says about those subjects." She printed a study on God's teaching about idolatry for the ladies to take home and study after the session. She knew this teaching was "disturbing" so she did not demand instant acceptance of it. In time, their adoration of Mary discontinued. They continued to respect her, but prayer and trust was in Christ alone.

Carol also felt that since there was no local church established for this "social group" that it would be suicidal to try to integrate these ladies prematurely into a church that would threaten their social and family position. (Actually, it had been tried previously, and a doctor and his wife finally left the gospel.) She preferred to wait until God brought men to work with their husbands. She prayed that in God's time he would bring a Latin American pastor who could minister and relate to professionals. Today upper-class men are beginning to come to Christ.

Eventually, these distinct basic philosophies of ministry made working together difficult. Sensing that Janet was displeased, Carol offered to step aside and let Janet teach. About a month after Carol left, a group of the ladies looked her up and asked her to teach them at a local hotel. This experience was painful, but finally she felt she could not abandon these babes in Christ who had decided not to continue in Janet's study. Since then, the group has grown greatly, and many of their children, maids, relatives, friends, and even husbands have been born again.

> *Discussion.* Which specific trust bond model would you begin with in studying this case? List the differences of lifestyle revealed in the case. You can look into chapter 11 to understand something more of the differences between the two missionary's lifestyles. Which one was right? How might they have achieved mutual respect and developed a strong style of team leadership? Was Carol justified in teaching the ladies in the hotel? Discuss.

Do, Re, Mi

A young man who had attended church and a Bible institute suddenly decided to leave it all and go to work and live in the South. We later found out that on a Bible institute trip he had met a young girl whom he started to date. He began working at a local "supposedly" Christian radio station. While there, he received several visits from former Bible institute teachers and missionaries. Although he welcomed them warmly, they were amazed to find out that the quality of the programming was 80 percent "worldly" and popular music. He had become the most popular disc jockey of the area. He knew all of the artists by nickname and was up-to-date on their hits and lifestyles. It seemed that he was receiving a ten-to-twelve-hour-per-day "brainwashing," as he was the operator as well as the speaker. His looks began changing to be more in line with his popularity. He felt he was one of the town's focus points, especially among the high schoolers who visited the studio and mobbed him for autographs, etc.

> *Discussion.* Was the concern of the missionaries appropriate? Discuss. How might they have achieved mutual respect with this young man and been of help to him? Were the things they rejected in his life potential blockages to his returning to "a walk of faith"? How might the acceptance of these things in his life have aided the missionaries' approach to the young man?

Highfalutin Lady

Melissa arrived at the airport with boxes, trunks, and elegant suitcases full of pretty clothes and fine household items for her first term in Bolivia. She was stunning as she strolled into the waiting room in her suit, high heels, and fashionable hairstyle. She looked like an oil company employee rather than a missionary.

As Melissa settled into the mission guest house, she quickly transformed her room into a fashionable suite.

Before going to Bolivia, Melissa had worked as a registered nurse. Her attire and manner were indicative of the professional circle of friends to which she had previously related in the States.

Language study was Melissa's first hurdle, and she enrolled at the Maryknoll Catholic Language School, where classes were on a one-to-one basis (one student to one teacher with a different teacher each hour). Her progress in the Spanish idiom was excellent. Friendships were soon formed with the single lady teachers who invited her to their homes, birthday parties, afternoon teas, and other social functions. Other missionaries had also attended the Maryknoll School and had opportunities now and then to testify for Christ, but they otherwise had had little contact with the teachers who were from middle-upper-class backgrounds. They had asked prayer for these teachers on several occasions.

Often the teachers, who dressed fashionably in spite of their limited incomes, complimented Melissa on her appearance, saying, "You look so smart always! Why don't the other missionaries keep themselves well-groomed like you do? Many are so sloppy and careless in their dress."

Meanwhile, back at the mission house, indirect remarks were being made by American, Canadian, and British missionaries about the "highfalutin lady" with her wigs, who had come to work with the national churches that were made up of mostly rural people.

(The upper classes had been virtually untouched with the gospel.) Melissa got along well with other single missionaries, but there was a distinct difference in their lifestyles.

Eventually, Melissa bought herself a small Honda motorcycle, a mode of transportation used by several of her Bolivian friends (most of the missionaries rode bicycles). Slowly, friendships deepened with her teachers and their families, and as she became more fluent in Spanish, she found herself listening to their problems and on many occasions sharing Christ and biblical solutions.

> *Discussion.* Was Melissa asking the prior question of trust with the teachers? Was she asking it with her colleagues? If she had been more consistently asking it with her colleagues, what differences may have resulted in attitude? in the relationship? in their appearance? How might Melissa have developed a trust bond with the rural people even as she did with the upper-class people?

My Hippie Brother[1]

I pushed open the door of Luigi's Pizza Parlor and entered another world—a world in which I was an alien, marked by short-cropped hair, tweed sports coat and shined shoes as identifiable with the Establishment. Funny how uncomfortable I felt as I walked to a back table, followed all the way by suspicious eyes. It was 10:30. My wife, Anne, had been late coming home from prayer meeting, but by the time she came in I was certain that I had to go out. If my information was correct, my kid brother was back in town and I had to see him.

As I sat down and scanned the room for a familiar face, I wondered for the thousandth time if I was being wise. Would I know Jim? Could my brother be like the rest of these young people, with their strange garb and incomprehensible lingo? Would I be able to communicate with him when I did see him? And how would he feel about this unrequested rendezvous? Would he resent his big brother's interest in his life?

But it was too late to worry about those things. I was here now, in the one spot in town where I might be reasonably sure of seeing him. And the waitress was tapping her pad, waiting for my order. "Black coffee," I ordered, and studied the room, table by table, once more. I sipped my coffee slowly and thought back over the events that had led to my sitting here in this coffee house.

Jim and I had grown up together—a couple of years between our ages—in a comfortable, middle-class Christian home. We went together to an Evangelical church, and what we learned there was reinforced by teaching at home. If my parents had been a bit too concerned about making money, who was to criticize? Surely they were not more materialistic than the average Christian family. They faithfully tithed what they had and gave generously to missions. As we grew older, I became interested in the many enterprises which my father undertook—from house construction to crop spraying, while Jim merely scorned the drive that pushed my family to work.

After he completed high school, Jim got a good job but soon dissolved his connections and disappeared from town. The haunting question—"Why?"—broke my mother's health and subtly transformed my dad from an outgoing and confident businessman to one who was tense, nervous, and introspective. And yet we knew that even by answering that question, by assigning the blame to one or the other thing in our lives, we would never solve the problem of the Jim we didn't know, the vanished son and brother.

It was this enigmatic Jim whom I was waiting to see. My parents did not know that he was back in town—a friend had phoned me that afternoon to confide the news.

And then I saw him enter the room. His brown wavy hair was shoulder length and neatly combed. His beard was clipped short and topped by a long, flowing moustache. A coarsely woven poncho, handmade pants and moccasins comprised his outfit. But in spite of this garb, he was unmistakably my brother, and I found it hard to keep myself from rising in greeting. Would he acknowledge me? I wondered.

But I didn't have to wait long. Jim had obviously seen me before I had seen him, and without hesitation he walked toward my table, calling greetings to his friends as he passed.

He sat down without a word. "Have a coffee?" I invited. He nodded. "Thanks." I ordered another cup for myself and one for Jim.

As we drank our coffee, we made small talk about our lives. I tried not to ask the questions that were burning in my mind: What have you been doing? Where have you been? When are you going to come back to us? Instead, I finally asked, "Can I give you a lift to your pad?" He grinned at my self-conscious handling of hippie lingo. "Sure," he said. And we walked out to the car.

Near the river, where we could look across at the skyline our city was gradually piling up, we parked the car and talked. Jim didn't need many questions—he seemed more than anxious to pour out to me his complaints and bitternesses; a little less anxious, perhaps, to inform me about his activities. It was past midnight now, and I was a working man, so when the flow of talk ebbed, I offered to take him around to where he slept. As I pulled up to the flophouse where he directed me, I reached for my pen and scribbled a number on a card. "Here's my phone number, Jim," I said. "If you want to visit more, give me a call."

Next afternoon the phone rang at 5:10—not a minute after I had come in from work. "Jim here," my brother's voice said. "Got an hour or two?" I picked him up and brought him up to the house for supper. It was strange to have so otherworldly a visitor at our table and to know he was my brother. He was at his courteous and pleasant best—even helped Anne with the dishes before we went out for another drive and talk.

As we sat parked at the end of an unused runway at the abandoned Air Force base, I began to ask some questions. They were not ones of particular family interest, but ones which I felt might give me some clues to this hippie brother of mine. "Do you remember that Sunday night about fifteen years ago—when I was eleven? While Pastor Thom was speaking, I suddenly realized my need to accept Jesus Christ as my own Lord and Savior."

Jim looked at me for a minute. I could see he didn't care to remember that night. Then he looked away. "I remember it, man."

"Remember how I stayed to pray with the pastor after the service? And when we got home, remember how Mom and Dad turned to you?"

Jim looked out the window. "Yeah, I remember. They said, 'Don't you think you should do this, too?'"

"You do remember, then."

"Yeah."

"Jim—is that the only experience of 'salvation' you ever had?"

There was a long silence. "What are you getting to?" he asked defensively.

"Did you really become a Christian that night?"

Jim shrugged under his poncho. He seemed resentful of my question. "Do I look like a Christian?" he taunted.

"That's not the point," I said. "It's what you are—not how you look."

"No," Jim said finally. "No, I'm not a Christian." There was a momentary silence, and then his tone was bitter again. "Any reason why I would be? So I can get a holy feeling by going to church on Sundays? And get God to help me make a pile? No. From all I've seen, this Christianity kick is just not where it's at."

"Then 'where is it at'?" I queried.

"Don't know. But I'm going to find out. That's what all this [he indicated his clothes and hair with a sweeping gesture] is about. This is the first time I've done anything that is me; the first time I've been a person apart from the rest of you."

"Ever read your Bible anymore?" I tried to sound casual as I pursued my quest.

"Sure. All the time. Along with the sacred writings of every other religion I can get my hands on." He became reflective. "You know, I met a very cool guy. He's a lama. When I'm down at the gulf, I take instruction from him once in awhile. Sometimes I think that I might just find the truth and be free. . . ."

A red light suddenly pulsated in the night sky behind us and Jim snapped from his reverie. "The fuzz again," he spat. "They'll nail me for something just because I am the way I am."

"They're just checking us out," I consoled, and stepped out of the car to meet the police officer. Routine check of license, registration, insurance—and we were alone again. But Jim was bitter and launched into a tirade against police that gradually widened to include invectives against all authority. When at last he had spilled out his bitterness, we sat in silence together looking out into the spring darkness. Finally he turned to me.

"Think I should go see the folks?"

"If you want to. I think they would like it if you did."

"Think so?"

"Yeah, I'm quite sure."

"Let's go around to the house."

And so we went. I didn't really expect a replay of the gospel account of the prodigal's homecoming. But I was as unprepared as Jim was for the barrage of questions that Mother and Dad launched.

"Do you have to look so . . . so grotesque?" Mother asked, surveying Jim with disfavor.

"Planning a stop at the barber's sometime?" My dad tried to be jocular, but there was no laughter.

"I'll get that tweed coat you left hanging in your closet—" Mom suggested.

"How could you do this to us?" was the unspoken question behind every question. And all the questions were asked—the where's and what's and why's. There were more.

Finally Jim turned to me and snapped, "Let's get out of here."

"Thought you said they'd like to see me," he snarled as we drove down the street toward his place.

"I thought they would," I said, feeling as betrayed as he.

"It's just like I thought it would be. Just like it always has been. Like it always will be. They don't really care about me. They care about my clothes, the impression I'll make on others, the way I've ruined their reputation. They won't accept me as I really am. Well, that's just too bad for them." He paused for a long minute. "And for me, I guess," he added, disappointment choking his words. And so my vanishing brother vanished again.

That was a year ago, and I haven't seen Jim to talk with him again. He is back in our state these days, with short hair and clipped moustache. He is a young man with a purpose. He tours with another young fellow, holding pacifist rallies. Just where and how he got involved in New Left activity, I don't know. Just how much he understands of his involvement I am not sure either.

But I am haunted by questions. In a New Left cell somewhere did he find acceptance which he failed to find in his own Christian home? Did some older organizer show Jim the attention his Christian Dad had always been too busy to evidence? Will my brother ever find his way to the Truth that will set him free from this new entrapment? And will I ever again answer my phone to hear my kid brother say, "Jim here. Got an hour or two?"

> *Discussion.* This is an excellent case for discussing the problems arising from rejection of the person in model 1. It can also extend to a discussion of conflict of norm in model 2.
>
> I personally use this case in every entry level course I teach in crosscultural communication. I first have a small group of students prepare out of class to present it in dramatic form; and then at the beginning of the discussion period, they present their skit. Hippies are out of date, of course, but there is always a functional equivalent the team can use to depict the problems of rejection within the family or the church. The skit helps the case come to life. Everyone begins to enter into the dilemma of Jim and his older brother. This facilitates discussion.
>
> Once debriefing starts, I divide the larger group into small groups of four or five to facilitate discussion. I urge them to follow the debriefing sequence of feelings, what went on, and what they have learned about acceptance/rejection.
>
> A simple way of adding depth to the discussion is to have the team reverse roles and have "straight" Jim look in on his "hippie" family. This adds an interesting dimension to the discussion, for one begins to realize that all parties are in reality rejecting each other in some way.

The Long Coat

One cool autumn day the missionary's wife received the visit of a national woman whose son was active in the church. After a prolonged afternoon (tea and all) the woman prepared to leave. It was a chilly evening, and it was raining. The missionary's wife offered to let the visitor wear her coat. The woman said that she would return it on Sunday, or if she didn't go to church, she would leave it with the other missionary at the church parsonage. The missionary's wife stressed the need of having her coat as soon as possible because of the inclement weather. The woman said not to worry. The missionary felt that she had done the right thing.

As the days and then weeks wore on, nothing was seen of the coat (or the woman or her son). The missionary's wife sent a message to remind her of the coat—all to no avail.

Finally, about two months later, the two ladies met on the street. To the missionary wife's amazement, the woman was wearing the coat—and she could see the marks where the hem had been turned up and the coat had been ironed (without a cloth on top).

> *Discussion.* How would you work with this woman so that both of you could maintain full authenticity as persons yet achieve a satisfactory resolution of the coat affair in the context of mutual respect?

Mutual "Arreglos"

Jose was driving his car through the downtown section. Preoccupied with various worries, he went through a stop sign. He was immediately stopped by the police. He received a ticket which would have been worth at least a half month's salary.

The first thing Jose thought of was his friend Waldo who worked in the "ticketing" office of the traffic court. As soon as Waldo heard about Jose's problem, he assured him that he should forget all about it because he was going to take care of it. He was going to use his position or influence. And he did.

Some months later, Waldo's car broke down and he needed a special repair that was very scarce and very expensive. He remembered his friend Jose who worked at the main Ford accessory department in the city. Needless to say, the piece was soon found at half price.

On another occasion, one of Jose's friends needed an ID card. Usually one had to stand in a long line for many hours in order to get it. Jose called Juan Rodriguez, a detective in that department, and everything was done in half an hour.

Sometime later, Juan Rodriguez's father needed a heart pacer, which was only available in the United States. He talked to Jose, who in turn talked to his brother (my husband), who talked to the mission officials, who called the New York office. The heart pacer was flown down the next day as an "emergency case." The operation took place that same day, and the father is still happily living and using it.

Discussion. This is a Latin American setting where the extended family is foundational to all interpersonal relationships. Jose would contact family and friends when in difficulty, whereas the North American would hire something done and not expect favors when involved with other nonpayable services. Who is right? Was Jose warranted in what he did? In what ways might rejection be triggered in a friendship with Jose? How can the North American work with the Latin American and effect mutual respect?

Model Two:

Social Structure

Add Onions

In the mountains of North Thailand and Laos, there is a group of tribal people known as the Meo. They have lived in the mountain forests for hundreds of years, sustaining themselves on a slash-and-burn type of agriculture and the growing of opium. In recent years, some of these Meo have turned to Christ from their animistic ways. Many have been uprooted from their mountain villages and have been forced down into the plains by the Communists.

On one occasion, a group of Meo Christians was gathered for a short-term Bible school. Periods of Bible study were arranged. There were also times for recreation and for meals taken together as a large family. Some of the wives of the believers shared in the cooking.

The local missionary who was doing some of the teaching joined the Meo for a noon meal. They were all happily enjoying the food and conversation together until the missionary tasted one of the dishes and grimaced openly, remarking in a loud voice, "This food tastes flat. Didn't you put any onions in it?" A hush fell over the group, and reluctantly one of those working in the kitchen replied, "Nzoe doesn't care for onions, so rather than offend him, the cooks refrained from putting onions in the food." Nzoe was a gifted young Meo with a keen mind and a deep desire to follow the Lord. Although quiet and reserved as a person, he was faithful and well respected by his peers. When the missionary heard this explanation, he bristled and said loudly for all, including Nzoe, to hear, "Next time, put in the onions. If Nzoe doesn't like it, he can go without. The rest of us want onions in the food." A few darting glances were exchanged among the Meo, and then everyone went back to eating.

The teaching sessions continued, with the missionary taking part. The Meo appreciated the opportunity to study the Word of God, to fellowship with one another, and to be together for the short-term Bible school.

> *Discussion.* This is a valuable case for both models 1 and 2. For 1, probe to determine who asked the prior question of trust and who did not. What was the effect on the group? Suppose the outspoken missionary later recognized his error. How might he have corrected the matter?
>
> For model 2, it is helpful to discuss the deprivation of norm model to determine which participants in the case handled their own deprivation the best. Who willingly accepted deprivation of norm? Who failed to handle it? Why? With whom did you identify? Why? What can be learned from this case to help you in your everyday life?

International Marriage

Alfonzo was an outgoing and talented student at the Latin American Bible Institute. Bonnie was an attractive single missionary who had come to be the secretary for the mission director. The two met at a church social, and there was immediate attraction. Almost everyone knew that Alfonzo had a fiancée in another city, a former Bible school student (in fact, Bonnie was probably number three).

Before long, Alfonzo secretly asked Bonnie to become his *novia* (fiancée) but made her promise not to tell anyone. Then he went on a trip to the capital city, where he had lived as an orphan. It was there that he had been led to Christ by an older single missionary lady. At one point in his life, friends had ridiculed Alfonzo because of his relationship to her.

Upon returning to Cochabamba, Alfonzo was overwhelmed to learn that his girlfriend had resigned her position as mission secretary and had written to her mother at home and told everyone about their "secret" engagement.

Not wishing to humiliate the missionary nor discredit his masculine and nationalistic identity (or honor), he quietly went along with the situation rather than confronting her and clarifying his intentions.

People reacted in many ways. "He's finished! Marrying a missionary or a foreigner will cause him to lose respect with his own people." "He's just marrying her for her money," some judged. Others said, "She shouldn't marry a national; there are too many cultural differences." Students began commenting on Bonnie's forwardness in phoning Alfonzo continually at the institute, saying how this humiliated and disgusted him.

One afternoon Bonnie was perplexed when Alfonzo completely ignored her at the youth center as he played volleyball and talked with others. Missionaries tried to caution Bonnie to go easy and read these "danger signals," but she was head over heels in love and could not listen to reason.

In the meantime, Bonnie's mother arrived to meet her future son-in-law. A wedding in the homeland was planned, and Bonnie took off to get ready for the big event. Alfonzo stayed behind just long enough to scrape together travel money.

During the succeeding days, Alfonzo began to act strangely. He was unable to sleep and became ill and nervous; and he couldn't stand the noises in the institute, especially the ringing of the bells. Students asked daily when he was to leave for the wedding, but he gave them no definite reply. Alfonzo tried to avoid the subject. No one knew if or when he was going. The Bible institute director encouraged him to go and helped arrange his travel. Bonnie sent him travel money for, as an orphan and a student, he had no source of income. One day the students woke up to find that Alfonzo was gone.

Shortly after the wedding, Alfonzo had a nervous attack. He began throwing things and reacting in violent ways. Although filled with fear, Bonnie decided to go ahead and return to South America, hoping that her great love for him would help him adjust to married life.

Alfonzo was invited to be the dean of students at the Bible institute, and thus they were given an apartment in the building that housed the institute and the main national church.

During the first few months of married life, things seemed to go well in spite of the fact that Alfonzo had some periods of deep depression and many times refused to eat Bonnie's cooking.

One day, however, the pastor and his wife on the third floor heard someone anxiously knocking on their door. There stood Bonnie, weeping uncontrollably as she poured out her story. "Alfonzo is out of his head. He's breaking everything in our apartment, including all our wedding gifts. He even tried to choke me, but I managed to escape."

Alfonzo was taken to a psychiatric institution, and Bonnie, with the aid of friends and doctors, tried to help him. At times he was loving, but he would change without warning, telling her he didn't love her and to get out of his life. Bonnie began to fear for her own life. Finally, the counsel of national church leaders persuaded her to return to her homeland, family, and church. In less than two years, her intended career missionary service was ended.

> *Discussion.* In how many ways did Alfonzo express the behavior of conflict? Did Bonnie help him? How might she have helped him? How might the mission director have helped the couple? How might prayer have aided each participant in the case? Many people suggest that culture is no problem and differences of culture do not need to be taken into account when marriage is contemplated. Is this so? How do you think differences of culture and social structure aided/harmed the relationship? Be specific.

Their Translation

Ray and Joyce had been the first missionaries to enter the tribe twenty-five years ago. They had started at once to learn and write the language, and they launched into translation and literacy work. They were considered by those who came later as the authorities in all matters of language and translation. Their goal was to translate the New Testament before their second furlough. Working rapidly with one informant, they were able to see it finished. The manuscript was hurriedly sent off to the publisher, and when the New Testaments arrived, they were hailed with great joy.

However, as younger missionaries arrived on the field and started to use the New Testament, they came to realize that it was a literal, wooden translation, often wholly incomprehensible to the nationals if they were not taught its special language.

Those who attempted to suggest changes to the translation couple found their suggestions taken as a personal affront to them. It was as if Ray and Joyce's integrity were at stake each time anything in "their" translation was questioned.

As the years went by, the Indian Christians spoke often of the need for revision, and the Bible society urged that work be started on a new translation, but the couple's defensive attitude stalemated all hope of having an improved version. It seemed unlikely that anything could be done until their retirement, which was still ten to fifteen years away.

Soon after John and Marge began work in a neighboring language group, they learned of this situation. John saw the temptation to become "the authority" in the language and wondered how the translation he was working on could belong to all the Christians and not be considered his alone.

From the beginning of language study, he sought correction from nationals and his fellow workers. He decided the translation should be a committee effort. Then as each book was finished, he mimeographed it and sent it to all his fellow missionaries and the leading literates of his tribe—both Christians and non-Christians—asking them to read it critically and send in to him corrections or suggestions for improvement. He was always happy when someone would come to him with an idea, for that person would feel he had had a part in putting God's Word into his own language.

Most of all, John was glad to find he never needed to defend his work or feel hurt when it was criticized, for he constantly sought constructive criticism.

The younger missionaries working with the first couple envied John's program and chafed at the frustration they felt in their own situation. They wondered what they could do to help Ray and Joyce have a change of attitude; or should they just "sit it out" until the day the couple would no longer be on the field?

> *Discussion*. What problem do we face here? Is this a cultural attitude or a personal one? Detail John's efforts to make the translation a group effort. Is it a better translation because of this effort? Is it more correct? In what ways might it be more correct? less correct? Explain. What responsibility did the field leaders have toward the translation couple? How might they have worked to alleviate the situation? How might the national church have helped?

One of Them

The young missionary couple was very pleased when they found a national who could help them in their home with their children. They bent over backwards to make her feel like one of their family. They joked with her and insisted that she eat with them at the table.

When other nationals came to eat, the missionaries noticed that they avoided carrying on conversation with the maid. To make up for it, they themselves continued bringing her into the conversation and joking with her, although she seemed to feel a little uneasy. Sometimes the missionary's wife felt uncomfortable because of her husband's joking. When the missionary couple visited in nationals' homes, they noticed that the girls or women who helped them did not eat at the family table but ate in the kitchen. They felt uncomfortable about this and once even went so far as to insist that it would be all right with them if the maid wanted to eat at the table. They insisted that there was plenty of room.

Several missionary families mentioned that they had had problems because their help had become too familiar and insisted upon privileges that really could not be considered. They were puzzled as to which was the right thing to do.

> *Discussion.* Read my book *A Look at Latin American Lifestyles* prior to discussing this case. Recognizing that there are status distinctions in Latin American society and that the maid is at times the mistress of the man of the house, what cautions should the missionaries have exercised with the maid? Is the householder-maid relationship the same in Latin America as in North America? Should it be? If it need not be, how might the missionaries have treated the maid? What further behavior did their openness encourage? Were the North Americans prepared for such behavior? What might the missionaries learn from the nationals?

That Experience

Drew came to a Christian college from a small town in Minnesota where his father was a minister at the First Covenant Church. His Evangelical upbringing was very similar to that of many of the other students. Church was a sacred place to attend with reverence, but the sobriety often seemed stifling. He could well remember one Sunday morning when startled church members gave disapproving stares to a certain visitor from North Carolina who shattered the service's monotone with a loud and emphatic "Amen, brother! Hallelujah! Glory be!"

Drew had learned to worship quietly and reverently. The atmosphere at school was quite similar to that back home. Then he met a group of fellows who really seemed to be "on fire for the Lord," as Drew put it. They spoke of being "turned on to Jesus." Drew felt he could see real "power" in their lives, and in an attempt to find this power for himself, he joined their group.

These fellows had their own get-togethers. The loose informality of the unstructured sharing times was strange to Drew. The group kept urging him to have the same experience with Jesus as they had had, and to ask the Holy Spirit to fill him completely. This was the only way, they said, that he could have a powerful Christian life.

Drew felt a little frightened but decided that if this was the way to do it, then he wanted this experience. The group prayed over him as he sought for this experience, but it did not come.

Surely there was some obstacle, some unconfessed sin holding him back. Drew began to confess things before this group that he would have never dared to tell even his father, but still he received no such experience. "You've got to want it real bad," they told him. He agonized on his knees for hours but to no avail. Where was the power? What was wrong?

> *Discussion.* What do you think was wrong? Was this a spiritual problem or one of social and cultural background or both? Did Drew's background have anything to do with his inability to be filled with the Spirit? How? Was this a bad thing? How does God work through our personal identity to reach us? to help us grow? to impact the world for Christ? Discuss your own experiences of this.

Choosing a Team

Walter and Ron, youth leaders of the Evangelical Christian Union, had decided to form a ten-member gospel team and lead it on a two-week ministry to the Bolivian cities of Oruro and La Paz.

Every night for a month music practices and orientation sessions were held. Both Walter, the Bolivian leader, and Ron, the missionary, emphasized repeatedly that only ten of the twenty young men attending the sessions would be chosen to make the trip. As the deadline approached, the two leaders met several times to compare notes and make the selections. Walter was assertive and firm concerning his ten choices. So was Ron, and happily they agreed.

When they called the twenty together to announce the ten, for some reason, Walter backed off and let Ron lead the session. Ron seemed only too happy to do so.

Silence fell over the group when they heard the announcement. Finally Alfredo spoke up.

"I've been counting on this trip, and I want to go, too."

"That's understandable," responded Ron. "All twenty would love to go. But you also understand, Alfredo, that we can only take ten fellows on this trip. Take heart! There will be more trips. If you keep trying, you will probably be selected on a future team."

"But I want to go now," retorted Alfredo, as the atmosphere grew tense. Disgusted that Walter would say nothing, Ron countered, "The answer is no, you can't go."

"I still want to go."

Launching into a fatherly lecture, Ron reminded Alfredo and the other youths, "We all have to mature and grow up. Sometimes the answer is no, but we must learn to accept that.

"Ron," Walter broke in, "what you don't realize is that many of us Bolivians aren't mature, even at forty years of age."

Walter had finally spoken, much to Ron's chagrin. Nonetheless, the missionary stuck to his guns, and Alfredo was not among the team members that left for Oruro in the "Cucaracha," a 1949 Chevy van.

Halfway through the first meeting, Ron almost fell off the platform when Alfredo walked in the back door of the church and sat down.

At the conclusion of the service, all the team members, led by Walter, gave Alfredo a warm welcome, inviting him to spend the night with them. Ron looked on mutely as they included Alfredo in the team's music ministry. The real stinger came four days later when Alfredo was invited to pile into the "Cucaracha" and continue on to La Paz as an authentic team member.

Live and direct, Ron was receiving some of his most important orientation lessons to the Bolivian culture.

Discussion. Was Ron justified in refusing to let Alfredo go? How did Walter fail his associate? in keeping quiet? in not sharing with Ron beforehand what he might expect in Bolivian decision making? What if the remaining nine had done the same as Alfredo? How might you have handled the case? Was Ron wise in saying no more after Alfredo joined the trip? What did Ron need to learn following this case? What did Walter need to learn? How might one proceed to work with Alfredo? Is this a case similar to that of John Mark in the Book of Acts?

The Surf-Riders

One of the groupings most natural to Hawaii is that of the surf-riders. Three of the regulars in our young peoples' group were surfers. Had I understood them better before my church planting experience in Hawaii, much more could have been attempted in acknowledging the validity of their group and in accepting the powerful restraints which membership in the group afforded. And with this understanding, perhaps a greater influence could have been exerted on them.

The following is a summary of the identification features of a Hawaiian surfers' group:
  I. Physical items
    A. A beach
    B. A surf

C. A surfboard
II. Sociological items
  A. A name—surfers
  B. Its own language. This is basic surfer terminology with added flavor from Pidgin English, e.g., nose, tail, skeg, hang five, hang ten, going through the tube, wipe out.
  C. A meeting place—the beach
  D. A time of meeting—when the surf's up
  E. Membership. A surfer must be a surfing *kamaaina* (old-timer) as over against a surfing *malihini* (newcomer).
  F. Means of identifying members—surfboard, surfers' cross, bleached hair worn long, surfers' knots (calluses on knees and across toes), uke.
  G. Leadership—the most skilled surfer; in case there are two, the biggest one!
  H. Rules. The surfer riding wave has the right of way. Don't surf without wearing surfers' cross.
  I. Discipline—continuous waxing of board for better toe grip, training for international meet at Makaha.
  J. Mechanisms to induce loyalty—stories of group heroes, previous group winners at Makaha, guys who braved waves at most dangerous Sunset Beach.
  K. Privacy. The group is usually limited to twenty or fewer because of limited good surfing areas and danger of overcrowding.
  L. Authority. The leader selects surfer sites.
  M. Perpetuation—no off-season in Hawaii; skill continues to determine group leader; surfers' cross serves as protecting charm.
  N. Means of defense—fist fights for best surfing areas.

Discussion. Do you feel this is an authentic group? How might you reach group members for Christ? How might you incorporate them into your church? How might you help new converts grow as Christians in such a group? Could you identify a group in your own setting that needs special attention as this one did? How would you go about entering it?

Pilate the Slave

The most complex case I ever dealt with during my term as governor of Judea involved the leader of a religious protest group who was feared by the Jewish leaders because of his rising political popularity.

The Jews, who have never accepted Roman rule, were

growing extremely restless around this time. Demonstrations against enforced taxation and compulsory government service were growing more and more frequent. Soldiers in the occupational forces were having to quell riots and marches at the risk of their lives. The secretary of the Bureau for Territorial Development had been putting increasing pressure on me because of this seething turmoil. Only the week before this trial, he had informed me that if this trend of riots and demonstrations continued, I would lose my job and my position within the governmental hierarchy. With the Passover bringing its hordes of tourists and Jewish pilgrims the next week, I expected the growing tension to explode.

All was relatively controlled, however, until the Jewish leaders brought this man to me, claiming that he was spreading anti-Roman propaganda and stirring up political opposition among the people. This amazed me, for I knew that the Jewish local leaders had been encouraging anti-Roman sentiment themselves. I was convinced, therefore, that this was a trumped-up charge, but I was forced to conduct a court trial because they had already bound him over for trial in a municipal council hearing.

I am ashamed to have had a part in such an outrageous mockery of justice. These same municipal officers who had convicted the defendant were the witnesses for the prosecuting attorney. What profanity and outright perjury these men used!

The atmosphere in the courtroom became so heated that tension spilled over in loud outbursts from the audience. At this point, I began to question the defendant myself. I was taken aback by his poise and calmness in the situation. He answered me calmly and directly. He claimed indeed to be the Deliverer of the Jews, but he said that he brought spiritual deliverance—that he was King of a heavenly empire. He was bringing truth to all people. Well, we all could use a little truth right now; and if he thinks he's got it, who am I to say he doesn't? After all, who knows what truth is anyway? I didn't exactly follow all his ideas, but I sure couldn't find anything wrong with him. So he had a few big ideas about himself. Everybody has a few weird ideas.

I adjourned court to consider the verdict, although I had nothing for which to convict the man. While I was gone, the Jewish officials stirred up the audience (which, by the way, was huge because of the defendant's renown) so that the courtroom was in an uproar when the session reconvened.

I quieted the people and told them that I couldn't find anything wrong with the man. The clamor in the courtroom was deafening! Everyone began yelling at once! I told them I could release this man as innocent, based on a custom of their Passover celebration. But they all began clamoring for the release of a convicted thief and murderer and for the crucifixion of the defendant.

As the incensed crowd began chanting, "Crucify him, crucify him!" I began to resent intensely my forced loyalty to Caesar and his Rome. I felt as though I were in a box which was fast closing in around me.

The Jewish officials calmly informed me that acquitting the defendant constituted treason against Caesar. I realized suddenly that I had no defense whatever against any reports these men might choose to spread.

I had to get the people out of there before violence erupted. What could I do? Not only my job, but my very life was at stake.

I had never sentenced anyone to death of whose guilt I was not unequivocally convinced. I would not pass a death penalty if any doubt existed. But I had the welfare of the people to protect as well as the code of the Roman law. If revolution broke loose, and it was my fault. . . !

I cannot forget that man who claimed to have truth. I can no longer live with myself.

> *Discussion.* This is a well-known case. How was Pilate a slave? Could he have done anything about it? In what ways do you become a slave to people, to programs, or to knowledge? How do you operate when this realization strikes you? Can we learn from such experiences what it means to be a slave to God?

An M.K. Goes to College

I'm a missionary kid. I grew up in Burundi, Central Africa. I can recall the early times when "everything was the same as it always was." After dinner at noon, Mother always read to us out of the big blue Bible study book. The daily bath was as regular as dusk, and our dear African cook was eternal.

But after all, things do change, and I started going to the Belgian colonial school. Even my sister's left-handedness was soon overcome by the regimentation there, and she was made to write *comme tout le monde* (like everyone else).

As time went by, I saw some change and a certain variety in life, but basically things moved slowly and obeyed the Swahili axiom, *"Bado kidogo"* ("Wait a while"). The third grade arrived out of the dim future, and with it came a shocking change: My two oldest sisters and my older brother left Dad and Mom and us four younger kids and flew away to some place called America to go to high school.

Then the next year we went to America, too! The imprint left by that year's furlough wasn't quite erased when we came home to Africa again. Even it had changed with the fever of independence. But the ageless blue mountains across the lake in Zaire seemed to belie any change. Wasn't it the familiar old roosters who still roused the same Africans to just another day of hoeing on the family plot?

Another year-long furlough with its timid forays into American life split my high school years, which were spent at an American missionary boarding school in Kenya. Here, despite our khaki school uniforms, I began to understand the diversity in life. This school acted as a bridge to the accelerated pace of life awaiting me in America.

Too soon, the happy days with friends, familiar scenery, wildlife, and rugby games was ended, and suddenly I found myself in the registration hassle at college, ID No. 435685.

I thought I could comprehend variety and change, but now I couldn't take it. There was too much too fast! The host of churches in town all clamored for my attendance. The immensity of the chapel engulfed me. "That whole book read by next week!" "I'll try to remember, but you're the eighth Bill I've met today!" I imprudently ventured into the library and blew my mind just browsing through the magazine rack.

To a guy who'd had the same breakfast all his life, the choices in the dining hall were a pleasant problem. ("Move it! How long does it take you to make up your mind?") Freshman guys and dolls were already going steady, and I hadn't even thought about a date yet!

Everything seemed to blare out, "Do, taste, experience, buy, absorb, read, feel, be—and quick, before it's too late!" I was being swept away by the philosophy lying behind Howard Johnson's thirty-four flavors of ice cream and Evelyn Wood's speed-reading course.

Discussion. Reverse culture shock is sometimes more powerful than regular culture shock. Discuss why this might be. What were the evidences of shock? What might this person have done to reduce the effect of shock? How can principles of effective crosscultural communication aid one in the setting of shock?

The Leper

Mr. Glab is a smiling, energetic young Asian from the Central province of Thailand. He was afflicted with leprosy early in life, and it left its mark in the form of claw hands and difficult-to-heal sores on his feet. Through the ministry of missionaries who early became concerned for leprosy sufferers in the Central Provinces, Mr. Glab found medical help and heard of Christ. During his long stay at the Christian hospital, he received treatment for his leprosy, and it was arrested. His general health improved, and he professed to believe in Christ.

Mr. Glab had been a carpenter. As he regained his strength, he became able to help in small carpentry jobs around the hospital and in the workshop of the leprosy rehabilitation center. A new hospital was being planned in another province, and a carpenter was needed to become a part of the full-time staff. Mr. Glab was asked about serving in this capacity. He was pleased about the prospect and eagerly took up his new assignment. At the new hospital, he became active in the small group of believers and continued growing into a mature Christian.

A separate building was erected to house leprosy patients who came to the hospital for treatment—some staying for a number of weeks at a time. Mr. Glab was put in charge of this house, and this arrangement provided him with many opportunities to share the gospel with patients from far and near. As a leprosy sufferer himself, he could identify with them wholeheartedly. Each year a leprosy believers' conference was held on the hospital compound, and many gathered for this time of teaching and fellowship.

As one of these conferences approached, Mr. Glab was busy preparing the house to receive the guests from neighboring districts. The hospital director informed him that if he attended the conference, it would be without pay. Mr. Glab was thrown into a state of turmoil. He found it difficult—even impossible—to understand the doctor's reasoning in this decision. After considering this decision, he announced that he would not attend the conference if it meant losing his pay for those days.

But because Mr. Glab was to act as host to the leprosy guests, it really was essential that he attend the conference. Another missionary at the hospital tried to help the doctor to see the importance of Mr. Glab's being there. They also discussed the matter of docking his pay. The doctor insisted that since other hospital personnel were required to work, Mr. Glab would have to work or attend the conference without pay.

Mr. Glab failed to see the situation as the doctor saw it. Since he was a valid member of the hospital staff and of the church, he saw no dichotomistic breakdown of categories. He could not understand why he should be penalized by loss of pay while performing his expected role in the total hospital program.

Through the mediation of the other missionary, an arrangement was worked out whereby Mr. Glab might attend the conference and continue on the payroll. However, the time consumed by the conference would be considered part of his regular vacation time. Mr. Glab agreed to this solution. A serious conflict between the doctor and Mr. Glab was averted, and the leprosy believers' conference proceeded with Mr. Glab playing his expected role in the community.

> *Discussion.* Three points of view are represented in this case. Which is the biblical point of view? Can the Bible support all three? Assuming for the moment that each of the participants was following biblical guidelines, what kind of thinking could have averted the clash? Using the basic values model, profile the doctor. Then profile the leper. Might one predict the outcome on the basis of the different profiles? Did the solution work? Was it a good one? Could you generate a better one based on the basic values profiles? Was Mr Glab justified in refusing to attend the conference if his pay was to be docked? Without some form of mediation in this situation, what might have happened? With whom do you identify? How might the question of trust aid the men?

Stifling or Developing Leadership?

After seven months of language study, Dan and Ethyl were assigned to pastor a national church in a large city on Bolivia's *altiplano* (i.e., plateau area).

They were carefully instructed by their missionary predecessors as to which men in the church were responsible spiritual leaders.

"The three men presently serving as elders qualify according to biblical requirements, but no one else in the church does. Especially not don Epifanio and don Jose. It would be a terrible mistake to put either one of those fellows into leadership."

The new couple initiated their new ministry energetically. Dan set up weekly prayer and planning meetings with the three elders. While the elders were faithful in attending those meetings, they demonstrated minimal ability to plan and lead the church's ministry. In contrast, Jose and Epifanio demonstrated tremendous leadership potential.

Dan carefully checked out Epifanio and Jose with the three elders. Some of their comments demonstrated jealousy of the two (as if there was a leadership power struggle), but nothing they said disqualified the men from spiritual ministry.

While continuing the regular meetings with the elders, Dan also moved with Epifanio and Jose. Epifanio accepted an invitation to teach the adult Sunday school class. Jose began traveling with Dan to outlying areas, preaching in open-air meetings and teaching in two rural congregations.

Four months after Jose and Epifanio had become active in ministry, the church held its annual assembly, at which time leaders were chosen. These two, along with the other three, were appointed as elders.

During the next year, the church flourished. A steady stream of people were converted, and many were baptized. The Sunday school was reorganized to include seven instead of two classes. The adult class more than doubled, going from twenty to fifty regulars. On occasions when Dan and Ethyl were absent, the elders led the services, preached, and visited the sick; in short, they administered the church very capably. The key leaders were Epifanio and Jose.

Then came another change. The former missionaries returned from furlough and resumed their pastoral position in the church. Dan and Ethyl were reassigned to Cochabamba. One of the first actions of the returning missionaries was to remove Jose and Epifanio from leadership. Epifanio and his family left the church and went elsewhere. Jose and his family stayed. Church attendance dwindled, and reports of many problems filtered into mission headquarters. Discouraged, within six months the missionary was assigned to a different ministry. A Bolivian was invited to replace him as pastor.

Jose stayed in the church for several years, but all of his attempts to participate in its ministry were thwarted by the three elders. Finally, he frankly told them that he was going to leave the church and begin a new church in another area of the city. He was not bitter, he was just frustrated at not being able to serve the Lord in his own church. He did plant a new church, and God has blessed it. Today, eight years later, they have a membership of 150, own their building, and are constructing a Christian education facility. They have also planted two daughter churches and obtained a campsite for ministry to youth and children.

Conversely, the original church remains truncated and plagued with problems.

Discussion. It would be easy to focus on the concept of conflict and try to ascertain the reasons for the conflict. The trust bond is also involved and deserves extensive discussion. Enjoy those areas of concern, but do not fail to study such books as Nida's *Understanding the Latin American,* and my *A Look at Latin American Lifestyles,* and try to develop a culturally sound way of working with leadership within a Latin American community. What structure could be built into the church to help develop all kinds of leadership? How might the missionary be trained to make effective use of structures of the society to encourage different styles and types of leadership?

Pentecostalism in Italy

In the early part of this century, Pentecostalism was carried from Chicago to Italy, where it has had phenomenal growth. There are more than twice as many Pentecostals in Italy today—over one hundred thousand members of the Assemblies of God alone—as there are all other Protestants combined.

"What made Pentecostal growth possible in this Roman Catholic land?" asks Roger E. Hedlund, Conservative Baptist missionary to Italy. He then explains that southern Italy is a disintegrating society. He feels that identification with the Pentecostals has given a vital functional equivalent to formerly meaningful forms of worship lost through disillusionment with the Catholic church. The following excerpts from his article show how Pentecostalism entered the void and offered a meaningful option to the disoriented people of Italy:[1]

1. Recovery of "community"—a sense of caring and sharing. Conversion results in membership in a fellowship of loving concern.

2. A new dignity. In a disintegrating society the convert finds himself "belonging" in a community where he is "somebody," where he is important as a person.

3. A new interest. Life is drab, but now it takes on color. It is exciting to belong to an ongoing, aggressive body.

4. Replacement for Catholicism. Southern Italians are generally anticlerical, but they still are Catholics for the saving of their souls. The convert, however, finds salvation through another channel. Moreover, he is liberated from many fears and binding beliefs. Rather than merely sweeping these away, however, Pentecostalism replaces many of the old features with functional substitutes. At

first glance Pentecostalism appears a complete negation of
Catholicism. But it is more—a complete replacement.
The disciplined way of life, the many meetings, the drive
to witness—all these tend to replace the old system. Local
house church services and Bible studies replace the old
parish church. Activities in a larger, central "mother"
church replace the cathedral function. The characteristic
change of lifestyle brings a dignity and respect (despite
persecution)—a replacement of the monastic system of
the Catholic Church. The mass is replaced by the fervent
Pentecostal worship in which everyone participates together. Catholic sacraments are replaced by crisis experience and by believer's baptism and the occasional celebration of the Lord's Supper. A doctrine of bodily healing is
substituted for pilgrimages to Catholic healing shrines,
and the Holy Spirit takes the place of the emotions of
Roman Catholic pomp and ceremony and procession.

Growth among Pentecostals follows family lines. Stress on
witnessing compels the convert to share his faith, and his most
natural contacts are members of his family. Italian family closeness
is reinforced by the utilization of house churches.

It is difficult to isolate any one element as the key to
Pentecostal victory. "The first reason for the growth of Pentecostal
churches is that when a forgotten human being comes to one of
them, he feels himself loved and understood."

A simplicity of approach is no doubt one important reason for
Pentecostal success. Christianity is not dogma so much as spiritual
experience. It is therefore a living reality, and as such brings
meaning to life and victory over unseen powers (which is
important in spiritistic Southern Italy).

Pentecostalism brings, therefore, newness of life and a new
dignity to the individual . . . within the context of a church . . .
within the framework of the Italian family.

Discussion. The functional equivalent is dominant in this
case and provides examples to illustrate the principle discussed in chapter 15. The case is in this section, however, to
provide practice in isolating aspects of a culture that influence
decision making. Begin a list of these aspects. Compare them
with the dynamic processes operating in your own community. Discuss how they compare or contrast. Does God use
culture in this way to bring honor to his name? Do you have
other examples?

One House, or Is It Two?

Peruvian custom is such that there are essentially two laws governing behavior, one that is written and another that is practiced. The reality of these distinctions came to our full understanding when the following incident happened involving fellow missionaries.

They were renting a three-bedroom apartment which was the lower level of a building. The owner lived upstairs where she also had three bedrooms. As one looked at the building from the street, it appeared as though it were only one house. It had a garage door, a front door, a picture window on the lower level (the missionaries') and one on the upper level (the landlady's). The landlady would enter through the front door which led directly upstairs to her apartment only. The missionaries would enter their apartment through the garage door. Since they were first-term missionaries, they did not understand at first the reason for the odd arrangement, but they soon found out.

It seems that in Peru real estate taxes are computed on the basis of the number of dwellings in a particular building. In this case, there were two separate apartments, which the written law says should be counted as two houses. Since from all outward appearances the house was used by one family, the owner was paying half the legally required amount of taxes.

The landlady began attending the church the missionaries had begun, and before long, she was converted. Soon afterwards, the missionaries discovered the real reason for the unusual architecture of the building. They promptly confronted the landlady with the matter because they termed it deception and tax evasion. They knew that nearly every owner in Peru practiced this, and they knew also that in actual practice written laws were not binding on any level of society, but to them that was no excuse. "A Christian must not be involved in such corrupt practices," they said.

The landlady politely listened to their words of admonition but seemed completely unmoved by them. They continued to speak to her about the matter, using biblical references, but they saw no favorable results. Finally, they moved away.

Discussion. Who was right? the landlady? the missionary? What was the real problem here? Compare this case with the practice of freeway driving in the States. How many Christians drive no more than fifty-five miles per hour? Are they wrong to go faster than fifty-five? Do we have other social laws that differ from the written ones? How might the missionary have responded in this case? (Note: The way he did respond was most ineffectual.) How did the landlady see the Christian life? What message of Christian growth did she read from the missionary's behavior?

The Headman's Hidden Agenda

There were more people in Kiziza village early on that bright Sunday morning than I had ever seen there before. I was quite sure they had not been attracted by the prospect of hearing me preach, and I was right. They were having a cattle auction that morning, but they were perfectly content to delay their auction for a time to listen to the missionary. At that time, I am sure that I would not have delayed my service for the auction had I been requested to do so.

I preached on John 14:6 and afterward chatted with the village headman. Latching on to the gist of my message, in which I proclaimed Christ to be the way or road, and apparently in all innocence, he said, "You know, Bwana, if we had a road between here and the mission, we could get to church each Sunday."

I realized that he was testing me. Some time before this, the Congo administration, in an effort to get the population out of the boondocks and along the roads, had agreed to advance the price of a cement block house to any working man who would move out to the road. I could see that our headman, with this take-off on the word "road," was testing my gullibility with the idea in mind that perhaps the missionary would naïvely consider extending the mission road a quarter of a mile to Kiziza. His goal was to give the local Kizizites the possibility of having permanent houses without moving their village. I smiled, winked, and casually reminded him how admirably he had made the twelve kilometer walk to the Djomba market the preceding Friday without the aid of a road. "And besides," I said, "I am not here to prepare roads on earth but roads to heaven."

We laughed together and understood each other perfectly. Consequently, he was always on hand for those early Sunday morning messages in his village, and he even managed to get to church occasionally.

Discussion. Was the missionary reading the situation correctly? What behavioral cues indicated that he did or didn't? Would the national's behavior have been any different had the missionary acceded to his wishes? How do we "try to get the road extended" to suit our needs? Is this wrong to try to do? Would it have been so terrible for the missionary to extend the road? What makes us treat others differently than we ourselves want to be treated?

Furlough

Lois Smith was a skillful missionary nurse working in a mission hospital in Southeast Asia. The hospital administration was planning to establish a nursing school to train national nurses to serve their own people. The government had set up rather stringent requirements regarding the educational standards of teaching personnel. A Master of Science degree in nursing was required of the nursing school director and of other key personnel. Among the nurses, no one had that degree.

Lois was asked by the hospital superintendent and the field council to spend her forthcoming furlough in procuring her M.S. in nursing in order to be prepared to head up the nursing education program. She was pleased with this prospect, and so were the mission leaders.

As time for furlough drew near, Lois realized that there was a little conflict. According to mission policy, no one was to go home for furlough early except for valid health reasons. Lois realized that she must plan to leave the field in August so as to be prepared to enter the fall term at the university in mid-September; however, her four-year term was not complete until mid-October.

She decided to write a personal letter to the mission director requesting early furlough—early by a scant two months out of forty-eight. The reply she received from headquarters was, "No. Early furloughs are granted only for health reasons." Feeling this was a bit unreasonable under the circumstances, she felt constrained to write again. This time she was told that mission funds would not be expended unless she waited until her full four years were up. If she must go early, it would be at personal expense.

After carefully praying about the decision, Lois made plans to leave in mid-August and arranged for personal payment for an air ticket—costing $639 economy fare! Her furlough was a busy one, and demands on her were great. However, she earned her degree and returned to her post at mission expense.

Discussion. Why was Lois in conflict? Describe the two institutional systems underlying this conflict situation. Which one was correct? Who was to yield in such a situation? What did the mission have to lose in denying Lois's request? What did Lois have to lose by staying longer? Did Lois make the right decision? What behavioral indications were there that she did?

Deprivation

Seeing Clarise's immaculately groomed figure with its shining auburn hair bent over the old leper woman's extended feet as she carefully debrided the ulcerating sores, Paul was struck by the amazing contrast and stopped to reflect a moment. Clarise was chatting fluently in old Luala's language, trying to calm her fears—and perhaps, Paul thought, trying to keep her own mind off the stench, the flies, and the heat.

Paul respected Clarise as a very capable fellow doctor. She could have had an exclusive practice in America. Just before going to Africa, she had inherited nearly a quarter of a million dollars from her father. Few people even knew of this. From the time she had given her life to Christ as a teenager, she had looked forward to working among the lepers of Central Africa.

Paul never ceased to be amazed at her total acceptance of the land and its people with seemingly no sense of deprivation. She accepted her role with joy and spread a contagious thankfulness to God in all circumstances. It made the routine and drudgery in the hospital easier for them all. What a contrast with Miriam!

Miriam. This morning had brought another scene that had left Paul feeling helpless and wondering if his whole ministry in this country was futile. She had wanted him to take the day off to go to the beach with the children. She felt he owed it to his family and let him know he was failing her and the children. She seemed incapable of understanding his enjoyment of his work. As for the children, Judy and John, Paul was certain he did not neglect them. Through long evening hours they had been growing closer together as their parents' estrangement increased.

Miriam had never been happy since they moved to Dempala to direct the hospital. On the coast, they had lived in the capital city. There had been a circle of French friends with whom she could always spend an afternoon. Here in Dempala, her days were made up of drinking iced tea, visiting with the other missionary women when they were not too busy with their classes or hospital work, and reading women's magazines.

Miriam had been beauty queen the year Paul was a senior in college. He had felt himself the luckiest fellow on campus when a short courtship brought a June wedding soon after graduation. It had seemed so wonderful to him that she was a Christian from a good, though not well-to-do, family, and she seemed to be delighted at the thought of going anywhere in the world that he went. Now she never passed up an opportunity to say, as though it were a great joke, that she had married a doctor, not a missionary, and see what she had gotten stuck with.

Looking at her this morning, he had found it hard to understand how her beauty had coarsened so in just sixteen years. Her bitterness and discontent had brought a permanent drooping sullenness to her face, a face from which all delicateness had been blurred by weight which had been creeping on over the years. Although she only stepped on the scales behind locked doors, one guessed that she was carrying at least eighty excess pounds. With this addition had gone all interest in dressing carefully. A drooping slip or a safety-pin-anchored hem gave the final picture.

And perhaps hardest for Paul to bear was her antipathy to the nationals, whom he had come to sincerely love. Serving the Lord in this land was his whole life. Bringing his mind back to today's problems, he decided he would try to take the afternoon off. He would try to appease Miriam once more.

> *Discussion.* How many of the three outsiders were living in deprivation of norm in their host society? Discuss. What responsibility did Paul have toward Miriam? Might this extend even to his being willing to leave this field? What are the implications of such a move? When considering rank of values, should Paul place his family well-being over the work? Why do you feel as you do about this? Could Paul be more effective in the ministry were he to divorce Miriam and marry Clarise? How might they resolve the conflict in their lives? Can the children possibly be unaffected by the parents' conflict?

"But Mom and Dad, You Don't Understand!"

Collin, a sophomore at a midwestern university, grew up in a typical middle-class, Evangelical home. He was a good student in high school, was active in extracurricular activities, and was well prepared for college. He enjoyed being with people and was involved in helping others.

Collin's father was a hard-working, conscientious person who was very loyal to his country's ideals. He experienced the Depression, fought in World War II, and had worked hard to give his family the material things he never had as a young man.

His mother was a devout woman who was very concerned with the spiritual welfare of her family. She had had to sacrifice personal pleasures for the sake of her children.

His younger sister Mary was a freshman in high school. She idolized her big brother and had always been influenced by his opinions. She was beginning to rebel outwardly against her parents' religious views that all behavior should "conform to the Bible" as they understood it. Her frustration had driven her to succumb to peer pressure to use drugs and experiment with free love.

Collin was very concerned about his sister's feelings and behavior. He thought her actions were wrong on the basis of what his parents had taught him, but since he had been at the university, he had also begun questioning his family's value system and the principles of the religious training he had been taught in church.

He had discovered at the university that if a person wanted to be accepted, he must tolerate the views of everyone else. Thus, if another person seemed sincere in his views toward life, it was right for him. Truth became relative and subjective. As circumstances and time changed, truth would also change in order to keep pace with its environmental setting. Collin had learned that the only things that really counted were those things that were happening right then. His professors told him that the criterion for evaluating life issues was "that whatever we do, it should be done for the immediate good of people—man will work out the reactions later. This is what really counts."

But this philosophy bothered Collin. If this criterion was good and true, he wondered, why didn't mankind naturally practice this value system? Why did the outward manifestations of hate, strife, selfishness, greed, war, sickness, prejudice, pollution, and anarchy still exist? Why did the humanitarian teachings he had received seem so ineffectual?

These honest doubts caused Collin to question the meaning of life and of his own existence. This began affecting his attitude in other social relationships. He found himself asking: What constitutes friendship or love? Why not have sex if the other person agrees? Is homosexuality wrong? Some of these thoughts caused a tension between Collin and his girlfriend. He had less desire to share his faith with others. He became preoccupied with questions like: Is the Bible the relevant, objective criterion for evaluating contemporary life issues? Was Christ really God in the flesh? Am I playing "church" games? Is there really a hell or a heaven? Is man born with a sin nature, or does society make him that way?

Collin had lost much of his purpose and direction for his future goals. His moral judgments became cloudy, and he had a hard time making decisions. He began seeing people around him being manipulated and used for selfish reasons, but his cries were not heard above the noise of the political machinery. The teaching/learning process at the university began to lose its effectiveness, and he began wondering if he should even be in school.

Discussion. Why was Collin in conflict? Name the steps in the process leading him to experience conflict. How did Collin's sister try to resolve the tension? Was she justified in trying to work it out her way? How might one maintain his own principles and still deal with his sister in such a situation? How might you help Collin? Mary? the parents? yourself?

Blood of a White Chicken

Among the Tagbanwa people of the Philippines, rice is the staple food, but only a small percentage of the total amount of rice consumed is actually produced by the people on their own land. This is of the upland variety, sometimes referred to as dry rice. The fields are carved out of secondary forest growth on the sides of mountains by the slash-and-burn technique. The seed is planted by hand in small holes dug by means of a dibble stick. Because the growth of the rice depends on the rainfall, only one crop a year can be grown during the rainy season. Such fields are usually quite small, and the yield ration is low compared to other methods that depend on the use of the plow. Even when there is a good harvest, which is rare, the longest the supply has been observed to last is about two months.

Outsiders who visit the village of Banwang Daan, a Tagbanwa settlement located on Coron Island, are often struck with the fact that most of the arable land in the valley is not cultivated. Instead, it is given over to the tough, resistant "cogon" grass. Furthermore, no water buffalo can be seen anywhere in the village, and there are no plows.

If the visitor should inquire from the people why the land is not put to better use, they will likely reply that they are too poor to own a buffalo. If one knows a bit about the Tagbanwas, he might proceed to remind them of the very lucrative trade in edible birds' nests which they engage in during five months of the year. In response, the people would probably pose the problem of social conflict should one's water buffalo get loose and wander over into a neighbor's garden. If the outsider should point out that there are ways to handle the problem of straying buffaloes and suggest that the introduction of plowing with them could help the people to make economic progress, the Tagbanwas would respond with silence.

Why are the Tagbanwas reluctant to plow their own land?

Traditionally, they have never been plowers of the soil. This agricultural technique has come into the area with other ethnic groups who have migrated and taken over land formerly used by Tagbanwas. This is not to say that present-day Tagbanwa men do not know how to plow. Most of them have had experience in the construction of rice paddies through hiring out to Cuyonon and Tagalog landowners on the large, adjacent island. However, despite their know-how, rarely, if ever, have they been known to employ it on land which they themselves intended to utilize. This has been true even when water buffaloes have been available to them. There was one man who obtained two of these animals, but he never used them for plowing, and within a year he sold them to non-Tagbanwas.

There is also a deep-seated Tagbanwa belief that owning and utilizing objects that have not been contemporaneous with one's childhood experience is very dangerous and will likely lead to one's death or the death of a member of his family. And there is a very close association between a person and the land he utilizes, so that his use of the land is hedged about with many taboos and rituals designed not only to insure productivity, but also to maintain his health and that of his family.

The act of plowing is fraught with danger because it is perceived as an offense against the ground and is compared to wounding a person. Unless placated by a sacrifice, the ground will exact payment in retaliation for the offense by inflicting death on the person or on some member of his family. Through contact with Cuyonons, the Tagbanwas have knowledge of a certain ritual that could be used to protect themselves from such danger in the event that they took up plowing. But there is a hitch when it comes to performing this ritual. The ability to perform it is a matter of inheritance—one's father must have performed this ritual and have passed it on to him. This is done by the son holding on to the father's shoulders as the father performs it.

Apparently no Tagbanwa has inherited this ability. The only other known alternative would be to hire a qualified Cuyonon to perform the ritual. However, this seems highly unlikely. Perhaps the history of land-grabbing on the part of this ethnic group may account for the reluctance of the Tagbanwas to hire them for this service. Thus it is that most of the arable land in the valley is not being utilized for the production of rice.

As for the ritual itself, two intersecting lines must first be plowed in the field in the form of a cross, making sure that the intersection is at the approximate center of the area to be plowed. After this pattern has been formed, the plow is detached and placed at the intersection. Then a white chicken is sacrificed by severing its jugular vein, and its blood is made to drip on the plowshare.

Simultaneously, a chanted prayer is addressed to the ground. The gist of the prayer is that the debt incurred by opening up the ground is now being paid by means of the sacrifice. The ground is implored to accept this payment instead of retaliating against the family. No more plowing is done until the next day.

> *Discussion.* This case is particularly useful for discussing chapters 10 and 15. For 10, it is helpful to ask such questions as: How does the activity of rice planting have social, economic, and religious significance to the Tagbanwa? Why would an agent of change insisting on the Tagbanwa's using the plow cause deep disruption in the society? Does this mean there is no possibility of encouraging a more productive rice culture here? Why? Why may a change of activity amount to a change of norm? What positive and negative results might accompany the introduction of Christianity among these people?
>
> For chapter 15, it is helpful to ask such questions as: How do each of the tools of relationship give insight into a study of this case? Imagine you are either a government-sponsored agriculturalist or a missionary. Present possible solutions to the problem that is hindering beneficial change among the Tagbanwa. In what way might the casual outsider likely confuse form and meaning in this case? Can you suggest how a functional equivalent for the blood sacrifice might be encouraged as part of the people's festival cycle?

Bible Institute?

The mission had recently decided to start a Bible institute in the city. There had been problems with the one in the country because the city students did not want to break away and go to a rural school.

During the first year, two city boys were enrolled, so the mission leaders decided to also bring in three country students who had not finished their elementary school. The city boys had finished with high standing in their high school's graduating class.

The building was in an upper-middle-class or lower-upper-class neighborhood. The people there had maids, beautiful mansion-type homes, several cars, gardeners to take care of their lawns and expensive plants, etc. The Bible school director began to notice that the Sunday afternoon visitation team of the country boys was not leaving in a very happy mood for the door-to-door visitation in the area of their school. The two city boys had had some rather interesting encounters and enjoyed sharing their experiences. The country boys seemed to be retiring more and more into themselves.

One of the Bible institute teachers began sharing his negative results with the staff. He found that the good students were not trying very hard. They did not seem to have much motivation. The country boys did not seem to grasp the theological terms presented in the class lectures, nor could they understand the commentaries or theology books. As a teacher, he felt frustrated and shared that he had begun to dread meeting his classes.

After some of the national pastors visited, they began to show concern for the future of the Bible institute.

> *Discussion.* How many cultures/subcultures are represented in the case? How would you analyze the lack of motivation and interest on the part of the students? Do you think the culture of the missionaries was affecting this? Why? Does being "one in Christ" make a difference in a setting such as this? How could the teachers prepare each student for a better experience in the classroom as well as in Christian service? Discuss.

Marriage Will Solve It All

Dear Phil:

Greetings from out Ivory Coast way. It surely sounds like you're enjoying your graduate work, though I still don't quite understand why you're doing all that work in anthropology. I personally never felt the need of it. You know the Baoules have a proverb, "He who really knows ten will never be deceived with nine." If you really know your Bible and teach it just like it is, you won't need to worry about the culture that the anthropologists are always talking about.

You asked about conference. We had a good one. As usual, the first three days were given to the missionaries' reports of their work. The delegation from the national church which had been invited seemed too busy with other things to attend. One wonders sometimes if they really care.

Oh yes, some of the younger missionaries brought up the idea again of changing the conference in order to present papers pertinent to the work instead of having the reports which have always been such a blessing down through the years. One of the young women—I won't tell you who—even suggested that we assign someone to study the etiquette of the Baoules during the coming year and then ask him to present his findings at the next conference. I vetoed that quickly enough. Imagine what a waste of missionary time! None of us is an authority in this field. And since the rest of us would not be prepared to refute anything that might be presented, it didn't seem fair to operate in that way. Nothing more was said, so I hope that will be the end of that.

You mentioned Andre Tanoh. He is still troubled by pains in his stomach—or so he says. The doctor can't find a thing wrong with him. You remember when he was converted about six years ago and came to work in the bookstore as accountant? He was doing such fine work, and we were all so pleased until we found out one day that Aya, the "little sister" who had been living with him for several months doing his cooking, was not his sister at all, but his cousin—and she was pregnant.

Well, I surely didn't waste any time. I piled them in the car the same afternoon and took them out to their village to arrange for them to get married. I told him not to come back to the bookstore until the matter was regulated, though we needed him so badly. He tried to make all sorts of protests—his old pagan uncle who had raised him and paid for his education was opposed to the marriage. Aya, as a first cousin, was not acceptable as a wife to his family. He really didn't think he loved her, etc., etc. He even brought up their pagan ways, saying that, according to their customs, what they had done was normal and would lead to marriage only if both parties agreed and the two families were in accord. Well, I knew he was only a new Christian, and so I read to him what the Bible says about fornication and adultery and told him that before he could come back to his job, the marriage would have to be arranged.

He was away from work about a month but finally came and said he and Aya had decided to consider their marriage as final, though they would still have to work at getting the old folks' consent. As far as I know, they never have been able to move that hard old character of an uncle of his.

It was surely good I took a strong stand at that time on this matter, because I can see now how it served as an example for the church to follow when similar disciplinary cases came up. Funny isn't it, that after thirty-five years, the Christians in this land have never really learned God's pattern for courtship and marriage. Our finest young people—raised right in the church—will go along until they reach that age when they want to get a wife, and then they invariably revert to the old custom of *soman bole,* which, at best, can only be regarded as trial marriage. I've seen it happen again and again in the Bible school. If the girl is pregnant, we usually urge them to drop out a semester while they make their relation official, and then, if we feel they are repentant, they may return as a married couple.

But I started to tell you why it was so good that I had insisted that Andre and Aya go through with their marriage at once. Several years ago a similar case came up with a student in the seminary. He was one of our first students at the intermission seminary and had been quite a ladies' man before his conversion. Then during his first vacation from seminary, he had an affair with a real "bush" girl back in his village. When it was found out, the church leaders talked the palaver and insisted they be married if he wanted to continue in seminary. So they were, and now they have three beautiful children.

It's just too bad his wife has had no interest in even learning to read or in bettering herself in any way so that she can fit into the milieu for which his seminary training has prepared him. She will always be a drag on him, I'm afraid, and some people feel he is friendlier than he ought to be with one of the girls from the normal school. Oh, why won't these fellows think about the kind of wife they need before they dash into an affair?

Some have criticized the church's decision to insist on marriage in such cases. They say that forcing people into a marriage which would bring a number of children into the world without love is a greater crime than the original affair. But what can the church do under the circumstances? Its purity has to be maintained.

Things are going along fine as usual out here. Have a good time with your studies and don't forget to put first things first.

Yours in His Service,
Andrew

P.S. Phew! Before I got this mailed, I was called out for a palaver about Andre. It's funny that I had just been writing to you about him, so I'll clue you in. It seems that he has been in the process of taking another wife for several months, and none of us knew it. Aya has taken the children and gone back to their village. In fact, some of the Africans feel he has just done this to get rid of her. He makes no bones about the fact that he doesn't love her. Guess we're out a good accountant. And after all the hours I wasted on him, trying to teach him what a Christian marriage is all about. . . !

A. S.

> *Discussion.* It would be good to work through the different indications that the national believers have little respect for the missionaries, e.g., they don't attend the annual meeting. Discuss why this might be. Spend some time suggesting resolutions for the various problems the missionaries face. Are these all spiritual problems? social? How might the discipline of anthropology help them and support what they are teaching?

"Please, Jim, Do Something!"

"If he'd only do something!" Karen wailed to herself. "Why must I be the only one to face the unpleasant situations? If only he'd help to carry the load!" Then realizing how self-pitying she sounded, she just gave up trying to understand and felt again the old frustration that enveloped her so often.

She could hear her missionary husband, Jim, in the kitchen laughing with Pierre, who helped her with the cooking and housework. Today she had finally caught Pierre in the act of stealing part of the meat she had laid out for dinner. Long suspicious of how the portions of meat seemed to shrink between the time they were given to Pierre to cook and their appearance on the table, she had taken to counting the pieces. This morning when she had found three fewer Swiss steaks cooking than she had given him to prepare, she had searched until she found the missing ones carefully hidden under the sink, ready to be carried off to Pierre's yard after work.

Over their after-dinner coffee, Karen had explained to Jim what she had found and asked him if he would handle the situation by having a talk with Pierre and telling him once and for all that, if this happened again, they would have to consider dismissing him. Now she could hear Jim chatting with Pierre, asking him how his farm was doing and if his oldest boy had passed his exams last week. Disgusted, Karen decided to take a walk so that she wouldn't hear them talking. She was sure Jim would never face him with the ultimatum.

Jim was such a wonderful guy; why did he seem so "weak," so incapable of taking a strong position that involved confrontation with people? There was the matter of the Johnsons' chickens that had been ruining her garden. She had asked Jim to speak to Bill Johnson about it, but somehow he always "forgot" to do it. Then there was the shirt he had bought last week only to find an ugly fault in the fabric when he unwrapped it. She was sure that if it were to be returned to the store, she would have to do it.

Perhaps the hardest of his "do nothing" way was his reluctance to take an authoritative hand in disciplining the children. Why must she always fill the role of the disciplinarian while he could be the "good guy," the father the children loved and respected but who could be worked around in almost any situation? Again a voice which she would have been ashamed to call her own whispered, "If he really cared for me as he says he does, wouldn't he take his share of the unpleasant jobs to be done? I'll bet if he saw me being robbed, he'd be a perfect gentleman and look the other way."

But inwardly Karen envied Jim in a way. How often he

attained his goal without the hurt feelings that her abrasive and abrupt actions brought in their wake. Now she could hear Pierre whistling as he got on his bicycle to go home. His talk with Jim apparently had left him feeling self-confident and happy. He wouldn't be whistling if she had talked to him!

Karen glanced at her watch and turned back to the house with a sigh of futility. It was time for her to take her medication for that ulcer that seemed to be threatening.

> *Discussion.* What was likely causing Karen's ulcer? In what ways was she taking herself too seriously? Did she have sufficient reason to do so? Be sure to read the case of the tricycle in chapter 16 (p. 246) before completing this discussion. Was this a case of theft, or was it some practice controlled by the culture but not involving theft, e.g., group sharing practices of some kind or other? How could one tell? Suppose it turned out to be a clear case of theft? How could Jim have handled it? Suppose it turned out to be some group sharing practice? Would Karen have had to give up her point of view in accommodating herself to this culture? What kinds of things did Jim need to learn about his wife? What kinds of things did Karen need to learn about the culture? How might they have worked more together to accomplish their maintenance of principle in the process of adapting to the new lifestyle? What Bible teachings could help them? How might the basic values model help them understand each other better?

Model Three:

The Validity of Distinct Societies

Should the Left Hand Know?

One of the first pastors of the Baoule church had died, and the leading Christians of the Ivory Coast tribe of nearly a million had gathered with a number of missionaries to participate in his funeral. As is customary at Baoule funerals, a table was arranged to display the gifts of cloth that were given to the family. When a gift of money was placed on the table, the name of the donor and the amount was called out in a loud voice.

The missionaries, feeling that they wanted their giving to follow the injunction "Do not let your left hand know what your right hand is doing," told the church president that they preferred to offer their condolences to the widow and quietly slip her a gift of money later. This way it would not be announced publicly. A sizeable collection was taken up, and the mission director made a special trip to see her and present it.

About eight months after the funeral, a large memorial wake was held, at which time even larger gifts were given publicly. Realizing that they should make some public presentation and not just sit there as though totally unconcerned, the missionaries took up a collection. Because they had already given in their own unobtrusive way, the gift was not as large as the Baoule church president thought it should be. He nearly refused it, since refusing a gift is a perfectly acceptable and often practiced privilege among the Baoules. As it was, he accepted the token gift, but he let the incident rankle bitterly in his mind for months.

The missionaries see this sort of public giving as an ostentatious display. The Baoules say, "This is our way of showing esteem for the deceased and consolation for the family." The missionaries say they like to give personally and without fanfare (forgetting the wreaths they send to funerals in America). The Baoules say that things done secretly are suspect, as honest people want their actions to be open and known to all. The missionaries feel that by their example they can teach the correct way to give. The Baoules feel the missionaries are miserly and terribly ungracious in their rejecting of their customs.

> *Discussion.* Which approach to giving is correct? Do the Baoules have the right to give in their way? Can it be an honor to God? Can it honor God yet not be in keeping with the way the missionaries do it? Are the missionaries interpreting the verses on giving correctly? How are Americans overt and ostentatious in their giving? Is this an honor to God? Does it follow the correct teaching of the verses on giving in the Bible? How would you resolve such a conflict of norm? How can one work with the Baoule Christians to both aid them in understanding the Scripture and in practicing what God has for them in spiritual growth. How can one work with American Christians in these same regards?

Reciprocity

On one occasion, I, a missionary, had irked one of the Shan families in the town where we lived by kicking their young son in the seat of his pants for breaking a toy and then spanking him because he threw a stone at me. After realizing the mistake I had made, I looked for a mediator to resolve this delicate situation. Since the mayor was a nearby neighbor, I called on him, explaining my dilemma and asking for his intercession as a mediator.

The mayor and I went to the house of the family involved, and the consultative process began. The mayor talked with the father on the porch of the house while I listened and looked on. The mother was crying inside the house, claiming the child's spirit had been broken. The mayor then went inside to talk with her. After considerable deliberation, he returned to me on the porch. He said local custom required the payment of a fine because the child's spirit had been broken. This fine would be 300 baht ($15). I balked at this high fine but later yielded and paid the fine to the family. This eased the tension and cleared up the conflict.

Later on, another set of circumstances brought me into contact with the mayor. I had been invited by the governor of the province to accompany him and his party on a trek to a distant district which was reachable only by foot. This was a distance of about sixty-five miles, which normally took five days of walking. I was going to this area for an evangelistic trip, so I agreed to travel with the governor.

At the campsites each night, I accepted the governor's hospitality and mingled freely with the lesser officials in the party. The mayor of the town was in the group. The governor, the mayor, and one other official rode horses while the rest of us walked. Since the governor's party was traveling rather slowly, I determined on the fourth day to go ahead alone so as to be at our destination for Sunday. Later, I joined the governor's party as it returned home via another route using a truck.

A month or two later, I found myself summoned to appear before a government investigator from Bangkok. It seems the governor had submitted a padded expense account for this trip and had collected money far in excess of what was actually spent. The vice-governor had evidently reported this to Bangkok authorities; hence the investigation. On the evening prior to my appearance before the investigator, the mayor paid me a visit. He had never before been to my house. After I invited him in for a chat, he approached the subject of the investigation, saying he had heard that I had been called to testify. I nodded agreement and wondered what was coming next. He went on to say, "When they ask you questions, just tell them you don't know anything."

Immediately, I recognized the bind I was in. Earlier he had done me a favor by acting as mediator with the family I had offended by my behavior. Now I felt he was expecting me to reciprocate by conceding to his request. I felt that I could not do it and explained to the mayor that as a Christian I could not willfully lie. However, I added that if I did not know the answer to any question, I would say so. The mayor made his departure disappointedly. The next day I went before the investigator, who asked about the various aspects of the journey in which I had taken part. The questions were simple and direct and were designed to ascertain the what, how many, and when aspects of the journey. I tried to be honest and proffered as brief answers as possible. Later on, I learned that the governor had been suspended from government service.

Discussion. Was the missionary obligated to respond to the investigation? Could he have handled the situation more effectively? Was it appropriate that the governor was released from his office? Was the missionary to blame? How might he have handled the situation so as to be uninvolved? Should he have been uninvolved? Did he fulfill his commitment to the mayor, or was he an ungrateful friend? How are politics involved in the missionary's ministry? Is the role of a missionary political? Does he need to be trained in political science to do his job? How do you think the governor feels about him? How do you think the mayor feels about him? Should we never ask favors of others? For the first stage of this case, see "The Foreigner's Dilemma" in case studies model 4.

A Kiss for the Preacher's Daughter

Dear Ann Landers: I am a fifteen-year-old girl who is awfully mixed up. The first problem is that I am a preacher's daughter and everybody expects me to be perfect. My parents are very strict. They keep reminding me that I have to live up to my station in life. I hate feeling that I am different from other girls my age, but that's the way it is, and I have accepted it. Two weeks ago a very nice boy walked me home from choir practice. Just before we reached our block he kissed me. I felt so guilty I couldn't sleep. A week later it happened again. Although I have prayed for forgiveness, I feel I should tell my parents, but I can't bring myself to do it. I'm afraid I would be restricted for life. This morning I was so nervous I couldn't go to school. I told my mother I had a stomach ache (which was true), but I'm sure my worry caused it. Can you help?—*Ashamed of Myself.*[1]

Discussion. Have the parents raised their child effectively? How might they have helped her more? Has the girl responded effectively? How might she have helped her parents raise her in a way that prepared her to more adequately face the challenges that will come her way? Is a kiss a bad thing? What makes it a problem to this girl? Was the fellow helping her in her dilemma? How might he have been more help to her? Is this a social or spiritual problem? When did it become a spiritual one? How might the girl aid herself most? in the social realm? in the spiritual realm? How do we implicate God in a negative way when we are unable to work through our social problems?

First Corinthians 8

Setting: Filipino girl whose norm is not holding hands until engagement, begins dating American boy for whom holding hands is part of his norm during the pre-engagement period as well as during the engagement period.

1. In this situation, everyone feels that only the American boy's custom is the right one! But although being a "know-it-all" makes us feel important, what is really needed to build the church is love.
2. If anyone thinks he knows all the answers, he is just showing his ignorance.
3. But the person who truly loves God is the one who is open to God's knowledge.
4. So now, what about it? Should the Filipino girl hold hands with the American boy? Well, we all know that holding hands is amoral (neither here nor there).
5. According to some people, there are a great many alternatives as far as showing affection is concerned.
6. But we know that there is only one God, the Father, who created all things and made us to be his own (allowing for holding hands or not holding hands); and one Lord Jesus Christ, who made everything and gives us life, i.e., giving each one the choice of holding hands or not doing so.
7. However, some Filipino Christians do not realize this. All their lives they have been used to thinking that holding hands before engagement is wrong, and they have believed that it is wrong. So when they do hold hands, it bothers them and hurts their tender conscience.
8. Just remember that God does not care whether we hold hands or not. We are not worse off if we do not hold hands and no better off if we do.
9. But be careful, American boy, not to use your freedom to hold hands lest you cause some Filipino Christian sister to sin whose conscience is weaker than yours.
10. You see, this is what may happen. A Filipino girl who thinks that holding hands is a sin will accept a date from you, and you will try to hold her hand, since you know there is no harm in it. Then she will become bold enough to hold hands even though she still feels it is wrong.
11. So because you "know it is all right to do it," you will be responsible for causing great spiritual damage to a sister with a tender conscience for whom Christ died.
12. And it is a sin against Christ to sin against your sister by encouraging her to do something she thinks is wrong.
13. So if holding hands before engagement is going to make

your sister sin, do not hold hands if you do not want to do this to her.

Discussion. Is the holding of hands amoral? What makes it moral? To the Filipino girl was it amoral? What is the function of hand holding in the American culture? What is the function of hand holding in Filipino culture? Which culture is right? Which is wrong? Does an American gain or lose by yielding to the host culture? Is God pleased when he/she yields? What could the American lose by pressing the Filipino girl to hold hands?

Compromise or Functional Substitute?

Mario was thirty-nine years old, a single adult in a home Bible study for upper-middle-class people who were contacted through professional luncheons during an evangelistic campaign. His parents and relatives also attended the study, which began with couples but developed into a family study as they became burdened for their relatives and friends. Years before, Mario had had a heart operation which, instead of relieving him, had damaged a valve and caused him to suffer from insufficient oxygen. He was thin and sickly, but he managed to get to most of the studies. He enjoyed the group members immensely, and they ministered to him and prayed for him regularly.

One day he was given the opportunity to travel to Brazil for corrective surgery. The operation was not successful, and Mario died within a short time.

Since the family had only been attending the Evangelical church for a few months, having come from a Roman Catholic background, they asked the Bible study leader, a missionary, to perform the funeral. The service was held in Mario's home, and the Bible study group sang hymns of hope and gave testimonies of their love for the Savior and of Mario's saving faith in the Lord. This was quite a contrast to the funerals held by Catholic friends where wailing, desperation, and sorrow prevail. The family was so comforted and thrilled with the positive testimony that when friends asked if there would be a nine-day mass to pray for Mario, they approached church leaders and asked, "Could we have a memorial service in the church to remember Mario? There we could explain to our loved ones and friends that Mario is now with the Lord according to the sure promises of God's Word, and he doesn't need the prayers of others." "He decided his destiny while on the earth," another remarked.

The pastor and elders of the church were hesitant to consent to a service of this kind because of their own Roman Catholic backgrounds, and they did not want to give the impression that the Evangelical church was copying the Catholic church or praying for the dead. It was pointed out, however, that the Evangelical church had a parade on Resurrection Sunday similar to the Catholics' parade on Good Friday, which had been very positive. At the insistence of the family and the encouragement of the Bible study leader, the church agreed. A service was held in which a clear presentation of God's plan of salvation was given. Since that time, two more members of the family have come to Christ. But the church has never had another service like it, before or since.

> *Discussion*. Do you feel the church did right in holding a memorial service for Mario? Would it have been wise to hold others in light of the good reaction to this one? Why or why not? Would this have been a "Catholic" service? Do we need to consider the past experience of believers in contextualizing the message and organization of the new faith? In what ways has Western Christianity adopted secular practices and sacralized them? Is this a wise practice? What guidelines might be followed in allowing for such a practice?

It Is More Blessed to Give

"Give to everyone who asks you . . ." (Luke 6:30). Lend to [your enemies] without expecting to get anything back" (v. 35).

If a person on the island of Truk has a need and goes to a friend who he knows has what he is in need of, the friend is required by custom to give it without any hesitation. Trukese, hearing a missionary preach on Luke 6:30 yet not seeing him practice it fully as they naturally do in their culture, are puzzled. They often come to the missionary and find their requests are refused even though they know he possesses what they need.

Once a fellow who owned an outboard motor asked me to give him some gasoline. I had only one drum left and did not know when the next shipment would arrive. There was no other gasoline on the whole island. I wanted to keep this one drum for an emergency. Sometimes accidents happened, and we would have to go to another island to call for help. Without any gasoline at all, we might be stranded.

I tried to explain this to the Trukese. I reminded him that he used to go fishing without an outboard motor, and I felt he should do it again until there was more gasoline available. Of course he considered me stingy.

Not only I, but Trukese Christians, have felt the effect of practicing this Scripture passage literally. Each church has a treasurer who keeps the books and the money. One treasurer was keeping about $250 in his house, which was to them a very large sum. Some people who knew about this money found themselves in need, and so they went to the treasurer to ask for help. To have refused them would have meant loss of face for him. So he gave (according to Scripture?) the church's money to all those who came and asked for it.

Finally, the amount dropped down to about $80, and the treasurer decided to spend the rest himself before anyone else came asking for it. He resented the others' benefiting from the church's money when he, who had done the hard work of keeping the books and hiding the money, should go empty-handed. Of course no one ever brought the money back, since to the Trukese borrowing implies no obligation to return an object borrowed.

When the Christians found out what had happened to their church funds, they elected a new treasurer. He agreed to accept his duties under the condition that he would only keep the books and the missionary would keep the money.

> *Discussion.* Was the first treasurer a thief? Do you think he really had to loan (give) the money to one who asked it? How might he have avoided doing so without offending his countryman? Was the missionary responsible in allowing the treasurer to keep the money in the first place? Should he have known better? Was the final solution the best? Is this teaching good stewardship?

The Black Beads

Suina and her husband were young Christians, both young in years and in their Christian walk, when an accident took the life of the husband. Suina carried on in the believers' class where converts were prepared for baptism. She seemed to be growing in Christ. The class was completed, and the date for baptism was set. Then Suina came to us and, holding out the string of black beads she was wearing, said, "I can't be baptized."

As we talked to her and to the African evangelist, we came to understand that the beads had been put on her by her husband's family to show that she belonged to the spirit of her departed husband. The ceremony to free the spirit of the dead man had not yet been held, so she was considered married to his spirit. At the time of this ceremony, the beads would be removed and she would be given her husband's brother, at which time she could refuse to be the brother's wife but would stay in his village and be cared for by him until another man paid the *lobola* (bride price) for her to her husband's brother.

Suina felt that she could not be baptized as long as she was wearing the black beads, and her in-laws had refused to take them off. We asked the evangelist if he could talk to the in-laws about removing the beads, and he said that would be asking to take her for his wife.

Suina waited two years until after the ceremony and then was baptized.

> *Discussion.* In Western thinking, two years is a long time to wait. In Africa, where Suina was raised, family responsibility is so important that two years is no time at all to wait. Had the evangelist urged her to go against her cultural ways, Suina would have been thrown into conflict, and her husband's family would have thought little of the gospel. As it was, they stood a good chance of responding to Suina's faith, for she showed firmly her sense of responsibility to them. The biggest challenge would have been the evangelist's, as he would have the responsibility of explaining his and Suina's actions to his mission leaders and his supporters. How might he best go about this task?

Model Four:

Effective Ministry

The Foreigner's Dilemma

My name is Noi, which means "little one." I am eight years old, and I live in a remote northern province of Thailand. Our town is a provincial capital. It isn't very large, but we enjoy life. I live with my parents and four brothers and sisters. My father is a barber.

A family of white foreigners came to live in our town, and they rented a small house just down the street from my house. I liked to visit their house, especially on Saturday nights. They let us come inside for a children's meeting where we sat on the floor, sang songs, played games, and then listened to stories about the white man's religion. Lots and lots of my friends came to the meeting each week.

Sometimes during the week I would visit the foreigner's house. His children had many toys. One day I stopped to play with the toys, and somehow I broke the wheels off one of the trucks. The foreign teacher was at home that afternoon, and he saw me with the broken toy in my hands. He yelled at me, "What are you doing, breaking Jamrut's toys like that?"

He started down the stairs of the house after me. I was afraid. He grabbed me and gave me a boot in the seat and told me to go home. This made me angry, so I picked up a stone and heaved it at him. He started to chase me, so I ran under a neighbor's house, but he came right after me. My heart began to pound as he dragged me out and spanked my bottom with his hand. I wailed with fright and ran home to tell my father.

"Father, the foreigner kicked me, and then he beat me," I cried. (To point with the foot or to kick anyone is extremely impolite among our people because feet are despised but the head is highly honored.) This made my father angry, so he went immediately to the man's house and, standing in the street in front of the house, he said, "Why did you kick and beat my son? If he did something wrong, why didn't you come and tell me?"

The teacher replied, "Please come up in the house and we'll talk it over together." My father was too disturbed and refused to go into the house. Later, the foreigner must have felt sorry. Suddenly I saw him heading toward my house accompanied by the district officer, the highest official of the area. They came up on our porch, and the district officer explained that he had come with the foreign teacher to make amends for upsetting the peace. My father and a group of neighbor men sat on the porch talking softly. My father suggested that the D.O. talk with my mother, who was sitting inside the house crying her eyes out. Leaving the white man on the porch with the men, the D.O. came inside to talk with my mother.

It is our practice to have a middle man help talk over important matters. The foreign teacher looked sad and didn't seem to know what to say. He tried apologizing to my father, but my father just nodded and agreed with him. Soon the D.O. returned to the porch and spoke with the foreign teacher. He said, "Ahjan [Teacher], the boy's mother says the spanking caused her son's spirit to break. You must pay a fine of 300 baht [$15] in order to bring healing for this offense."

"But that's too much money!" replied the teacher. "There is nothing wrong with the boy; the spanking likely did him good."

The D.O. tried to explain how my people handle an affair like this. The foreigner didn't understand very well. He had never been in trouble before. After almost two hours or so of conversation, he consented and paid the 300 baht to the D.O., who gave it to my father. He in turn assured the teacher that all was well now. Farewells were exchanged as the D.O. and the teacher descended the porch stairs. It was now dark. Many people had gathered. The foreigner appeared perplexed but much relieved and grateful that the official had served as a friend and mediator.

After that, I didn't feel like playing with the foreigner's children any more. In fact, I don't think I went to any more Saturday night children's meetings either.

Discussion. Did the missionary do right in spanking the child? in using a mediator? in hesitating to pay the fine? How might the situation have been handled in a way that helped all parties? For a second stage of this case, see "Reciprocity" in case studies model 3 (p. 368).

The Marriage Vow

While my wife and I were in language study, we lived for six months on a small Micronesian island called Oneop. A mission station has been there for about thirty years, and now the church is in the care of a national minister and two assistants. Before the influence of the gospel came, the inhabitants fought with the neighboring islanders, killing and robbing each other.

One day the minister excitedly told us of an event that had taken place the night before. The whole island was talking about it. A young man had been found sleeping in the house of his fiancée. The minister asked me if I would be willing to pray with the two young people involved. Before doing so, I set out to ask some questions.

After careful inquiry, we found an unwritten law was operative in such cases: If a young man had sexual relations with his fiancée before the marriage ceremony, they could not speak their vows and have a marriage celebration in the church. It was customary in such cases for the minister or missionary to have a brief prayer with the couple, and the new marriage would be considered established. Many couples, we were told, got married that way. We felt there must be some reason for this behavior, and so we continued to ask questions.

We found that the main reason seems to be the fear of making a vow before God, who is to them a righteous judge. He would take account of their vow, and it would be dangerous to incur his wrath by not keeping it. But they also know their own weakness, which, in a sense, is stronger than their fear of God.

The Trukese custom used to be that a man would live with his wife until she no longer pleased him. Then he would send her away and live with another woman. But now a binding vow complicates the process and threatens punishment from God. The perfect solution seemed to be to avoid making a vow yet to still receive the blessing of the minister.

We were not willing to accept this view. After receiving permission, we set to work to find a better solution in this case. We called the young couple for several counseling sessions in our home. We also talked with their parents about their responsibilities. Both families were of high rank and hesitated at first to listen. Since the marriage vow was highly respected, we set out to convince them that it would be a blessing for them and would help them to stay together rather than divorcing in an easy way. After the counseling session, when I felt they understood what a Christian marriage should be, I performed an official marriage celebration with sermon and vow. I did not perform it in the church building, however, but chose a classroom. It would have greatly offended the minister and the congregation if I had conducted the ceremony in the church. The close relatives on both sides attended, and after the service, everyone seemed happy.

We found there is also a financial reason for not getting married in the church. An unwritten rule says that the family of a couple married in the church must feed all the people who attend the wedding. If a couple is from a lower social rank, they cannot make a big feast because they do not have enough money to feed a few hundred people. Often those from higher ranks do not want such a big feast either. I occasionally met this problem by conducting weddings in private homes where I could show them the importance of a Christian marriage and the vow regardless of the place where the ceremony was performed.

> *Discussion.* How do you react to the alternate solutions of the missionary in this case? Were the solutions Christian? biblical? useful? Why do you think the other missionaries were unable to come up with alternate solutions? Do you think they could accept these? Do we do things because they help people? Can we be biblical and still do things that help people? How do those things that we do automatically as Christians at times hinder the spread of the gospel? the growth of other Christians?

Sunday Soccer

Luis was a deeply committed Christian in his second year of studies at the Cochabamba Bible Institute. He was also a talented striker on the Aurora professional soccer team. Things were going well for Luis in every way until the missionaries met for their 1966 field conference.

After the missionary director of the Bible institute gave his annual report, questions from the floor were welcomed. "Is it true," queried an Australian missionary, "that one of your full-time students is also a professional soccer player and is involved in matches every Lord's Day?" Fortunately or unfortunately, Luis's game had been improving, and the Sunday before the missionary conference began, he had kicked two goals, and his name was splashed all over the sports page on Monday.

"That's correct," responded the director. Pandemonium broke loose on the conference floor as one missionary after another took shots at Luis and the institute director.

"I turned down an invitation to play on the first fifteen of a top Australian rugby team, just so I could come to Bolivia and serve the Lord," volunteered the Australian brother. "What kind of testimony do you think it is when one of our institute students constantly desecrates the Lord's Day?"

"Certainly you can't believe that the Lord will bless our Bible institute when we demonstrate such a lack of spiritual standards, can you?"

"And what about all the young people in our churches Luis is leading astray through his negative example?"

Quietly but firmly, the institute director defended Luis's right and privilege to engage in professional soccer. He also clarified that it was Luis's sole source of financial income for himself and his new bride. Three other missionaries supported the director in his defense of Luis.

By this time, the mission director had intervened and proceeded to define and decide the issue.

"What would our supporting churches think if they knew we had no standards concerning observance of the Lord's Day?"

"Sunday sports has always been a stone of stumbling for Bolivian Christians. It took Jack five years to wean Antonio away from Sunday soccer."

What the mission director and most of his colleagues did not realize was that Antonio and many other Bolivian church leaders were regular spectators at Sunday afternoon soccer matches.

"You must give Luis an ultimatum. Mr. Bible Institute Director. Either he drops out of professional soccer, or he is through in our Bible institute."

A week later when Luis was read the ultimatum, he decided to drop out of the institute, at which point the righteous indignation of the missionaries subsided.

Discussion. What were the aspects of the ethical problem faced by Luis? by the institute director? by the missionaries in general? by the mission director? Is the argument from Australia a valid one? In what ways is it valid? In what ways is it invalid? How might the situation have been dealt with to advance the cause of Christ in the area? Was it valid to bring in the Christian leaders' attendance at Sunday soccer games? How much in tune were the missionaries with Bolivian culture? with the people among whom they ministered? Is it of value to get close to the people? Can one be contaminated in his Christian life by being too close to the people among whom he serves? Discuss this case with members of your own culture as well as with people of different cultures.

Soni

It was a typical warm, muggy morning when we first made our acquaintance with Soni. She came to our home primarily in search of help to obtain food, medicine, and clothing for herself and her children. Soni and three of her preschool-age children, one an infant, were received into our *salla*—an area of the house where guests are received. They were dirty, unkempt, lice-infested, sickly, undernourished specimens of humanity. The children, particularly, were covered from head to toe with running ulcerous sores. After opening remarks, we asked her the purpose of her visit. We had, however, surmised the reason why she had come when we first saw her and her children. Nevertheless, we did not have the heart to send them on their way without first giving them refreshments—a customary practice when guests are received—and hearing her out. For the next hour and a half or so, we mostly listened as she poured out her woes. After she left, we made inquiries about her. This information, together with that which we had learned from talking with Soni herself over a period of time, shaped into the following story of tragedy, hardship, and struggle to survive.

At an early age in life, Soni became an orphan. She was adopted by a middle-aged couple who had no children of their own. They also had adopted a son about the same age as Soni but not related to her. These foster parents were both public school teachers and were well able to care for themselves and their two adopted children.

Up until the time that Soni was in high school, she was the favorite in the family. However, instead of completing her high school training as desired by her foster parents, she eloped with one of her classmates. Soni's foster parents, particularly the mother, were very much offended and put to shame by her rash action. However, she and her husband were received into the home and lived with the foster parents for several years. In the course of time, three children were born into the family.

Jobs were scarce, and Soni's husband had been having difficulty getting regular employment to take care of his family. He then decided to return to his home area, which was on another island several hundred miles away. Soni's foster mother refused to let Soni and the three children go. As a result, her husband left by himself. After a year or so had passed, word was received that he had "remarried" in his home area.

Beginning with Soni's elopement, the affection which her foster parents had had for her was transferred to her adopted brother. This was especially true of the affection of the mother. A new will was made out, and all of the inheritance and property rights which were previously Soni's were given over to the son. Soni's name was entirely left out of the new will.

Soni's foster father had loved her before her marriage, and she felt that he continued to love her even though he was hurt by her marriage. As she reported, he was always sympathetic and kind to her and her children. After Soni's husband left for his home area, her foster mother became, in Soni's words, "jealous of her." She felt that the reason behind it was the attention and affection that her foster father continued to show toward her and her children. The situation in the home became unbearable, and Soni, looking for an escape, remarried. Her new husband was a Moslem; and, as it turned out, he already had a wife and several children.

When Soni left her foster parents' home, her mother refused to let her take her first-born child, a girl, with her. From that time on, Soni was never granted admittance to the home whenever her foster mother was present. She was, to her, counted as one dead. Her foster father, however, continued to help Soni on occasion. But after several years had lapsed, they retired from the teaching profession and moved to another part of the country where they had invested in land. They took with them Soni's eldest child.

Soni was brought up in a Christian or Roman Catholic culture. When she remarried, she married into a Moslem culture. She had an inferior status as a second wife, but a greater problem to her acceptance in the new culture was her being a "Christian." For the first year or more, Soni lived in the city where there was a large number of "Christian" people, but the predominant group was still Moslem. Their home was a simple one-room dwelling about ten by ten feet, constructed from native materials (thatch) with a split bamboo floor. Her husband's first wife lived in a similar type house but somewhat larger and located in the country among his people. His relatives did not own the land on which they lived. They were sharecroppers, and their livelihood was quite meager.

When Soni's husband lost his job in the city, he, together with Soni and the children, moved into the country to be among his own people. Soni had with her two of her children from her first marriage and an infant fathered by her Moslem husband. All were undernourished and sickly. The difference between Soni's way of life in the home of her foster parents was in great contrast to that which she experienced since her remarriage. The kind of house she lived in was different; the food was different; the sleeping habits were different; the system of values was different; the religion was different; the language was different; and there were many more differences. In their new surroundings in the country, the children became afflicted with ulcerous sores. Native remedies were used to try to rid the children of the sores and other illnesses which they had, but to no avail. Soni and her children experienced great hardship.

The day came when Soni began her break from this situation. Without informing her husband or his relatives of the true purpose of her trip, she made her way into the city to work, beg, or steal to get food and medicine for herself and her children. If they had known what she was up to, they would not have allowed her to go; for, if she were to beg, it would bring shame upon her husband and his people. It was during one of Soni's first trips to the city that we met her.

As time went by, Soni's practices were found out, and she suffered for it. She was put under the guard of an elderly lady and lived together with her in a small hut. During this time, one of Soni's children by her first husband died. Several months later she gave birth to another son. After that, the old lady prohibited Soni's husband from sleeping with her. Later, Soni made treks back into the city and was able to get a job as a waitress in a small cafe. She worked about a week before her husband found out about it. In a rage, he came to the cafe, threatened the life of the owner, beat up Soni, and took her back to the country.

Soni was fearful of cohabiting again with her husband lest she become pregnant once more. After a while, she "escaped" and together with an old lady began living in the city. The old lady cooked and watched over the children while Soni went out to try to get something for them to eat each day. It has been and perhaps still is a difficult and constant fight for existence for Soni and her children. She contracted tuberculosis as did at least one of her children. She and her family need help, but the kind of help and how it should be given so that she can maintain her own authenticity as a person needs deep and thoughtful consideration. In our efforts to help, we have often been both baffled and frustrated by the problem.

In our efforts to help her, we fed her and her children when they came to our home, we washed off their sores and bandaged them, we accompanied them on occasion to doctors, we purchased medicines, we gave them vitamins and rice, we gave her a small start in selling vegetables in the market to earn a living, we gave her suitable clothes so that she would look clean when she looked for a waitress job, we prayed with her and for her, yet we often felt frustrated over her situation and what we could do to really help her.

On the other hand, we felt that she respected us and did deeply appreciate the help that we gave to her, feeble though it may have been. She felt that we at least cared for her to some extent and would listen to her. When we met her on the street or in the market, we recognized and greeted her. From her reactions, she seemed to appreciate this very much; her face would always light up into a bright smile. On one occasion, with tears in her eyes, she shocked my wife by suddenly kneeling down and kissing her feet because of something that my wife had done for her and her children. Before we left for furlough, she came over to our home alone just to say goodbye and then kissed our hands in departure.

Discussion. What do you think the kissing of the missionaries' hands meant to Soni? Did the missionaries really help Soni? In what ways? How might they have done more? Was their help worthwhile? How would you characterize in about twenty-five words how these people helped Soni? Was their help the same or different from the way the foster parents helped her? her husbands? her other friends?

How would you characterize Soni's condition? Was it primarily spiritual? What aspects of her life needed to be cared for so that her spiritual life could grow and develop? How might one help her in personal and social adjustment? Are there Bible verses that could guide one in doing so? What aspects of the trust bond could be called upon to help her? social organization? tools of relationship? the educational process?

Addendum to Soni Case Study

Elopement

Elopement, as far as I know of Philippine culture, is frowned upon by all of the subcultures in the Islands: Christian (Roman Catholic and Protestant), Moslem, Buddhist, and pagan. To curb young women from getting married without their parents' permission, at least until they are of age, the government has enacted a law stating that until a young woman is twenty-one years of age, she cannot get married without the signed consent of her parents or guardians. When a young man and woman elope, they often do not immediately go to a justice of the peace and get married unless the girl is of age (twenty-one) and prior arrangements have been made for the wedding in a municipality away from their home area. What is commonly done in some areas of the Philippines is for the couple to cohabit with one another for a short period. If they have been together intimately, consent for the girl to marry is usually given quickly by the parents; however, and understandably so, there is a great amount of shame experienced by the parents in this kind of a situation. There often may be an attempt to lessen the shame by saying that the girl was abducted. The couple is separated, and arrangements for the wedding are negotiated between the parents or guardians. Preliminary negotiations are often made through a third party.

Among Moslems, when a couple elopes, they try to get to the boy's relatives or to the person entitled *sara* (religious court) as fast as they can. If they are overtaken by the girl's relatives, the young man may lose his life.

Employment

For those who have not graduated from high school, it can be difficult to get regular employment. This is especially true if the person has no particular skill or craft, such as carpentry, mechanics, etc. In Jolo there are a number of unskilled, laboring jobs available, but the number of job seekers greatly exceeds the number of job openings.

Soni's husband was not born and raised in Jolo. How he came to go to school there, I do not know, but I can venture a guess. He probably was brought there by one of his relatives to help out in his or her home. It is a common practice in the Islands for a brother or sister to take one of his or her younger siblings into his or her own home to help with household tasks and other jobs. That person in turn provides his food, clothing, and shelter, and often helps him through school as well.

When Soni and her husband got married, they moved into the home of her foster parents. It is also a very common practice for young couples to live with their parents or in-laws for a time after their marriage or until they can financially take care of themselves. After several years went by and Soni's husband was still having difficulty getting regular employment, he decided to return to his home area near Dadiangas, Cotobato, where employment was then more readily available.

Family

It is not uncommon for a husband to remarry when he leaves his wife and children behind in order to seek employment in another area. This is particularly true if his wife refuses to go or if her family refuses to let her go with him. A man may precede his family, with his family joining him after he has obtained employment and a place to live. If a man's family does not join him, the man commonly takes another wife. In the Philippines, the government does not grant divorce, so in circumstances such as those above, the man's second wife is in reality a concubine. Before the law, his first wife remains his legal spouse.

Inheritance

I am not certain concerning the inheritance laws of the subculture to which Soni's parents belonged. However, the writing of wills is not commonly done except among business people, professionals (doctors, teachers, etc.), and landowners. Where there is no formal will drawn up, there is, nevertheless, an understanding among the heirs as to who gets what and how much. Adopted children may or may not receive any inheritance, depending upon their inclusion in a will and/or their good standing with the other heirs. Soni, by her behavior, lost the favored position she held in the family and with it her inheritance.

Polygamy Implications and Requirements of the Wife in This Relationship

Plurality of wives is an accepted part of Islamic culture but not of the Christian culture in which Soni had been raised. She was married in accordance with Islamic wedding regulations. She could not be married before a judge nor have her wedding registered with the government, for she already had a husband who was still living.

From what we were made to understand, she did not know at first that the Moslem fellow whom she married already had a wife when she married him. There are a number of instances where a girl from a Christian culture marries a Moslem only to find out later that he already has a wife. Some women are really deceived, while others suspect or know the real situation beforehand but marry crossculturally anyway.

Usually, the second wife will be subservient to the first wife, particularly if they live in the same house. If they have separate dwellings, each can do pretty much what she likes in her own home. There is, of course, competition for the husband's affection and for the money he earns.

Illness Remedy

I am not sure what was used in these instances, but the Moslems have a number of quack doctors. They brew medicines from herbs, roots, etc., which may be drunk or applied directly to the sores. The sores may be left open or may be covered with leaves. When the medicine is administered, it is accompanied with sacred sayings in Arabic. There are others who present food offerings and perform certain rituals at holy places to placate "spirits," or demons, that have caused the illnesses.

Moslem Male

The Tausug Moslem male is proud of his Tausugness and his religious heritage. He is very quick to fight and will fight until death when he feels his honor or that of his family, tribe, or religion has been offended. In regard to his wife or wives, he has a strong sense of their belonging to him and will not tolerate any other male giving flirtatious attention to them.

> *Discussion.* This is the second part of a two-stage case study. It is wise to get respondents to commit themselves to considerations in the first stage of the case prior to discussing the implications of the information in stage two. The key question in stage two is how the information on social structure and social relations in the cultures influencing Soni help one in resolving this larger case. Does it cause you to change your considerations in stage one? your attitude toward Soni? your suggestions as to how to help her? Do not be quick to judge someone until you know where that person is coming from.

NOTES

Chapter 1

1. In the Philippines, a person of higher status than the father of the family is named sponsor of a newborn child. This is similar to the godparental relationship in Spanish background societies. The "tests" are numerous, and one is generally unaware that they are being made. For example, the Filipino will state that a baby is on the way. If the response is, "Great! Keep me informed!" the family assumes you are willing to be named sponsor. If one does not want to be named sponsor, it is expected he will be noncommittal at a time like this, saying, "I'm glad for you both," or even, "So what!"

2. See my *A Look at Filipino Lifestyles* (Dallas: Summer Institute of Linguistics Museum of Anthropology, 1980).

3. Stratification is needed in society to define one's relationship to others so that the work of society can be done. The strata rank system of social stratification (see chap. 7) operating in the Philippines places everyone on a status level either above or below everyone else. One's standing is thus established, not in relation to one's social role or job responsibility, but in relation to everyone above and everyone below him. He tends to guard his position very carefully so that anyone moving up the status ladder becomes a threat to him and is thus resisted.

Chapter 2

1. Many illustrations of this phenomenon could be cited. There is perhaps no more tragic experience for the members of a society than to be forced to learn a national or trade language and in the process lose their own language before they are fully fluent in the new. They could speak of the superficial matters that concern them in their daily lives, but they would lose out in the deeper, more meaningful concerns of life.

2. See Tom Brewster, *Language Acquisition Made Practical* (Colorado Springs: Lingua House, 1976).

Chapter 3

1. From a column of Ann Landers.
2. Gwen Bailey, a student.

Chapter 4

1. The drive to be accepted is confirmed continually in the research and writings of psychologists, sociologists, and anthropologists. See the works of Peter Berger, Carl Rogers, Paul Tournier, and many others.

2. Alan Holmberg, "The Wells That Failed," in Edward H. Spicer, *Human Problems in Technological Change* (New York: Basic Books, 1952), pp. 113–23.

3. Carl Rogers, *On Becoming a Person* (Cambridge, Mass.: Riverside, 1961), pp. 50–55.

4. It is unfortunate in any age that "man looks at the outward appearance." However, we may be grateful that the Lord looks at the heart (1 Sam. 16:7).

Chapter 5

1. See George Dalton, *Tribal and Peasant Economics* (Garden City, N.Y.: Doubleday, 1967); and George M. Foster, *A Cross-Cultural Anthropological Analysis of a Technical Aid Program* (Washington, D.C.: Smithsonian Institute of Social Anthropology, 1951); *Traditional Cultures and the Impact of Technological Change* (New York: Harper and Row, 1962); *Applied Anthropology* (Boston: Little, Brown and Co., 1969).

2. For a fuller discussion of the concept of cultural relativism, see Melville Herskovits, *Cultural Dynamics* (New York: Alfred A. Knopf, 1964), pp. 49–64. Also refer to chapter 17.

3. Joseph Fletcher, *Situation Ethics* (Philadelphia: Westminster, 1966), p. 26.

4. Ibid., pp. 29, 36.

5. Paul Tournier, *The Meaning of Persons* (New York: Harper and Row, 1957), p. 22.

6. Keith Miller, *A Taste of New Wine* (Waco: Word, 1965), p. 22.

7. Provided by R. Campbell.

Chapter 6

1. From a column of Ann Landers.

2. See Vilhelm Aubert, *Elements of Sociology* (New York: Scribner, 1967); and Peter L. Berger, *The Sacred Canopy: Elements of a Sociological Theory of Religion* (Garden City, N.Y.: Doubleday, 1967).

3. See George M. Foster, *A Cross-Cultural Anthropological Analysis of a Technical Aid Program* (Washington, D.C.: Smithsonian Institute of Social Anthropology, 1951); *Technological Change* (New York: Harper and Row, 1962); and *Applied Anthropology* (Boston: Little, Brown and Co., 1969).

4. See Helen Merrell Lynd, *On Shame and the Search for Identity* (New York: Science Editions, 1958); Julian Pitt-Rivers, *People of the*

Sierra (Chicago: University of Chicago Press, 1961); and Paul Tournier, *Guilt and Grace* (New York: Harper and Row, 1962).

5. See Eugene Nida, *God's Word in Man's Language* (New York: Harper and Row, 1952); *Customs and Cultures* (New York: Harper and Row, 1954); *Message and Mission* (New York: Harper and Row, 1960); *Religion Across Cultures* (New York: Harper and Row, 1968); and Alfred G. Smith, *Communication and Culture* (New York: Holt, Rinehart and Winston, 1966).

Chapter 7

1. *Structure and Function in Primitive Society* (London: Cohen and West, 1959), pp. 188–204.

2. *Churchman,* 1968.

3. Auto repair manuals are systems manuals as are some medical textbooks and some systematic theologies.

4. See Talcott Parsons, *Essays in Sociological Theory: Pure and Applied* (Glencoe, Ill.: Free Press, 1949); and Robert K. Merton, *Social Theory and Social Structure* (Glencoe, Ill.: Free Press, 1957).

5. A series of case studies in cultural anthropology is available from Holt, Rinehart and Winston, Inc., 383 Madison Ave., New York, N.Y. 10017.

6. See A. L. Kroeber and C. Kluckhohn, *Culture: A Critical Review of Concepts and Definitions* (New York: Random House, 1970).

7. See Harry C. Bredemeier and Richard M. Stevenson, *The Analysis of Social Systems* (New York: Holt, Rinehart and Winston, 1967), pp. 146–76.

8. The concept of hierarchy utilized in this discussion is that discussed by Kenneth L. Pike, *Language* (The Hague: Mouton, 1967), p. 32.

9. See S. F. Nadel, *The Theory of Social Structure* (Glencoe, Ill.: Free Press, 1957), pp. 12–14.

Chapter 8

1. "The Decision-Making Process in Japan," *The Chicago Tribune,* April 23, 1972.

2. Herman Kahn, *The Emerging Japanese Superstate: Challenge and Response* (Englewood Cliffs, N.J.: Prentice-Hall, 1970), pp. 44–45.

3. *Wildfire: Church Growth in Korea* (Grand Rapids: Eerdmans, 1966).

4. John Calvin, *Institutes of the Christian Religion* (Philadelphia: Westminster, 1960).

5. J. William Pfeiffer and John E. Jones, *A Handbook of Structured Experiences for Human Relations Training,* vol. 2 (Iowa City, Iowa: University Associates, 1971), p. 14.

Chapter 9

1. See Herbert A. Simon, *Models of Man: Social and Rational* (New York: John Wiley and Sons, 1957); Abraham Kaplan, *The Conduct of Inquiry* (San Francisco, Calif.: Chandler, 1961); and Robert Redfield, "The Folk Society," in *Human Nature and the Study of Society,* the papers of Robert Redfield, ed. Margaret Park Redfield (Chicago: University of Chicago Press, 1962), vol. 1.

2. The concept of model is useful in objective consideration of another society. Everyone utilizes a conceptual model, e.g., everyday speech. Scientific, academic, humanistic, etc., models compete with the everyday usage model. Some are more helpful and some are less. The crosscultural models utilized in this volume have proven significantly useful in ministry within a distinctive cultural context and surprisingly valuable when facing one's own culture.

3. For a more complete listing of ways people group, consult any basic introductory anthropology or sociology textbook.

4. See A. H. J. Prins, *East African Age Class Systems* (Groningen and Djakarta, 1953); and R. H. Lowie, "Plains Indian Age Societies: Historical Summary," *American Museum of Natural History, Anthropological Papers* (1916), vol. 11.

5. Alan R. Beals, *Gopalpur: A South Indian Village* (New York: Holt, Rinehart, and Winston, 1962), pp. 58–72.

6. See my *A Look at Filipino Lifestyles* (Dallas: Summer Institute of Linguistics Museum of Anthropology), pp. 19–25.

7. L. H. Morgan, *League of the Iroquois* (New York: Dodd, Mead, 1904), pp. 79–87.

8. J. William Pfeiffer and John E. Jones, *A Handbook of Structured Experiences for Human Relations Training,* vol. 1 (Iowa City, Iowa: University Associates, 1971), p. 24.

Chapter 10

1. W. Vincent Lucas, "The Educational Value of Initiatory Rites," *International Review of Missions,* 16:62 (April 1972): 192–98.

2. The classical work is Arnold Van Gennep, *Rites of Passage* (Chicago: University of Chicago Press, 1960).

Chapter 11

1. See Herman A. Witkin, "Cognitive Styles Across Cultures," in J. W. Berry and P. R. Dasen, *Culture and Cognition* (London: Methuen, 1974); and Talcott Parsons and Edward A. Shils, *Toward a General Theory of Action* (Cambridge: Harvard University Press, 1967).

2. From my *A Look at Filipino Lifestyles* (Dallas: Summer Institute of Linguistics Museum of Anthropology, 1980), p. 91.

3. Marshall McLuhan, *Understanding Media: The Extension of Man* (New York: McGraw-Hill, 1964), p. 36.

4. Mary Stewart Van Leeuwen, "Cognitive Style, North American Values and the Body of Christ," *Journal of Psychology and Theology* 2 (1974): 77.

5. Sherwood G. Lingenfelter and Marvin K. Mayers, *Ministering Cross-culturally: An Incarnational Model for Personal Relationships* (Grand Rapids: Baker, 1986), pp. 53–67.

6. J. Anthony Paredes and Marcus J. Hepburn, "The Split Brain and the Culture Cognition Paradox," *Current Anthropology* 17 (1976): 121–27.

7. Marvin K. Mayers, Lawrence Richards, and Robert Webber, *Reshaping Evangelical Higher Education* (Grand Rapids: Zondervan, 1972), pp. 120–30.

8. See Claude Levi-Strauss, *Structural Anthropology* (Garden City, N.Y.: Doubleday, 1967); N. Chomsky, *Syntactic Structures* (The Hague: Mouton, 1957); and J. A. Fodor and J. J. Katz, *The Structure of Language* (Englewood Cliffs, N.J.: Prentice-Hall, 1964), for insight into the generative process.

Chapter 12

1. To use as a case study, consult Marvin K. Mayers, "Two-Man Feud in the Guatemalan Church," *Practical Anthropology* 13 (July-August 1966): 115–25.

2. For a fuller discussion of the results of tension in an individual's personal life, consult the materials of psychology, psychotherapy, and social psychology.

3. Kalervo Oberg, "Culture Shock: Adjustment to New Cultural Environments," *Practical Anthropology* 7:4 (1960): 177.

4. William Smalley, "Culture Shock, Language Shock, and the Shock of Self Discovery," *Practical Anthropology* 10:2 (1963): 49–56.

5. Louis Luzbetak, *The Church and Cultures* (Pasadena, Calif.: William Carey Library, 1984), p. 98.

6. Oberg, "Culture Shock," pp. 178–79.

7. Smalley, "Culture Shock, Language Shock," pp. 49–56.

8. J. William Pfeiffer and John E. Jones, eds., *A Handbook of Structured Experiences for Human Relations Training*, 8 vols. (Iowa City, Iowa: University Associates, 1973–81).

Chapter 13

1. From William A. Smalley, "The Cultures of Man and Communication of the Gospel," a paper presented at the twelfth annual convention of the American Scientific Affiliation, August 27–29, at Gordon College, Beverly Farms, Massachusetts.

2. For discussion of language and culture as symbolic, see Edward T. Hall, *The Silent Language* (Garden City, N.Y.: Doubleday, 1959; reprint, Westport, Conn.: Greenwood, 1980); Joyce O. Hertzler, *A*

Sociology of Language (New York: Random House, 1965); Eugene Nida, *Message and Mission* (New York: Harper and Row, 1960); Edward Sapir, *Selected Writings in Language, Culture, and Personality,* ed. D. G. Mandelbaum (Berkeley, Calif.: University of California Press, 1949); and L. A. White, "The Symbol: The Origin and Basis of Human Behavior," in *The Science of Culture* (New York: Farrar, Straus and Co., 1949).

3. Philip K. Bock, *Modern Cultural Anthropology*, 3rd ed. (New York: Knopf, 1978).

Chapter 14

1. See John Madge, *Tools of Social Science* (New York: Doubleday, 1965); and Pertti Pelto, *Anthropological Research: The Structure of Inquiry* (New York: Harper and Row, 1970), for research tools and methodology.

2. For studies utilizing participant observation, see Jules Henry, *Jungle People* (New York: Random House, 1964); Bronislaw Malinowski, *Argonauts of the Western Pacific* (New York: E. P. Dutton, 1961); and T. R. Williams, *Field Methods in the Study of Culture* (New York: Holt, Rinehart and Winston, 1967).

3. For studies utilizing interviewing, see Oscar Lewis, *The Children of Sanchez: Autobiography of a Mexican Family* (New York: Random House, 1961); and Benjamin D. Paul, "Interview Techniques and Field Relationships," in A. L. Kroeber, ed., *Anthropology Today* (Chicago: University of Chicago Press, 1953).

4. For studies utilizing experimentation, see Gardner Lindzey, *Projective Techniques and Cross-Cultural Research* (New York: Appleton-Century-Crofts, 1961); and Evon Z. Vogt, "Navaho Veterans: A Study of Changing Values," in *Papers of the Peabody Museum of American Archaeology and Ethnology* (Cambridge: Harvard University Press, 1951), 41:1.

5. Such as my *Pocomchi Texts* (Norman, Okla.: The Summer Institute of Linguistics and the University of Oklahoma, 1958).

Chapter 15

1. By Gene Olsen.

2. See Edward T. Hall, *The Silent Language* (Garden City, N.Y.: Doubleday, 1959; reprint, Westport, Conn.: Greenwood, 1980); and *The Hidden Dimension* (Garden City, N.Y.: Doubleday, 1969).

3. See Eugene Nida, *Message and Mission* (New York: Harper and Row, 1960); Clyde Kluckhohn, "Navaho Witchcraft" in *Peabody Museum of American Archaeology and Theology Papers* (Cambridge: Harvard University Press, 1944), 22:2; and Harry C. Bredemeier, "The Methodology of Functionalism," *American Sociological Review* 20 (1955), pp. 173–80.

4. See my *Pocomchi Texts* (Norman, Okla.: The Summer Institute of Linguistics and the University of Oklahoma, 1958), pp. 138–39.

5. For more on this concept, consult Harvie M. Conn, *Eternal Word and Changing Worlds Theology, Anthropology, and Mission in Trialogue* (Grand Rapids: Zondervan, 1984); David J. Hesselgrave, *Communicating Christ Cross-Culturally* (Grand Rapids: Zondervan, 1978); Charles H. Kraft, *Christianity in Culture* (Maryknoll, N.Y.: Orbis, 1979); and Eugene Nida, *Message and Mission* (New York: Harper and Row, 1960).

6. Don Richardson, *Peace Child* (Ventura, Calif.: Regal, 1976), p. 288.

7. Norman L. Geisler, *Ethics: Alternatives and Issues* (Grand Rapids: Zondervan, 1971), pp. 60–78.

8. See Karl Hess, "Free the Schools," *The Orange County Register*, January 19, 1986.

9. See Paul's discussion of the parts of the body in 1 Corinthians 12:12–26.

10. See Millard Erickson, *The New Evangelical Theology* (Westwood, N.J.: Revell, 1968).

11. See Pertti J. Pelto, *Anthropological Research: The Structure of Inquiry* (New York: Harper and Row, 1970), p. 130.

12. *Beyond Culture* (Garden City, N.Y.: Doubleday, 1976); *The Hidden Dimension* (Garden City, N.Y.: Doubleday, 1969); and *The Silent Language* (Garden City, N.Y.: Doubleday, 1959; reprint, Westport, Conn.: Greenwood, 1980).

13. Adapted from Eugene Nida, *God's Word in Man's Language* (New York: Harper and Row, 1952), selected passages by Tim Black, Lisa Espinelli, Joyce Houggy, Paul Lewis, and Jim Savage.

Chapter 16

1. Two valuable books in this regard are Everett M. Rogers, *Modernization Among Peasants: The Impact of Communication* (New York: Holt, Rinehart and Winston, 1969); and Everett M. Rogers and F. Floyd Shoemaker, *Communication of Innovations: A Cross-Cultural Approach* (New York: Free Press, 1971).

2. By Dick Muzik.

3. This is not the place to argue the ethics of drinking alcoholic beverages. The concern here is not with the individual's decision about whether he should drink or not, but with the way one's decision is expressed through behavior in various social contexts. I personally am a total abstainer on the basis of conviction. However, such considerations should not enter the discussion at this point lest the significant point of one's adaptation or lack of adaptation to another culture or subculture in some way adversely affect the other by pressing that one to abandon principle and become an ethical relativist.

4. An older but useful book dealing with crosscultural ethics is *The Ethical Imperative* by Richard L. Means (Garden City, N.Y.: Doubleday, 1969). Dr. Means is a philosopher dealing with a sociological approach to ethics in American society.

5. *Cultural Dynamics* (New York: Alfred A. Knopf, 1964), pp. 49-64.

6. There are many parallels within North American society. One is the freedom a North American has, having paid the hotel bill, to take with him items provided for the convenience of the guest but which could also be used by another, e.g., soap, shampoo, shoe horn, etc., though not towels and sheets. He in no way intends theft. I have talked to members of other cultures who, in the same setting, would never think of taking such items with them, as they see that as stealing from the hotel.

7. For a careful look at this problem from the anthropologist's point of view, read the works of Clyde Kluckhohn, Margaret Mead, and Ruth Benedict. Also, numerous anthropologists have been professing Christians. Bronislaw Malinowski was a member of the "low church of England" and A. R. Radcliffe Brown was "high church." Robert Redfield was a member of the Episcopal church.

8. See Ashley Montague, *The Humanization of Man* (New York: Grove, 1964).

9. Edward J. Carnell, in *The Theology of Reinhold Niebuhr* (Grand Rapids: Eerdmans, 1950), p. 108, says that "Christ is a moral absolute which stands outside of history to exhaust the freedom of man but sufficiently in history to clarify history's possibilities and limitation." Note: For Carnell's usage of "history," read "culture." I suggest that Christ is God's act of supernatural intrusion and the nucleating factor of supernatural precept, i.e., always divine and always human with no dichotomies. See also H. M. Kuitert, *The Reality of Faith* (Grand Rapids: Eerdmans, 1968).

10. See Joseph Fletcher, *Situation Ethics* (Philadelphia: Westminster, 1966), p. 164.

11. Ibid., p. 26.

12. A German viewing the case finds it significant that she sought out a German guard rather than a Russian. An American likely misses this nuance.

13. In a later development of the case, it appears that certain doubts arose within the mind of the husband, and tension increased. Such additions to the case would force a new study of the now "new case," yet they would not invalidate the insights gained from the above considerations. Apparently, his wife actually had a norm more like norm A, whereas he had a norm more like norm B, and after living with the situation for a while, he had second thoughts.

14. I personally feel, from my understanding of the Word of God, that if she were a true Christian, her norm would change over time,

i.e., from norm A to norm B. Having said this, I also gain a great deal of insight by leaving my own norm open to the leading of the Spirit in my own sense of family responsibility. If her norm did not change over time, then I would be forced to reexamine my own understanding of Scripture, take a new look at her norm, take a fresh look at mine, and develop the patience of which James speaks in chapter 1 of his epistle. Compare this point of view with the five presented in *Christ and Culture* by H. Richard Niebuhr (New York: Harper and Row, 1956).

15. See A. Berkeley Mickelson, *Interpreting the Bible* (Grand Rapids: Eerdmans, 1963), pp. 159–72.

16. Carnell, *Theology of Niebuhr,* p. 69.

Chapter 17

1. Lionel Whiston, *Are You Fun to Live With?* (Waco: Word, 1969), pp. 37–38.

Chapter 18

1. From Paul Turner, *Journal for the Scientific Study of Religion* 18 (1979): 252–60. Edited to its present form by Samuel Scheibler.

Case Studies: Model 1

1. *Moody Monthly*, October 1969. Reprinted by permission. © 1969 by the Moody Bible Institute of Chicago.

Case Studies: Model 2

1. Roger E. Hedlund, "Why Pentecostal Churches Are Growing Faster in Italy," *Evangelical Missions Quarterly* 8:3 (Spring 1972): 129–36.

Case Studies: Model 3

1. From a column of Ann Landers, 1968.

BIBLIOGRAPHY

Abt, Clark C. *Serious Games.* New York: Viking, 1970.

Adams, D. M. *Simulation Games: An Approach to Learning.* Worthington, Ohio: Charles A. Jones, 1973.

Altman, Irwin, and Dalmas A. Taylor. *Social Penetration: The Development of Interpersonal Relationships.* New York: Irvington, 1983.

Alves, Rubem A. *Protestantism and Repression: A Brazilian Case Study.* Maryknoll, N.Y.: Orbis, 1979.

Asante, M. K.; E. Newmark; and C. A. Blake. *Handbook of Intercultural Communication.* Beverly Hills, Calif.: Sage, 1979.

Associates of Urbanus. 3919 Willoughby Road, Holt, MI 48842. Games and Materials.

Aubert, Vilhelm. *Elements of Sociology.* New York: Charles Scribner's Sons, 1967.

BaFa BaFa. Intercultural Press, P.O. Box 768, Yarmouth, ME 04096.

Barber, Bernard. *Social Stratification.* New York: Harcourt, Brace and World, 1957.

Barnett, H. G. *Innovation: The Basis of Cultural Change.* New York: McGraw-Hill, 1953.

Barton, Richard F. *A Primer on Simulation and Gaming.* Englewood Cliffs, N.J.: Prentice-Hall, 1970.

Bartos, Otomar J. *Simple Models of Group Behavior.* New York: Columbia University Press, 1967.

Beals, Alan R. *Culture in Process.* New York: Holt, Rinehart and Winston, 1967.

_____. *Gopalpur: A South Indian Village.* New York: Holt, Rinehart and Winston, 1962.

Benedict, Ruth. *Patterns of Culture.* New York: Penguin, 1946.

Bennis, Warren G.; Kenneth D. Benne; and Robert Chin. *The Planning of Change.* New York: Holt, Rinehart and Winston, 1969.

Benson, Dennis. "The Fine Art of Creating Simulation Gaming," *Learning Games for Religious Education.* Nashville: Abingdon, 1971.

Berger, Peter L. *Invitation to Sociology: A Humanistic Perspective.* Garden City, N.Y.: Doubleday, 1963.

_____. *The Sacred Canopy: Elements of a Sociological Theory of Religion.* Garden City, N.Y.: Doubleday, 1967.

Berkowitz, Leonard. *Cognitive Theories in Social Psychology.* New York: Academic Press, 1978.

Bernard, H. Russell, and Pertti Pelto, eds. *Technology and Social Change*. New York: Macmillan, 1972.

Berry, J. W., and P. R. Dasen. *Culture and Cognition: Readings in Crosscultural Psychology*. London: Methuen, 1974.

Biddle, Bruce J. *Role Theory: Concepts and Research*. New York: John Wiley, 1966.

Birdwhistell, Ray L. *Kinesics and Context*. Philadelphia: University of Pennsylvania Press, 1970.

Bittner, John R. *Each Other: An Introduction to Interpersonal Communication*. Englewood Cliffs, N.J.: Prentice Hall, 1983.

Blake, Robert. *The Managerial Grid*. Houston: Gulf, 1964.

Bochner, Stephen, ed. *Cultures in Contact, Studies in Crosscultural Interaction*. Oxford: Pergamon, 1982.

Bock, Philip K. *Modern Cultural Anthropology*. New York: Alfred A. Knopf, 1974.

Bonthius, Robert H. *Christian Paths to Self-Acceptance*. New York: King's Crown, 1948.

Boocock, Sarane S., ed. *Simulation Games in Learning*. Beverly Hills, Calif.: Sage Publications, 1968.

Bredemeier, Harry C. "The Methodology of Functionalism." *American Sociological Review* 20 (1955): 173–80.

————, and Richard M. Stevenson. *The Analysis of Social Systems*. New York: Holt, Rinehart and Winston, 1967.

Brewster, Tom. *Language Acquisition Made Practical*. Colorado Springs: Lingua House, 1976.

————, and E. Brewster. *Bonding and the Missionary Task*. Colorado Springs: Lingua House, 1984.

Brislan, Richard W. *Cross-Cultural Encounter: Face-To-Face Interaction*. New York: Pergamon, 1981.

Brougher, Toni. *A Way With Words: How to Improve Your Relationship Through Better Communication*. Chicago: Nelson-Hall, 1982.

Brown, Charles. *Communication in Human Relationships*. Skokie, Ill.: National Textbook, 1973.

Brown, Ina Corrine. *Understanding Other Cultures*. Englewood Cliffs, N.J.: Prentice-Hall, 1963.

Buchler, Ira R., and Hugo G. Nutini. *Game Theory in the Behavioral Sciences*. Pittsburgh: University of Pittsburgh Press, 1969.

Calvin, John. *Institutes of the Christian Religion*. Philadelphia: Westminster, 1960.

Capelle, Ronald G. *Changing Human Systems*. Toronto: International Human Systems Institute, 1979.

Carnell, Edward J. *The Theology of Reinhold Niebuhr*. Grand Rapids: Eerdmans, 1950.

Carr, Jacquelyn. *Communicating and Relating*. Dubuque, Iowa: Brown, 1984.

Casse, Pierre. *Training for the Cross-Cultural Mind,* 2d ed. Yarmouth, Maine: Intercultural Press, 1981.

Casteel, John L. *The Creative Role of Interpersonal Groups in the Church Today.* New York: Association, 1968.

Cathcart, Robert S., and Larry A. Samovar. *Small Group Communication.* Dubuque, Iowa: Wm. C. Brown, 1979.

Chomsky, Noam. *Syntactic Structures.* The Hague: Mouton, 1957.

Churchman, C. West. *The Systems Approach.* New York: Dell, 1968.

Clifton, James A. *Applied Anthropology: Readings in the Uses of the Science of Man.* Boston: Houghton Mifflin, 1970.

Clignet, Remi. *Many Wives, Many Powers.* Evanston, Ill.: Northwestern University Press, 1970.

Condon, John C., and Fathi S. Yousef. *An Introduction to Intercultural Communication.* Indianapolis: Bobbs-Merrill Educational Publishing, 1975 (1980).

Conn, Harvie M. *Eternal Word and Changing Worlds: Theology, Anthropology, and Mission in Trialogue.* Grand Rapids: Zondervan, 1984.

Cooper, Ken. *Nonverbal Communication for Business Success.* New York: AMACOM, 1979.

Covert, Anita, and Gordon L. Thomas. *Communication Games and Simulations.* Urbana, Ill.: Clearinghouse on Reading and Communication Skills, 1978.

Dalton, George. *Tribal and Peasant Economics.* Garden City, N.Y.: Doubleday, 1967.

Davey, William G. *Intercultural Theory and Practice: A Case Study Approach.* Yarmouth, Maine: Intercultural Press, 1981.

Davis, Morton D. *Game Theory: A Nontechnical Introduction.* New York: Basic Books, 1970.

De Bono, Edward. *The Five-Day Course in Thinking.* New York: Basic Books, 1967.

Duck, Steven W. *Personal Relationships and Personal Constructs.* London: John Wiley, 1973.

Duke, Richard D. *Gaming: The Future's Language.* Boston: John Wiley, 1974.

————, and Cathy S. Greenblat. *Game Generating Games.* Beverly Hills, Calif.: Sage, 1979.

Durkheim, Emile. *The Elementary Forms of the Religious Life.* Glencoe, Ill.: Free Press, 1947.

Dye, Wayne T. *Bible Translation Strategy: An Analysis of Its Spiritual Impact.* Dallas: Wycliffe Bible Translators, 1980 (revised 1985).

Eisenberg, Abne M., and Ralph R. Smith, Jr. *Nonverbal Communication.* Indianapolis and New York: Bobbs-Merrill, 1971.

Elder, C. D. "Problems in the Structure and Use of Educational Simulation." *Sociology of Education* 46 (Summer 1973): 425–54.

Ellington, Henry; Eric Addinall; and Fred Percival. *Case Studies in Game Design*. London: Kegan Paul, 1984.

————. *A Handbook of Game Design*. London: Kegan Paul, 1982.

Erickson, Millard. *The New Evangelical Theology*. Westwood, N.J.: Revell, 1968.

Erikson, Eric. *Childhood and Society*. New York: Norton, 1965.

————. *Identity, Youth and Crisis*. New York: Norton, 1965.

Evans-Pritchard, Edward E. *The Institutions of Primitive Society*. Glencoe, Ill.: Free Press, 1954.

————. *The Values of Primitive Society*. Oxford: Blackwell, 1954.

Fabun, Don. *Dimensions of Change*. Beverly Hills, Calif.: Glencoe, 1971.

————. *The Dynamics of Change*. New York: Prentice-Hall, 1970.

————. *Three Roads to Awareness*. Beverly Hills, Calif.: Glencoe, 1970.

Fast, Julius. *Body Language*. New York: Simon and Schuster, 1971.

Filbeck, David. *Social Context in Proclamation: a Socio-cognitive Study in Proclaiming the Gospel Cross-culturally*. Pasadena: William Carey Library, 1985.

Filley, Alan C. *Interpersonal Conflict Resolution*. Glenview, Ill.: Scott, Foresman and Co., 1975.

Firth, Raymond William. *Elements of Social Organization*. London: Watts, 1952.

Fletcher, Joseph. *Situation Ethics*. Philadelphia: Westminster, 1966.

Fodor, J. A., and J. J. Katz. *The Structure of Language*. Englewood Cliffs, N.J.: Prentice-Hall, 1964.

Forbess-Greene, Sue. *The Encyclopedia of Icebreakers*. San Diego: Applied Skills, 1980.

Ford, Leroy. *Using the Case Study in Teaching and Training*. Nashville: Broadman, 1969.

Foster, George M. *Applied Anthropology*. Boston: Little, Brown and Co., 1969.

————. *A Cross-Cultural Anthropological Analysis of a Technical Aid Program*. Washington, D.C.: Smithsonian Institute of Social Anthropology, 1951.

————. *Traditional Cultures and the Impact of Technological Change*. New York: Harper and Row, 1962.

Frazer, James G. *The Golden Bough*. London: Macmillan, 1911–15.

Gatheru, R. Mugo, *Child of Two Worlds*. Garden City, N.Y.: Doubleday, 1964.

Geertz, Clifford. *Local Knowledge, Further Essays in Interpretive Anthropology*. New York: Basic Books, 1983.

Geisler, Norman L. *Ethics: Alternatives and Issues*. Grand Rapids: Zondervan, 1971.

Gibb, Jack R. *Climate for Trust Formation*. New York: L. P. Bradford, 1964.

————. *Trust: A New View of Personal and Organizational Development*. Los Angeles: Guild of Tutors, 1978.

Gibbs, G. I. *Handbook of Games and Simulation Exercises*. Beverly Hills, Calif.: Sage Publications, 1974.

Giffin, Kim. *Basic Readings in Interpersonal Communication*. New York: Harper and Row, 1971.

————, and Bobby R. Patton. *Fundamentals of Interpersonal Communication*. New York: Harper and Row, 1977.

Gillispie, Philip. *Learning Through Simulation Games*. New York: Paulist, 1973.

Glazier, Ray. *How to Design Educational Games*. Cambridge, Mass.: Abt Associates, 1969 (4th ed., 1973).

Goffman, Erving. *The Presentation of Self in Everyday Life*. Garden City, New York: Doubleday, 1959.

Goldstein, Kenneth M., and Sheldon Blackman. *Cognitive Style*. Canada: John Wiley, 1978.

Goodenough, Ward Hunt. *Cooperation in Change*. New York: Russell Sage Foundation, 1963.

Greenblat, Cathy S., and Richard D. Duke. *Gaming-Simulation: Rationale, Design and Application*. New York: John Wiley, 1975.

————. *Principles and Practices of Gaming-Simulation*. Beverly Hills, Calif.: Sage, 1981.

Grossman, Lee. *The Change Agent*. New York: AMACOM, 1974.

Grove, Theodore G. *Experiences in Interpersonal Communication*. Englewood Cliffs, N.J.: Prentice-Hall, 1976.

Grunlan, S. A., and M. K. Mayers. *Cultural Anthropology, A Christian Perspective*. Grand Rapids: Zondervan, 1979.

Gudykunst, William B., and Young Yun Kim. *Communicating with Strangers—An Approach to Intercultural Communication*. Reading, Mass.: Addison-Wesley, 1984.

Hall, Edward T. *Beyond Culture*. New York: Doubleday, 1976.

————. *The Hidden Dimension*. Garden City, N.Y.: Doubleday, 1969.

————. *The Silent Language*. Garden City, N.Y.: Doubleday, 1959. Reprint Westport, Conn.: Greenwood, 1980.

Harris, Marvin. *Culture, Man, and Nature*. New York: Thomas Y. Crowell, 1971.

Hastings, Adrian. *African Christianity*. New York: Seabury, 1976.

Hawley, Robert C. *Value Exploration Through Role Playing*. New York: Hart, 1975.

Hedlund, Roger E. "Why Pentecostal Churches are Growing Faster in Italy." *Evangelical Missions Quarterly* 8:3 (Spring 1972): 129–36.

Hegarty, Witt. "Changes in Student's Attitudes As a Result of Participation in a Simulation." *Journal of Educational Psychology* 67 (1975): 137–40.

Henry, Jules. *Jungle People*. New York: Random House, 1964.

Herskovits, Melville. *Cultural Dynamics*. New York: Alfred A. Knopf, 1964.

Hertzler, Joyce O. *A Sociology of Language*. New York: Random House, 1965.

Hesselgrave, David J. *Communicating Christ Cross-Culturally*. Grand Rapids: Zondervan, 1978.

Hiebert, Paul G. *Anthropological Insights for Missionaries*. Grand Rapids: Baker, 1985.

_____. *Cultural Anthropology*. Grand Rapids: Baker, 1983.

Hinde, R. A. *Non-Verbal Communication*. Cambridge: Cambridge University Press, 1972.

Hocker, Joyce L., and William W. Wilmot. *Interpersonal Conflict*. Dubuque, Iowa: Wm. C. Brown, 1985.

Hoebel, E. Adamson. *Anthropology: The Study of Man*. New York: McGraw-Hill, 1972.

Hollander, Edwin P., and Raymond G. Hunt, eds., "Leadership, Power, and Innovations," *Current Perspectives in Social Psychology*. New York: Oxford University Press, 1967.

Holmberg, Alan. *Nomads of the Long Bow*. Garden City, N.Y.: Natural History, 1969.

Horn, Robert E., ed. *The Guide to Simulations/Games for Education and Training*. Cranford, N.J.: Didactic Systems, 1970.

Inbar, Michael, and Clarice S. Stoll. *Simulation and Gaming in Social Science*. New York: Free Press, 1972.

Jennings, Jesse D., and E. Adamson Hoebel. *Readings in Anthropology*. New York: McGraw-Hill, 1972.

Johnson, David W., and Frank P. Johnson. *Joining Together: Group Theory and Group Skills*. Englewood Cliffs, N.J.: Prentice-Hall, 1975.

Jones, Ken. *Simulations: A Handbook for Teachers*. New York: Nichols, 1980.

Kaplan, Abraham. *The Conduct of Inquiry*. San Francisco: Chandler, 1961.

Karlin, Muriel S. *Classroom Activities: Desk Book for Fun and Learning*. West Nyack, N.Y.: Parker, 1975.

Katz, Albert M., and Virginia Katz. *Foundations of Nonverbal Communication*. Carbondale and Edwardsville, Ill.: Southern Illinois University Press, 1983.

Keesing, Felix M. *Culture Change*. Stanford, Calif.: Stanford University Press, 1953.

Kelley, Harold H., and John W. Thibaut. *Interpersonal Relations: A Theory of Interdependence*. New York: John Wiley, 1977.

Kenyatta, Jomo. *Facing Mt. Kenya*. London: Secker and Warburg, 1938. New edition, 1962.

Klemm, Herb. *Oral Communication of Bible*. Pasadena: William Carey, 1984.

Kluckhohn, Clyde. "Navaho Witchcraft." Cambridge, Mass.: Harvard University. *Peabody Museum of American Archaeology and Ethnology Papers,* 22:2, 1944.

Knapp, Mark L. *Social Intercourse: From Greeting to Goodbye.* Boston: Allyn and Bacon, 1978.

Kohls, R. *Survival Kit for Overseas Living.* Chicago: Systran, 1979.

Kraft, Charles H. *Christianity in Culture.* Maryknoll, New York: Orbis, 1979.

Kraft, Marguerite. *Worldview and the Communication of the Gospel.* Pasadena: William Carey, 1978.

Kreitler, Hans and Shulamith. *Cognitive Orientation and Behavior.* New York: Springer, 1980.

Kroeber, A. L., and C. Kluckhohn. *Culture: A Critical Review of Concepts and Definitions.* New York: Random House, 1970.

Krupar, Karen. *Communication Games: Participant's Manual.* New York: Free Press, 1973.

Kuitert, H. M. *The Reality of Faith.* Grand Rapids: Eerdmans, 1968.

LaHaye, Tim. *Spirit-Controlled Temperament.* Grand Rapids: Zondervan, 1967.

Landers, Ann. *Ann Landers Says Truth Is Stranger. . . .* Englewood Cliffs, N.J.: Prentice-Hall, 1968.

Larson, Bruce, and Ralph Osborne. *The Emerging Church.* Waco: Word, 1970.

Larson, Donald N. *Guidelines for Barefoot Language Learning.* St. Paul: CMS, 1984.

Levi-Strauss, Claude. "Social Structure" in Nelson Graburn. *Readings in Kinship and Social Structure.* New York: Harper and Row, 1971.

————. *Structural Anthropology.* Garden City, New York: Doubleday, 1967.

————. *The View From Afar.* New York: Basic Books, 1985.

Lewis, Oscar. *The Children of Sanchez: Autobiography of a Mexican Family.* New York: Random House, 1961.

Lindzey, Gardner. *Projective Techniques and Cross-Cultural Research.* New York: Appleton-Century-Crofts, 1961.

Lingenfelter, Sherwood G. *Yap: Political Leadership and Culture Change in an Island Society.* Honolulu: The University Press of Hawaii, 1975.

Lingenfelter, Sherwood G., and Marvin K. Mayers. *Ministering Crossculturally: An Incarnational Model for Personal Relationships.* Grand Rapids: Baker, 1986.

Livingston, Samuel A., and Clarice Stasz Stoll. *Simulation Games: An Introduction for the Social Studies Teacher.* New York: Macmillan, 1973.

Loewen, Jacob A. *Culture and Human Values: Christian Intervention in Anthropological Perspective.* Pasadena, Calif.: William Carey, 1986.

Loss, M. *Culture Shock: Dealing with Stress in Cross-Cultural Living*. Winona Lake, Ind.: Light and Life, 1983.

Lowie, R. H. "Plains Indian Age Societies: Historical Summary." *American Museum of Natural History, Anthropological Papers*. 11 (1916): 877–984.

Luzbetak, Louis. *The Church and Cultures*. Pasadena, Calif.: William Carey Library, 1984.

Lynd, Helen Merrell. *On Shame and The Search for Identity*. New York: Science Editions, 1958.

Madge, John. *Tools of Social Science*. New York: Doubleday, 1965.

Maidment, Robert, and Russell Bronstein. *Simulation Games: Design and Implementation*. Columbus, Ohio: Charles E. Merrill, 1973.

Malinowski, Bronislaw. *Argonauts of the Western Pacific*. New York: E. P. Dutton, 1961.

_____. *Coral Gardens and Their Magic*. London: G. Allen and Unwin, 1935.

_____. *The Dynamics of Culture Change*. New Haven: Yale University Press, 1945.

Massey, Morris. *The People Puzzle: Understanding Yourself and Others*. Reston, Va.: Reston, 1979.

Mayers, Marvin K. *A Look at Filipino Lifestyles*. Dallas: Summer Institute of Linguistics Museum of Anthropology, 1980.

_____. *A Look at Latin American Lifestyles*. Dallas: Summer Institute of Linguistics Museum of Anthropology, 1982.

_____. *Pocomchi Texts*. Norman, Okla.: The Summer Institute of Linguistics and the University of Oklahoma, 1958.

_____. "Two-Man Feud in the Guatemalan Church." *Practical Anthropology* 13 (July-August 1966): 115–25.

_____; Lawrence Richards; and Robert Webber. *Reshaping Evangelical Higher Education*. Grand Rapids: Zondervan, 1972.

Mayers, Philip, ed. *Socialization: The Approach from Social Anthropology*. New York: Tavistock Publications, 1970.

McConnell, William T. *The Gift of Time*. Downers Grove, Ill.: InterVarsity, 1983.

McGavran, Donald A., ed. *Church Growth and Christian Mission*. New York: Harper and Row, 1965.

_____. *Understanding Church Growth*. Grand Rapids: Eerdmans, 1969.

McGuire, Christine H.; Lawrence M. Solomon; and Philip G. Bashook. *Construction and Use of Written Simulations*. New York: The Psychological Foundation, 1977.

McLuhan, Marshall. *Understanding Media: The Extension of Man*. New York: McGraw-Hill, 1964.

McQuown, Norman A. *Language, Culture and Education*. Stanford: Stanford University Press, 1982.

Mead, Margaret. *Coming of Age in Samoa*. New York: William Morrow, 1928.

————, ed. *Cultural Patterns and Technical Change*. New York: Mentor Books, New American Library, 1957.

Means, Richard L. *The Ethical Imperative*. Garden City, N.Y.: Doubleday, 1969.

Megarty, Jacquetta, ed. *Aspects of Simulation and Gaming*. London: Kegan Paul, 1977.

Merton, Robert K. *Social Theory and Social Structure*. Glencoe, Ill.: Free Press, 1957.

Mickelson, A. Berkeley. *Interpreting the Bible*. Grand Rapids: Eerdmans, 1963.

Miller, Keith. *A Taste of New Wine*. Waco: Word, 1965.

Mills, Watson E., ed. "The Behavior of Tongues," *Speaking in Tongues, Let's Talk About It*. Waco: Word, 1973.

Montague, Ashley. *The Humanization of Man*. New York: Grove, 1964.

Morgan, L. H. *League of the Iroquois*. New York: Dodd, Mead and Co., 1904.

Morris, Desmond, et al. *Gestures*. New York: Stein and Day, 1980.

Myers, Gail E. *The Dynamics of Human Communication: A Laboratory Approach*. New York: McGraw-Hill, 1973.

Nadel, S. F. *The Foundations of Social Anthropology*. Glencoe, Ill.: Free Press, 1951.

————. *The Theory of Social Structure*. Glencoe, Ill.: Free Press, 1957.

Nida, Eugene. *Customs and Cultures*. New York: Harper and Row, 1954.

————. *God's Word in Man's Language*. New York: Harper and Row, 1952.

————. *Message and Mission*. New York: Harper and Row, 1960.

————. *Religion Across Cultures*. New York: Harper and Row, 1968.

Niebuhr, Richard. *Christ and Culture*. New York: Harper and Row, 1956.

Nisbet, Robert A. *The Social Bond*. New York: Alfred A. Knopf, 1970.

Norton, R. *Communication Style: Theory, Application and Measure*. Sage Series in Interpersonal Communication. Vol. 1. Beverly Hills, Calif.: Sage Publications, 1983.

Oberg, Kalervo, "Culture Shock: Adjustment to New Cultural Environments." *Practical Anthropology* 7:4 (1960): 177.

O'Conner, Elizabeth. *The Eighth Day of Creation—Gifts and Creativity*. Waco: Word, 1971.

Olson, Bruce E. *Bruchko*. Carol Stream, Ill.: Creation House, 1978.

————. *For This Cross I'll Kill You*. Carol Stream, Ill.: Creation House, 1973.

Ortner, Donald J., ed. *How Humans Adapt*. Washington, D.C.: Smithsonian Institution, 1983.

Paredes, J. Anthony, and Marcus J. Hepburn. "The Split Brain and the Culture Cognition Paradox." *Current Anthropology* 17 (1976): 121–27.

Parshall, Phil. *Beyond the Mosque: Christians Within Muslim Community.* Grand Rapids: Baker, 1985.

———. *Bridges to Islam: A Christian Perspective on Folk Islam.* Grand Rapids: Baker, 1983.

———. *New Paths in Muslim Evangelism: Evangelical Approaches to Contextualization.* Grand Rapids: Baker, 1982.

Parsons, Talcott. *Essays in Sociological Theory: Pure and Applied.* Glencoe, Ill.: Free Press, 1949.

———, and Edward A. Shils. *Toward a General Theory of Action.* Cambridge: Harvard University Press, 1967.

Parvin, Earl. *Missions USA.* Chicago: Moody, 1985.

Paul, Benjamin D., "Interview Techniques and Field Relationships," in A. L. Kroeber, ed., *Anthropology Today.* Chicago: University of Chicago Press, 1953.

Pelto, Pertti J. *Anthropological Research: The Structure of Inquiry.* New York: Harper and Row, 1970.

"Person to Person." *Interaction Kit: Tuning into Others.* San Diego: Creative Learning Systems, 1978.

Peters, George. *A Biblical Theology of Missions.* Chicago: Moody, 1972.

———. *Saturation Evangelism.* Grand Rapids: Zondervan, 1970.

Pfeiffer, J. William, and John E. Jones. *A Handbook of Structured Experiences for Human Relations Training.* Vols. 1–3. Iowa City, Iowa: University Associates, 1971. New edition. San Diego: University Associates, 1983.

Phillips, Gerald M. *Communication and Human Relationship: The Study of Interpersonal Communication.* New York: Macmillan, 1983.

Pigors, Paul, and Faith Pigors. *Case Method in Human Relations: The Incident Process.* New York: McGraw-Hill, 1961.

Pike, Kenneth L. *Language.* The Hague: Mouton, 1967.

Pitt-Rivers, Julian. *People of the Sierra.* Chicago: University of Chicago Press, 1961.

Prins, A. H. J. *East African Age Class Systems.* Groningen and Djakarta, 1953.

Radcliffe-Brown, Alfred R. *Structure and Function in Primitive Society.* London: Cohen and West, 1959.

Raudsepp, Eugene. *How Creative Are You?* New York: Academic Press, 1981.

Redfield, Robert. *The Folk Culture of Yucatan.* Chicago: University of Chicago Press, 1941.

———. "The Folk Society," *Human Nature and the Study of Society.* The papers of Robert Redfield, ed. Margaret Park Redfield. Vol. 1. Chicago: University of Chicago Press, 1962.

—————. *The Little Community*. Chicago: University of Chicago Press, 1955.

—————. *The Primitive World and Its Transformation*. Ithaca, N.Y.: Cornell University Press, 1953.

Reed, Lyman E. *Preparing Missionaries for Intercultural Communication: a Bicultural Approach*. Pasadena: William Carey, 1985.

Reich, Charles A. *The Greening of America*. New York: Random House, 1970.

Reichert, Richard. *Simulation Games for Religious Education*. Winona, Minn.: St. Mary's College, 1978.

Reina, Reuben. *The Law of the Saints*. Indianapolis: Bobbs-Merrill, 1967.

Richardson, Don. *Lords of the Earth*. Ventura, Calif.: Regal, 1977.

—————. *Peace Child*. Ventura, Calif.: Regal, 1976.

Robertson, James. *American Myth, American Reality*. New York: Hill and Wang, 1980.

Rogers, Carl. *Freedom to Learn*. Columbus, Ohio: Charles E. Merrill, 1969.

—————. *On Becoming a Person*. Cambridge, Mass.: Riverside, 1961.

Rogers, Everett M. *Modernization Among Peasants: The Impact of Communication*. New York: Holt, Rinehart and Winston, 1969.

—————, and F. Floyd Shoemaker. *Communication of Innovations: A Cross-Cultural Approach*. New York: Free Press, 1971.

Ruben, Brent D. *Communication and Human Behavior*. New York: Macmillan, 1984.

—————, and Richard W. Budd. *Human Communication Handbook: Simulations and Games*. Rochelle Park, N.J.: Hayden, 1975.

Samovar, Larry A. and Richard E. Porter. *Intercultural Communication: A Reader*. Belmont, Calif.: Wadsworth Publishing Company, 1976.

Sapir, Edward. *Selected Writings in Language, Culture, and Personality*. ed. D. G. Mandelbaum. Berkeley, Calif.: University of California Press, 1949.

Scherer, Roy. *Wildfire: Church Growth in Korea*. Grand Rapids: Eerdmans, 1966.

Scott, Osgood D., and Christopher Peterson. *Cognitive Structure: Theory and Measurement of Individual Differences*. Washington, D.C.: V. H. Winston and Sons, 1979.

Seelye, H. Ned. *Teaching Culture Strategies for Intercultural Communication*. Lincolnwood, Ill.: National Textbooks, 1984.

Segall, Marshall H. *Cross-Cultural Psychology*. Monterey, Calif.: Brooks/Cole, 1979.

Sharan, Shlomo, and Yael Sharan. *Small Group Teaching*. Englewood Cliffs, N.J.: Educational Technology Publications, 1976.

Sharp, J. Lauriston. "Steel Axes for Stone-Age Australians" in Edward H. Spicer, *Human Problems in Technological Change*. New York: Basic Books, 1952.

Shears, Laura, and Eli Bower. *Games in Development and Education*. Springfield, Ill.: Charles C. Thomas, 1974.

Shubik, Martin. *Game Theory in the Social Sciences*. Cambridge, Mass.: MIT Press, 1982.

Simon, Herbert A. *Models of Man: Social and Rational*. New York: John Wiley and Sons, 1957.

Smalley, William. "Culture Shock, Language Shock, and the Shock of Self Discovery." *Practical Anthropology* 10:2 (1963): 49.

_____, ed. *Readings in Missionary Anthropology*. Pasadena: William Carey Library, 1974.

Smith, Alfred G. *Cognitive Styles in Law Schools*. Austin, Tex.: University of Texas Press, 1979.

_____. *Communication and Culture*. New York: Holt, Rinehart and Winston, 1966.

Smith, Dennis, R., and L. Keith Williamson. *Interpersonal Communication: Roles, Rules, Strategies and Games*. Dubuque, Iowa: Wm. C. Brown Publishers, 1985.

Spicer, Edward H., ed. *Human Problems in Technological Change*. New York: John Wiley and Sons, 1967.

Spradley, James P., and David W. McCurdy. *Conformity and Conflict*. Boston: Little, Brown and Co., 1971.

Stadsklev, Ron. *Handbook of Simulation Gaming in Social Education*. Parts 1 and 2. Montgomery: The University of Alabama, Institute of Higher Education Research and Services, 1974.

Stewart, Edward C. *American Cultural Patterns*. Chicago: Intercultural Press, 1972.

Summer, W. C. *The Challenge of Facts*. New Haven: Yale University Press, 1914.

Sutlive, V. H.; N. Altshuler; M. D. Zamora; and V. Kerns. *Missionaries, Anthropolgists, and Cultural Change*. Williamsburg, Va.: College of William and Mary, 1985.

Taylor, John L., and Rex Walford. *Learning and The Simulation Game*. Beverly Hills, Calif.: Sage Publications, 1978.

Thiagarajan, Siv Asailam, and Harold Stolovitch. *Instructional Simulation Games*. Englewood Cliffs, N.J.: Educational Technology Publications, 1978.

Thompson, John F. *Using Role Playing in the Classroom*. Bloomington, Indiana: Phi Delta Kappa Educational Foundation, 1978.

Tippet, Alan R. "Polygamy as a Missionary Problem: The Anthropological Issues." *Practical Anthropology* 17:2 (March-April 1970): 75–79.

Toffler, Alvin. *Future Shock*. New York: Random House, 1970.

Tournier, Paul. *Guilt and Grace*. New York: Harper and Row, 1962.

_____. *The Meaning of Persons*. New York: Harper and Row, 1957.

Van Gennep, Arnold. *Rites of Passage*. Chicago: University of Chicago Press, 1960.

Van Leeuwen, Mary Stewart. "Cognitive Style, North American Values and the Body of Christ." *Journal of Psychology and Theology* 2 (1974): 77.

Verhey, Allen. *The Great Reversal, Ethics and the New Testament*. Grand Rapids: Eerdmans, 1984.

Verma, C., and C. Bagley. *Self-Concept, Achievement and Multi-cultural Education*. London: Macmillan, 1982.

Vogt, Evon Z. "Navaho Veterans: A Study of Changing Values." Cambridge, Mass.: Harvard University Press. *Peabody Museum of American Archaeology and Ethnology Papers*, 41:1, 1951.

Ward, Ted. *Living Overseas*. New York: Free Press, 1984.

Watson, O. Michael. *Proxemic Behavior: A Cross-Cultural Study*. The Hague: Mouton, 1970.

Weeks, William W.; B. Pederson; and R. W. Brislin, eds. *A Manual of Structured Experiences for Cross-Cultural Learning*. Yarmouth, Maine: Intercultural Press, 1977.

Werkman, Sidney. *Bringing Up Children Overseas, A Guide for Families*. New York: Basic Books, 1977.

Werner, Roland, and Joan Werner. *Bibliography of Simulations: Social Systems and Education*. La Jolla, Calif.: Western Behavioral Sciences Institute, 1969.

Whiston, Lionel. *Are You Fun to Live With?* Waco: Word, 1969.

White, L. A., *The Evolution of Culture*. New York: McGraw-Hill, 1959.

_____. "The Symbol: The Origin and Basis of Human Behavior," in *The Science of Culture*. New York: Farrar, Straus and Co., 1949.

Wicklund, Robert A., and Jack W. Brehm. *Perspectives on Cognitive Dissonance*. Lawrence Erlbaum Associates, Publishers, 1976.

Williams, T. R. *Field Methods in the Study of Culture*. New York: Holt, Rinehart and Winston, 1967.

Wilson, Clifford A., and Donald W. McKeon. *The Language Gap*. Grand Rapids: Zondervan, 1984.

Winter, Ralph, and Steven C. Hawthorne. *Perspectives on the World Christian Movement*. Pasadena: William Carey Library, 1981.

Witkin, Herman A. "Cognitive Styles Across Cultures" in J. W. Berry and P. R. Dasen, *Culture and Cognition*. London: Methuen, Ltd., 1974.

_____. *Cognitive Styles: Essence and Origins*. New York: International Universities Press, 1981.

_____, and Donald R. Goodenough. *Cognitive Styles: Field Dependence and Field Independence*. New York: International Universities Press, 1981.

Wohlking, Wallace, and Patricia J. Gill. *Role Playing*. Englewood Cliffs, N.J.: Educational Technology Publications, 1980.

Wolf, Margret S., and Mary E. Duffy. *Simulations/Games: A Teaching Strategy for Nursing Education*. New York: National League for Nursing, 1979.

SUBJECT INDEX